CATHERINE LE NOBLE

Daughter of James and Elizabeth Le Serrurier, emigrants; the wife of Henry Le Noble and the mother of Mrs. René Louis Ravenel. (From an original oil painting in the possession of Mrs. R. Y. Dwight, Pinopolis, S. C.)

The Huguenots of Colonial South Carolina

BY

ARTHUR HENRY HIRSCH, Ph.D.
Professor of American History in Ohio Wesleyan University
Fellow of the Royal Historical Society

Southern Historical Press, Inc.
Greenville, South Carolina

Originally Published 1928

SOUTHERN HISTORICAL PRESS, INC.
PO BOX 1267
Greenville, SC 29601

ISBN #978-1-63914-061-9

Printed in the United States of America

To

THE MEMORY OF

MY FATHER AND MY MOTHER

PREFACE

This study is an attempt to disentangle from the network of colonial history the contributions made in Carolina by the French Protestants. The initial impulse for the work was received and the beginning was made in a seminar conducted by Professor Wm. E. Dodd.

In their original form three of the chapters of this volume were submitted in fulfillment of the thesis requirements for the degree of Doctor of Philosophy at the University of Chicago. To these several chapters have been added, bringing the work into its present form. In its preparation the endeavor has been to produce a narrative embodying the principles of sound scholarship, though also readable and interesting. As no history of the Huguenots of South Carolina has hitherto been attempted, new ground has been broken and much source material heretofore unused for this purpose has been examined and utilized. In all cases the author has tried to get at the truth, regardless of current theories or traditions.

A perusal of the bibliography will show that a study has been made of primary and secondary material available in the United States and in England, more particularly in Charleston, Columbia, and Pinopolis, South Carolina; the Library of Congress; the Chicago Libraries; the New York Public Library, the libraries of Philadelphia, and the archives in the Bodleian Library, Oxford; Fulham Palace, the Royal Society Collection, and the British Public Record Office, in London. For transcripts from the English archives I am indebted to Mr. R. A. Abrams, of Oxford University, and Miss R. Catton, of London.

While the author does not want to have it appear as though he wishes to cancel the indebtedness thereby, he desires to make grateful acknowledgment to those who have materially assisted in making the load lighter.

In addition to the officers and staffs of the several libraries mentioned above, my deep appreciation is herewith expressed to Mr. Alexander S. Salley, Jr., Secretary of the South Carolina Historical Commission and the Hon. R. M. McCown, formerly Secretary of the State of South Carolina, for special privileges and numerous courtesies extended during the pursuit of the work, and to the Vestries of St. Philip's and St. Michael's Episcopal Churches of Charleston, to the Trustees of the Congregational Church of Charleston, to the Colonial Dames of South Carolina and to the officers of the South Carolina Society, for the privilege of examining their valuable records. Mr. Thomas Wright Bacot, ex-President of the Huguenot Society of South Carolina; Mr. Daniel Ravenel, the Secretary; the late Doctor Robert Wilson, its former President; the Rev. Florian Vurpillot, formerly Pastor of the Huguenot Church of Charleston; Professor Yates Snowden; Miss Isabelle De Saussure; Mrs. Louisa Smythe; Mr. Isaac Porcher; Mrs. H. F. Porcher; Mrs. R. Y. Dwight; Mr. Samuel G. Stoney; Mr. Arthur Mazÿck and Mr. Alston Reed generously opened their private collections to unrestricted examination, or assisted in numerous other ways to further my endeavors. Without the assistance of Mr. Henry R. Dwight, of Pinopolis, the photographic illustrations found in this volume could not have been procured. With generous coöperation and zeal, under trying circumstances and many obstacles, he obtained photographs of a number of oil paintings and pastels of the Huguenots of the colonial period. My debt of gratitude to him is great. For the unselfish assistance in research on the part of Mr. D. E. Huger Smith and Miss Mabel Webber, both of whom also read nearly all of the early drafts of a portion of the manuscript and whose critical though kindly counsel has saved me from a number of errors, I am especially indebted. To Professors Andrew C. McLaughlin, William E. Dodd, and Marcus W. Jernegan, of the University of Chicago, who have followed my work at every step with many helpful suggestions and who read much of the first draft of the prepared manuscript, and to Professor Charles M. Andrews, of Yale University, who read and criticized all of the first draft, my deepest appreciation is hereby expressed. To Miss Katharine Mazÿck, whose constant counsel and unfailing encouragement have been like beacon lights through the years, my debt of gratitude is beyond measure. In its final form the manuscript had the distinct benefit of a careful reading by the late W. C. Miller, Esq., a former President of the Huguenot Society of South Carolina, Miss Katharine Mazÿck, the Society's Historian and a member of the Executive Committee, and Daniel Ravenel, Esq., its Secretary. To each of them my gratitude is great. All of these, however, should be relieved of responsibility for errors that may appear. To Professors William K. Boyd, Paull F. Baum, and Louis M. Sears of Duke University, who gave the final manuscript and the galley proof a careful reading and made many helpful suggestions, and to the Duke Press, through whose interest in the work the volume is brought out in its present form, a special expression of appreciation is fitting.

It is hoped that perchance there can be recovered from oblivion some of the great and noble recollections that deserve to live in the memory of man and of which France herself may have reason even now to be proud.

ARTHUR H. HIRSCH.

Delaware, Ohio.
March, 1927.

CONTENTS

ILLUSTRATIONS

ABBREVIATIONS

Acct. of Ga. – Account of Georgia.

Brit. Transc. – British Transcripts.

Cal. St. Pa. – Calendar of State Papers.

Cal. St. Pa. (Am. & W. Ind.) – American and West Indies.
(Dom.) – Domestic.
(Col. Am. & W. Ind.) – Colonial American and West Indies.

Ch. Wardens Acct. Bk. – Church Wardens' Account Book.

Coll. N. Y. Hist. Soc. – Collections New York Historical Society.

Coll. S. C. Hist. Soc. – Collections South Carolina Historical Society.

Col. Dames Archives. – Colonial Dames Archives.

Col. Rcds. N. C. – Colonial Records of North Carolina.

Council Jrnl. – Council Journal.

C. T. – Charles-Town and Charleston.

C. T. Yr. Bk. – Charleston Year Book.

Ga. Col. Rec. – Georgia Colonial Records.

Hist. Fr. Refugees. – History of the French Refugees.

Hist. Presbyt. Ch. S. C. – History of the Presbyterian Church of South Carolina.

Hist. S. C. – History of South Carolina.

Hug. – Huguenots.

Hug. in Am. – Huguenots in America.

Indian Bk. – Indian Book.

Jrnl. – Journal

Land War. – Land Warrants.

Pro. H. Soc. Am., Pro. Hug. Soc. Am. – Proceedings of the Huguenot Society of America.

Pro. H. Soc. London, Pro. Hug. Soc. London. – Proceedings of the Huguenot Society of London.

Pub. Hug. Soc. London. – Publications of the Huguenot Society of London.

Pro. R. H. Soc. London. – Proceedings of the Royal Historical Society of London.

Pr. Doc. Mass. – Probate Documents of Massachusetts.

Pr. Ct. Rcd. – Probate Court Records.

Rcds. – Records.

Rcds. Ct. of Ordinary. – Records of the Court of Ordinary.

Rcd. Bk. – Record Book.

Reg. Rcd. – Register's Record.

Sec'y. Rcd. – Secretary's Record.

S. C. Gaz. – South Carolina Gazette.

S. C. Hist. Com. – South Carolina Historical Commission.

S. C. H. & G. Mag. – South Carolina Historical and Genealogical Magazine.

S. P. G. – Society for the Propagation of the Gospel.

S. P. G. Abs. – Abstracts; S. P. G. Dig. – Digest; S. P. G. Transc. – Transcripts.

T. H. S. S. C. – Transactions of the Huguenot Society of South Carolina.

The Huguenots of Colonial South Carolina

CHAPTER I

THE EUROPEAN BACKGROUND AND THE BEGINNINGS IN CAROLINA

The persecution of French Protestants and their journeys to America constitute a familiar chapter in the history of migrations. Driven from France, nurtured in England and carried across forbidding seas, scores of thousands of refugees, seeking shelter from political and religious adversity, found a home in the colonies of the New World. During the last quarter of the seventeenth century and the first half of the eighteenth, great numbers of these persecuted Huguenots fled from Europe to America.[1] Thousands of families settled at various convenient points along the Atlantic coast. South Carolina was one of their most favored retreats and became known as the home of the Huguenots in America. In this province they made eight settlements, six in and about Charles Town, one to the extreme south of the province, and one in the distant back-country.

The European background for the history of the Huguenots in South Carolina centers naturally in two events: the Edict of Nantes, issued in 1598, and the repeal of that famous decree in 1685. The Edict of Nantes was but a confirmation of various treaties and other agreements concluded between Catholics and Protestants. It presumed to cancel all past grievances and injuries. Sentences that had been imposed upon Protestants on account of their religion were annulled. The legitimacy of Protestant children, settled abroad, was conceded, and prisoners were set free. Wherever Catholic worship had been interrupted, it was restored. Unlimited freedom of conscience was guaranteed. Special courts were set up to administer religious cases. This solemn edict was given perpetual and irrevocable character, and when proclaimed it was heralded as a star of promise

[1] Estimates of the total Huguenot exodus from France to other parts of the world vary from 300,000 to 1,000,000. See Anderson, *Commerce*, III. 258, 297.

and the beginning of a new era of historical development and religious toleration.[2] But, alas, its postulates soon lost their force and the Edict became a dead letter. In many provinces, where Catholic authority was still heavily chained to mediaeval narrowness, and where the Protestants persisted in running risks of liberty, the force of the Edict was publicly annulled. Widespread proselyting, unbridled persecution, and intemperate outrages followed—excesses that enthusiasm can easily encourage and fanaticism accelerate—with the result that in 1685 the famous Edict of Nantes was revoked. The extensive migrations from France quickly followed.

It is interesting to note then that seventy-five or a hundred years before the Revocation, hundreds of Protestants were leaving France on account of the opposition directed against them in local politics, because of restraints of trade and other reasons, social and political. Many of the clauses in laws and charters were in practice only dead letters.[3] It is clear that before the repeal of the Edict of Nantes the Huguenot leaders were forced to face the prospect of a great exodus. Employers of labor were making arrangements for a transfer of their industries to places of greater safety.[4]

These people found a welcome in all parts of Europe and America. Especially cordial was their reception in the British Isles and in America. England gave asylum to all who fled from persecution. For more than a hundred years, in one way and another, she encouraged the Protestants of France. It is not strange then that thousands of Frenchmen sought shelter in England. So great was their number and so genuine the welcome accorded them and so complete the tolerance, that French churches were founded and entire freedom of religion was granted them. The parish registers of the English churches contain thousands of French names, attesting

[2] For the text of the Edict of Nantes see Abbé Soulier, *Histoire du Calvinism,* 598.

[3] Levasseur, *Cours d'Économie,* etc., 179; Clément, *Lettres, Instruc. et Mémoires de Colbert,* II, part 1, Intr., 149 f.; Lavisse, *Histoire de France,* VII. 220; Voltaire, *Siècle de Louis XIV.* (ed. Bourgeois), 696; Clément, *Histoire de Colbert,* II. 398; Thompson, in *Am. Hist. Rev.,* XIV. 38.

[4] See *Mémoires Inédits de Dumont de Bostaquet,* Preface, xxiii; *Pub. Hug. Soc. London,* XLX, Intr.

to the fact that many readily identified themselves with Anglican religious bodies. Scores of these French names reappear in the records of South Carolina.[5]

Though Huguenots were heartily welcomed in the British Isles, there were a number of reasons for their emigration to America. As we shall see, English economic policy lay in the background. The British Crown had granted a patent for the Carolina region and the Proprietors wanted it inhabited. French Protestants were therefore encouraged to go to America. Here was a hardy race, skilled in numerous trades, expert in the culture of wine, silk, and oil, perturbed in spirit by persecution, inured to labor, fatigue, and privation, yet enthusiastic in religious zeal. This is the very material needed for successful colonization under adverse primitive conditions. Because honorable toil is a balm to persecution and hard work an outlet for religious zeal, they were considered admirable subjects for encouragement. Besides, it was a time when conformity to the Church of England was urged with great earnestness and when the persecutions of Protestant dissenters in England were at their height. The strict laws against nonconformists drove many from England.[6] Clergymen not ordained by the Bishop of London did not enjoy the same ecclesiastical standing as others, and to make matters worse, the possibility of a "popish successor" was greatly feared.[7] It was a time too when competition in England was bitter and intense, especially after the Huguenot immigration. English tradesmen and craftsmen were complaining.[8] Anxiety pressed the people on every hand. In the charity bureaus it was equally trying. So great was the demand for "poor relief" that even the most deserving found it difficult to obtain aid.[9]

[5] See in bibliography lists of parish registers, etc.

[6] Ramsay, *Hist. S. C.*, I. 3.

[7] Burgess, 8; Ramsay, *Hist. S. C.*, I. 3-4; Carroll, *Coll.* II. 311, 407.

[8] It is estimated that about 120,000 Huguenots went to England, either temporarily or permanently. They were refugees of all ranks, soldiers and sailors, ministers, merchants and mechanics, teachers and traders, lawyers and laborers. (See Smiles, *Huguenots*, 230.)

[9] Among the refugees were a large number of professional men, for whom the earning of a livelihood was difficult. These were among the

But besides these conditions there were other temptations to lure them to their new home in America. America was looked upon as a place inhabited by placable natives, a place of salvation and informal life, where the children of the old races of Europe could without difficulty live in comparative innocence, free from the rigid requirements of antiquated religious limitations. Furthermore, the proprietors promised large tracts of land to their friends as inducements for booming the new colony. To all emigrants of proper quality smaller grants were offered. The Carolina Charter promised liberty of conscience. These things at a time when dissenting bodies were persecuted in England and Protestants were driven out of France, proved especially inviting to French refugees.

In South Carolina the religious sympathies of the people were aroused and the destitute were generously assisted. Subscriptions were raised to support them; liberal allotments of land were bestowed. The poor were received with generous hospitality. The alien born were naturalized. Privileges and immunities were granted them to induce them to remain.

Generations before the first successful colonization in Carolina, French Protestants sought there a shelter from political and religious persecution. Admiral Coligny dreamed of it as a haven for destitute countrymen, at a time when the coasts of Florida proper, Georgia, and the Carolinas, were still vaguely designated Florida.

In 1555 the first expedition under Durand de Villegagnon had landed at the mouth of the Rio Janeiro, in Brazil. Here a fort was constructed on the island that was named for the intrepid enthusiast, Coligny, patron of the colony. But the

first to be relieved by the "poor fund". Weekly allowances and pensions were maintained for them. Next in rotation for relief came the aged and sick. This left little for the able-bodied, destitute classes, who had no primary claims on English charity (*ibid.*, 252). So great did the need become that disorderly assemblies, held by persons in the last stages of misery, had to be broken up by the clergymen of the London French churches themselves. (See *Cal. St. Pa.* (Dom.), 1689-90, 227.) During the years 1681-5 £14,631,000-11-7½ was given in London for the relief of the French. The bulk of this sum was paid out before Sept. 23, 1683. About £3,500,000 of this was collected among the churches in London. (See MS documents of Guild Hall, London, quoted in *Pro. R. H. Soc. London*, V. 343.)

small settlement was finally betrayed by Villegagnon, and in time entirely failed.

The second expedition, 1562, under Jean Ribaut and René de Laudonniere, touched at the mouth of the Saint John's River, in Florida. Here a column of stone, bearing French arms, was erected. Not satisfied, the party proceeded thence up the coast to Port Royal harbor, within the bounds of the present South Carolina. Here on a small island, now called Parris Island, Charlesfort was constructed and the foundations of a colony were laid. These adventurers, however, returned to France, but the country received the name Carolina, a name later retained by English colonists.[10]

In the third expedition, which was undertaken in 1564, with Ribaut and Laudonniere again in charge, Fort Carolina was built at the mouth of the St. John's River (River May) in Florida. But this expedition, though consecrated with fervent prayer and dedicated by the blood of martyrs, was throughout doomed to disaster. The mistakes and misfortunes of earlier undertakings were repeated. The adventurers neglected the culture of the soil and yielded to the temptation of quarreling among themselves. In the end the fort was destroyed by the Spanish, under the leadership of Pedro Menéndez. Then a fierce storm broke its fury upon the coast, finishing the work of destruction which Menéndez had begun. Carolina, thus occupied for this brief moment, by French Protestants, relapsed into decay. The ruins of the fortifications were overrun by savages, and for nearly a hundred years it gave but little promise of resuscitation.

In view of such things one need not be surprised to find that in 1629 French Protestants were once more in communication with Charles I, of England, for the purpose of establishing a colony in Carolina.[11] The patent that was issued to Sir Robert Heath, as sole proprietor of the region, grew out of the proposals of Soubise (Duc de Fontenay), representing the Huguenots in England. The Baron de Saucé

[10] Baird, *Huguenot Emigration to America;* MS Col. Doc. S. C., XIII. 48; Godin, *Memorial of S. C.*

[11] *Pro. H. Soc. Am.,* III. 117.

and M. de Belavene, both Frenchmen, are said to have been the originators of this fruitless design of settling French Protestants in Carolina.[12] The promoters were so certain of the success of the enterprise that the Crown issued particular instructions respecting the creed and other matters of those who would go to the new settlement; and William Boswell, one of those interested in the undertaking, gave power of attorney to Peter l'Amy to receive all his rights and profits accruing from the project.

Accordingly, in 1633, a colony of French Protestants sailed for Carolina from England in the Mayflower, with Edward Kingswell, their first Governor. But miscarriage in the passage landed them in Virginia instead. Owing to the carelessness or else wilfulness of Samuel Vassal, the contractor, or of the captain, they got no farther. After an eight-months' stay in Virginia, waiting for a vessel to take them to Carolina, Kingswell, in May, 1634, started for England.[13] He ultimately received £611-1-14 from Vassal and Andrews for damages and losses. What became of the families that remained is not known.[14]

Records of similar attempts are found in the years that follow, good examples of which are such efforts as those of 1663, 1670, 1677, 1687, etc. In 1663, when Charles II granted all of the area comprised in the two Carolinas to a company of English gentlemen and the lots in Charles Town were distributed, three men whose names seem to be French, Richard Batin, Richard Deyos, and Jacques Jours, were invested as free tenants and given all of the rights of English subjects. In the records that survive are found individual grants to John Bullon in 1677, to John Bazant in 1678, to Richard Gaillard in 1678, and to Mary Batton in 1683. Possibly some or all of these were persecuted French Protestants, though the complete evidence to support such a conclusion is wanting. In January, 1670, the ship *Carolina,* which was one of a fleet of three, sailing from London,

[12] MS S. C. Papers (Saintsbury Papers) in N. Y. Public Library.
[13] MS S. C. Papers (Saintsbury Papers) in N. Y. Public Library.
[14] *Ibid.*

carrying Huguenots, arrived in Carolina. This enterprise started in 1667. After sending Sayle over to survey the coast, the proprietors in England had decided to found a colony in the section previously surveyed by Robert Sandford, Secretary and Chief Register for the Lords Proprietors.[15] The colony was to be composed of emigrants from England, supplemented by additions from Barbadoes, Ireland, and the Bermudas. Preparations required two years in time and £120,000 in money. In 1669, three vessels were purchased and equipped with the purpose of settling two hundred people in the new territory. Joseph West was put in charge of the fleet, until it should reach Barbadoes, where Governor Sayle was to take command. On August 17, 1669, the three vessels, the frigate *Carolina,* the *Port Royal,* and the sloop *Albermarle,* were at rest in the Downs.[16] The *Carolina* contained ninety-three passengers and supplies of all kinds, ready for the sea.[17] The list of passengers on this ship contains the names of Mellicent Howe, Robert Doné, (alias Donne), Abraham Phillips, and Thomas Gourden (Gourdin), presumably French, and all servants.[18] The lists of passengers on the other two vessels are lost, but it is highly probable that they contained a number of Huguenots, also bound for Carolina.

These were the beginnings of permanent French colonization in Carolina. The three ships, after touching at points in Ireland and Barbadoes, headed for the American coast. The frigate *Carolina* reached there August 30, the *Albermarle* and the *Port Royal,* under stress of weather, tossed on the

[15] *C. T. Yr. Bk.,* 1883, 259 ff.; Hewat, in Carroll's *Collections,* I. chaps. 1 and 2; Drayton's *View,* 200; Holmes, *American Annals,* I. 405 (1670). French names are spelled as in local usage.

[16] *Cal. St. Pa.* (*Col. Am. and W. Ind.*), 1669-74, no. 97.

[17] *Coll. S. C. Hist. Soc.,* V. 136, gives 92 as the number.

[18] *Ibid.,* 134; *Council Jrnl.* (Salley) 1671-80, 7. Though Philippes (or Phillips) at first blush does not seem to be a French name, there is evidence to support the supposition that it was French. Persons of this name are found to be identified with the Threadneedle Street Huguenot Church, London. See *P. H. S. London,* XVIII. 333. In South Carolina the name appears in the same form. See MS Reg. Rcd. 1675-96, 536 and *Coll. S. C. Hist. Soc.,* V. 328. Peter Philippes and his wife Jeanne apprenticed their daughter Charlotte to René Ravenel and his wife.

sea some six weeks, and though reported lost, reached harbor.[19] The colonists settled in the country of the Cacique of Kiawha, twenty leagues north of Port Royal. Dissatisfied with the location, they soon moved to a point on the Ashley River, almost directly across from the present site of Charleston. But in 1682 a second move of the seat of government was made to the neck of land formed by the confluence of the Cooper and the Ashley Rivers. Huguenots are found there when Charles Town was first laid out.[20]

It is not known when Richard Deyos, Richard Battin, his wife, and George Prideaux, a servant, who were in the province by 1672, arrived. George Gourdon (Gourdin), John Bullen (Bulleine), Richard Gilliard (Gaillard), and Thomas Fluelline and wife were there by 1679. William Argent, the record states, came "in the first fleet", probably in 1670.[21] In January, 1672, Joseph Dalton, a passenger on the *Carolina,* wrote Lord Ashley, from Charles Town, "that 337 men, 71 women, and 62 children, a total of 470, had arrived in the province and that of this number, 43 men, 2 women, and 3 children had died." Sixteen others were absent when the enumeration was made, leaving a total of 406 in the province.[22] How many of these were Huguenots can probably never be ascertained.

It is not difficult to come to the conclusion that the French Protestants reaching Carolina before 1680 were in the main individual adventurers, who escaped from France to the British Isles and then went to Carolina with others of their

[19] *Cal. St. Pa.* (*Col. Am. and W. Ind.*), 1669-74, nos. 105, 434, and p. 622.

[20] Holmes, American Annals, I. 408. By 1682 there were a hundred houses in Charles Town. Carroll, *Collections,* II. 24. Cf. letters of Thos. Newe, in *Am. Hist. Rev.* XII. 323. —The name of the city was spelled Charles Town before the American Revolution. At present it is written Charleston.

[21] *Land War.* (Salley), 1672-9, 55-6, 134, 137, 139, 186, 196, 24, 39; *C. T. Yr. Bk.,* 1883, 460-1; *Coll. S. C. Hist. Soc.,* V. 329; *Land War.* (Salley), 1680-92, 5. There is some doubt whether Bullen and Gourden were French.

[22] *T. H. S. S. C.,* V. 7; XI. 15 f.; *Cal. St. Pa.* (*Am. and W. Ind.*), 1669-71, preface and no. 736; *Land War.* (Salley), 1680-92. All persons under 16 were considered children; *Cal. St. Pa.* (*Col. Am. and W. Ind.*), 1669-74, Preface.

nationality, many of whom had been denizened in England.[23] The first important accession on record of Huguenot refugees as a colony, is that of 1679-80. In that year the first large company of French Protestants came to Carolina under the direction of René Petit, the King's Agent at Rouen, and Jacob Guerrard, gentlemen from Normandy. These two men, on February 10, 1678-9, presented a petition to the Lords of Trade and Plantations, asking leave to settle about eighty families of foreign Protestants, "skilled in ye manufacture of silkes, oyles, wines, &c.," in Carolina and requesting that the £2,000 necessary outlay on the part of the undertakers be reimbursed from the first money accruing to the King's customs by bringing into England the commodities of the new colony.[24] This request was referred to the Lords of Trade and Plantations, who required the consent of the Lords Proprietors.[25] Consent was given in writing on March 5, 1678.[26] Thereupon a third petition was sent by the undertakers, stating that fifty or sixty planters were ready to go immediately. This again was referred, though this time, through the Lords of the Treasury, to the Commissioners of Customs.[27] The latter reported unfavorably upon the project, advised that the refugees be persuaded to remain in England and proposed that the Proprietors and not the King bear the expense of the voyage if it were undertaken.[28] The King in council, on May 28, however, gave his consent to the plan of the petitioners and agreed that as soon as the latters' promises were fulfilled, ships would be fitted out.[29] This long routine of necessary official procedure, which is a good example of what others encountered, continued until October, 1679, when still another petition appeared in the King's council. It suggests that since

[23] For explanation of term *denization* see pp. 109f. below.

[24] MS Col. Doc. S. C., I. nos. 69, 77; *Cal. St. Pa.* (*Am. & W. Ind.*), *1677-80,* nos. 875, 888.

[25] *Cal. St. Pa. (Am. & W. Ind.), 1677-80,* 918.

[26] *Ibid.*, no. 919; MS Col. S. C., I. 69.

[27] *Cal. St. Pa. (Col. Am. & W. Ind.), 1677-80,* nos. 919, 920.

[28] *Ibid.*, nos. 967, 999.

[29] *Ibid.*, nos. 1006, 1167, 1233. They came on the frigate *Richmond.*

the Crown had granted the request of the petitioners, and owing to the fact that many of the families had already arrived in London and little extra expense would be incurred by allowing them to go to Carolina on the ship *Richmond,* then almost ready to sail for Barbadoes, the *Richmond* be commissioned to make the voyage to Carolina, after touching at Barbadoes.[30] The petition also stated that since the remainder of the families would not be ready to go until December, when they should be transported, a list of the persons concerned in the entire undertaking would be submitted. This was agreed to. Then on the bonded promise of the two undertakers they were loaned £1,400 with the understanding that in due time they would submit the list of the persons conveyed to Carolina.[31] By the *Richmond,* loaded with freight for Barbadoes and forty-five French Protestants for Carolina, went a letter to the Governor and Council of the province recommending those on board and requesting for them such treatment as would encourage others to follow them.[32] Extracts from the log-book of the *Richmond* show that on December 17, 1679 above five o'clock A.M. they went aboard and that they landed at Oyster Point, in Carolina, on April 30, 1680.[33] This group of refugees, like other large groups arriving later, was gathered by promoters. René Petit and Jacob Guerrard were well repaid for their efforts, for on their arrival in Carolina each was granted a manor of 4,000 acres.[34]

The supposition that one or more other vessels, loaded with Huguenots, followed the *Richmond* immediately, is not based on extant material.[35] Other ships are mentioned in the records, as the *Swan,* the *Oxford,* and the *Saphire,* but apparently none of these went to Carolina, or carried French immigrants thither. The *Oxford* carried Lord Culpepper to

[30] MS Col. Doc. S. C., I. 92.
[31] *Ibid.,* I. 93, Oct. 17, 1679.
[32] Letter of "Thomas Ash Gentleman", clerk on board the *Richmond, T.H.S.S.C. XII.* 19; MS Col. Doc. S. C., I. 95.
[33] *Coll. S. C. Hist. Soc.,* I. 102.
[34] MS Col. Doc. S. C., I. 96.
[35] *Cal. St. Pa.,* 1677-80. Supplement.

Virginia, but did not touch at Carolina.[36] It seems therefore that the King loaned only one ship, the *Richmond,* in 1679, for the transportation of French Protestants, and that the promise to submit a list of passengers was never fulfilled.[37] Here then is a colony of French refugees, solicited in continental Europe, assembled in London, and transported to Carolina to produce wine, silk, and oil.

Naturally enough, emigration of Huguenots continued with greater activity after 1685 than before, owing to the fact that the persecutions in France were not only more severe, but extended over a wider territory.[38] Dragoons were now sent to Normandy and other sections, which had been exempt prior to this time. Persecutions in France continued through practically the whole of the eighteenth century, resulting in the continuation of the stream of emigrants from that country into England and from there to South Carolina.[39] A large part of the contingent of 1687, numbering six hundred, consisting chiefly of artisans, and laborers, to whom even their tools were given, came to Carolina. They were the recipients of a royal bounty. The English Revolution of 1688 opened anew the channels of immigration. No large groups, however, are known to have reached South Carolina then until the arrival of the French Protestants who came with the Purryburg settlers in 1732, and thereafter none until 1764, when 371 French Protestants arrived. Nevertheless, throughout the period individual families and small companies of emigrants of French nativity went to Carolina, to escape the rigors of the law in France and to satisfy the never-dying hunger for liberty of conscience.

[36] *Ibid.; T.H.S.S.C.,* XII. 23.

[37] *Ibid.*

[38] Smiles, *Hugenots,* 192.

[39] Floquet, *Histoire du Parlement de Normandie,* quoted in Smiles, *Hugenots,* 250. *The S. C. Gazette* of Oct. 3, 1752, published a letter from Nismes, in Languedoc, dated June 6, 1752, which describes the persecutions in Languedoc and states that they continue with more vigor than ever; that M. Benefor was condemned in the morning for attending religious service and was executed the same day; that M. Fletcher, a Protestant clergyman was under sentence of death. See also *London Gazette,* Apr. 13, 20, May 4, 11, etc., 1699; Antoine Court, *Mémoires Historiques,* 94; *Bulletin de la Société de l'Histoire du Protestantisme Français,* 69; *Cal. St. Pa. (Domestic),* 1689-90, 119.

CHAPTER II

THE HUGUENOT SETTLEMENTS

Charles Town

Probably the richest and most populous center of Huguenot activity in South Carolina was Charles Town. Its harbor was the gateway through which most of them entered. The only known exceptions were the small colony that came to Santee, overland from Virginia, and the small groups of individuals and families, who migrated by land from New York, Pennsylvania, and other colonies.[1]

In the chapter on the Huguenot churches it will be seen that before 1706 Charles Town and the Santee section contained a number of Frenchmen, and the Goose Creek area, Orange Quarter, and St. John's Berkeley had small groups. French Protestants were also found after 1706 in St. Stephen's in considerable numbers as well as in Granville County, St. John's Colleton, St. Luke's Parish, St. Matthew's, Christ Church Parish, etc., but in none of these places were purely Huguenot churches maintained after 1706, nor separate and distinct settlements founded or established except in the city of Charles Town, in Orange Quarter, and in Hillsboro Township.

Among the original lot-holders of Old Charles Town, situated on the west side of the Ashley River, who had moved from the settlement at Port Royal, were Richard Deyos, who owned lot 19, Richard Battin, owning lot 13, and others.[2] But there were French emigrants there prior to the removal of the seat of government to Oyster Point, in New Charles Town, as we have seen.[3] In October, 1692, the fol-

[1] See bibliography for list of parish registers, etc., giving details.

[2] *Council Jrnl.* (Salley), 1671-80. 40 f.; *Land War.* (Salley), 1672-79. 55.

[3] MS Council Jrnl., 1671-1721, 98. On the *Royal Jamaica,* a privateer vessel, in April, 1692, came the following Huguenots: "Daniel Horry; Peter Girard, Sr.; Peter Girard, Jr.; Peter La Salle; Isaac Massique" (Mazÿck) (*Council Jrnl.* (Salley), 1962, 61). Some of these may have

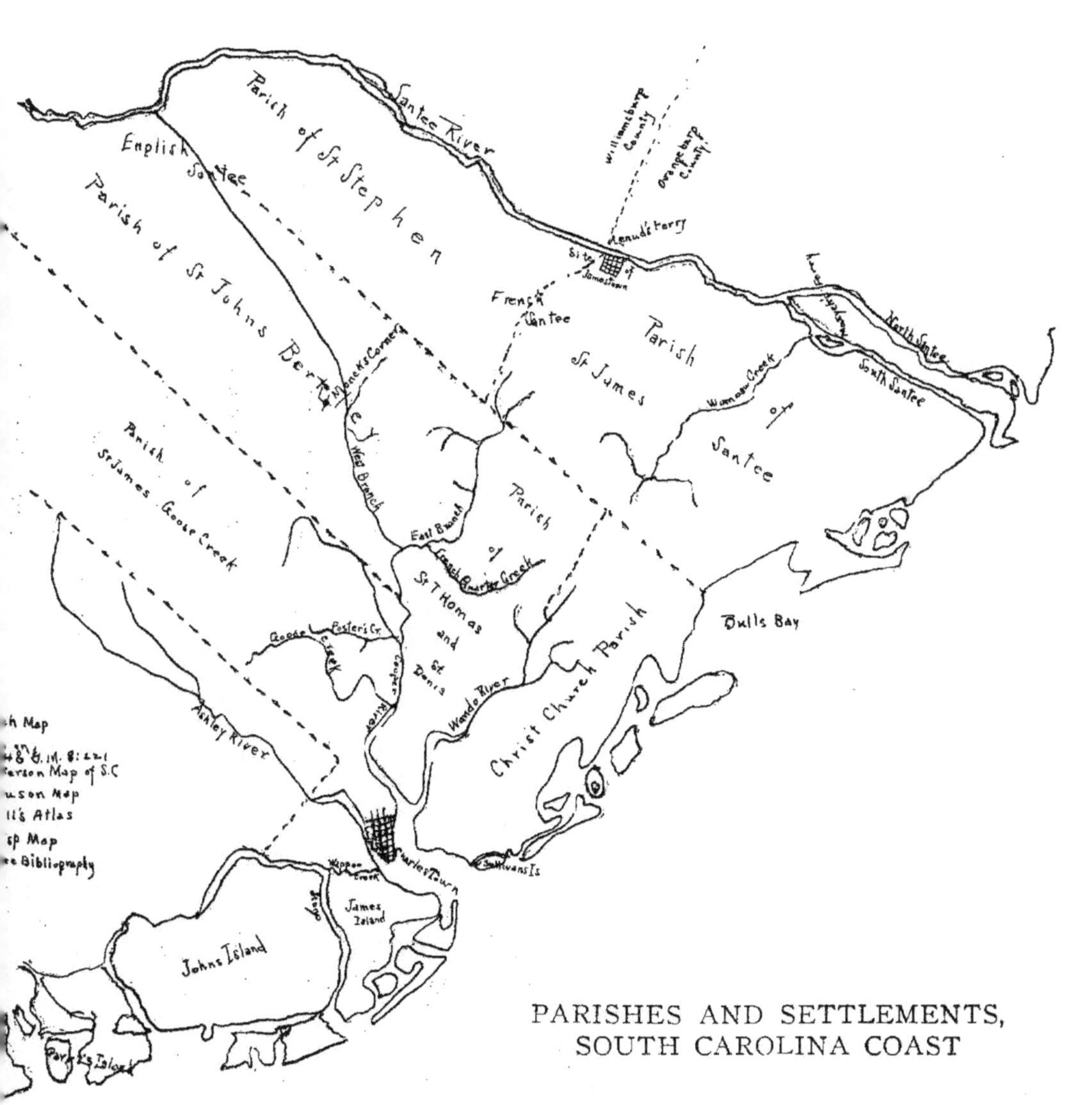

PARISHES AND SETTLEMENTS,
SOUTH CAROLINA COAST

lowing received grants of lots in Charles Town: "Peter Le Chevalier, Sr.; Isaac Dugue, Sr.; Ja. Dubourdeaux, Jr.; Jonas Bonhoste; Peter Le Chevalier, Jr.; and Jas. DeBourdeaux, Sr."[4]

Santee

The largest settlement of Huguenots in the province outside Charles Town during the early life of the colony, was on the Santee River, sixty miles north of Charles Town. How early its plantations were occupied is not known, but by 1690 about eighty families of French had settled there, distributing themselves along the waterfronts of streams, from Mazÿck's Ferry, South Santee, two miles below Wambaw Creek, in what became St. James Parish by the Acts of 1706 and 1708, to within a few miles of Lenud's Ferry, and thence back from the river into the parish of St. Denis, called Orange Quarter.[5] The area south of the Santee comprised the parishes of St. James Santee and St. Stephen's. The boundary limits north of the river were not fixed before the American Revolution. By 1706 there were a hundred families of French and sixty families of English in the district.[6] The settlement immediately south of that made by the English was known as French Santee. Though the date of the original settlement can not be fixed, a number of grants of land are found in that area in 1685. This leads

made their first trip to Carolina earlier than this. Owing to errors of phonetic spelling, common in those days, and other mistakes frequently made by clerks, in public records, it is impossible to ascertain with any degree of certainty whether all these were names of Frenchmen or not. Thomas Newe, of Exeter College, Oxford, and his father, were among the earliest settlers. His letter of May 17, 1682, written at Charles Town, stated that they arrived on May 12 of that year. Their vessel carried 62 passengers, several of whom were lost during the voyage. Two were seamen; one died of scurvy and the other fell overboard. Besides, a woman died of childbirth, and her child also. He says the town in 1680 had only three or four houses, but that in 1682 it had one hundred, all built of wood. See Rawlinson MS D. 810, folio 52b, Library of Congress.

[4] *Ibid.*

[5] See map, p. 00. Also James, *Life of Marion,* 9; Cooper, *Statutes,* II. 282 f., 328. These statements are based on numerous records still presevcd in the office of the Secretary of State, Columbia.

[6] Cooper, *Statutes,* II. 268; *C. T. Yr. Bk.,* 1895, 352; Dalcho, 295.

one to suppose that a number of French families settled there at that time. On October 10 of that year, for example, a land warrant was issued for 600 acres to Joachim Gaillard in "Jamestown Precinct."[7] A grant of that size to Mr. Gaillard can not be found in the records, but three grants of 200 acres each, adjoining each other on the Santee River, were recorded on January 18, 1688.[8] They are made out to Jean François de Gignillat. On May 5, 1690, they were conveyed to Joachim Gaillard and his sons Bartholomew and John, 200 acres to each.[9] Warrants of land were issued also to the following: Moreau Sarazin, Jacob Satur, Andrew Rembert, René Ravenel, and others.[10] Tombstones in the Santee burial ground still bear inscriptions of Colonel Elias Horry, 1707-1783; Hannah Simons, 1748-1787; and Lewis Dupré, 1767-1787.[11]

In this area the refugees settled on their plantations to cultivate the vine, olive, and silk worm and to produce naval stores.[12] Jamestown was the principal center and the only town of the settlement.[13] It was laid out after the inhabitants of that region, at a meeting held on January 29, 1705-6, had passed resolutions that 141 acres on the banks of the Santee be set aside for a town and that a remaining 219 acres be disposed of at the best advantage.[14] The inhabitants appointed Mr. Bartholomew Gaillard the surveyor and made

[7] *Cal. St. Pa. (Am. & W. Ind.)*, 1685-88, 451; H. A. M. Smith, in *S. C. H. & G. Mag.*, IX. 222. An item in *S. C. Gaz.*, Oct. 26, 1769, states that Mrs. Marian C. Porcher, daughter of Philip Gendron, was one of the first to settle in Santee about 1685.

[8] MS Proprietary Grants, vol. XXXVIII, Office Hist. Com. Columbia.

[9] MS Record Bk. "F", p. 158, Office Hist. Com. Columbia; MS Bk. "P" no. 3. 172 in Mesne Conveyance Office, C. T.

[10] MS Plat Bk., I. 321, 324, 328, 350. Sec'y. of State's Office, Columbia.

[11] *S. C. H. & G. Mag.*, XII. 153 f.

[12] Ravenel MS.

[13] The proprietors had given the name Jamestown to that section before the town was built, naming it as was customary in the laying out of townships. (See Gaillard MS.) The Jamestown on James Island should not be confused with this one. The former was laid out in accordance with an act of Council passed Dec. 1761. *Council Jrnl.* (Salley), 1671-80, 91 and *Coll. S. C. Hist. Soc.*, V. 369.

[14] Gaillard MS. Lots 19 to 24 inclusive were about three times as large as lots 1 to 18.

Santee River

Town ▫ {Church and ▫ Cemetery} Common

1	2	3	4	5	6	7	8	9	10	11	12	13	14	15	16	17	18

24	23	22	21	20	19
25	26	27	28	29	30
36	35	34	33	32	3

Philippe Jandron

James Boyd

Plan of Jamestown.

Plan copied from original attached to deed of conveyance drawn and signed by the three Commissioners appointed by the inhabitants of the vicinity of Jamestown

John Gaillard

"Le Plan cy desans est le veritable plan – et la forme de deux cents dix neuf acres de terre Vendües par les habitans des frecinct de Jamestown, au Sieur Jean Gaillard – confrontant au Nord les terres de Jamestown, a L'est les terres du Jacques boyd, au Sud celles dudit, Jean Gaillard et au West les terres du S philippe Gendron fait et certifié le fev 171$\frac{5}{6}$ par moy

B Gaillard Survd Dep.

Deed Signed by B Gaillard.
Elie Horry.
P. Robert.

PLAN OF JAMESTOWN

him one of the commissioners with directions for laying out the town lots. Lots 1 to 24 both inclusive were valued at 40 shillings each; 25 to 30 both inclusive, at 60 shillings; 31 to 36 both inclusive at 40 shillings; the rate being proportioned by the proximity to the river, the nearest being highest in price. Jean Guibal, René Ravenel, Bartholomew Gaillard, Pierre Gaillard, Jr., and Henry Bruneau were commissioned to sell lots in town and Thomas Gaillard assisted in the surveying.[15]

In this region the center of religious and political life was the church, situated within the town, less than five yards from the river, overlooking the stream at the north end of the central street on land appropriated for the commons.[16] It was built of wood and stood on a foundation of brick.

Mr. Lawson, Deputy Surveyor General for the British Government, in his tour of South Carolina in January, 1700, visited the Santee settlement and in his account of the trip states that he visited the homes of the Hugers, the Gaillards, and the Gendrons, and met the French at noon emerging from their religious service. Though he makes no mention of a town or of a church building, he states that the French were very friendly and their homes neat and clean.[17] He

[15] MS Memorial Bk., IV. 402; Gaillard MS. The following were purchasers of lots: Bartholomew Gaillard, nos. 1 and 36; John Gaillard, no. 2; Alexander Chastaigner, no. 3; John Guibal, no. 4; René Ravenel, no. 5; Philip Gendron, no. 6; Pierre Robert, no. 7; Paul Bruneau, no. 9; Peter Gaillard, no. 10; Nicholas Le Nord, no. 29; Ducros de la Bastie, no. 11; Isaac Dubose, no. 12; Peter Cadeau, no. 13; Étienne Thibout, nos. 16, 19, 30; Jedion Foucherou, no. 18; Andrew Rambert, no. 21; Moyse Carrion, nos. 23, 26, 35; Antoinette Lejau, no. 24; James Seron, no 27, 34; Peter Couillandeau, nos. 28, 33.

[16] There had been a church here before the town was laid out. No mention of the town is found before that contained in the record of a grant of 360 acres, dated September 15, 1705, to René Ravenel, Bartholomew Gaillard and Henry Bruneau, for themselves and the rest of the inhabitants on the Santee River, for the purpose of laying out a town. See MS Memorial Bk., IV. 402. There is mention, however, of a Jamestown Precinct, assigning 600 acres of land in Jamestown Precinct to Joachim Guillard (Gaillard) Oct. 10, 1687. See *Cal. St. Pa. (Am. & W. Ind.)*, 1685-88, 451; and Ravenel MS.

[17] Lawson, *Jrnl.*, 7-15. Lawson spells the names: Eugee, L'Jandro, LGrand, Gallians. The French Doctor was Porcher.

comments with feeling on the wholesome community spirit among them and their kindly coöperation in time of need.

Jamestown never prospered. The river was given to freshets and the climate was not salubrious, but the territory surrounding it continued to be inhabited by French Protestants until the nineteenth century. In November, 1708, René Ravenel, a vestryman, relinquished the money belonging to the Jamestown church and prepared to leave.[18] As the years passed he was followed into the more northerly regions of the province by numerous families. In this way St. Stephen's and St. John's Berkeley were replenished with population. This migration, though it did not entirely depopulate the region, continued about twelve years, namely, to about 1720.[19] To-day much of the old Santee section is almost a wilderness. Here and there an old ruin marks the spot where once a plantation house stood, but the river flows through miles of waste area, desolate and lonely.

Until the Revolution the principal occupation of the settlers was the culture of rice and indigo. The so-called "long cane" cotton was introduced into the province about 1770, but before its appearance most of the planters who could do so had removed to the tide lands on the Santee. This was a limited area between the salt water at the mouth of the river, and the head of the tidewater.[20] The site where Jamestown once stood was eventually abandoned and sold as a plantation.[21] Even its name is to-day but a memory, for the site for decades was known as Mount Moriah. How generally the lots of the village were improved by buildings and other additions is not known. It never became a large town. Its location was unsuited to inland trade and it was too far from

[18] Gaillard MS.

[19] *Ibid.* The emigration thus begun was continued with less persistence until the Revolution. In spite of this fact and during the continued renewal of population, the French were fairly well represented there until 1790.

[20] *Ibid.* "Long-cane cotton" derives its name from the region where it was popular, along Long Cane Creek.

[21] MS Memorial Bk., VII. 375 (Office Hist. Com. Columbia); MS Rcds. Bk. "F", no. 10, p. 116 (Mesne Conveyance Office, C. T.).

Charles Town and too inaccessible to serve as a distributing station for foreign goods. The losses sustained by these emigrations were compensated for in part by accessions from Virginia. In 1712 a portion of the settlers of Manikintown moved to Carolina and settled on the Santee. Many of them had gone to Virginia between 1690 and 1702 and were naturalized by the special Act of 1702.[22] Owing to a church quarrel in which there seems to have been more heat than religious zeal, the colony was split. The Governor and Council were appealed to that the strife might be settled. Part of the colony went to the Trent River, in North Carolina, but the Rev. Philippe De Richebourg, formerly a Roman Catholic, associate-pastor of the Anglicised Huguenot Church, in whose favor the adjudication of the Governor and Council was given, drew most of his sympathizers with him to Carolina.[23] There Dr. Isaac Porcher, a relative of the Rev. Philippe De Richebourg, was one of the foremost planters.[24] De Richebourg was made rector of the French-Anglican Church and served it until his death in 1718.[25]

In spite of adverse circumstances, numerous French Protestants grew rich on the soil in St. James Santee. The advertisements in the *Gazettes* show that many of the planters had acquired large tracts of land. Isaac Mazÿck in 1731-2 advertised the sale of 5,500 acres on the south side of the Santee River.[26] In 1735 he advertised 1,650 acres for sale.[27]

[22] *Cal. St. Pa. (Am. & W. Ind.)*, 1700, Preface, lxix and no. 681. Williams, *Hist. N. C.*, I. 178; Rawlinson MSS, Brit. Transc., no. 271, folio 9, Library of Congress; Hening, *Statutes*, III. 228.

[23] *Cal. St. Pa. (Am. & W. Ind.)*, 1702, 472; *Pub. Va. Hist. Soc.*, V. 69 f. According to Baird, *Hug. in America*, II. 177, De Richebourg went to Virginia in 1700 from England. According to the *Rawlinson MSS*, no. 271, De Joux, the associate of De Richebourg, went to Virginia in the same year, and De Richebourg is among the beneficiaries who receive a bushel of Indian corn per month, beginning Feb. 1700-1. See Rawlinson MSS, no. 271, folio 9, Library of Congress.

[24] No explanation can be offered for the connection between the names of Isaac Porcher, M.D., and the Rev. Philippe De Richebourg. The former mentions the children of De Richebourg in his will as objects worthy of compassion. MS Pr. Ct. Rcd., 1671-1727, 275.

[25] See chapter three.

[26] *S. C. Gaz.*, Feb. 19, 1731-2.

[27] *Ibid.*, May 31, 1735.

Theodore Gaillard, in 1735-6 offered 1,500 acres in Santee, 550 in Winyaw Parish, and 400 on Minion Island. Peter Horry offered 1,000 acres.[28] The year following Daniel and Élias Horry advertised 1,250 acres of rice and pine land, while in 1737 Frederick Gaillard offered 1,400 acres.[29] In 1744 Jane Douxsaint sold 1,000 acres.[30] Benjamin De St. Julien offered 3,400 acres in 1753.[31] Abraham Satur, in 1754 had an estate of 4,300 acres and with it advertises the sale of 50 negroes. The heirs of Abraham Dupont in 1761 disposed of over 3,000 acres of good land that had belonged to him.[32] It is evident that people of French descent continued to reside here far into the eighteenth century, for in 1741, when the new chapel of Echaw was proposed, all but six of the subscribers to its erection were French.[33] Noah Serre, in 1726, was still a resident of Santee, for he appends to his will: "done at my house at Santee".[34]

These are but a few of many such references found in contemporary records.

Goose Creek

Early in the life of the colony Goose Creek became a favorite residential resort for Charles Town people and others. English and French settlers were attracted to the rich lands at the "head waters" of the stream. No enumeration

[28] *Ibid.*, Jan. 17, 1735-6; Jan. 31, 1735-6.
[29] *Ibid.*, Dec. 11, 1736, Jan. 8, 1737.
[30] *Ibid.*, Jan. 3, 1744.
[31] *Ibid.*, June 18, 1753.
[32] *Ibid.*, Aug. 29, 1754, March 7, 1761.
[33] By Act of March 8, 1741, the Assembly appropriated £200 and appointed Noah Serre, Paul Bruneau, and Theo. Gaillard Commissioners. See Cooper, *Statutes*, III. 580. The following French Protestants are in the list of donors, "If built of brick and wood":

"Noah Serre, £450; Dan'l Horry, £50; Élias Horry, £25; Paul Trapier, £25; John Mayrant, £10; Wm. Thomas, £30; Tacitus Gaillard, £31-6-0; André DeSerruliette, £10; Dupont, £6; Allen Gaillard, £10; Isaac Mazÿck, £25; Dan'l Horry, £50; John Perdriau, £10; Michael Bonneau, £10; Alex. Chovin, £20; Peter Robert, £20; Elias Jaudin, £10.

For list see MS Pr. Ct. Rec., 1749-51, 134. Appended to this list is another of donors who would contribute if another certain form of structure would be constructed: John Gendron, £100; Abr. Satur, £50; Dan'l Jaudon, £50; Paul Brunneau, £51; Theo. Gaillard, £55; Paul Labilliere, £10; Andrés Rembert, £5; and Benj. Perdriau, £10.

[34] MS Pr. Ct. Rec., 1729-31, 88.

of Huguenots living there has been preserved, except possibly that of Peter Girard, who states that in March, 1699, there were thirty-one.[35] Land in this vicinity was granted to Huguenots as early as 1680. The George Gourden (Gourdin) grant of 300 acres, is dated November 15, 1680, and recites that he was then in possession of the land.[36] According to an incomplete enumeration preserved in Mrs. E. A. Poyas' *Peep into the Past,*[37] the following were tax payers at Goose Creek in 1694. She says:

"I have seen an assessment of the inhabitants of Goose Creek, for January 1694, which gives property as follows: Peter Villepontoux, Madame Elizabeth Gaillard, £2,234; Peter St. Julien, for Louis Pasquereau £350; Francis Guerin, Peter Guerin, Abraham LePlain, Gideon Fisherau (Fouchereau), Benjamin Marion, Mr. Mazÿck, Moses Moreau, Benjamin Godin."

From various sources we gather that Goose Creek must have been a rather large settlement and that a number of French families lived there either on cultivated plantations or, in the later period, at fashionable country seats.[38] In 1702 the Rev. Mr. Thomas wrote to the Society for the Propagation of the Gospel in Foreign Parts that many of the settlers "taking part in the government" lived at Goose Creek, and that some of the members of the Governor's Council and of the Assembly were there.[39] Among the French families prominent in this region were those of Antoine Prudhomme, John Boisseau, Abraham Fleury, Sieur de la Pleine, Peter Bacot, Henry Bruneau, Abraham Du-

[35] Letter, P. Girard to Lords of Trade, MS Col. Doc. S. C., IV. 75; Rivers, *Sketch.* 477.

[36] MS Register's Rcd., 1675-96, 120, Office Hist. Com. Columbia.

[37] See pp. 25, 36, 37.

[38] *S. P. G. Abs. and Dig.* in N. Y. Public Library and St. Philip's Home, Charleston; *S. C. Gaz. Council Jrnl.* Humphrey's *Hist. of the S. P. G.*, in Carrol's *Collections,* II. 540, mentioning Dr. Le Jau, states: "His own parish (Goose Creek) had about 100 families, making up 1,000 persons, much the greater number of which were members of the Church of England." This refers to the year 1706.

[39] Letters, Rev. Mr. Thomas to S. P. G., reprinted in *S. C. H. & G. Mag.,* vol. V.

Pont, Pierre Dassau, Isaac Fleury (alias De France), Gideon Faucheraud, Elias Prioleau, Anthony Bonneau, Charles Franchomme, Benjamin Godin, Francis Guerin, Benjamin Marion, John Postell, Dr. Isaac Porcher, J. DuGue, Philip Trouillart, Paul Mazÿck, Isaac Peronneau, Ann LeBrasseur, Élie Horry, and Zachariah Villepontoux.[40]

By the Act of 1706, as we shall see, the French lost their Huguenot ecclesiastical identity, but they continued to support the Established Church with liberality and took part in the political and ecclesiastical activities.

St. Thomas and St. Denis, and Orange Quarter

Except for the portion which was closely associated with the life of the local Huguenot church, little is known of the distinctly French settlement called Orange Quarter, or French Quarter. No town was established, but in the first division of the country into parishes, this area was named St. Thomas Parish.[41]

The Parish of St. Thomas was created by an act in 1706 which established religious worship in the province. In later geographical divisions Orange Quarter was part of St. Thomas Parish.[42] St. Thomas was situated northwest of Wandoe and southeast of the Cooper River, extending from the *Silk Hope* plantation to the headwaters of the east branch of the Cooper River.[43] Under provisions of the Act of 1706,

[40] MS Pr. Ct. Rcd., 1671-1727, 51 and 1754-58, 357 f.; *T. H. S. S. C.*, XVI. 42 f.; *Sims Mag.*, I. 217. Gideon Faucheraud settled there in 1707 and added to his estate until he owned 3,300 acres; see *S. C. Gaz.*, Feb. 12, 1737 and *T. H. S. S. C.*, XVI. 42. Benj. Godin was a Charles Town merchant who lived at Goose Creek; see *S. C. Gaz.*, Aug. 31, 1734. Shortly before 1748 he retired to his country seat at Goose Creek. His death occurred Apr. 27, 1748. The *S. C. Gaz.* of that date bore the following testimony to his noble life: "A gentleman of unblemished character for Integrity, Benevolence and every Moral Virtue." According to the *S. C. Gaz.* of Feb. 2, 1733-4, Paul Mazÿck owned a plantation of 900 acres. The house on it contained eight rooms. There were two stables, 60 x 30 and 60 x 20 ft. respectively, coach houses, stock barns, sheep pens, negro houses, etc. See also *S. C. Gaz.* Feb. 28, 1735-6; May 15, 1736, and Jan. 7, 1751.

[41] Cooper, *Statutes*, II. 236. For a more complete account of the church see chapter on French churches.

[42] S. P. G. MS Tr., Series B, IV, no. 88; Hassell to S. P. G.

[43] *Ibid.*, nos. 88 and 46; Cooper, *Statutes*, II. 236.

known as "The Church Act", Orange Quarter was constituted a parish for the French under the name of "The Parish of St. Denis". This was separate from the Parish of St. Thomas. In an Act of December 18, 1708, the church of the parish is called the "Church of St. Denis".[44] This was formerly the Huguenot Church of Orange Quarter. Its inhabitants were a colony of an unknown number of families the first of whom came to Carolina between 1680 and 1690.[45] Save for the mechanical lists of residents of this portion of Carolina, little can be written concerning it. Advertisements in the *South Carolina Gazette* reveal to us some of the names of the planters who lived there in the period after 1731,[46] while among the names of French families in the early records are many that are familiar in later decades.[47]

St. John's Berkeley

The Huguenot settlement of St. John's Berkeley, as it became known after 1706, was the child of the Orange Quarter and the Santee sections.[48] Located near the fertile banks of the Cooper River thirty miles nearer Charles Town

[44] See Cooper, *Statutes,* II. 282, 328.

[45] This estimate is based upon a study of Salley's *Land Warrants.* See also table in the Article by H. A. M. Smith in *S. C. H. & G. Mag.,* XVIII. 114 and the article by Thomas W. Bacot, in *T. H. S. S. C.,* XXIII. 40.

[46] *S. C. Gaz.,* July 27, 1734; Sept. 14, 1734; Dec. 21, 1738; Jan. 4, 1739; Feb. 26, 1741; March 5, 1741; June 8, 1747; Sept. 14, 1747; May 21, 1753. Daniel Jaudon, James Bilbeau, the Trézvants, Varambants, Henry Videau, Anthony Bonneau, Henry Mouzon, John Dutarque, and Benjamin Simons.

[47] *T. H. S. S. C.,* V. 66; St. Julien List, ed. 1888, 62 f.; *Land Warrants;* Probate Court Records; etc. Aunant, Bochet, Bordeau, Belin, Bremar, Bonjeau, Brabant, Boisseau, Besselleu, Bossard, Bourdin, Boyneau, Carriere, Carteau, Chovin, Cordes, Caretonau, Combe, Dupre, Durand, Dutarque, De Hay, De Veau, Dubois, Dulette, De la Motte, De Longuemar, De St. Julian, Foure (or Faure), Goudin, Gibert, Guerin, Gabeau, Huger, Horry, Jaudon, Juin, Joly, Lejau, Lesesne, Lenoir, La Bruce, Lachicotte, Le Coulier, La Pierre, Laporte, Laurens, La Roche, Legare, Leroux, Manigault, Marbeuf, Marion, Marboeuf, Micheau, Monier, Mouzon, Morquereau, Morraine, Moze, Normand, Neufville, Perdriau, Poideuin, Poitevin, Picar, Peyre, Petineau, Prioleau, Peronneau, Poinsette, Poyas, Purry, Ravenel, Roche, Rembert, Roulain, Sarazin, Simons, Sallens, Savineau, Serre, Soulege, Trézvant, Tartre, Torquet, Tarque, (or DuTarque), Trouchet, Trouillart, Videau, Varine, Varambant.

[48] Howe, *Hist. Presbyt. Ch. S. C.,* I. 112.

than the Santee region, overgrown with pine forest and containing less swamp land and a better quality of high land, it was a far more favorable place in which to live than was the Santee River district.

This colony is said to have been led by Anthony Cordes, M.D., who had arrived in Charles Town in 1686, with ten families of Huguenots.[49] They were organized into a church by the Rev. Florente Trouillart, colleague of the Rev. Elias Prioleau, of Charles Town. The Huguenot life as an element in the community has continued to the present day. Great plantations were maintained where stock raising became a leading industry and horse breeding one of the most popular activities.[50]

James St. Julien, until 1746, operated a large stock farm, the stock of which was sold at auction after his death.[51] Isaac Mazÿck, René Ravenel, and Joseph St. Julien, probably neighbors, appear as executors of the sale.[52] Joseph De St. Julien's estate was advertised for sale in 1749. It included fifty slaves, most of them country born, horses, sheep, hogs, plantation tools, etc.[53] Mrs. Jane Du Pré lived in the parish until 1750, conducting a plantation of 534 acres of corn, rice, and indigo land.[54] Gabriel Guignard owned Wampee plantation, three miles from Stone Landing, a tract of 870 acres of rice and indigo land.[55] Henry Laurens, famous as statesman prior to and during the American Revolution, lived here on large estates.[56] In 1764 Daniel Huger advertised his intention to return to France and offered for sale his plantation in the parish, 120 slaves, horses of English breed, and all of his cattle, hogs and sheep.[57] John Guerrard

[49] S. P. G. MS Tr., Series A, vol. X, no. 9; Howe, I. 112.

[50] Irving, *Hist. of the Turf in S. C.*

[51] *S. C. Gaz.*, July 14, 1746.

[52] The original parchment indenture of 93 acres of this land, dated November 26, 1726, is still in the possession of Dr. and Mrs. R. Y. Dwight, of Pinopolis. It names Henry Gignilliat, Jean Garnier, and Anthony Poitevine as witnesses of the transaction.

[53] *S. C. Gaz.*, Jan. 19, 1749.

[54] *Ibid.*, June 18, 1750.

[55] *Ibid.*, June 3, 1751.

[56] MS Laurens Letter Book, 1762-66, *Library Pa. Hist. Soc.*

[57] *S. C. Gaz.*, Feb. 25, 1764.

owned extensive domains.[58] His executors after his death disposed of more than 5,000 acres of land. Isaac Porcher was one of the great planters of his generation, a prominent leader in political activities and a successful stock raiser.[59]

Many of the plantations in this section were known by name: *Somerton,* formerly the home of the Ravenels, was bequeathed to Daniel Ravenel. Here in the burial ground under the trees are the remains of many of those once active in the community, especially members of the Ravenel family. *Wantoot* and *Hanover,* the erstwhile seats of the St. Julien family, were secured by the Ravenels through marriage with the St. Juliens. *Ophir, Mexico,* and *Peru* figured prominently in the family of Porchers. Peter Porcher settled one of these plantations on each of his three sons. *Somerset* was the property of the Mazÿcks.[60] *Eutaw,* the residence of the Sinklers, was one of the battlefields of the American Revolution. On it stood a large brick house used as a fortification by the British. *Dawshee* was formerly the home of the Gignilliats and was later owned by the Gaillards. *Chelsea* is one of the oldest plantations in the parish. It was the home of the Porchers, St. Juliens, and Ravenels. *Pooshee* was originally granted to Pierre de St. Julien, in a grant of 1,000 acres. René Ravenel and Henry Le Noble later made it their home. At *Woodboo* the Mazÿcks kept open house for all of their relatives and friends.[61]

The plantation record books and the commissary account books of the Ravenel families are interesting documents to peruse.[62] They contain the names of numerous St. John's planters and merchants and enumerate in some cases the extent of the ownership of stock and negroes. The Ravenel

[58] *Ibid.,* Nov. 5, 1764.

[59] In 1681 Isaac Porcher married Claude Cherigny, native of La Rochelle. After a married life of nearly 45 years she died August 10, 1726. In his family Bible Isaac Porcher wrote at the time: "God give me grace to make an end as Christian as she has done." See Porcher Bible, in the possession of Isaac Porcher, Esq., Pinopolis, S. C.

[60] See *T. H. S. S. C.,* XIII. 72 f.

[61] *Ibid.*

[62] These books are in the possession of Mrs. H. F. Porcher and Dr. and Mrs. R. Y. Dwight, of Pinopolis, S. C.

ledger marked "A" covering the years 1750 to 1776, contains the names of the following families of the neighborhood: Daniel Ravenel, Sr., Daniel Ravenel, Jr., Samuel Ravenel, Peter Mazÿck, Stephen Mazÿck, Catherine Taylor, daughter of Catherine Le Noble, Samuel Richebourg, Peter Gretélait, Benjamin Marion, and Henry de St. Julien. The Ravenel day-book "A" beginning with 1748, contains the record of the plantation of René Ravenel, Jr., and shows accounts with Susannah Gignilliat, Peter St. Julien, Samuel Richebourg, René Ravenel, Sr., Daniel Ravenel, Jr., Peter Gretélait, and Thomas Cordes.

The Huguenots of this parish were principally planters; a life of exceptional freedom and comfort was theirs. Their parlors were rich with mirrors, drapery, elegant furniture and silverware. Their libraries contained the best books.[63]

Here amid the gardens, where the primitive trees of the original forest survived in all their natural glory, stood the homes of these rich planters. One can almost see, even at this distance, with the centuries of years intervening, the beautiful landscape presented by noble houses, clustered closely about with trees and stately terraces and banked behind with skies of beautiful blue.

St. Stephen's

St. Stephen's parish was created by emigration from the parish of St. James Santee. As a parish it was established in 1754, though it was recognized to be the residence of numerous French families long before. Twenty years prior to the emigration from St. James Santee, St. Stephen's was a garden spot of South Carolina. The land was not liable to the sudden and frequent freshets so common along the Santee. Dubose wrote of the region:

> The exceeding fertility of the soil rendered labor scarcely necessary to make a wilderness of vegetable luxuriance; the quantity of decomposing matter and the myriad of insects incident thereto with the abundant yield of seeds furnished by the

[63] Numerous inventories of property, Pr. Ct. Rcds., Charleston; Ravenel Rcds., 104.

rank weeds and grass caused the poultry yard to teem with a well-fed population and the pastures of crab-grass and cane poured into the dairies streams of the richest milk. Nor were swine in abundance and countless fish of the finest quality wanting to fill up the measure of the peoples' comforts. . . . I have never listened to representations of comfort more perfect and exhuberant than those often given me of the scenes which I am attempting to describe, by those who had known them and loved them.[64]

Such was the country that attracted the French of St. James Santee and induced them to abandon their homes to seek a place more congenial to the growth of indigo, then the chief source of their increasing wealth.[65] In a few years it became the most thickly populated country area in the province. *Milford* plantation, a tract of between 300 and 400 acres of swamp land and 100 acres of high land, is an example indicative of the wealth of this section of the province.[66] It was purchased before the American Revolution for 6,000 guineas sterling by Samuel Cordes.

Here lived the Porchers on plantation *Mexico*. The Marions lived at *Belle Isle*. Between *Belle Isle* and the river road was the residence of Peter Couturier. The Duboses, the Richebourgs, the Sinklers, the families of Porcher and Cordes, the Peyres, the Dutarques, the Besseaus, and others, all of Huguenot stock, made this their home.

No Huguenot church was maintained there after 1706, but the vestry book of St. Stephen's Parish, (1754 *et seq.*) and the *South Carolina Gazettes* indicate that the French Protestants lived there and were affiliated as members and officers of the Established Church.[67]

[64] Dubose, *Reminiscences of St. Stephen's Parish,* 38.
[65] *Ibid.,* 40.
[66] *Ibid.,* 67.
[67] MS St. Stephen's Vestry Bk., *entry* Apr. 20, 1767; Apr. 4, 1768; March 27, 1769; Apr. 23, 1764; May 19, 1767; May 31, 1754; Apr. 16, 1759; Apr. 8, 1765; *S. C. Gaz.* Feb. 17, 1757; May 7, 1764; July 20, 1765. The following families were well known: Villepontoux, Sinkler, Dubose, Richebourg, Gaillard, Peyre, Porcher, Bonneau, Gignilliat, Simouét, Mouzon, Bochét, LeQuex, Boisseau, Couturier, Cordes, and Marion.

Purrysburg

A portion of the population of South Carolina, often counted among the Huguenots, were Frenchmen, but inhabitants or natives of Switzerland.[68] Pursued by their oppressors, both after the massacre of St. Bartholomew's and after the repeal of the Edict of Nantes, many had fled from France into the mountains of Switzerland, not far from their estates, which they had temporarily lost and to which they could easily return and claim in case the opportunity should be offered.[69] Emigration to Switzerland continued until far into the eighteenth century. It is estimated that 60,000 French Protestants found refuge in Switzerland. With many thousands of Swiss colonists emigrating to North America during the eighteenth century, directing their course chiefly to Pennsylvania and Carolina, came a sprinkling of French Protestant refugees. Two colonies were established in Carolina under Swiss leadership, one in New Bern, North Carolina, in 1710, the other at Purrysburg, South Carolina, in 1732. The latter is of special interest to us in this chapter. Among the refugees of this group who went to South Carolina, during the early years of its history were, for example, the families of Laurens, De la Bastie, Gautier (Cottier),[70] May, Leher, Jean François Gignilliat, Pierre Robert, Honore Michaud, Jean Pierre Pele, etc.,[71] but much larger numbers went under the alluring and oft repeated solicitation of Jean Peter Purry, of Neufchatel,

[68] At the time they were classed as Frenchmen, though they were born in Switzerland. See Cooper, *Statutes,* II. 59.

[69] See Moerikofer, *Geschichte der Evangelischen Flüchtlinge in der Schweiz.* Among the French-speaking areas in Switzerland were the following: Corcelles, Bern, Basil, Langel, Le Roy, La Ferrière. See Faust and Brumbaugh, *Lists,* 41, 43, 45, 61, 62, 76; Combe, *Les Refugiécs de la Revocation en Suisse.*

[70] Cottier (also written Gautier) came from a respected peasant family. Because of his peasant stock he was looked down upon by fellow students at school. See Faust and Brumbaugh, II. 4. Henri-Louis Bouquet, born about 1715 in Rolle, served first in a Swiss regiment in Holland, then in Sardinia, when he became captain. See Faust and Brumbaugh, *Lists,* II. 37, and *Dictionnaire biographique des Genèvois et des Vaudois.*

[71] Howe, *Hist. Presbyt. Ch. S. C.,* I. 115; MS Pr. Ct. Rcd., 1694-1704, 406; Pr. Ct. Rcds., 1754-58, 357.

Switzerland, formerly Director General of the French East India Company, advertiser and solicitor.[72] The provincial government was fearing the results of a great increase of negro population and was adding greater inducements for settling Carolina in order to counteract the effect of the great number of blacks. In June, 1724,[73] he began his attempts to convince the British authorities that he could transport 600 French and Swiss to Carolina, providing he were offered proper inducements for making the attempt. He asked for "four leagues square of land"[74] located according to his own choice, that he be constituted a colonel and a judge with power to nominate his own officers, and that the emigrants, after being transported to Carolina free of charge by his Majesty, should be regarded there on "the same and equal basis" with Englishmen and that they be organized into a military regiment, whose officers should have brevets from the King of England.[75] The British Government, in 1725, made a contract with Purry in which the former agreed to give passage to 1,200 persons from England to Carolina, 600 of whom were to be transported that autumn, and to grant Purry 24,000 acres of land in the province.[76] The 600 persons, however, after four years, should be required to pay annually a revenue of £300 sterling to the proprietors. This project became a "speculation bubble". The British government, after a large number of people had waited at Neufchatel for nearly a month for means of transportation to England, failed to carry out its part of the contract. Vernett, one of the adventurers, disappeared for want of sufficient money to take the people on the journey and Purry absconded to avoid the fury of the people, who had neither

[72] Howe, *Hist. Presbyt. Ch. S. C.,* I. 115; Col. Rcds. S. C., XVII. 294; XI. 132. The name is spelled *Purry* and *Pury* in the records; the former is preferred.

[73] See MS Col. Rcds., S. C., XI. 132; Dalcho, 385.

[74] Col. Doc. S. C., XI. 132-33.

[75] Popple to R. Skelton, June 11, 1725, Col. Doc. S. C., XI. 132.

[76] *Ibid.,* XI. 282, 320-1; Rawlinson MSS no. 271, folio 3, Library of Congress transcripts. The South Carolina Assembly contracted to supply the provisions for the company for nine months.

food nor shelter, nor money to buy either.[77] Jean Watt wrote on October 31, 1726:

> So many people offered themselves on the sight of the vessel, prepared, that I am persuaded if one had money, above 600 volunteers might have been procured.[78]

There was evidently considerable disturbance and possibly riot, for four days later he wrote that the magistrate of the city had quelled the tumult by "giving them each 75 'bats' of their own country". A band of about forty went to England by way of Holland, not daring to face the reproaches of their friends at home. They were led by Mme. Vallet, who took her four children, aged six to twelve, with her. Mme. Vallet and a few of her company succeeded in making only a part of the journey. Out of this scattered and numerous host of six hundred persons, twenty-four finally reached Charles Town, arriving there December 6, 1726, after a six weeks' voyage.[79]

Defeated in this first undertaking, Mr. Purry waited nearly four years before making another attempt, though meanwhile carrying on his publicity. In 1730 he went again to South Carolina to look over the available territory.[80] He wrote and published a glowing account of the province and then returned to England. In perusing the pamphlet now, one is led to wonder that the statements it contains could have been taken seriously by anyone. Many of the arguments it presents are illusory and chimerical. Nevertheless, it had the desired effect of inducing a good many disheartened foreigners to go to South Carolina.[81] Purry agreed with the English authorities in return for 12,000 acres of land to

[77] MS Col. Doc. S. C., XII. 153-4, Jean Watt to Monsr. de Valagne, "at Giles's Coffee House in Pell Mell, London"; dated Neufchatel, Oct. 31, 1726.

[78] *Ibid.*

[79] *Ibid.*, XII. 190 f.

[80] *Ibid.*, XVI. 122.

[81] MS Col. Doc. S. C., XIV. 243, 112, 237; *Coll. S. C. Hist. Soc.*, II. 127, 179, 182; Letter, Chas. Purry to a friend, *S. C. Gaz.*, Sept. 23, 1732.

transport six hundred emigrants to South Carolina within six years at their own expense. A £6 bonus for each effective person brought over was promised him by the South Carolina legislature.[82]

In 1731, one hundred and fifty colonists were brought over.[83] In addition to other perquisites obtained in America,

[82] *Ibid.*, XVI. 122; Carroll, *Collections*, II. 121 f.; MS Col. Doc. S. C., XIV. 112, 237, 243; *Coll. S. C. Hist. Soc.*, II. 127, 179, 182. The Swiss French emigration reached its height about 1734-35. By that time it had reached such proportions that it may be called an "emigration fever". A Bernese official at the time coined for it the appropriate expression "Rabies Carolinae". Efforts were made at Bern to restrain the movement. See Faust and Brumbaugh, *Lists of Swiss*, II. 17 *et seq.*

At various times financial aid was given to refugees who went to Carolina, e.g., Jaques Bernhardet, wife and two children received a viaticum of two thalers each (*ibid.*, 18).

On March 19, 1735, the *Bernische Avis Blättlein* contained the following notice: "For the good of those who have no scruples against leaving their fatherland and going to a strange country, the following extract from a letter from a citizen of Bern residing in London is here inserted.

London, February 4, 1735.

There have arrived here 340 Swiss who have no money left to pay for their passage to Carolina and who are in the direst need because of Mr. Pury's little book in which Carolina is represented as much better than it is and no mention is made of the difficulties, expenses, nor how to plan the journey, so that they are forced to accept any conditions, however hard they may be, to reach Carolina. Finally they have all departed in a little ship in which twice as many were placed as it will probably hold, so that in all probability many will die on the way. . . . Not only are they taken to the hottest part and to the border-lands of Carolina, but Mr. Pury requires of them a threefold ground-rent, and as I have said, makes them agree to pay over a sixth of the produce of the land to him. I have also heard that Mr. Pury treats the German Swiss very badly; he makes them work for him a half year before he assigns their land to them; he also sells rum to those who like to drink, in return for which they must work his land for him, and so Mr. Oglethorpe who is a member of Parliament (Parlaments-Herr) and trustee of Georgia, had the bottoms of all the casks broken, since it is a practice very harmful to the people to sell them this liquor, so that when the people complained, this gentleman, when he was in that country, put them under the supervision of a German, in order that Mr. Pury should no longer have control over them."

The following appears under date of June 4, 1735: "Reliable account of the people from Bern who recently set out in three ships for the English colony of Carolina: After they left here they were 53 days on the way to Rotterdam because of bad weather and water, but contrary to expectation they passed the Rhine safely . . . but with three times as much expense as they expected, and on May 19 . . . arrived in Rotterdam and on May 21 . . . embarked there 300 . . . in one ship." (See Faust and Brumbaugh, *Lists of Swiss*, II. 25).

[83] *Proposals of Peter Purry for Protestants;* Description of South Carolina, Carroll, *Collections*, II. 121 f.

Mr. Purry received from the British government £4 sterling for each effective person he brought.[84] The assembly appropriated £5,150 for expenses occasioned by Mr. Purry's trip and the laying out of the new township. In 1732 the town of Purrysburg was laid out. It contained 400 acres on the Savannah River. Besides, 300 acres were set aside for a church and cemetery and 100 acres for a common and a glebe.[85] In a company of 260 that came in 1734, 40 were persecuted and poverty stricken refugees who had temporarily settled in the Piedmont.[86] A collection was taken for them in England, which netted them enough for the purchase of tools, provisions, and cattle on their arrival in South Carolina. Their names are not extant, but the names of those who arrived on the 22nd and 23rd of December, 1732, are preserved, as well as the age of each.[87]

On March 12, 1732-3, Colonel Purry made affidavit in the court house at Charles Town, that he had brought the following consignments of French and Swiss to Charles Town.[88]

[84] See Holmes, *American Annals,* 1753 and MS Assembly Jrnl., (Col. Doc. S. C.), 1728-33, 960.

[85] *Council Jrnl.,* V. 74-6; Cooper, *Statues,* III. 301; *Coll. S. C. Hist. Soc.* III. 306; MS Council Jrnl., 1730-34, 208, 277. Four thousand eight hundred acres were marked off for the new settlers (*ibid.,* 376).

[86] *S. C. Gas.,* Nov. 16, 1732.

[87] The list contains the names of both French and Swiss. Only the French names are given here: "David Hugenin, age de 60; Susanna Seccot, sa femme, 47; Daniel Huguenin, son fils, 14; David, son fils, 8; Abraham, son fils, 10; Marguerite, sa fille, 12; Josue Robert, 56; Joshue, son fils, 21; Marie Madeline, 29; Anne Vallo, veuvre de Pierre Jeannerret, 49; Henry, son fils, 19; Jacques Abram, son fils, 17; Jean Pierre, son fils, 14; Marie, sa fille, age de 21; Rose Marie, sa fille, 9; François Buche, 45; Margaretta, sa femme, 50; Jean Pierre, son fils, 4; Dan'l Henry, son fils, 1; Abram, son fils, 2; Susanne, sa fille, 8; Henry Girardin, 32; Marguerite, sa femme, 32; David, son fils, 7; Henry, son fils, 4; Anne, sa fille, 2; François Bachelois, 46; sa femme, 36; Batiste, son fils, 6; François, sa fille, 3½; Marie, sa fille, 1½; Laleuve Breton, 53; Jean Pierre Breton, son fils, age de 17; Ulric Bac, age de 50; Jacob Calame, age de 60; David Giroud, age de 19; Madame Varnod; Abram Varnod, son fils; François, son fils; Trantions, sa fille; Mariannee La fille; Andrians Richard; Monsieur Purry; Monsieur Buttal; Monsieur Flar."—MS Commissions and Instructions, 1732-42, 4, Office Hist. Com. Columbia.

[88] *Ibid.,* p. 6.

November 1, 1732, in the ship *Peter and James,*
61 men, women and children.
December 13, 1732, in the ship *Shoreham,*
42 men, women and children.
December 15, 1732, in the ship *Purryburg,*
49 men, women and children.

To this list should be added 150 who arrived in 1731 and 260 who reached Charles Town in 1734.[89] At least 87 were French.[90]

Mr. Purry died about 1738-39 leaving an estate of personal property valued at about £3,600, in addition to his land holdings.[91] His youngest son who died in Lisbon in 1786 left an immense fortune valued at £800,000 sterling. During his lifetime the latter presented to his native city, Neufchatel, a gift of £50,000 sterling for the erection of a state-house and a hospital. In recognition of the gift he was honored with the title of Baron, by the King of Prussia. In his will he bequeathed £140,000 sterling to his native city.[92]

In 1764, as we shall see, Granville County Frenchmen secured their final additions of countrymen, prior to the American Revolution, by the arrival of thirty-one French Protestants. This was a section of a larger company of about 370 French refugees, who went to South Carolina with the intention of settling in Hillsboro Township, but who separated from the rest in a quarrel. Thereby they lost the protection of the provincial government and the promised bounty.[93] Forced to shift for themselves, they sought land in Granville County.

[89] *Ibid.*, 6; *S. C. Gaz.*, Nov. 16, 1743.

[90] Col. Doc. S. C., XVI. 121. An unknown number of persons of French extraction went from Charles Town and other places to settle in Granville County with the newcomers. This fact is attested by the presence of names in Granville County formerly familiar in other places.

[91] Pr. Ct. Rcd., 1736-39, 65.

[92] Extract from a letter from Neufchatel, dated July 1, 1786, printed in *S. C. H. & G. Mag.*, V. 191 and in the *State Gazette of S. C.*, Nov. 6, 1786.

[93] MS Council Jrnl., 1763-64, 179-80.

The Back-Country Movement

Following the settlement of Granville County began the movement into the back-country. The entire Atlantic water-front from North Carolina to Georgia was now occupied. Much of the tide-water area had been appropriated by the large land holders, and the rich-soil sections had been seized by land-hungry settlers of all classes. Prior to 1750 a few outposts were established on the margin of the "up-country" and a few settlers had ventured into the danger-area of the hostile Indian and the wilderness of swamp and pine-barren or rich back-country districts. Some of these settlers were from the tide-water and from England, but others, following the great valleys and adjoining plateaus that ran in a general south-westerly direction from New England, moved into the Pedee, Hillsboro, and adjoining sections.[94]

John Dubose was among the first of the Huguenots to move into the Pedee region, near the Welch settlement. He came from Santee to Lynch's Creek. Both he and his sons were men of means.[95] Isolated families, rather than large groups of French, first made their appearance in these regions. In 1760 Claudius Pegues went to Pedee and settled on the east side of the river, not far from what later became the state line. He had fled from France after the Revocation and with his wife, a Swiss, settled in London. In South Carolina he was an active citizen in St. David's Parish. He was in 1768 elected to the legislature and in 1770 was a church warden.[96] The tendency found for successive generations among the French Protestant families, to move farther and farther into the back-country, is seen in the family of Bacots. The emigrant, Pierre Bacot, of the vicinity of Tours in France, and his wife, Jacquine Menesier, together with their two sons, Daniel and Pierre, went to Charles Town, South Carolina, late in the seventeenth century. In 1696 and in 1700 grants of land were made to

[94] Calhoun, *Works*, I. 400; Brevard, *Digest*, Intr., *Coll. S. C. Hist. Soc.*, II. 75; Logan, *Upper S. C.*, etc.
[95] Gregg, *Old Cheraws*, 91.
[96] *Ibid.*, 93-5.

Pierre Bacot, the elder, in St. Andrew's Parish, lands that are now a part of the well-known *Middleton Place,* near Charleston. He died in 1702. His wife, it seems, died in 1709. The two sons who survived moved over into the Goose Creek section, about twenty miles from Charles Town, not far from what is now Ladson's Station. In 1769, Samuel Bacot, grandson of the emigrant and the eldest son of Peter Bacot by his second wife, moved into the Darlington District, far into the back-country. In 1741 he had married Rebecca Foissin. The family was one of the highly respected and efficient planter and merchant class, several of whom entered public life. Thomas Wright Bacot, of the Charles Town branch of the family, was appointed Postmaster at Charleston by President George Washington in 1794. He retained the position with increasing honor for more than forty years.[97] In the Darlington District were found also the families of Leonard Dozier and John Prothero. Sometimes driving their animals before them and carrying their possessions in wagons and carts, at other times making their way through unbroken wildernesses afoot, they went forth to overcome the difficulties incidental to the frontier.

The back-country movement was not without its French clergymen, one of the best known of whom was Paul Turquand. He was recommended to the Bishop of London by William Bull in February, 1766, after a sojourn of several years in the province. During this time "he kept a grammar school of some reputation" and because he was conducting his life "according to the precepts of Religion and good order", he was invited to accept the leadership of the Established Church in St. Matthew's Parish, and in due course he was recommended to the Bishop of London for ordination.[98]

In St. Matthew's Parish, he continued his abundant and efficient services until his death in 1784. Regardless of the

[97] MS Bacot Papers. The denization records show that one Peter Bacot and one John Bacot were granted papers of denization in 1699 in London. See *Pub. Hug. Soc.*, London, XVIII. 312-13.

[98] Fulham MS 315, no. 169, Bull to Bishop of London, February 1, 1766. Charles Town, South Carolina.

fact that his Anglican rectorship would ordinarily lead him to be loyal to the British government, he became one of the most active patriots in the cause of the American colonies in the Revolution. Elected to the Constitutional Convention of South Carolina and to the State Legislature he continued his work in defense of the American side until the British seized Charles Town and overran South Carolina. It was not until then that, foreseeing the possibility of being apprehended on charges of treason, owing to his Anglican ordination, he left his family in charge of friends, and, in company with Tacitus Gaillard, also an ardent patriot, fled to New Orleans. Though eventually both of these men were captured, Turquand was released; his friend Gaillard probably died in prison. When the war closed Turquand returned to Charles Town. Accompanied by a faithful negro servant, who had been his escort on the trip, he threaded his way through the vast Indian wilderness between New Orleans and Georgia afoot. On his return to South Carolina he resumed his duties in St. Matthew's Parish. Paul Turquand represents a tendency, prevalent, as we shall see, several generations prior to this time in young men of French nativity or parentage, resident in England, to turn to Anglican orders rather than continue in Calvinistic circles. The period of polemic discourses and sensitive distinctions had to a large extent passed both in South Carolina and in England, but he carefully considered both sides of the question. He had made a visit to South Carolina as a young man and after studiously weighing the matter he returned to England persuaded that he ought to embrace Anglicanism. He was probably helped into this decision by Pastor Boundillon, of London, an Anglicized Huguenot clergyman, and by the Rector of the Purrysburg Congregation, Mr. Geisendammer, who, together with other influential men, had been addressed by Turquand on the subject. On his return to England, after visiting South Carolina, he had entered the Winchester School, the records of which reveal his residence in 1757, and according to current practice give the date of his baptism as October 25, 1736, at Spitalfields. His family was one of the oldest and most respected of the merchant and professional class of France, who under persecution had gone to London in search of protection and an opportunity to make a living under British rule. Paul Turquand during his rectorship in St. Matthew's Parish projected a plan for the founding of a college with a faculty composed of educators gathered from England and France. With this in view he had collected a large classical library and a considerable amount of manuscript material as a nucleus, but the approaching Revolution put an end to his contemplations.[99]

With the establishment then, as we shall see, of the Hillsboro district, individual families of French Protestants emigrated thither by way of the back-country. For example, James and Mary Petigru (Petigrew) journeyed from France to Ireland, thence to Pennsylvania, and finally by way of the back-country moved into Abbeville District.[100]

These pioneers were an interesting people, fearless and dauntless. Their heroism made the frontier less dreaded, and their tireless toil made the back-country wilderness smile with generous harvests.

In 1764, shortly after the conclusion of the Peace of Paris, 1763, which ended the Seven Years' War, the last large groups of French Protestants to go to South Carolina, landed at Charles Town. They settled in Hillsboro Township and comprised a total of 371 persons. Like several of the other colonies these people left France "on account of their religion", brought their ministers with them, and established a Protestant Reformed Church, of the Calvinistic faith.[101] The sagacious governor of the Province was not insensible to the value of these newcomers. He wisely wrote to Patrick Calhoun, father of John C. Calhoun, the statesman: "I expect you will do every friendly office for them

[99] MS Turquand Papers; Pierce Family Records; David G. McCord Papers; MS Letter, Boundillon to Turquand,—all in possession of Mrs. Louisa Smythe, Charleston.

[100] Grayson, *Life of James Petigrew,* 19.

[101] MS Col. Doc. S. C., XXIX, 375 f.

which besides discharging your own conscience by doing will most certainly if this colony shoud thrive and become very Populous as it will if properly encouraged now promote the value of all the Neighbouring Lands these being men who fly from the religious oppressions in france will be followed by many also the account of enjoying Civil and religious Liberty here."[102] The Rev. Jean Louis Gibert was the pastor of one of the groups. With him was associated the Rev. Jacques Boutiton.

There was abundant reason for the continued emigration of Protestants from France to South Carolina. Persecution, though at times diminished, had not ceased.[103] Besides, it must have been generally known on the continent of Europe that the poorest classes in South Carolina and even the middle class could live better there than in Europe. Of those intending to go to the Hillsboro section the first group embarked from Plymouth, England, January 2, 1764, after two years of negotiations through their agent, John Lewis Gibert, with the British authorities, and arrived in Charleston, on April 12.[104] Gibert's correspondence with the English authorities shows him to have been a man of unique leadership. He had carefully studied the problems that would confront the new colony and had scrutinized the difficulties of the Georgia and other settlements near by. His frank boldness and characteristic courtesy were outstanding traits.[105] These people were furnished accommodations in Fort Lyttleton, at Beaufort, at a total cost of £12-17-0 for the summer and returned to Charles Town in August, having lost only one of their number.[106] A tract of land, known as Hillsboro Township, on Long Cane Creek, immediately north of the settlement made shortly before by Irish immigrants, was allotted to them. Michael Smith undertook the task of transporting them from Charles Town to Hillsboro

[102] See MS Council Jrnl., 1763-64, 262.
[103] Glen to Lords of Trade, 1751, MS Col. Doc. S. C., XXIV. 303.
[104] *Ibid.*, XXIX. 375.
[105] *Coll. S. C. Hist. Soc.*, vol. II.
[106] MS Council Jrnl., 1763-64, 144-47.

Township. His remuneration was £840.[107] These people went to South Carolina under written contract between John Lewis Gibert and his colleague, Mr. McNutt, on the one hand, and the English authorities on the other hand. The "undertakers", as they were called, were to transport two hundred French people to South Carolina and furnish a "proper vessel" for the voyage. Even the details concerning the accomodations are preserved. The passengers should be furnished with berths 6 x 1½ feet each and wholesome provisions in quantities as follows: six pounds of bread, six of beef, and one pound of butter per week, and two quarts of water each day for each passenger.[108] They were to receive land grants at the rate of one hundred acres to each family head and fifty acres to each black or white man, woman or child in the family. The rent rate was fixed at four shillings proclamation money per 100 acres, to begin at the expiration of two years.[109] Both on account of their indigent condition and their value to the province they were allowed ten years' exemption from rent, and the expenses of surveying the township and transporting them from Charles Town to the place of final settlement were paid by the provincial treasury in addition to the bounty of twenty shillings per capita for provisions and tools.[110] They named the village in the center of the township, New Bordeaux, because many of their number had come from Bordeaux, in France.[111]

Immediaely after their arrival in August and September, Patrick Calhoun, grandfather of the famous American statesman, John C. Calhoun, with the aid of the Frenchmen, surveyed the township and laid it out in vineyard lots, plantations, and a village on a New England plan. The township embraced 26,000 acres, 24,000 of which were

[107] *Ibid.*, 328.
[108] *Ibid.*, XXIX. 378.
[109] *Ibid.*, 160.
[110] *Ibid.*, 381.
[111] Bull to Lords of Trade, Aug. 20, 1764 (*ibid.*, XXX. 185).

designed to be reserved for the French.[112] For land already occupied in other grants 2,000 acres had been allowed in the survey. The surveyed portion was situated on the two main forks of Long Cane Creek, three and one-half miles from the Savannah River, forty miles above Augusta and nine miles south of Fort Boone. The lot surveys in the village were completed by October 5.[113] In spite of the "distemper" among them, they had built a fort, a mill, and a number of houses by January, 1765.

A tract of 800 acres, which comprised the village of New Bordeaux, the vineyards, glebelands, and commons, was situated on the spot where the Long Cane Creek and the Northwest Fork meet.[114] These 800 acres were apportioned as follows:

"1. Lots of 2½ acres each, embracing 100 acres . . 100
2. A fort, church yard, parsonage, market-place, parade ground, 1 acre for a public mill, and streets 25
3. A common reserved for the government 200
4. A glebe for the minister and the Church of England 300
5. 175 acres to be divided into 4-acre lots for vineyards and olive gardens 175
Total . . . . 800"[115]

In 1765 word was sent in the form of a petition, signed by fifty-eight persons, to the Board of Trade, informing them that the subscribed twenty families of destitute French Protestants were in London, that relief had been sought from the French churches in the city, "which already swarmed with poor", but without avail; and that unless they be transported to some colony they "would starve for want

[112] Inscription, original Calhoun map of Hillsboro Township, Office S. C. Hist. Com. Columbia.
[113] Patrick Calhoun to Council, MS Council Jrnl., 1763-64, 330.
[114] Original Calhoun pen map, Office Hist. Com. Columbia.
[115] MS Council Jrnl., 1763-64, 261-67.

in this land of plenty".[116] They expressed a desire to go to South Carolina and to join the colony under the care of John Pierre Gibert and Mr. Boutiton.[117] Help was given them and they united with the settlers already situated in Hillsboro Township.

At New Bordeaux the inhabitants at once organized a local form of government. It seems to have been a sort of branch political system, making reports to the head of the provincial government in Charles Town and referring disputes to the colonial assembly. Roger (Rogers) took up the duties of Justice of the Peace and was supplied with a copy of Simpson's *Justices' Guide*. Due was made Captain of the militia; Leorion was chosen Lieutenant; Le Violette, Ensign; and the Rev. Joseph Boutiton assumed the duties of spiritual guide, associated with the Rev. Mr. Gibert. For each five persons a cow and a calf were purchased. These and the horses were branded so as to distinguish them from those owned by persons outside the French community.[118]

Jacob Anger, one of the Frenchmen of Hillsboro, in 1765 petitioned the Council for a bounty sufficient to enable him to return to Great Britain and France with the purpose of trying to induce many of his relatives to emigrate to South Carolina. He sets forth in his petition that he had come to the province very poor, that he had left about twenty-five

[116] MS Col. Doc. S. C., XX. 261.

[117] The list follows: "Claude Chabor sa femme & quatres Enfans Laboureurs de Terre—6; Pierre Boyan Charpantier—1; Jean Jacques Gransar, sa femme & quatres Enfans Tisserand & Ouvrier de Terre—6; Paul Chauvet Ouvrier de Terre—1; Claude Barnier sa femme & unfils Labourer de Terre—3; Pierre LeRiche sa femme & cinc enfans Tisserand—7; Jean Dron sa femme & un Enfant. Tisserand—3; Jacques Chamberland. Iardinier & Boulanger—1; Claude Chauvet sa femme & un Fils, Laboureur de Terre & Fabriquant en Laine—3; Jean Pierre Blanchet & sa femme Iardinnier—2; Jacques Le Gros sa femme & quatres Enfans, Jardinnier—6; Pierre Chenton, Laboureur de Terre—[1]; Pierre Vaillant, Travailleur de Terre & Tailleur—1; Louis Salleri, sa femme & trois enfans ouvrier de Terre—5; Mathew Poitvin & sa femme Laboureur de Terre—2; Iean Plisson sa femme & un fils Tisserand—3; Joseph Roulland & sa femme, Jardinnier & ouvrier de Salpetre—2; Jacques Paulet Tonnelier—1; Louise Marechal—1; Pierre Villaret & sa femme Iardinnier—2; Jean Berard, Charpantier—1; Pierre Commer Boulanger—1; Laurrant Augustin, Boulanger—1." Total 58.

[118] MS Council Jrnl., 1763-64, 259 f.

relatives in France, among whom were tradesmen who said they would settle in South Carolina in case it would be advantageous for them to do so, and that he believed that he could, by returning, induce them to go to South Carolina. He states that he is "afraid to write" lest his letters be intercepted and be of great detriment to his friends in France.[119] This indicates that as late as 1765 matters were so disturbed in France as to compel Protestants to flee and to make it unsafe for those who remained to declare publicly their Protestant persuasions. The Council ordered that £100 currency be given him out of the township fund.[120]

The last two installments of French Protestants to go to South Carolina before the American Revolution went under the direction of M. Dumese de St. Pierre, who in 1767 was taking a number of French and German Protestants to occupy lands granted them by the government at Cape Sable, in Nova Scotia.[121] St. Pierre and his French followers also left France on account of religious persecution, for St. Pierre states in his petition to the public that he could not live on his estate in Normandy, because he had been "devoted to death" for his perseverance in religion and his inviolable attachments to the commercial interests of Great Britain.[122]

Owing to severe weather the vessels were driven far from their course and put in at Charles Town after being sea-ridden 138 days and having buried ten of their number overboard.[123] Sick of the sea they decided to remain at Charles Town rather than pursue their journey further and were given the benefit of the bounty ordered by the law of 1761. Accordingly £1,197 was voted by the assembly to M. de St.

[119] MS Council Jrnl., 1765-66, 578-9. The substitute of an *X* for a signature at the close of the petition may supply an additional reason for his being "afraid to write".

[120] *Ibid.* There is no evidence that he ever returned, nor that he induced his relatives to emigrate to South Carolina.

[121] Petition of Lewis Dumesnil de St. Pierre to Council, dated March 9, 1765, MS Col. Doc. S. C., XXXIII. 91. Copy of St. Pierre's Account of Vine Culture in New Bordeaux, Library of Congress, Washington, D. C.

[122] *Ibid.*

[123] *Ibid.*

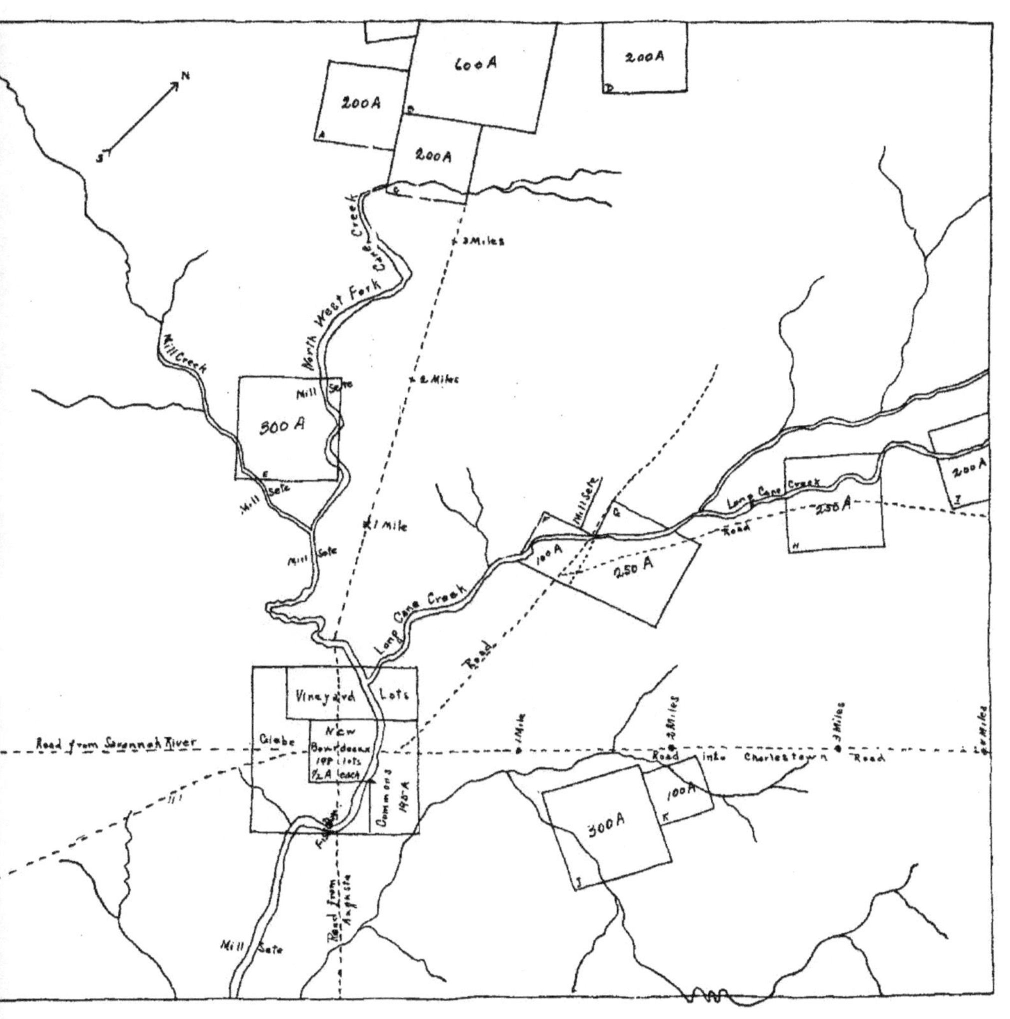

HILLSBORO TOWNSHIP

Pierre.[124] These people settled in Hillsboro Township and St. Pierre immediately entered public life. He became one of the Justices of the Peace and was made captain of the militia of the French colony of New Bordeaux. He was one of the most successful cultivators of the vine in the province.[125] In 1772 he returned to England and France to purchase grape vines and incidentally induced twenty-seven families to return to South Carolina with him. One-third of these bore French names.[126]

These groups, going to America and settling in Hillsboro Township, as we have seen to be the case in the early history of South Carolina, were assembled by brokerage agents in Europe. Direct commissions to the extent of £209 were paid to these brokers for the Hillsboro emigrants alone.[127]

Though most of the settlers in New Bordeaux were distressingly poor, occasionally one can be found who was in good circumstances. Among the latter were Antoine Gabeau and his mother, who went to South Carolina under the guidance of Jean Lewis Gibert. Antoine at the time of his arrival in the province was only seven years of age. His mother, driven out of France by persecution, was the widow of Pierre Antoine Gabeau, the owner and operator of extensive champagne vineyards near Bordeaux.[128] She brought with her to South Carolina the title deeds of two vineyards, a few personal treasures, and enough money to make herself and her son comfortable. Through her agent in France, into whose charge her property was committed, she received regular remittances, the earnings of her French estates. Though for years they yielded a good return, they were eventually lost to a "squatter". Mme. Gabeau seems to have been more fortunate than most of the refugees, for there are but few hints that they profited by their holdings in France after emigrating to South Carolina.[129]

[124] MS Council Jrnl., 1768, 101.
[125] MS Col. Doc. S. C., XXXIII. 91-122.
[126] *Ibid.*
[127] *Ibid.*, XXX. 176 f.; XXXIII. 91.
[128] Memorial Bk., C. T. Huguenot Church and *T. H. S. C.*, XIII. 84.
[129] *Ibid.*

The Huguenots in the Hillsboro section settled down in comfort and peace, but the storms of the American Revolution were soon to break forth. Like the French of the tide-water section, they mingled freely with persons of other blood and married early into the families of English, Irish, Welsh, and Germans who were numerous in that part of the province.[130]

Coeval with the arrival of the last colonizers among the French Protestants to South Carolina occurred what was perhaps the most extensive exodus among the descendants of the original emigrants. Small companies had gone to other colonies from time to time, but in the 1760's, a large number, principally from the tide-water, emigrated to Georgia, settling to the south of the Altamaha River, or between it and the Savannah River. This land, it was claimed by interpreters of the South Carolina charter, was a part of the tract granted to the province of Carolina.[131] A fort had been built on the Alatamaha River before 1721 and in that year accidentally burned. Petitions for grants aggregating nearly 23,000 acres, and grants of land aggregating over 17,000 acres to a list of persons altogether different in personnel from those represented in the petitions, give hints of the extent of the emigration.[132] Wealthy Frenchmen, such as Cornelius Dupont, sold their large holdings in South Carolina, where the price of land was increasing and the productive power of the land diminishing and moved to the newly opened districts, beyond the Savannah in Georgia.[133] Other familiar names are Henry Laurens, Theodore Gourdin, Joseph Porcher, Benjamin Mazÿck, Michael Bonneau, Jean Sinkler, etc. While it is possible that some of those

[130] See chapter on Absorption of the Huguenots; see also *T. H. S. S. C.*, V. 83.

[131] MS Col. Doc. S. C., XV. 76 f.

[132] MS Council Jrnl., 1763, 43-53; MS North American Papers, Instructions and Orders, Am. Br., 1704, 211 f., Library of Congress.

[133] Dupont advertised for sale his plantation of 1,706 acres on which was a new Dutch-roofed house, framed in yellow pine. His advertisement also mentions indigo vats, water reservoirs, a rice-pounding machine, etc.—*S. C. Gaz.*, Aug. 31, 1765.

who received grants remained in South Carolina, no doubt most of them moved to their newly acquired tracts. The scheme had been undertaken in England as well as in America, and a canvass had been made of the continent of Europe for indigent Protestants who would go to Georgia.

With the opening of Georgia as a new province in 1732, came the opportunity for the purchase of virgin soil at a low price.[134] James Oglethorpe, one of the trustees of the new province, sailed in 1732 from England with a company of emigrants bound for Georgia. The citizens of South Carolina made elaborate preparations for their arrival. At the request of Governor Robert Johnson and his Council, James St. Julien, a prominent French Protestant, was sent to wait on His Excellency, the Honorable James Oglethorpe and to assure him of the hearty support of South Carolina in the settlement of the new province.[135] Among the names of the first trustees of the new colony, appointed by George II, is that of John La Roche, a name for decades familiar in South Carolina among the French Protestants.[136] Thomas La Roche appears on the list of councilmen.[137] In order to secure military protection for the new colony by the arrival of able-bodied men, land tenure was at first made easy, but owing to the fact that negroes were excluded from the province except by special license and owing to the fact that the Indian was still in the regions near by, settlements were made with reluctance by whites other than foreign Protestants.

Georgia was called upon to undergo experiences similar to those of her neighbor province, nearly a century before. In both cases Huguenots became willing settlers, eager to profit by the returns of cheap virgin soil and ready to endure the hardships incident to the life of a thinly settled country. The success of the Georgia settlement was largely dependent on the inhabitants of South Carolina. In 1735 the English Parliament, strongly influenced by a memorial sent to the

[134] Martyn, *Acct. of Ga.*, London, 1741, 1-2.
[135] MS Council Jrnl., 1730-34, 254.
[136] *Ga. Col. Rec.*, 1732-52, I. 12.
[137] *Ibid.*, I. 14.

King by the Governor of South Carolina, gave £26,000 sterling toward settling and colonizing Georgia, and so its trustees at once took steps for settling the region near the Alatamaha (Altamaha) River.[138] The purpose was to raise raw silk.[139] A French silk expert from Piedmont went to Georgia in the first group from England.[140] On reaching America, this company cast anchor at Charles Town, and it is possible took with them to Georgia a number of planters from the southern metropolis, attracted by the added protection given them.[141]

[138] Martyn, *Acct. of Ga.*, 19.
[139] *Ibid.*, 11.
[140] *Ibid.*
[141] *Ibid.*, 12, 22.

CHAPTER III

THE FRENCH-PROTESTANT CHURCHES

The eager searcher looks in vain for extant church records to furnish information about the French congregations in South Carolina. The fires that consume wherever they may took their accustomed toll of such material, and, where moth and rust did not corrupt, a careless custody of priceless treasures made possible the destruction or loss of all that once existed. Consequently one must turn to other sources, such as reports sent to the British authorities by clergymen and missionaries, the records of the Society for the Propagation of the Gospel in Foreign Parts, the parish records, the Council and Assembly minutes, and many similar places to which the investigator is prone to turn, hopeful that they will yield something to reward his search.

Naturally the life of the Huguenots escaping religious persecution abroad was closely associated with their French churches. Wherever they settled, prior to the Church Act of 1706, they established their own worship and built their own meeting houses. We have seen that before the American Revolution there were French Protestants in almost every part of the inhabited area of the province. Nearly every parish having extant records bears testimony to the presence of Huguenots and their descendants in larger or smaller numbers.

The French Protestants are known to have established six Churches of the Reformed and Calvinistic polity and doctrine in South Carolina. They were: The Huguenot Church at Charles Town, The Huguenot Church at Goose Creek, The Huguenot Church at Orange Quarter, the Huguenot Church at Jamestown, French Santee, The Huguenot Church in St. John's Berkeley, and The French Protestant Church at New Bordeaux, in the township of Hillsboro.

The first five were founded before 1706 and of these the one at Jamestown was the first to succumb to the conditions making inevitable the necessity of embracing the polity and doctrines of the Established Church. It was anglicized in April, 1706, at its own request.[1] Those at Goose Creek, Orange Quarter, and St. John's Berkeley were absorbed by the act of 1706.[2] The French Church in New Bordeaux, founded in 1763,[3] remained Presbyterian until the American Revolution.

The Huguenot Church in Charles Town has weathered all of the adversities incident to its long history, maintaining in unbroken form and preserving the Calvinistic worship in singular purity from the time of its foundation to the present day.[4]

The polity of these Huguenot Churches, during their existence as such, was presbyterial, in accordance with the principles laid down and explained in *Le discipline Ecclésiastique des Églises Reformées de France.* This in Carolina was supplemented and adjusted to suit local conditions. The polity of these Churches was thoroughly democratic and representative. It provided for several officers. The minister was ordained in conformity with the Calvinistic tenets and was nominated by the elders of the church to the corporation.[5] With the corporation lay the power of choosing or rejecting the nominee. It also determined the length of his term of service and his salary and had the power to dissolve his connection with the church. The elders or "anciens" elected by the corporation at the January meeting of each year, were overseers or "surveillants" and were all laymen. They had charge of the common seal and the communion plate.[6] They

[1] MS Assembly Jrnl., 1702-6, 496.

[2] Cooper, *Statutes,* II. 268-9.

[3] Pierre Moragne, *Private Journal,* reprint in W. G. Morangne's published address, Appendix.

[4] On April 12, 1912, the "French Protestant Church in the City of Charleston" as it is now known in its corporate name, celebrated the 225th anniversary of its founding, with fitting ceremonies. Its venerable minister, the late Rev. Charles S. Vedder had been its pastor since 1866. He resigned in 1914, after a pastorate of forty-eight years. The Rev. F. Vurpillot was until recently the minister.

[5] *Government of the French Church,* preamble, p. 3, and article 5, p. 6.

[6] *Ibid.,* articles 9 and 13.

had the power of appointing the clerk and the sexton[7] and they nominated the minister to the corporation. It was their prerogative to sit with the minister to adjudicate matters of local importance. The fact that the Charles Town Church had elders appears in the will of Anthony Prudhomme.[8] There is no evidence of the existence of deacons in the Carolina French churches, though that office probably existed there. The deacon's function was to collect and distribute, with the advice of the consistory, moneys to the poor, the sick, and the imprisoned, and to visit and take care of them.[9] The provincial officers, vestrymen, and church-wardens functioned in the same capacity. Some cases of aid to needy French refugees are recorded in the St. Philip's vestry and church-wardens' records. The corporation was the ruling body as in the Congregational polity.[10] It was dependent on no outside body and consisted of all white members of the church in regular standing. It held two regular meetings each year, and other meetings might be held at the call of the elders. One-third of the members constituted a quorum, but at least eight were required to be present regardless of the number of members in the church. It elected a president, a secretary, and a treasurer by ballot, each to serve one year.[11] It chose its own minister and stipulated the length of his term and the amount of his salary. The consistory, or session, consisted of the minister and elders, or overseers, of the church.[12]

The body of doctrine of the churches was Calvinistic, according to the tenets contained in the "Confession de Foi,

[7] *Ibid.*, article 4.

[8] MS Pr. Ct. Rcd., 1671-1727, 51; 1692-93, 227.

[9] Quick, *Synodicon,* p. 30.

[10] *Government of the French Church*, Article 14. According to Agnew, I. 65, the first Reformed Synod, which met May 28, 1559, and the days following, drew up a *confession de foi* in 40 articles and a *Discipline Ecclésiastique* in 40 precepts. These are printed in Haag and Haag, *La France Protestante.* The office bearers were of three orders: Pasteurs, Surveillants, and Diacres. The spelling in local usage is followed; *Philip's* and *Phillip's* are both common.

[11] *Government of the French Church,* Article 2.

[12] Quick, *Synodicon,* p. 30; *Discipline of the Reformed Church of France,* Chapter V, canon 1.

faite d'un commun accord par les Églises reformees du Royaume de France" and contained forty articles. They were prepared under Calvin's supervision in May, 1559, and taught the total depravity of man's nature, the indispensible necessity of the operations of the Holy Spirit in conversion, the satisfaction of the law in the sacrifice of Christ, and "justification by faith in His name unto eternal life".

The worship in the churches was liturgical and in conformity with the Calvinistic service established in 1543 as a basis.[13] The one in use in the Charleston French church was introduced in 1713 by the churches in the principality of Neufchatel and Velangen, to which several additions have been made since.

There being no records of the Huguenot churches of South Carolina extant, as we have seen, it is impossible to write a history of their detailed activities from primary material contained in such records. There was probably little dissimilarity in the life of the several church organizations. They had been established according to custom as soon as the Huguenots reached their several places of abode and as soon as possible buildings were erected in which to conduct their worship, which prior thereto had been conducted in the homes of the refugees. The Huguenot ministers traveled circuits in accordance with the time-honored custom of frontier life, dispensing drugs to the sick, giving aid to the poor, distributing books to such as would read, and consoling the spiritually needy.

Charles Town

The little that is known about the Reformed French Protestant Church in Charles Town is gathered from materials collateral to its immediate life and activities. Tradition holds that after war, fire, and floods had done their worst in the devastation of written and printed materials, such records as survived were carried to Cheraw, South Carolina, for safe keeping, during the war for Southern Independence, but they were never recovered after the cessation of hostilities.

[13] Howe, *Hist. Presbyt. Ch. S. C.*, I. 32.

It is probable that the church was founded soon after the repeal of the Edict of Nantes, though no building is known to have been erected until later.[14] The will of Cæsar Mozé, which for generations has been quoted as proof of the organization of the church as 1687, makes no mention of the Charles Town French Church, but bequeaths £37 to the church near Mozé's plantation. Mozé lived in Orange Quarter.[15]

The Charles Town French Church was an extension, or perhaps better, a transferred reëstablishment of the French Protestant Church of Pons, France, whose pastor was Élias Prioleau. He, with his congregation, in April, 1687, witnessed the destruction of their church building in that place by their Catholic enemies.[16] While it was being demolished Mr. Prioleau gathered his congregation about him, and after he had addresed them regarding their plans for the future, they determined to embark for England. How many followed him is not known, but the names of a number of French families denizened the same day that Mr. Prioleau and his family were denizened in England, names that in later years are familiar in Carolina, indicate reasons for the supposition that at least a number followed their spiritual leader to England and subsequently to South Carolina.[17] Others probably followed as it became possible. Hands ruthless in the destruction of visible buildings were unable to destroy the church organization. It reasserted its life on American soil.

At this distance from the facts and owing to the scarcity of extant material it is uncertain whether the Charles Town Church was founded before Mr. Prioleau reached there or not. The Rev. Florente Trouillard was in Charles Town,

[14] The Charleston French Church has officially designated 1687 as the supposed date of its founding.

[15] MS Rcds. Ct. of Ordinary, 1672-92, 282.

[16] Weiss, I. Bk. 4, Chap. 1.

[17] Peter Bellin, Peter Burtel, James Benoist, Peter Chardon, David Godin, Peter de St. Julien, Caesar Mozé, Stephen Mazÿck, Isaac Mazÿck, Alexander Pepin, Peter Videau, Henry Augustus Chastaigner de Cramahé, Paul Douxsaint. See *Pub. H. Soc. London,* XVIII. 182 f.

according to the Ravenel manuscript, in 1686, and may then have been in charge of the Charles Town French Church. It is possible in that event that the Prioleau congregation united with the church already organized. Mr. Prioleau, his wife Jane, and their two children, Jane and Elias, were denizened April 9, 1687, in London.[18] There is a possibility of their having gone to Carolina before that date, for after having taken the oath of allegiance, papers of denization could have been issued to them *in absentia* on the above date. Mr. Prioleau was not naturalized in Carolina until June 14, 1697.

Thus we see the greater part of a congregation, forsaking Pons, in France, emigrating by way of Great Britain, where they were presented with letters of denization, and being transported as a church organization led by its minister, to continue its life in South Carolina. Mr. Prioleau there was associated with the Rev. Philippe Trouillard.[19] This church represents the principles of the Reformed Church of France in its purest period. These people came as the professors of its faith. They brought over and established its worship in Carolina.

A complete and authentic list of the succession of ministers of this church is now impossible. From various sources as indicated we learn of the following who served the congregation as pastors and readers:

1686. Philip Trouillard was in Charles Town. He may have been minister of the French Church.

[18] *Pub. H. S. London,* XVIII. 190.

[19] Tablet, Huguenot Church, Charleston. Fothergill's list of emigrating ministers to America, who received the Royal bounty of £20 passage money, names the following French Protestants who went to South Carolina: Stephen Coulet, Aug. 3, 1731; John la Pierre, Feb. 23, 1707-8; Francis le Jau, Nov. 27, 1705; Timothy Mellichamp, June 6, 1732; Chas. F. Moreau, Feb. 16, 1773; Peter du Plessis, June 3, 1736; Albert Pouderous, Nov. 9, 1720; John James Tissot, Aug. 5, 1729; Paul Turquand, May 1, 1766; Francis Vernod, Aug. 7, 1723. None of these so far as is known became regular ministers of the Charleston Huguenot Church; receiving the bounty would have required the abjuration of their Huguenot faith. John la Pierre served it as supply a short time, after he had taken Anglican orders. See Rawlinson MS C. 943, Bodleian, Oxford.

1687. Élias Prioleau takes charge of the church.[20]

1700 (December) to (March) 1719. Paul L'Escot served the church.[21]

1712-1713. John La Piere and Mr. Boisseau were associated with Mr. Paul L'Escot.[22]

1717. Philip de Richebourg served temporarily.

1722. Pierre Stoupe.

1728. John La Pierre.

[20] Ravenel MS; Memorial tablet, Charleston Huguenot Church; Weiss, 300.

[21] Letter of commendation presented to Paul L'Escot by his congregation on his departure for England (Rawlinson MS B. 376, folio 154, Bodleian Library, Oxford):

Nous Anciens et chefs de familles composaus L'Eglise Françoise recucillée à Charlestown in Caroline dans L'Amerique Septentrionale Certifions que Monsieur Paul L'Excot fidele Ministre du Saint Evangile a fait entre nous la Fonetion de Pasteur de notre Eglise pendant l'espace de Dixheret ans et deux mois, c'est a dire depuis Noël en l'anneé 1700 cusau 'an commencement de Mars 1719 et quel nous a toenoeurs bien edefie tant par sa conduite et ses moers qui ont ete sans reproche et de bon exemple parmi nous. Et comme de temps de son engagement avec nous est fing et que se trouvant libre il desire fortement de quitter ce pais cy pour se retirer à Geneve et y finis ses yours aupres de ses amis se Dieu le permet ne pouvans resister à son desir ne lieu refuser le conge qu'il Touhaitte. Nous le recommandons inslamment a la Grace de Notre Seigneur et à tous les bons offices de nos Freres. Fait a Charlestown en Caroline ce 14 a de Mars. 17¹⁸/19

Benj a De La Conseillere
Ancient.
Also signed by B. Godin

Samuel Peronneau
Elisée Prioleau
Jean Beauchamp
Samuel Prioleau
Jean Gendron
Peter fillieux
Chars Franç'homme
Andre Dupuy
Paul Douxsaint
cha Marchè
P. Bacot
B. Marion
Abraham Le Sueur
Adam Beauchamp
Ettienne Taunroy
James Mazÿck

Endorsed Dec. 6, 1719.

After his return to England he served the church at Dover (Rawlinson MS B. 376, folios 154 and 171, Bodleian Library, Oxford).

[22] Ravenel Rcds., 266; Tablet Huguenot Church, Charleston; Rawlinson MS C. 943.

1731. Paul L'Escot returns from England and remains with the church until 1734.[23]

1734-[52]. Francis Guichard.[24] The length of his incumbency is uncertain. The *South Carolina Gazette,* Jan. 24, 1735-6 announces the death of the wife of the Rev. Guichard, Minister of the Charles Town French Church. The will of Mathurin Boigard mentions Guichard as Minister of the French Church.[25]

1735-37. David Deléscure, Reader in the French Church.[26]

1742. Francis Varambant, "Lecturer."[27]

1753-58. Jean Pierre Tetrard.[28]

1759-72. Bartholemi Henri Himeli.[29]

1774-80. Pierre Levrier.[30]

All through its early years it was difficult to find suitable men to supply this church, but in 1710 the Charles Town Huguenot church must have sunk to the lowest stage of its disappointment. Its history holds no darker days than those which mark these years. Paul L'Escot, ever sagacious, alert, liberal, and affable was still its minister. The British archives, though silent as to the major phases of this era, contain one letter which throws a little light on the situation, not only by what it actually says, but by what it implies. The leaders of Anglicanism had not been indifferent to what had taken

[23] MS Rcd. Bk. A, p. 126, and MS Rcd. Bk. B, 140, Mesne Conveyance Office, Charleston; MS Pr. Ct. Rcd., 1752-56, 26. Will was made Aug. 24, 1752 and proved Oct. 13, 1752. *C. T. Yr. Bk.*, 1885, 305.

[24] *C. T. Yr. Bk.*, 1885, 305; Fulham Palace MSS, S. C., Box 315, no. 31. *S. C. Gaz.*

[25] See MS Minutes of the Charles Town Circular Church, 1732-96, 59; MS Rcds. Bk. *"AA"*, 320-6, Mesne Conveyance Office, Charleston; and list of subscribers to a volume of sermons by Rev. Samuel Quincy, published in Boston, 1750, flyleaf.

[26] *S. C. Gaz.*, Jan. 17, 1735-6; March 26, 1737.

[27] *Ibid.*, May 22, 1742. He also taught a private school in Charles Town. The Rev. Peter Du Plessis may have been a minister in the Charles Town French Church. The inventory of his property appears in MS Pr. Ct. Rcd., 1739-43, 210, date 1743. Varambant died in Sept. 1767, at the age of 68 years. Seven weeks before, he had married Miss Anglica Latour. See *S. C. Gaz.*, Sept. 28, 1767.

[28] *Coll. S. C. Hist. Soc.*, I. lxvii, 248; MS *Pr. Ct. Rcd.*, 1752-56, 479 f.

[29] *S. C. Gaz.*, July 19, 1760; Nov. 28, 1771; Ann Manigault Diary; MS Pr. Ct. Rcd., 1752-56, 439; Howe, *Hist. Presbyt. Ch. S. C.*, I. 326.

[30] *C. T. Yr. Bk.*, 1885, 306.

place in the crisis of 1706. After that contest was ended only one French church remained unconquered outside the Anglican fold. Commissary Johnston, forever advancing the interests of his church and government, had suggested to the Secretary of the Society for the Propagation of the Gospel that L'Escot might be induced to transfer his own allegiance and possibly that of his congregation, then very small and weak, to the Church of England. No doubt the "venerable Society", as was its policy, offered him a living through its regular missionary allotments, so that L'Escot, who then faced the possibility of being without a church in case his congregation should fail, would not be left unprovided for. Johnston had cultivated the friendship of L'Escot from almost the very hour he arrived in Charles Town and in the time of the church's distress made good use of the advantage it afforded. In those numerous conversations which their growing friendship afforded them L'Escot had evidently expressed his favorable attitude toward Anglicanism. Johnston cautiously advancing toward a conclusion based on such a friendship and such remarks wrote to the Secretary of the Society in London what his impressions were and even asked that Paul L'Escot be diplomatically approached on the subject of embracing Anglicanism. In fact the Society's letter to L'Escot was sent through Commissary Johnston, who delivered it in person. The Society for the Propagation of the Gospel offered to send him enough Anglican Books of Common Prayer to supply his congregation in their public service, as a beginning toward certain assimilation. L'Escot was not unresponsive to Johnston's attentions. He had examined the confession and creed of the Established church and expressed himself friendly to its tenets.

Furthermore, L'Escot expressed the conviction that his "duty and his conscience compelled him to make this sincere profession", that "though his Charles Town congregation" was "nonconformist, the majority of its members consider the Anglican Church with respect". His letter leaves the impression that L'Escot himself looked favorably upon Anglicanism and that if his congregation would not accept conformity it was only because of a lingering attachment which they might still have for the service practiced formerly in the churches of France. Evidently Paul L'Escot was convinced that the time was not yet ripe for a change. His reply to the Society shows this conclusively. He politely declined the offer of Books of Common Prayer because, as he states, "there might be people among us who must have a certain false zeal, inspired by ignorance, which might lead them to be unwilling to accept them, that this might cause trouble" and even "division in the congregation". But he adds, as if to reassure the Society of his own personal belief: "When it shall please God that the situation come I shall take my position there with pleasure and even if I do not dare say openly what my desire would be I could at least make it clear without disguise that it would be extremely agreeable for me that we all have perfect conformity in the service of God, since we have already arrived at it in matters of faith." There is no denial of the fact that already the public services of the Charles Town Huguenot Church were experiencing many points of contact with the Anglican formularies. The next step toward complete conformity would, it might seem, have been easy to make. Whether the conservative element in the congregation prevented its minister from going the full distance may forever be a matter of conjecture, for information on that point is lacking. L'Escot remained at his post, serving his people with entire satisfaction until 1719, but the church held continually to its own forms and practices.[31]

[31] British Transcripts, S. P. G. Series A, vol. 7, Sept. 2, 1711, no. 3: Lettre du Monsr. L^{d}. Escot South Carolina September 2^{d}. 1711.
Monsieur

J ay recu de Monsieur Johnston avec autant plus joye l'honneur de la lettre qu il vous a plu de m'ecrire n aurois osé l esper l' attendre, et les favorables Sentimens que La Tres Illustre et Venerable Societé daigne pour moy et que vous avez eu la bonté de Mexprimer par son ordre me remplissent d'un profond respect pour Elle et d'une Entiere reconisance. C'est un bonheur qui me donne une joye d autant Plus Sensible que je sais que je l'ay merité le moins, car s'il est le fruit de la liaison et de l'amitié que j'ay eu le bonheur de contracter dans ce pais cy avec Monsieur Johnston, c étoit déja beacoup d'honneur et un fort grand plaisir pour moy de recevoir des Marques bien douces et bien expresses d'amitie d'un homme de son merite, et auquel je n'ay pu refuser mon estime et beacoup plus que cela Monsr. Johnston n'est pas plutôt arrivé dans ce pais cy quil má fait la grace de m'accorder son amitié et de m'en donner des preuves que m'ont eté douces, et dout la plus grande et celle qui me touche le plus est qu il a bien voulu rendre de moy un bon temoignage à La Tres Illustre et Venerable Societe, et faire que je leur sois connûe que j'estime un honneur et un avantage bien pretieur pour moy. La Tres Illustre Societé veut aussi me faire la grace de me temoigner par vous qu' Elle est satisfaite des Sentimens qu' Elle a appris que j'ay pour l'Eglise Anglicane. Depuis que j'en ay Soigneusment Examiné la Confession et tout le Service, ma Conscience et mon devoir m'ont fortement obligez a donner à cette Eglisse mon respect et ma Veneration, Elle est pure et n'a rien que de conforme a la Sainte Doctrine de Jesus Christ de ses apotres et du Salut et, à ce que la Primitive Eglise Chretienne à cru et pratique, Et je suis et seray toujours tres eloigné de l'entetement de tous ceux qui en jugent au contraire Souhaittant avec passion qu ils rendent justice à Sa pureté et à Sa Verité. Et comme mon devoir et ma Conscience M'engagent à faire cette profession Sincere touchant L'Eglise Anglicane, je recois Comme un tres grand honneur ce que la Tres Illustre et Venerable Societe veut bien m'en temoigner par Votre moyen Son Approbation et Sa bienveuillance. Il est vray que le Troupeau au Service duquel Dieu m'a appellé icy n'est pas Conformé, mais ceux qui le Composent, on pour le moins la meillure partie considerant L'Eglise Anglicane avec le Respect qui luy est dû, et S'ils ne recoiverit pas la Conformité ce n est que par un reste d'attachement et de respect qu'ils ont encore pour le service pratiqué autrefois dans les Eglises de France qu'ils ont eû jusque icy la liberté de conserver. Quelque Veneration legitime que j'aye pour L'Eglise Anglicane, et pour son service, il ne seroit pas en mon pouvoir de changer celuy que nous retenons encore, c'est ce que le temps amenera. Ainsi, Monsieur, Oserray je vous dire que je ne vois pas qu'il soit encore necessaire de nous envoyer des Livres de Prieres Communes pour les Introduire dans notre Service, il Pourroit y avoir des gens parmi nous qu'un certain faux Zele guidé par l'ignorance porteroit à ne vouloir pas les recevoir ce qui causeroit peut etre du trouble et de la Division dans ce Troupeau qui est bien peu Nombreux, et vous jugez bien qu'il est toujours Convenable que la forme du service public s'establisse d'un commun et paisible Consentement de tous; quand il plaira à Dieu que cela arrive je m'y rangeray avec joye et si je noise pas declarer tout ouvertement que ce seroit mon desir, du moins faysé connoitre sans deguisement qu'il me seroit fort agreable que l'on néust tous qu'une parfaite conformité dans le service de Dieu puis que lon est deja enherment conformes dans tous les Points de la foy. Notre Service a deja beacoup de rapports avec celuy de L Eglise Anglicaine, nous nous Servons comme elle de Formulaires ce que ceux qui ne veulent point avoir d' accord avec Elle Condamnent fort injustement; il ne nous reste que de nous Servir du meme Formulaire de celuy de L Eglise Anglicane qui est tres beau et tres propre a inspirer la Devotion. Au reste j'ay communiqué la lettre que vous m'avez fait l'honeur de m'ecrire aux Personnes de ce pais qu'y y Sont nommies et que la Tres Illustre et Venerable Societe à voulu remercier des honnetetez qu'elles (ont en pour Monsr. Johnston et le leur bons Sentiments pour l'Eglise Anglicane, et Elles m'ont prié de vous temoigner) leur Reconnoisance pour l'honneur que la Tres Illustre Societé leur a faite. Je finiray en presentant mes tres humbles et profonds Respects à La

The Charles Town French Church after the the death or departure of its first ministers and especially after the departure of Paul L'Escot by 1719 found it increasingly difficult to supply its pulpit with desirable men of Huguenot descent. The Protestant theological schools of France had been closed, while ministers trained in England naturally drifted to the Establishment. L'Escot, though himself inclined to Anglicanism, had somehow succeeded in holding his congregation together until 1719, when he returned to England. The letter of recommendation given by heads of families of the Charles Town Huguenot Church to Mr. L'Escot at the time of his departure is full of interest. It is an expression of the appreciation of a grateful congregation for the services he had rendered. Subscribed to it are the names of twenty-one men, heads of families of the church and probably a complete or nearly complete list of the heads of households of the Charles Town French Church in 1719.[32] It seems that even Paul L'Escot was unable longer to resist the encroachments of the Established Church and was on that account unwilling longer to contiue his service to a Huguenot church, for immediately on his arrival in England, on the recommendation of M. de Guhlen, he was or-

Tres Illustre et Venerable Societé suppliant Le Seigneur quil repande tres abondamment ses benedictions les plus saintes et les plus pretieuses sur tous les Venerables Prelats et toutes les autres Personnes qui composent La Tres Illustre Societé, Quil fasse reussir toujours a Sa grand gloire et a l'avancement du Regne de J Ch tous ses pieux et tres Zelez desseins, en Sorte que par ses soins qui ne peuvent jamais assez etre loüez la a lumiere de l'Evangile et du sault soit portée jusqu' au bout de la Terre. Je prie aussi le Seigneur qu'il vous comble de ses graces et de ses benediction, agreez que je vous assure que je suis avec becoup de Respect Monsieur

Votre Tres humble et tres
obeissant Serviteur
L Escot

A Charlestown en Carolina ce 2e. de Septembre 1711.
See also Rawlinson MS B. 376, fol. 154.

[32] MS Rawlinson transcript, Library of Congres. B. 376, fol. 154: B. Godin, Samuel Peronneau, Élisée Prioleau, Jean Beauchamp, Samuel Prioleau, Jean Gendron, Prr Fillieux, Charles Franc'homme, André Du'puy, ————? [————] Bacot, James Mazÿck, Benj. de la Conseillère, (Ancient) Paul Douxsaint, Charles Marchè, P. Bacot, B. Marion, Abraham le Sueur, Adam Beauchamp, Adrienne Taun u roy.

dained an Anglican priest and became the rector of the French Anglican Church at Dover.[33] Two letters written by Isaac Mazÿck, dated 1724, and addressed to Mr. Godin, in London, manifest the despondency of members of the Charles Town French Church. They complain that owing to the absence of Huguenot ministers the church "was going over to the Episcopal worship" and show plainly the extreme difficulty in securing desirable clergymen. L'Escot's Charles Town congregation, left without a shepherd, became a weakened, scattered, unsheltered people. That this church weathered the storm and remained unseduced in the midst of such painful circumstances is remarkable. It is not known exactly when, but sometime later than 1728, L'Escot after a sojourn in England was induced to return to his former Charles Town congregation. The author is inclined to place the date about 1731-32, for in 1731 the London Walloon Church received a letter from the Charles Town French Church asking for a minister. A salary of £80 was offered and an additional £25 for passage. The letter is signed by Peter Fillen (Fillieu), Éstienne Mounier, Mathew Boigard, Jean le Breton, André de Veaux, Anthoine Bonneau, Jacob Satur, Joel Poinset, Jean Garnier, Jacob le Chantre, and C. Birot. It seems that soon after this Paul L'Escot returned to Carolina. He served the Charles Town French Church then until 1734.[34] In the interim of weakness cited above the church was forced to content itself with a French clergyman who had been ordained in the Anglican communion. Alexander Garden's letter to the Bishop of London under date of November 8, 1732, is a commentary, not only on the weakness of the congregation at this time, but also on the subject of conflict over practices and policies. The Anglican authorities held that even though Guichard was the settled minister of the Charles Town French Church, the fact of his ordination in the Church of England made it incumbent upon

[33] MS Rawlinson B. 376.

[34] Rawlinson MSS B. 376, C 943; Burns, *Hist. Fr. Refugees,* 19; *C. T. Yr. Bk.,* 1885, 305-7.

him to use the Anglican ritual, that all clergymen thus ordained "were bound by their subscription as a Condition of their Ordinaon, to use the Liturgy of the Church of Engld in their ministraon & no other." Guichard, it is clear, made light of this exact interpretation and consequently was cited for criticism by Commissary Garden.[35]

Santee

The French Church of Santee was numerically probably the strongest to be found in the province outside of Charles Town. One hundred families were settled there by 1700.[36] These in all probability, however, would not make a very much larger church affiliation than that of the Charles Town Huguenot Church, whose membership in 1699 was 195.[37] The Church building was situated on the spot that after 1695 was the center of the village of French Jamestown, on the margin of the Santee River, overlooking the stream.[38] The

[35] "But my Lord, there's lately come over also a french minister, (whose name is Guichard,) for the Calvinist meeting here in Charles Town, who says he was Ordained by your Lordship and yet uses only the Calvinist or French Protestant Liturgy in that meeting. I have talked with him on the subject; but he seemd to make light of it; said it was usual 'mong the French Ministers to use the one or other Lityrgy as the People were minded, & that he thought the matter of no consequence. I observed to him that however those who had only Geneve or Presbyterial Ordination, were at Liberty to use any Protestant Liturgy they may think fitting, yet as to those who rec' Orders in the Chh of England the case was not so; but they were bound by their subscription as a Condition of their Ordinaon, to use the liturgy of the Church of Engld in their ministratraon, & no other. Now as this is an unusual case; and in noch as the Person has no Living, Stipend, or Salary in the Church of England, I know not well how to proceed agt him, to any Purpose, and being that the French (who have always kept on good terms with the Ch of England here, many of them frequenting it & coming over to its Communion are generally a pretty humorsum & captious people on Points of this nature; and therefore tho such Process should not prevail, wou'd yet be apt to make much ado about it, take up much Prejudice agt the chh upon it, & run it into a Party Quarrel. I have therefore determined first to acquaint your Lordship of this affair & to wait your Direction how to conduct myself in it.

A. Garden."

See Fullham MSS S. C., no. 31.

[36] *S. P. G. Abs.*, 1712.

[37] Gaillard MS; *Cal. St. Pa. (Am. & W. Ind.)*, 1699, 107; Rivers, Sketch, 447.

[38] Gaillard MS.

church, however, was erected before the town was laid out. It is not known when it was built nor when the church was organized, but the probabilities are that these things occurred almost as soon as Huguenots settled there. The first French minister known to have preached in Carolina was the Rev. Pierre Robert, a refugee, who went to the province in 1686 with Captain Philip Gendron and settled on the Santee, in St. James Parish.[39] He was a clergyman of Swiss parentage and birth and became minister of the French congregation of St. James Santee.[40] In 1699 the church had 111 members.[41] Pierre Robert was the son of Daniel and Marie Robert. The register of the old Huguenot Church in Basle, Switzerland, bears record of his ordination, February 19, 1682, and the baptism of his son, Pierre, May 9, 1675. His wife's name was Jeanne Broye.[42]

The Huguenot Church on the Santee, as such, had a short existence. In April 1706, seven months before the famous Church Act of 1706 was passed, at the request of the French settlers themselves this was constituted a Church of England parish, in conformity with the doctrines and usages of the Established Church.[43] Pierre Robert remained its minister until 1710, the year of his death.[44] Being in Anglican orders he was eligible to a rectorship in the Establishment. The change thus accomplished in the church was complete and thorough, for the time being, for the only concession that was made to the Huguenots was that they might conduct their worship in the French language, provided they would use the John Durel translation of the Book of Common Prayer. Was there something unconquerable in the spirit of

[39] MS Memorial Bk., C. T. Huguenot Church.

[40] Pr. Ct. Rec., 1694-1704, 406.

[41] *Cal. St. Pa. (Am. & W. Ind.)*, 1699, no. 341; Rivers, *Sketch*, 477; MS Col. Doc. S. C., IV. 75.

[42] MS Memorial Bk., C. T. Huguenot Church, p. 45.

[43] MS Assembly Jrnl., 1702-6, 496; Cooper, *Statutes*, II. 268.

[44] The record of Daniel Huger, in possession of the Huger family, Charleston, states that on January 25, 1709-10, his son Daniel Huger was married to Elizabeth Gendron, by the Rev. Peter Robert, Minister of the Holy Gospel (T. H. S. S. C., IV. 11). Howe (I. 151) says that Pierre Robert was minister from 1700 to 1710.

these people? They yielded to the legal specifications, but for generations they held to the French language and traditions, yielding up only reluctantly the cherished Calvinism for which they had suffered and which they had passed through even the fires of adversity to maintain. There was no delirium of excitement: only a silent, courteous submission to the inevitable. It is clear too that long after the Church Act of 1706 was passed the Church of England provided clergymen of French nativity to supply the pulpit of this place. Philip de Richebourg succeeded Pierre Robert as minister. Albert Pouderous was next in the succession. The date of the beginning of his incumbency is fixed by his own letter, under date of April 25, 1724, in which he says: "it has been three years and Seven Month that j am send a Missionary."[45] He was a native Frenchman and a convert from Romanism who refugeed from France under persecution, preached in London three years and then was sent to South Carolina by the Society for the Propagation of the Gospel. His broken English did not deter him in his zeal to serve his generation. Like others who preached at Santee, he lived on the main highway to the up-country, and there being no taverns at which travelers could be accommodated, his home became the rendezvous of this class. Here he almost daily dispensed succor to the poor and needy and even medical aid to the sick. The human heart responds with sympathy as one reads the brief excerpts from his letters to those in London who were his supervisors. Though good sense would counsel against such a location, circumstances seem to have compelled the building of the parsonage on the very banks of the river, where the overflow even in winter annoyed and freshets caused great inconveniences and loss. Albert Pouderous' letter of January 20, 1723 states that he had "above seven foot" of water in his house, "the greater part" of his "Household goods damaged and crops entirely lost."[46] His death

[45] Fulham Manuscripts, S. C., Box 315, no. 197; Fothergill, *Emigrants, 1690-1811*, p. 50.

[46] S. P. G. MS Tr. Series B. IV. 137; Fulham MSS, S. C., no. 278; Fulham Manuscripts, South Carolina, Box 315, no. 1: Albert Pouderous to the Bishop of London, April 25, 1724:—

occurred February 7, 1731, while still in charge of the Santee Church.

How can the ironies of fate be explained that seem to have directed the next step in the Santee congregation? Though the vestry addressed a letter to the Bishop of London, requesting another minister, but one who had never been a Roman Catholic, Stephen Coulet, a convert from Catholicism, was sent to South Carolina in 1731 and directed to fill the vacancy in the Santee parish. He died in 1733.[47]

"j am Milord a french minister that abandoned every thing for the cause of the Gospel and j have worck with great Zeale for the oppressed church in french, afterwards j suffered verry much, j have imbraced with all my hart the church of england sins many years finding her conform with the worth of god and with the primitive church j preached three years it london j am Sendet by the late milord bishop of London and the Society. . . . j am obliged without charite to assist the Sicke poor people and to keep phisic to cure her Some kine there be at my charge two month befurst to recouverd her held . . . [paper broken] ruined the plantations, some time the water come Six food high into the houses my house is Situated upon the common passage every j am obliged to loged and to nourish the passenger being no Taverns of ins in this parish and everything is very deart because the parish is 60 mils distante of the town."

A letter dated April 20, 1731, at Charles Town, from Commissary Garden to the Bishop of London mentions the death of Mr. Pouderous. Mr. Garden spells it "Poudrous". The following is found in the letter; the reference is to Santee: "That Parish was at first settled with French Refugees, but as many of the present Inhabitants are the posterity of those first Settlers, and to whom the French is become a learned Language, while the old ones that still remain understand but little or nothing of the English; they therefore also Request that the Gentleman, who shall be now sent them, may be one who is capable to officiate in both Tongues." See Fulham Palace Manuscripts, S. C., under date.

[47] Fulham Palace MSS, S. C., nos. 36, 37; A. Garden to Bishop of London, July 24, 1733:

"I am sorry that Mr. Coulet has troubled your Lordship with any complaint of the English Parishioners of Santee. He had no just grounds for so doing: and at least, when those he apprehended to be such were removed & all Matters of Deferrence 'twixt him and them set to rights, (as they were, as soon as he wrote to me of them; 'bout the same time, it seems as he wrote to your Lordship;) he ought to have acquainted your Lordship of the same also. The whole Account of that Affair wou'd be as tedious, as now also it is needless to trouble your Lordship with. Only is Sum, it appear'd on the Enquiry, that Mr. Coulet, as he was sickly, so he was captious and humorsom; but chiefly that he had declined to officiate in English at all, and sought under various Pretences wholly to avoid it. Being sufficiently informed of this, I wrote a pretty sharp letter to Mr. Coulet expostulating the mat-

Joseph Bugnion served in the church after 1733. Coulet was French and Joseph Bugnion was of Swiss extraction. Bugnion brought over a company of French-Swiss families to settle in Carolina. He had embraced Anglicanism in England and was ordained in London to the priesthood of the Established Church.[48] With the families of French-Swiss that he brought over, he settled first at Purrysburg. A quarrel between Purry, the Proprietor, and Bugnion resulted in a division in the Purrysburg Established Church, with which the French-Swiss families had affiliated. Thereupon Bugnion requested the Bishop of London to appoint him to the Santee Church. Coulet had died in 1732 and had been succeeded by Colladon in 1733. His tenure was very short, for Alexander Garden in a letter of December 28, 1733 mentions both his arrival and his death and says that he was acceptable to both the French and the English. He died on the fourth day of his illness, of fever. Bugnion found in the Santee section a more agreeable situation than the Purrysburg section had afforded him.[49]

Almost immediately upon his arrival in South Carolina Bugnion had aroused the Anglican clergymen. He "declined to officiate in the English language and saught wholly to avoid it." This was one of the things that stood against him at Purrysburg. At Santee the same objection to his ministry

ter with him & advising him to alter the measures, wch either his own Inclinaons or partial Advise, or both perhaps, had led him into and to divide his Labors 'mongst the People of his Charge, in such manner as allmight equally (as near as could be) partake of the Benefit of them. This Advice he immediately comply'd with, dropt his former measures. & officiated by Turns in French and English; on which all Differences subsided, and he thenceforth lived easy and contented to the time he died. I have assured Mr. Colladon, (as I also take leave to do your Lordship), that if he will only do, what every good Clergyman will desire and choose to do, viz, divide his labors 'mongst the People of his charge impartially, or so as all may equally (as near as may be) partake of the Benefit of them; Ill engage none of the matters complain'd of by Mr. Coulet, shall give him any the least Trouble: and in any other Difficulties that may happen, if he will let me know in time, I shall be always ready to assist him with the best offices in my Power."

[48] Fulham Palace MSS, Box 315, No. 31.

[49] Fothergill, *Emigrants,* 50; S. P. G. Abstracts, 1723, 45; Fulham Palace MSS, S. C., Box 315, no. 75.

was raised, and Bugnion, who had not mastered the English language sufficiently to officiate in it, found that the English portion of his parish were opposed to employing him. This fact threatened a split in the Santee church because the French portion refused to apply for any other minister. The French had an advantage in this case in the fact that the vestry consisted "chiefly of French and their descendants" and, "being that the several vestries here" were then "empowered to employ any lawful minister to supply their cures in case of Vacancy" they were determined to secure Bugnion, "though contrary to the late law", which provided that the minister must officiate in English. When the English of the parish threatened to withhold the salary provided by law, Mr. Bugnion came to the rescue of his countrymen by expressing his willingness to abandon French entirely, and "learn the English tongue". Owing to his destitute condition, with a family of four small children, the English agreed to be patient under this arrangement.[50] Bugnion struggled on under great distress, but was compelled finally to give up his efforts to satisfy the people. He came to know at what a cost one of alien birth strives to serve a congregation of two languages and two allegiances. He had to contend with carping critics. In 1734 the petulant faultfinders had their way, for the vestry was no longer able to employ him and hold the church together. A fever of unrest and dissatisfaction was spreading. Though remaining in the parish he withdrew from his ministry and ministered to a few French families who clung to him.[51] It would seem as though Bugnion now turned to farming as a makeshift. At least he became a rich landowner, for in 1739 he advertised for sale 3,900 acres of land and 42 slaves. Had the time passed when even the parishioners of this distinctly French section were no longer willing to suffer the discomforts that must certainly have been their portion, as they listened to their minister trying to

[50] Fulham Palace MSS, S. C., Box 315, no. 75.
[51] *Ibid.*

expound the scripture in broken English and reveal the mysteries of religion in a language that he understood not?[52]

The London archives still hold a number of letters bearing on the period. The communications that passed between Alexander Garden and the Bishop of London leave the impression that two separate vestries, in the Santee parish, representing the two groups, operated officially and unofficially, each after its kind and in its own behalf. The date of Bugnion's dismissal is fixed by one of the vestry letters, dated April 14, 1735, in which it was set forth that they had been without a minister for eighteen months. Emphasis is placed on the fact that a minister is desired who can speak French, because some in the parish cannot understand English, while others, who can understand English, prefer to hear sermons in French. Probably the portion of the parish that was unfamiliar with the French language and saw no good reason for continuing it in Carolina, who chafed under a public ministration carried on in broken English by one who, though in Anglican orders, was still imbued with a strong Calvinistic and French individualism, were not least among the disturbers of the peace.[53]

The Santee vestry, in April, 1735, renewed their request to the Bishop of London for a clergyman. Rev. Mr. Du Plessis arrived in September 1736, to gather the broken pieces of the church together and carry forward the work of the ministry.[54] The transition was in progress. Santee, as the older French people were moving away or dying, was becoming more and more inclined to accept the practices and usages of the majority of the province. This was only natural. The things for which the fathers had suffered were but dim in the minds of the children, except where by daily precept and example the elders impressed upon the youths the overmastering power of their convictions.

[52] *Ibid.*, MS Council Jrnl., 1734-37, 186, 328; MS Assembly Jrnl., 1735-36, 392-3.

[53] Fulham Palace MSS, S. C., Box 315, nos. 36, 75, 131, 188; *ibid;* Box 316, no. 274.

[54] *Ibid.*, Box 315, nos. 131, 188; MS Council Jrnl., 1734-37, 328.

Goose Creek Church

The earliest mention of a French congregation at Goose Creek is in the will of Anthony Prudhomme dated 1695 in which he bequeathed a cow and two heifers to the people who worshipped there.[55] The church building was located about four miles north-west of the Episcopal Church now known as the Goose Creek Episcopal Church, built in 1711-12, and one and one-half miles from Ladson's Station, about twenty miles from Charles Town.[56] A granite cross erected by the Huguenot Society of South Carolina now marks the spot where the building stood. It was on a tract of land granted to Abraham Fleury de la Pleine in 1696.[57]

The existence of a French Protestant Church organization at Goose Creek is proved by many documents: the Peter Girard enumeration of the membership of the Goose Creek Church, the will of Anthony Prudhomme, the John Purcell map (which indicates the location of the Church), many references in the S. P. G. reports, and the correspondence of the Rev. Mr. Thomas, Missionary of the Society for the Propagation of the Gospel.[58] This section was "erected into a parish" by the Act of 1706 and its boundaries defined, but prior to that time the active life of the French in the settlement had begun.[59] French inhabitants were there as early as 1680.[60] It is evident, however, that by 1702 the French were already pretty completely absorbed by the Established Church, for the Rev. Pierre Thomas, a Missionary of the Society for the Propagation of the Gospel, wrote to the Society in London that there were only five families there who

[55] MS Pr. Ct. Rcd., 1671-1727, 51; 1692-93, 227.

[56] The Joseph Purcell map, 1791, shows the "ruins of French Church". The Goose Creek Established Church was completed about 1711-12; see MS S. P. G. Rcd.; MS Journal of the Board of Commissioners of Indian Affairs, March 9, 1710-11, 4, and Apr. 17, 1711, 6.

[57] MS Pr. Ct. Rcd., 1671-1727, 167.

[58] *Ibid.*, 57; Rivers. *Sketch,* 447; MS Joseph Purcell Map; Record Bk. "G", 95, Mesne Conveyance Office, Charleston; MS Transcripts of Letters of Thomas to S. P. G. in possession of the Hon. John P. Thomas, Columbia; MS S. P. G. Transcripts, Series A, vols. I-XX.

[59] Cooper, *Statutes*, II. 282 f.

[60] MS Register's Rcd., 1675-96, 120.

still retained the Calvinistic belief.[61] There were two churches at Goose Creek, an Anglican and a French Protestant. Thomas was missionary to the Anglican church and Le Jau succeeded him and became the first rector of the parish. The French Protestant Church near by probably died out and the membership affiliated with the Anglican body after 1706. Benjamin Godin, a prominent French Protestant, was the first donor of the land on which the Episcopal Church of Goose Creek now stands. The tract contained sixteen acres. In 1688-89 the Goose Creek Huguenot Church had thirty-one members.[62] There is no evidence of the Huguenots having had a minister of their own nativity prior to 1706, when Francis Le Jau, born and reared a Huguenot in France and Episcopally ordained in London, came to Carolina to officiate in the Anglican church of Goose Creek.[63] He arrived in Carolina, from Virginia, on October 13, 1706. Le Jau was at this time fully committed to his Anglican allegiance as can be shown by his letter of December 2, 1706, to the Secretary of the Society for the Propagation of the Gospel, in London. He asks for four more ministers, several teachers, etc. Then he adds:

> If some french minister would come here, there is the same maintenance from the country for two of them & if they could serve an English Parish 'twould be better. I will now and then, as I am able, visit the French plantations, but will chiefly behave my self according to the Commands and receive from His Grace the President of the Hon[ble] Society.[64]

[61] A copy of his letter is in the possession of the Hon. John P. Thomas, Columbia. Its date is not recorded, but circumstantial evidence contained in the letters accompanying it shows that this one was written before July, 1702. Thomas went to England in 1705 and returned the year following. He died on Oct. 3, 1706, a few days after his return to Charles Town. Humphreys, S. P. G., 48; MS S. P. G. Tr., A, vol. III. no. 68.

[62] *Cal. St. Pa. (Am. & W. Ind.)*, 1699, no. 431; Rivers, *Sketch*, 447.

[63] *S. P. G. Abs.*, 1706, 32; Humphreys, *S. P. G.* 84; *Dalcho*, 245. Le Jau was in London in November, 1705, for on Nov. 27 he appeared for Royal Bounty to cover his expenses in going to America (Fothergill, 40).

[64] S. P. G. MS Tr., Series A, vol. III, no. 68. This plan he fulfilled, for on September 23, 1707, he wrote to the Secretary of the Society for the Propagation of the Gospel: "I design to go on Sunday next to

FRANCIS LE JAU, D.D.
1665-1717
First Rector of St. James Church, Goose Creek, 1706-1717.
(The painting from which this photograph was taken was painted from the original by Dr. John B. Irving. It is now in the possession of the Rev. Francis Le Jau Frost, West New Brighton, N. Y.)

He was the first clergyman exclusively assigned to this church and with his rectorship the organic life of the parish begins.[65] The nearby Huguenot Church was with others absorbed or anglicized a month after his arrival.[66] Le Jau had been a canon in St. Paul's Cathedral and had been honored with the degree of Doctor of Divinity by his alma mater, Trinity College, Dublin.[67] He was sent to the Goose Creek congregation in conformity with the policy of the English government to cater to the desire of the French portion of the population in the province. His ministry was rewarded by the rapid growth of his church.[68] Doctor Le Jau was a constructive religious statesman, fearless in his convictions, a builder and organizer of rare skill and insight. He was a thoroughly anglicized Frenchman, having served established churches in the British Isles before going to South Carolina. Probably no clergyman in the province left a more voluminous body of correspondence behind. During the early part of the eighteenth century, he was, next to the Commissary, the most influential Anglican clergyman in South Carolina. During the Commissary's absence in England he served St. Philip's Church, Charles Town, and acted as Deputy to the Commissary. The records of the Society for the Propagation of the Gospel in Foreign Parts are replete with evidences from his own hand of his active interest and participation in every movement of public importance in the province. He wrote to the Bishop of London regularly and kept the Secretary of the Society for the Propagation of the Gospel informed of practically every detail of administration and doctrinal controversy, as well as of events of gen-

visit the French settlement in the Orange Quarter and administer the Holy Communion among them. The families are 32 and the number of communicants 50" (S. P. G. MS Tr., Series A, vol. III, no. 146). Under date of June 30, 1707, he reported 50 communicants in the French Settlement of St. Denis (*ibid.*, no. 142).

[65] *Ibid.;* Cooper, *Statutes.* II. 286-8.

[66] Cooper, *Statutes.*, II. 268.

[67] *S. P. G. Digest Missionary Roll*, 1702-1892, 849.

[68] *S. P. G. Abs.* 1715, 9; *Ibid.*, 1709-10 to 1710-11, 39. Lejau letters to Bishop of London, S. C. Letters, Fulham Palace, London.

eral interest in South Carolina, during his active life there.[69] Dr. Le Jau took a great interest in the negroes and Indians of his parish. From time to time he reported his activities in this direction. For example, in 1711-12 he says that from forty to fifty negroes were being catechized in his parish. He urged the people to give them the advantage of Christian instruction and baptism.[70] Herein he was materially helped by the work in the parish mission school, which was established as a result of Le Jau's efforts. The salary of the missionary-teacher was paid by the Society for the Propagation of the Gospel in London. Le Jau brought Benjamin Dennis over from Virginia, in 1711 to take charge of the school. He devoted all of his time and effort to its work, which consisted not only of giving daily instruction to the children of the parish in secular education, but also of catechising servants and negroes, instructing them in religion and preparing them for baptism and admission to the church. He says in one of his reports to the London Secretaries: "I catechize those that are ignorant twice a day and those more perfect twice a week." In this school, in 1713 there were two Indians getting regular instruction.[71]

In 1711 Le Jau undertook the construction of a much needed church building, which after anxiety-ridden delays was finished in 1712. The passion and patience of missionary effort in the world are not infrequently recorded in bits of unconscious record and hints dropped with no thought at all of the heroism with which the effort is girt around. The Chamberlayne letter, dated January 4, 1711-12, leaves no doubt that Le Jau "had been forced to pass his own word for the payment of things necessary for finishing" the church and house. And Le Jau adds: "else we were like never to see the End of that tedious work." Then, as though he suddenly remembered his own indigent condition, he appends

[69] Fulham Palace MSS, Records of the S. P. G., London.

[70] Le Jau to S. P. G., MS Letter S. P. G. Trans., Series A. vol. VI. May 26, 1712; also no. 12, 403. Series A. vol. VI. no. 104.

[71] *Ibid.*, A. vol. VII. no. 12, p. 403; vol. VI. no. CIV; vol. VII. no, 9.

this comment: "I hope the Parishioners will not suffer me to loose too much."[72]

How well the work was done is distinctly manifested in the building itself. It stands today a memorial to his life of service and sacrifice, a monument to his devotion and skill. Built of enduring brick and stone, these more than two centuries of time have not destroyed it and above its altar still repose the emblems of the British authority to which he was ever faithful and of the church in whose verities his faith never faltered. And even as one might suppose Le Jau himself would have it, it occupies its place humbly beside the road, and though bearing the marks of its age, it gives promise of standing another century and then perhaps another. This was in every true sense of the word Francis Le Jau's church.

After Dr. Le Jau's return from a visit to England made necessary by ill health, his activity was focused on creating interest in and erecting a free school at Goose Creek, "for instructing children in the knowledge and practice of the Christian religion."[73] The Huguenots were well represented in the subscription list. They promised to pay the amount opposite their names each year for three years as follows:[74]

Zachariah Villepontoux	£50.
Cornelius Dupré	5
Gideon Dupont	7
Benjamin Mazÿck	15
Gideon Fauchéraud	10
James Marion	5
Peter Porcher	15
Isaac Porcher	5
Rachel Porcher	5
C. Fauchéraud	100
Paul Mazÿck	50

Francis Le Jau died September 10, 1717, after a lingering

[72] S. P. G. Transcripts, Series A. vol. VII. no. 8.
[73] Dalcho, 255-6. *S. P. G. Abs.* 1732 f.
[74] Dalcho, 255.

illness of eighteen months, during which, "through an Extreem weakness" he was deprived of the use of his lower limbs and his speech. The destitution of his family after his death is a lamentable fact.[75] The Society for the Propagation of the Gospel which Le Jau had so faithfully served, came to the rescue with a gratuity of £30, in addition to the salary due at the time of his death.

With characteristic definiteness Francis Le Jau saw the tendencies of his day. He laments the prevalence of so-called "profane literature", widely read in the province and he publicly denounced other deep-seated evils of the day. To counteract such tendencies he personally undertook the distribution of literature and handled large consignments of books sent over from London for this purpose.[76] In the summer of 1717, then in ill health, he seriously considered moving to Barbadoes, but he died before the arrangements were completed.[77]

On October 25, 1732, the Rev. Timothy Mellichamp, a French Protestant, but also in Anglican orders, arrived, sent over by the Society for the Propagation of the Gospel.[78] He found there a large and regular congregation. On Christmas day he was formally chosen to be their minister. He is the only rector of French blood, except Dr. Le Jau and Francis Guichard, known to have served the church prior to the American Revolution.[79]

The Rev. Francis Guichard served the church until 1752. He then sold his well improved plantation of 448 acres after advertising for ten years.[80] In the advertisements he expressed a desire to return to his native country.[81]

[75] S. P. G. MS Tr., B. vol. IV. no. 95.
[76] *Ibid.*
[77] S. P. G. MS Tr., A. vol. XII. p. 171.
[78] S. P. G. Abs., 1732, 67; Fulham MSS, S. C., Box 315, no. 31; Dalcho, 254. Son of Richard Mellichamp, of Abdon, Salop. See Fothergill, 45.
[79] *S. C. Gaz.*, Jan. 7, 1751.
[80] *S. C. Gaz.*, Dec. 21, 1741; Jan. 7, 1751; Jan. 22, 1752; Nov. 27, 1752.
[81] *S. P. G. Dig.*, Missionary Roll, 1702-1892, 849:

Orange Quarter

The settlement known as Orange Quarter and also as French Quarter was located on the East Branch of the Cooper River, a little south of the intersection of the East Branch and the Cooper Rivers, and was inhabited at first

---

Goose Creek Vestry to Bishop of London. October ye 29th 1717

May it Please your Lordship

Wee the Vestrymen and Church Wardens of the Parish of St. James on Goosecreek in the Province of South Carolina; Do with grief & Affliction, but as our Duty obliges Us; hereby Inform your Lordship of the Death of our late Minister Dr. Francis Le Jau, who departed this life on the 10th day of September last past; After a very Long & tedious fitt of Sickness

We do therefore humbly Pray your Lordship to Supply Us with an English Divine to Succeed him So Soon and So Qualified as in your great Wisdom you shall think fitt

Rt Revd. Sr our former Minister; being a Missioner from the Most Noble & Rt Honble Society; for Propogateing ye Gospell in foreighn Parts; the Bounty he Received from then; was the greatest Part of his Support Amongst Us; for tho' the Sallery here is £100 Pr. Annum; of this Country Mony; it is Not to be Value'd at Above £25 Sterling; Which is one of the ill Consequences; that has befell this Colony; by our Indian Warr; besides Which the Vast Expences We have been at; And ye Present Charges we are forst to be at; daily to Defent our-Selves; from these our Barbarous Enemies; Renders Us So low; that we are truly Objects; worthy that Noble Societys Charity; and therefore are humble Petitioners to your Lordship; as A Member; of that Most Honble Christian Society: (to whom we have Address'd our Selves by this Same Opportunity) to Advocate in our behalf, and we as in Duty bound, Shall Continue to Pray for your Lordships happiness, and Prosperity & Remain with all Dutyfull Respects your Lordships Most Obedient humble Servants.

Edd. Smith
Jno. Gibbes
Churchwardens
Robt. Howes
Arthur Middleton
Rogr. Moore
Benja. Schenckingh
Thos. Smith
Vestrymen

Addressed To

The Rt Reverend
Father in God Dr. Jno. Robinson
Lord Bishop of London
In
London

Endorsed S. Carolina 1717 Ch. Wardens & Vestry of Goosecreek.

British Transcripts. Fulham Palace MSS, Box 315, no. 116, Oct. 29, 1717. See also S. P. G. Abstracts, 1732, 67.

almost exclusively by French Protestants.[82] A creek, known as French Quarter Creek, derives its name from this settlement. On the banks of this creek the French built their church.[83] Probably the main body of the colonists, about thirty families out of forty-five, said to have been brought over by René Petit and John Guerard, settled in this area.[84] Though the year is unknown the organization of the church society was probably accomplished at about the same time as the one on the Santee River, though a church building was probably not erected until after 1687. In his will, dated June 20, 1687, Caesar Mozé bequeathed thirty-seven pounds sterling to the organization "to be used in the construction of a temple for French refugees."[85] A deed of conveyance from Pierre Faure to Pierre de St. Julien and a grant of land to Nicolas de Longuemar show that the place was occupied as early as January or February, 1684-5. The congregation was served most of the time by ministers of other churches, viz., Francis Trouillart, Elias Prioleau, and Francis Le Jau.[86] St. Denis was included in the boundaries of St. Thomas Parish.[87] Its "erection" into a separate parish was for the convenience of the French residents. The Act of 1706 provided that as soon as services should be performed in English the church of St. Denis should become a chapel of ease to the parish of St. Thomas.[88] Elias Prioleau was minister here until the Rev. John La Pierre took charge of the church and many of the French met in their own church (built in 1708) whenever they had a French minister.[89] In 1698-9 the French Church had 101 members.[90]

[82] Gaillard MS.
[83] Ravenel MS; Gaillard MS.
[84] Weiss, 300 ff.
[85] MS Rcds. Court of Ordinary, 1672-92, 282-3.
[86] Howe, *Hist. Presbyt. Ch. S. C.* I. 112 ff.
[87] Fulham Palace MS Trans., Box 315, no. 227.
[88] Trott's Laws, 155.
[89] Humphreys, *S. P. G.*, 105; Weiss I. Bk. 4, chap. 1.
[90] *Cal. St. Pa. (Am. & W. Ind.)*, 1699, no. 431; Rivers, Sketch, 447. Parish of St. Thomas, S. C. Dec. 27, 1716.

Letter by Thomas Hassell to S. P. G. Sec'y. (Mr. David Humphreys). The Province of South Carolina was divided into Parishes about 1704 by an act to establish Religious Worship in the Province according to

The reports to the Society for the Propagation of the Gospel in London show that in 1721 there were thirty families of French refugees and their descendants in Orange Quarter and that the actual communicants of the Church of England numbered about forty, and that there were about forty families in the parish who professed themselves of the Church of England, exclusive of Orange Quarter.[91] In 1718-19 the St. Denis French families, because of a renewal of their former tribulations, split from the Anglican Church and embarked alone. Little is known of this incident, but La Pierre says in his letter to the Society for the Propagation of the Gospel in 1719, "I have made for sometime my practice to extend my care to them when the Inhabitants of the French Parish of St. Denis by their defection and falling from the church of England have rendered my functions ineffectuall amongst them."[92] La Pierre soon left

the church of England. "The Parish of St. Thomas so made by the above mentioned act of ye country (which I have ye care of)" is situated "upon a neck of land lying on up North West of Wandoe and South East of Cooper River, being in length from *Silk Hope* Plantation towards ye Head of ye Eastern branch of Cooper River inclusive which plantation belongs to Mr. Johnson (now in London) to ye plantation of Col. Danial our present Governor upon ye North West side of Wandoe River inclusive, about 25 miles and containing at present upwards of 100 families inclusive of ye French Protestants of Orange Quarter lying in ye middle of it."

The French Settlement of Orange Quarter "at the first division of the country into parishes was one part of the Parish of St. Thomas tho vary few of you ever attended ye English churches and that chiefly for want of ye Language the Major part of y^m^ always meeting together in a Small Church of their own, where they generally made a pretty full congregation and had sometimes a Calvinist minister among them but not being well able to maintain a Minister they made Application to ye Assembly of this Province to be made into a Parish and to have some publick Allowance for a Minister, upon which Condition they consulted to Conform to ye Church of England and to send for a minister Episcopally Oedained, who should use ye Liturgy of ye Church of England as Translated into French and Preach to ye in their own tongue . . . and then to be incorporated into ye Parish of St. Thomas. This Parish of St. Dennis has now a pretty good church, which ye Inhabitants built about ye same time with that of St. Thomas at their own charge and never had any other minister of it but ye present Incumbent the Reverend Mr. John LaPierre."

See S. P. G. MS Tr., Series B. vol. XIII. no. 88.

[91] S. P. G. MS Tr., Series B. vol. XIII. no. 103.

[92] S. P. G. MS Tr., Series A. vol. XIII. p. 210.

St. Denis to succeed Richebourg at Santee.[93] By 1726 the French had again all become identified with the Anglican Church, for Thomas Hassel reported then to the London Society that "all ye French of St. Denis's profess ymselves of ye Church of England" and he reported fifty families of the Church of England exclusive of the French of Orange Quarter.[94] In 1732 the settlement had thirty-two families, of whom fifty persons were communicants of the Established Church.[95] In a good account of the parish, rendered to the Society for the Propagation of the Gospel under the date of June 4, 1728, the facts are brought out that the parish church, 37½ x 27½ feet, was built in 1708. It was constructed of brick and had a porch. The chapel was built in 1704, but there was in 1728 no parsonage. The glebe consisted of 320 acres. The correspondent states that the parish was then (as in 1724) 20 miles wide and 35 miles long, and that there were 120 families within its bounds, including St. Denis in Orange Quarter in the middle of the parish. There were then about 30 to 35 families "who have a conformist minister among them who reads divine, and preaches to them in French." This was Rev. John La Pierre. The French were still worshiping in a wooden church built by their own contributions at the same time that the Anglican Church was built in 1708. He adds: "The inhabitants both English and French are much improved in their fortunes and manner of living."[96]

La Pierre preached in South Carolina nearly a quarter of a century, living much of the time in abject poverty. The words that Commissary Garden used in 1711 in writing to the Society for the Propagation of the Gospel, concerning La Pierre's financial status, were "miserably poor".[97] While the great service that he rendered was in the St. Denis dis-

[93] *Ibid.*
[94] S. P. G. MS Tr., Series B. vol. IV. no. 208.
[95] Humphreys, chap. 5; *S. P. G. Abs.* 1732.
[96] S. P. G. MS Tr., Series A. vol. XXI. p. 108. Fulham Palace MS, S. C., no. 285.
[97] MS S. P. G. Trans., Series A. vol. VII. no. 7. p. 388.

trict to the French refugees, he also served other vacant English parishes at convenient intervals. A letter of his, dated January 1, 1725-6, leaves no misgiving about the grim shadows that lay across his way, even on that New Year's day. There is reference to his family, who "are a great charge" to him, for there are "five small children". There is no lament recorded in those words, they are merely a matter-of-fact statement. But there was a wife as well, "who had lost her eyesight before their departure from England". Does not one's fancy naturally linger in that household, where a mother gropes her way amid the manifold duties of her home, or sits helplessly among the cares, with the full weight of her own handicap and of the family's poverty pressing down upon her? Her husband was then, in 1725, "officiating, going on the nineteenth year" in that place.[98]

La Pierre was a college graduate, being in possession of his A.B. degree before his elevation to clerical orders. He was ordained to the Anglican priesthood in 1708 by Compton, Bishop of London, who in turn recommended him to Johnston, the Governor of South Carolina. He was assigned to the French Church in the St. Denis parish, which according to his instructions, he was "to serve until the death of the old settlers who did not understand the English Tongue".[99] "So in the time of the new generation, who understood the said tongue in which they were born," La Pierre became an assistant to Rev. Hassell in the parish of St. Thomas, next to St. Denis. There he lived, "hoping of the two nations to make but one and the same people".

In one respect at least the Orange Quarter district was unique. Its settlers tenaciously held to the French language until the middle of the eighteenth century. The Huguenots who lived here had come before the repeal of the Edict of Nantes and were not so bitter against the French language and usages as were their French neighbors who had for-

[98] Fulham Palace MSS, Box 315, no. 5.

[99] La Pierre to Bishop of London, Oct. 9, 1733, written from New Brunswick, Cape Feare. Fulham Palace MSS, N. C. & Ga.; T. H. S. S. C., XXVI. 23.

saken France under the rigorous persecutions incident to the Revocation. Besides they were removed from immediate and constant English influence by their isolation and stoutly fought against English influence in their activities. They gave up their French Protestant usages with great difficulty and embraced the practices of the Establishment with reluctance. There was an Anglican Church at Pompion Hill, but the French worshipped according to the Reformed faith, unchanged, until 1706. Then poverty forced them to seek financial aid in the support of their ministry by submitting to the encroachments of the Established Church. But they maintained an independent Huguenot Anglican Church, until the original French refugees were all dead.[100] Here the Rev. Mr. La Pierre, their only Huguenot French minister, served the congregation, now Anglican in doctrine and polity, until his removal to Cape Feare in 1728.[101] He was succeeded by another of French descent, Rev. John James Tissot, an ordained Anglican clergyman.[102] The white population of this settlement continued to be essentially French in composition and life.[103]

[100] *S. P. G. Abs.*, 1758.

[101] Humphreys, *S. P. G.* 106; Dalcho, 289, errs in stating that La Pierre died in 1728. See MS Rawlinson C. 943., Bodleian, Oxford.

[102] *S. C. Gaz.*, July 9, 1763. He died Sunday, July 3, 1763, having been rector of the French-Anglican Church of St. Thomas Parish thirty-four years.

[103] MS Assembly Jrnl., 1702-12, 365; Humphreys, *S. P. G.* 105. A deed of gift of 100 acres by Nicholas Bochet and wife, members of the French-Anglican Church, of Orange Quarter, dated May 1, 1731, indicates the French nature of the church. It recites: "Nicholas Bochet of Berkely Country, Planter and Mary his Wife for & In Consideration of the love and Affection we bear unto the Evangelist of our blessed Lord & Saviour Jesus Christ & unto the Church of the Same Belonging to the French protestants and whereof they Profess themselves members Thereof do Give grant and Confirm (in the Method & With the Condition hereafter & herein mentioned & specified) One Plantation in berkeley County, containing one Hundred Acres of Land which the sd Nicholas Bochet Lately Purchased of Peter Johnson Sr." . . . give 100 acres for the use of a glebe to the Church belonging to the French Protestants as long as the French language is used in the congregation of the said parish. See MS Register, Bk. I, p. 311, Mesne Conveyance Office, Charleston. This land had been granted to Joseph Marbeuf, on June 4, 1701 and had been owned by Gideon and Gabriel Ferrow, Andrew Dupuy and the Rev. John LaPierre before Bochet held it.

The Rev. Mr. Alexander Garden in 1758 wrote to the Society for the Propagation of the Gospel, in London, that the French refugees were now all dead and that their descendants, understanding the English language, had united with the English speaking Anglican church.[104] By the recital of the Act of 1768 we learn that the families of French extraction who formerly worshipped at the French (Anglican) Church, "being then well acquainted with the English language" attend the Church of St. Thomas and St. Denis. This act authorizes the sale of the property.[105]

Grateful for the continued benefactions bestowed by Gabriel Manigault, Alexander Garden on May 6, 1765, when a new church building was under way in St. Thomas Parish wrote the following in a letter to the Secretary of the Society for the Propagation of the Gospel: "And have among other Benefactors, Gabriel Manigault, Esquire, of Charles Town merchant deserves notice, who besides his first generous Subscription of £50, sterling for himself and Son, has made a Present of 950 red Tile for flooring the Isles which cost him £10, sterling."[106]

St. John's Parish

A small wooden church was constructed by the French a little east of what is now Simpson's Basin, on the Santee Canal, but the extant records are silent as to the date of the organization of the church. This was the first church to be built in the parish. No church was built for worship in the English language until 1711, two years after Mr. Maule arrived to officiate.[107] By 1707 there was a small congregation of French Protestants there, whose minister was Florente Philippe Trouillard. Like the other Huguenot churches described, it was absorbed by the Act of 1706.[108] Mr. Trouillard, after that date, continued to serve the church,

[104] *S. P. G. Abs.* 1758; Humphreys, *S. P. G.*, 106.
[105] McCord, *Statutes,* IX. 225.
[106] See S. P. G. MS Tr., Series B. vol. V. no. 220.
[107] MS S. P. G. Tr., Series A. vol. X. no. 9, p. 77; Ravenel MS.
[108] Cooper, *Statutes,* II. 268 and 282.

but as an Anglican rector, retaining his congregation, though shifting to another allegiance. The change doubtless was a major factor in the transformation which now took place. The membership of the church dwindled to eight or ten families by 1709. Trouillard preached there once fortnightly, in French, in the Huguenot Church. On other Sundays many of his congregation heard Mr. Maule preach in the same building.[109] Maule had organized another Anglican Church in the area, for the English of the parish, and in response to their invitation used the French house of worship. Maule's new Anglican Church building was completed in 1711. The Rev. Mr. Maule died in the winter of 1716-17 of consumption.[110]

Mr. Trouillard had been one of the first ministers of the Charles Town Huguenot Church, associated with the Rev. Élias Prioleau.[111] Mr. Trouillard died at St. John's Berkeley in 1712.[112] His will was recorded March 19 and proved April 14, 1712.[113] He must have died between these two dates. His congregation was at that time ready to affiliate with the English-speaking Anglican congregation in the same parish and for two months worshiped with it, but the arrival

[109] MS S. P. G. Trans., Series A. vol. X. no. 9, p. 77.

[110] *S. P. G. Abstracts,* 1715; MS S. P. G. Transcripts, A. vol. X. no. 9, p. 77; Humphreys, S. P. G. 89; S. P. G. MS Tr., Series B. volume IV. no. 39.

Maule's letter to the Secretary of the S. P. G., 23 Jan., 1714, brings out that he was the first Anglican clergyman to reside in St. John's any length of time, having arrived there in 1707 (two men, Mr. Kendall and Mr. Guerard, preceded him as rectors in that parish, but neither was able to remain long because of the low salary); that in 1707 about eight or ten families of French lived there; they had their own minister, Mr. Trouillard; that he preached to them once a fortnight in a small church built by them "in their own charge"; that most of Trouillard's congregation came to hear Rev. Maule when their own minister was not there; that since Trouillard's death (1711) "several of the French have entirely Joyn'd themselves to the Communion of the Church of England"; that until the church was built for the English portion of the parish (which was dedicated September 1711), Maule made use of the French Church every second Sunday.

See S. P. G. MS Tr. Series A. vol. X. no. 9.

[111] In 1704 the proprietors granted Mr. Trouillard 216 acres in Berkeley County.

[112] MS S. P. G. Tr. A. vol. X. no. 9, p. 77 f.

[113] Gaillard MS.

of Philip de Richebourg from Virginia as pastor of the Santee Church and his willingness to administer the sacraments according to the Huguenot forms turned them from their former decision and drew them back into a long conflict over forms and usages.[114] In 1723 the missionaries of the Society for the Propagation of the Gospel reported 90 families living in St. John's, most of whom were members of the Church of England. Brian Hunt was chosen by the vestry of June 5, 1723, as its rector, and he, in 1724, reported 80 families in the parish. A letter to the Bishop of London, dated May 23, 1727, bearing 38 signatures, has only four French, namely, James Le Bas, John Bettison, Francis Le Jau, and Sam'l Dubordieu. Rev. John La Pierre served this church, among others, in the seventeen hundred and twenties.[115] His report declares that "Mr. Hazel's [Hassell] parish in ye parish of St. Thomas" consisted of "sixteen families french". He says that there is one service each Sunday, that most of the members live at a distance, that children are catechized regularly, but that there is neither a public nor a private school in the parish.[116]

During the period just preceding the American Revolution the Rev. Mr. Durand, an Anglican-Huguenot minister, served the church and lived in the district. Letters from Henry Laurens directed to him reveal the fact that his son Levi was Mr. Laurens' clerk, having been recommended to him by Mr. Manigault.[117]

Purrysburg

Students who are familiar with the history of South Carolina know how many times the claim has been made that a French Protestant church was established at Purrysburg. Occasional mischievous hints are found in the British records, which leave the impression that such statements are

[114] MS Rawlinson C., 943, Bodleian Library, Oxford.

[115] Fulham Palace MSS, Box 315, no. 198; *S. P. G. Abstracts,* 1723, 46; Unnumbered letter in Box No. 315, Fulham Palace MSS.

[116] Fulham Palace MSS, Box 315, no. 227.

[117] MS Laurens Letter Bk., 1762-66, 43 and 46. Pennsylvania Historical Society Library.

not entirely without foundation, in spite of the fact that complete evidence is not available. It is well known that an Established Church flourished there and that many persons of French and Swiss nativity identified themselves with it. In 1731 Joseph Bugnion, a French-Swiss clergyman, who had embraced Anglicanism in London and was ordained there, brought a colony of his countrymen to South Carolina. They settled at Purrysburg. Bugnion was appointed to the French Anglican Church in that place. All of the services which Bugnion conducted here during his incumbency were French. There is abundant evidence of this. Bugnion was unable for several years to use the English language at all, much less to officiate in it. It seems as though nearly all of his troubles in South Carolina, while in charge of churches, are rooted in this fact. In 1733 a quarrel between Bugnion and Peter Purry terminated in a church schism. Bugnion claimed that he had been mistreated by Purry, the Proprietor of the settlement, and that the promises originally made to him by Purry had not been fulfilled. Evidently much more was said than was written. What was said may be inferred from the malicious lines that are found in letters that passed between Charles Town and London. Purry had prejudiced the people against Bugnion and against the Church of England, and, "obeying a secret design to do away with him" had urged separation, causing a number of people to "attend Divine Worship by the Liturgy of Calvin". Purry, "whose pride pierced his cloak", himself selected a man in the community to officiate at the new service. There being no ordained clergyman available, he selected a layman, "partly enticing the people and partly overawing them to separation". "The Governor and Mr. Oglethorpe did both interpose in his (Bugnion's) behalf with Mr. Purry, but without success."[118]

One may not leap to the conclusion, however, that this was the beginning of a French Protestant Church. The di-

[118] Fulham Palace MSS, Box 315, nos. 75 and 9. Bugnion was naturalized Feb. 23, 1732-3 (MS Commissioner's Instructions, 1732-42, 2).

vision was evidently temporary. We know at least that Bugnion moved to Santee. Purry, satisfied in the accomplishment of his purpose in getting rid of Bugnion, seems to have returned to his former church allegiance. It is not unlikely that a petition, without date, praying for a new minister for Purrysburg, addressed to the Bishop of London, is the sequel to the unlovely incident described above. This petition contains thirty-five signatures and "Jean Pierre Purry Colonel & Juge a Paix" is at the head of the list.

The Bugnion letter of July 15, 1733, addressed to the Bishop of London, makes it clear that Bugnion went to the Purrysburg church before the legal requirements for its erection into a parish had been completed. As there were but sixty men in the settlement in 1733 and the required one hundred could not be assured before Mr. Purry could bring another company from abroad, Bugnion had no definite assurance of an income through the channels of the Establishment. Three-fourths of the Santee inhabitants being French, he avers, and the parish established, he expressed the desire to the Bishop of London of becoming the rector of the Santee Church. Schooled in the wisdom of his surroundings he clinched his request with a statement to the effect that he had been studying the language with this in view and hoped in a few months to make the service at Santee English.[119]

[119] Fulham Palace MSS, S. C. Letters, no. 43, etc.

Petition for new minister.

Les Inhabitants de Purrysbourg prennant la liberte de representer a votre Granderir, que comme Mr. de Ministre Bugnion a recen sa lettre de vocation de L'Eglise de Santee, et que ne pouvant ovlener de la Province, laspension annex'ee aux Paroisses parce que la notre, n'est pas encore Complette, et qu'ayant une grosses famille, avec jeu on point de bien, illn'aurait pes subsister parmy nous, outre que nous avons un bon nombre de Suisses Allemande, qui, n'entendent point la langne française, el que par consequent ils ne Souroient etre edifies; nous prenons la liberte de sufflier.

Signed by Jean Pierre Purry, Colonel and Juge Prix Jacques Richard, Major and Juge a Paix

Guilaume Bulot, Secy.	Jean Rodolph Nelleman
Daniel Brisbant	Henry Francois Bourquin
André De Monchard	René Mullier
Jean Babtiste Bourquin	Wattier Cuillat

St. Peter's Parish, of the Purrysburg area, was not established as such until 1746-7.[120] The Anglican Church was nevertheless continuous in its activities there. Upon Bugnion's departure for Santee, Rev. Henry Chiffelle succeeded him at Purrysburg. Chiffelle was a missionary sent by the Society for the Propagation of the Gospel, in London. He was an ordained clergyman of the Anglican Church.[121]

New Bordeaux, Hillsboro

The Huguenot Church of New Bordeaux was the last to be organized before the American Revolution. The French people in Hillsboro Township reëstablished the Protestant Reformed religion which they had professed in France, and built with their own hands a church of logs cut from the virgin forest. John Pierre Gibert in France and England had been the spiritual guide and business director of the group that arrived in South Carolina in April, 1764.[122] In 1761 Louis Gibert had gone to London to secure the coöperation of the British Crown in his plans to take a colony of Huguenots to America. In his letters to Secker, the Archbishop of Canterbury, he states that the colonists

Rosue Robert
Adam Cuillat
Dana Gerond
David Sousy
David Gautre
Francois Gabriel Ravot.
François Favre
Ludwig Vehl (in German Script)
Drobold Kiesler (in German Script)

Vanderrusz (in German Script)
imszler (in German Script)
Anthoine Theremin
Jean Pierre Dagallier
Joseph Raymond.
Jean Rodolphe Grand
mark of Jenais Henry Jeanneret
Jose Geradeon
Jans ris deroche

Jorg Mengersdorff (in German Script)
George Girardeu (Geardeau)
mark of de Francois Buchè
Henry Girardeu
Abram Pallotton
Miclansz Cronenbergen, (in German Script)
Jean Pierre Jeanneret
Abraham Jeanneret
Jacob Henri Meuron
Abraham Meuron

[120] Dalcho, 385.
[121] *S. C. Gazette,* Nov. 18, 1734.
[122] MS Col. Doc. S. C., XXIX. 279 and 379.

intend to become faithful subjects of the Crown and later asserts that they all intend to conform to the Anglican usages and to have bishops. Their plans in these particulars were not carried out, for, though in the original plat of the town 300 acres out of a total of 800 acres were reserved for a glebe "for the minister and the Church of England", no Anglican Church was founded prior to the American Revolution. In addition to the French Protestant Church at Hillsboro and the German Lutheran Church in Londonburgh there were six meeting-houses in the near vicinity, but not one was Anglican.[123]

In the French Protestant Church Mr. Boutiton was associated with Mr. Gibert as the first minister of the congregation after its establishment in New Bordeaux.[124] Immediately after his death, in 1772, Mr. St. Pierre petitioned the Board of Trade in London to provide funds for another minister.[125] Fifty pounds had been given annually by the Society for the Propagation of the Gospel. An equal amount each year was now asked for from the British government in order that the Rev. Peter Levrier, during the past seven years minister of the church at Pensacola, might be secured to serve the French Church in New Bordeaux.[126] This seems to have been granted, for Mr. Levrier arrived at Charleston, bound for Hillsboro Township, on May 7, 1772.[127] This church remained Calvinistic until the American Revolution.[128]

Naturally in a study of this kind, even though realizing the value of comparative inquiries, one is inclined, as far as possible, to hold rather steadily to the theme of direct discussion. And yet how evident it becomes as one proceeds that none of the churches of South Carolina lived to itself.

[123] *Ibid.*, 32, 371.
[124] MS Council Jrnl., 1763-4, 253f. and 179-80; *Private Journal of Pierre Moragne,* reprinted in *Moragne Address,* Appendix.
[125] MS Col. Doc. S. C., XXXIII. 147.
[126] *Ibid.*
[127] *S. C. Gaz.*, May 7, 1772.
[128] *Private Journal of Pierre Moragne,* reprinted in *Moragne Address,* Appendix.

This is shown again and again in these pages. Probably the best single source of contemporaneous material now in existence, giving in compact form a survey of all of the tidewater churches and congregations, is the report of Mr. Woodmason, covering South Carolina, North Carolina and Georgia. The portion pertaining to South Carolina is herewith given in full in the footnote, not so much because of the amount of information which it contains on the Huguenots, but because of its revelations of the general conditions in the province shortly before the American Revolution, including a description of the church equipment and the facilities with which the several congregations were able to carry forward their enterprises, as compared with the Huguenot Church of Charles Town.[129]

[129] British Transcript, Manuscript Division, Library of Congress, Box 316, no. 300.

Notes & Remarks
No. 1.

St. Philips Charlestown	This Church is allow'd to be the most elegant Religious Edifice in British America. It is built of Brick. Length 100 ft. Breadth 60 Height 40, with a Cupola of 50 feet, with two Bells, and a Clock and Bell. It has 3 Portico's before the West, North & South Doors. It was built from the Model of the Jesuit Church at Antwerp. Having Gallerys around, exceeding well plann'd for Sight and hearing. In this Church is a Good Organ, the Great Organ has 16 Stops—the Choir Organ 8. It is well Ornamented. Has rich Pulpit Cloths, & Coverings for the Altar and a very large Service of Plate. A Lecturer (or Assistant) is maintain'd here by the Publick. His Salary 200£ Stg p ann, as is also the Rectors; & his fees full as much. Divine Service is perform'd here with Great Decency & Order; both on Holidays & Week Days.
St. Michaels	Is a New built Church from the Model of that of Greenwich being Truss'd-Roofd & no Pillars. Is 80 feet by 60. Has a Tower & Steeple 196 feet high, and a Ring of 8 Bells lately hung. In this Church is a small Organ, but a large & Noble One is now in Hand, to be sent over. The Plate & Ornaments of this Church are superb. Divine Service is regularly perform'd here on Sundays Holidays & Week Days as at St. Philips—The Rector & Assistant's Salaries are the same as theirs, but the Fees are not above 100£ Stg p ann.

St. Andrews	Was lately consum'd by Fire, but is rebuilt, & is a pretty Edifice It has an Organ.—This parish has also a Chapel of Ease.
St. George's	Is a very handsome Brick Church, with a Steeple, 4 Bells, and an Organ. An Endowed free School in this Parish.
St. Johns Berkley County	Was burnt abt. 7 year ago, & not yet rebuilt, tho' the Money for it has been long collected. Here is a pretty Chapel of Ease a handsome School, well endow'd, & a House for the Master.
Christ Church	Is a pretty Brick Building—but very plain.
St. Thomas	Is a Good Church. Has a Chapel of Ease, and a Publick School Well endow'd.
Santee	This Church fell to decay some Years ago, and has not been since rebuilt. Service is perform'd at (what was formerly) a Chapel of Ease.
St. James's Goose Creek	This is one of the best Country Churches in the Province, and both it and the parsonage stand close by the Bridge, over which is the Greatest Flux and Reflux of People, in the Province, which makes it very troublesome & expensive to the Minister, as he is daily & hourly pester'd with Travelers calling for Lodging or Entertainment.
St. Matthew	Is a Parish just laid out—Has as yet no Church built, or parsonage House or Glebe laid out.
St. Helena	This Church is in the Town of Beaufort, Port Royal, which altho' the second Town in the Province, boasts the very meanest Church in it.
Prince William	This is the second best Church in the Province, and by many esteem'd a more beautiful Building than St Philips It is far more elegant than St Michaels, & is beautifully pew'd and Ornamented.
Prince George	This Church is in the Town of Georgetown—is 80 feet by 50 has 3 Isles, but no Galleries as yet—The Pulpit & Pews are well Executed, but the Altar Piece is not yet up. Here is a free School.

The other Parish Churches are all Timber Buildings—But the parsonage Houses of most of them are of Brick, and Good Structures. The Glebes of several are Valuable; Particularly St Andws. St George & St Stephens.

In Charlestown, is a publick provincial School, endowed with 100£ Stg p ann, besides Bye Scholars, which makes it a profitable Place The Free Masons, & other public Societies, maintain Charity Schools So that there is not a Beggar in the Province—Evry Parish maintains its own poor—But there are few, or none, out of Charlestown.

As the Province has undertaken to add 30£ Stg p ann to the Salaries of the Clergy, whereby their Stipends are now 110£ Stg. beside their fees, House & Glebe; It is almost a Sin for any of the parochial Clergy longer to receive the Mission Money—Nor are there but two who choose to continue on the Old foot, recg only 80£ Stg from the Treasury & 30£ from England. This Money could be better employed in Georgia.

Augusta	Is a Town high up on the River Savanna, and a Place of Great Resort for Trade with the Indians—It is a frontier Settlement. The Society maintains a Missionary here a 75£ Stg Salary. It is almost scandalous for the Rich Province of South Carolina to

receive the Societys Money, or to suffer them to maintain their Clergy—But the Reason why no more parishes are laid out arises from Political Motives, as it would encrease the Number of Assembly-Men; which Place is so troublesome and expensive, that few are to be found at an Election to undertake it.

Purrysburg Is a Town on Savanna River, between *Savanna* & *Augusta:* The Inhabitants chiefly *Switzers* & *Saltzburghers.* The Revd Mr Imber, who lately came over with the French protestants, was established at this place, But differing with the People, he now is among those he came over with, and *Stumpels* Germans.

Altho' the Country Parishes in So. Carolina are on one and the same Establishment, Yet some are more lucrative, others more desirable than the Rest. Hence, it is not uncommon when Vacancies happen, for Ministers to remove from one Parish to another. For Instance—St Helena & Prince George, being Towns, are more pleasant and profitable, than St James's or St Stephen, wch. are inland. St. Andrew & St George, by being near the Sea, and inhabited by Rich Planters, are more agreeable than Prince Frederic or St. Mark, which are inhabited by poor & illiterate People. While St. Mark & St. Matthew, tho' very undesirable on Acct of the want of sensible and literate Persons to make an incumbents Hours pleasing, are, on another Acct. preferable to all the Rest; for what they enjoy as to *Wealth,* these possess in respect to *Health,* no part of England being better, and none in the Province so good as to this particular.

Beside the two Episcopal Churches in Charlestown, there are those other Places for Religious Worship.

1. A Presbyterian Meeting, the Minister of the Kirk of Scotland, and acting by the Model of the Directory.
2. An Independent-Meeting, in Alliance with those of England.
3. A Baptist Meeting, in Harmony with those of Pensylvania.
4. A Quaker Meeting —Ditto—
   (N.B. There are but 2 or 3 Quakers in Town, so no Congregation of them)
5. An Arian Meeting, acting on *Whistons* System & Principles—There are but few Members, but it is Well endow'd.
   (N.B. All the Teachers of these Meetings wear Gowns, and have Good Salaries, paid them by their respective Congregations.)
6. A Dutch Lutheran Church. Service is perform'd here in the German Tongue; It has an Organ—The Pastor officiates in his Surplice and Cope, after the Manner of the Danish Church in Wellclose Square.
7. A French Calvinist Church.—Service is perform'd here in the French Tongue, after the Geneva Pattern. It has but a small Congregation, but is Rich, & well endow'd.
8. A Jews Synagogue.

In the Country, are 8 Presbyterian Meetings, supply'd wth Ministers from Scotland, who form a Presbytery, and govern their Members after the plan of the Scotch Kirk. Most of these Congregations are in decay tho' strongly supported from Home; And in Charlestown, most of the rising Generation, incline to the Church Establish'd, and will join it in Time. This is owing to our having of late Years, Good and Worthy Clergymen sent over: A Matter of most serious Concern: For the

Church has greatly sufferd through default herein. But the Parishes will not now accept unworthy Persons, but will reject them as they lately did two, One at *Beaufort,* the other *P. Frederick;* which rotten Members are now roving about *North-Carolina* in a starving Condition.

Methodism has been endeavour'd to be introduc'd in Carolina, but has made no Progress: They run to hear *Whitfield* out of Curiosity only, as an Orator, but will not adopt his Principles, or admit his Pupils He intended the Orphan House in Georgia, as a Seminary of Disciples to be entirely devoted to Him, and sent out as his Emissaries around: Some of them have appear'd in Publick—but were such Lame Tools, that their Master was as much asham'd of them, as the People despised them. He has now given up the House to the Publick of Georgia, to serve as a Publick College for that Colony.

The Greatest Harmony subsists between these Sectaries, and the Establishment—owing to the Candour, Prudence, and regular demeanour of the present Clergy, who are the best Sett of Men, that Carolina were ever blest with at one Time.

The People of South Carolina in General, may be said to be a sensible and Moral People. Divine Service is perform'd in the Country Churches on Sunday Mornings only. All the Churches have a Service of Plate—Surplices worn only in the three Towns.—Great Regard to Decency and proper Deference is observ'd by these provincials, as to Externals—As to Internal Righteousness, Holiness, and Purity, it lyes in small Compass. There are but very few Communicants, in any Congregation: Which is partly owing to the false Zeal of the Presbyterians, who by *forcing* their people indiscriminately to the Holy Ordinance, have made more *Deserters,* than *Volunteers* in the Cause of Religion.

Messrs. Smith—Cooper—Martin—and Keith—have acquir'd Genteel Fortunes since being in the Province

ENDORSED

Mr Woodmason's Account
of South Carolina, North
Carolina, Georgia &c

1766

CHAPTER IV

THE ASSIMILATION OF THE HUGUENOTS

The rapid assimilation of the French in Carolina into the Established Church and their intermarriage with other nationalities are remarkable features of their early history. The absorption into the Anglican church was indirectly coercive, rapid and thorough. The English institutions mastered and overpowered the French. The French became English in language and religion, British in sentiment and policies. The fulcrum by which it was accomplished was economic necessity, the lever was political preferment. We are slow to conclude that the change was made with graceful ease. On the contrary, it must have been accomplished with reluctance and in pain, despite the fact that the French had for centuries made political and social changes with comparative ease. Religious opinions and prejudices are not easily relinquished even now, however honest the purpose and sincere the effort. How much more was this the case in the eighteenth century. Only after a conflict, the temper of which is too remote to be easily understood today, did the French Protestants relinquish their church affiliation and embrace Anglicanism.[1]

Are we to assume that the original Frenchmen, had they gone directly from France to Carolina, could readily have given up their purely Protestant faith for one almost Roman Catholic in form and practice, for one largely Catholic[2] in doctrine? It was for their religion that they suffered, for their Protestantism they were persecuted. Because they loved it they forsook fatherland and fortune. Because they refused to abjure their Protestant faith they denied themselves their

[1] See chapter on the Dissenter Fight. The undertone of that struggle is heard in nearly every important political issue for twenty years; see MS Council and Assembly Records.

[2] It is now quite generally accepted among scholars that the English Reformation was anti-papal, rather than anti-Catholic and that its ecclesiastical accomplishments were not extensive beyond throwing off the papal yoke.

fondest possessions.[3] In South Carolina it was a struggle which, though not bloody, as was many a lesser one, abounded in bitter imprecations in public and private. By excited debate on the common green and in the Assembly and Council it threatened the safety of this infant government.[4] It was a conflict in which those who had been willing to lavish blood and treasure in defense of their convictions were made the subjects of implied and expressed reproach. The sacredness of their religion, the legitimacy of their children and the scriptural authority of their ministry all were challenged.[5] It was a struggle in which mob riot reigned five days.[6] At the close of the struggle their determined state of mind dictated allegiance to the Establishment, not by a voluntary choice, but as a result of economic, social and ecclesiastical necessity. In a period of great public or party distress opinions are sharply and clearly stated. Again and again in wills and other documents, reference, sometimes direct, sometimes deeply submerged, is made to the pain that the change engendered even a decade after it was accomplished.[7] Legacies are bestowed on condition that the Reformed practices continue to be used.[8] Burial services according to the Calvinistic religion are demanded in wills,[9] while on the other hand, the struggle may be inferred from such determined statements as that of André Rembert, who states in his will: "I wish to be buried according to the custom of the Anglican Church, of which I profess to be and am a member."[10]

[3] See the chapter on the Dissenter Fight.
[4] Rivers, *Sketch,* chaps. 6. 7 and 8; MS Hazard Transcripts, 1700-32; S. C. MSS no. 33, Library of Congress.
[5] *Ibid.,* and Carroll, *Collec.,* I. 103.
[6] Rivers, *Sketch,* chaps. 6, 7 and 8; Oldmixon, in Carroll, *Collections,* II. 25-9.
[7] MS Pr. Ct. Rcd., 1692-93, 18; *T. H. S. S. C.,* X. 36 f.
[8] Porcher, *Reminiscences,* 100; Philip Gendron's will, in MS Pr. Ct. Rcd., 1722-24, 301.
[9] Pierre Bertrand's will (*ibid.,* 1692-3, 9), proved Oct. 11, 1692; Arnaud Bruneau's will (*ibid.,* 1671-1727, 275; 1692-3, 172); Lewis Perdriau's will (*ibid.,* 1692-3, 182); Daniel Huger's will (*ibid.,* 1752-56, 282).
[10] *Ibid.,* 1736-40, 61.

But side by side with these facts we must remember that most of the French who went to South Carolina had lingered in the British Isles long enough to learn the essentials of Anglicanism and had come in contact with its doctrines, liturgy, polity, and practices to an extent sufficient to break down many of their prejudices through long familiarity.[11] There in their private life they were inclined to mingle more with the upper classes, the bishops and gentry of England, than with the dissenting lower classes and they became the willing recipients of the benefactions of the nobility, who in the main were high-churchmen. Persecution in France was the entering wedge to the change; contact with the Anglican Church in England was a second factor; the Dissenter fight in Carolina was the climax.[12] In highly organized society it is difficult to live in disunity. Under primitive conditions, in which people are very dependent on one another, this difficulty is magnified. It is there that their motives become active. In South Carolina such problems took definite form. Should they yield the cardinal principle of their church polity in order to secure a desirable social and political position? Their minister had been a pastor and teacher, but not the mysterious go-between embodied in the Anglican priest. The Established Church held to three orders in the ministry. The French-Protestants had but one. Anglicanism was pro-Catholic, Calvinism anti-Catholic. The Establishment was rigid and fixed; French Protestantism was liberal and elastic. Anglicanism was episcopal; French Protestantism was presbyterial. Nevertheless, in spite of the fact that the Huguenots agreed with the Anglicans in rejecting both the Apocrypha and the observance of Saints' days, in retaining the observance of festivals dedicated to the persons of the Godhead, in the simplicity of their baptismal ritual, and in the fact that the liturgy of the two polities was quite similar, the change meant that they must surrender the simplicity of their belief regarding the supper, baptism, absolu-

[11] Agnew, I. 69 f.
[12] See the chapter on the Dissenter Fight.

tion, and confirmation. In the change they must accept the polity of presiding bishops, a thing against which Calvin had persistently protested and against which Bishop Bossuet had discoursed at length. It was the point of attack on the part of the Catholics, the point which the Huguenots, while in France, were bound not to surrender. Did not Bishop Bossuet in his pastoral letter reproach them by the challenge: "Let them show the original of their ministry and like Saint Cyprian and other orthodox bishops, let them make us see that they are descended from an apostle."[13]

All of this in polity, doctrine, ancient practice, precedent, and tradition the Huguenots should relinquish in order to become adherents of the Established Church. Nevertheless, on the other hand there were a number of reasons why the Huguenots should be expected to make the change. As we have seen it was becoming increasingly difficult to supply the pulpits of their French churches with properly trained ministers.[14] Their theological schools had been displaced. The divinity students, fleeing from France, were taking orders in England and Ireland in the Established Church.[15]

[13] See Agnew, *Prot. Exiles from France,* 65 f. Dr. Durel, a French-speaking Englishman, fulfilled the desires of King Charles II regarding the worship of the Westminster French Church by undertaking a new translation. Therefore in 1662 Charles II issued a proclamation to the effect that henceforth the Durel translation and version of the Book of Common Prayer should be used in all of the French Churches in the British dominions which conform to the Established Church. When the King's orders were made known at Savoy, Pasteur Hierosme *(alias* Jerome) advised submission under existing circumstances, owing to the current of opinion in favor of it. Though the result pleased Dr. Durel, he was displeased with the reasoning, for he published a book to prove that the Calvinistic ritual of the French Church was as liturgical as the worship of the Church of England and that the services of the two churches were practically identical.

[14] See above, pp. 54f.

[15] Smiles, *Huguenots,* 245. Many of the most distinguished French ministers were admitted to degrees at English universities. See Anthony Wood's *Athenae Oxoniensis* and Gustave Masson, *The Huguenots,* 134 and 167. Under the administration of Archbishop Laud the attitude of the Established Church had been arrogant, but under his successors milder policies prevailed and many inducements were held out to Huguenot pastors to enter the Anglican fold. It was especially through the influence of Durel, who though not a refugee, had studied at the French Protestant University of Saumur, that Huguenot pastors entered the Established Church. See *Pro. H. Soc. London,* VIII. 4.

As a last resort a theological seminary, especially for candidates for the ministry among fleeing French Protestants, was opened at Lausanne, in Switzerland, with Antoine Court, the great preacher and organizer, as its founder. This school, though aided and supported by the rulers of Great Britain, Holland and Sweden, and by many wealthy persons in all parts of central Europe, was not opened until 1792, too late to affect the situation in South Carolina. Its tardy establishment was due largely to the fact that the refugee churches in Switzerland had degenerated into fanaticism and inspirationalism.[16]

The original ecclesiastical bond thus weakened must break sooner or later. The indigent circumstances of many of the Huguenots, especially before 1706, made it impracticable, if not impossible, to support the Established Church by taxation and their own church by subscription. In spite of the fact that there was a bond that united all Huguenots into one union—that of mutual sympathy because of bitter persecution—dissensions which divided them into factions and weakened their ecclesiastical potency made their appearance as they have in other religious bodies. The Established Church was able to take advantage of these divisions. The Huguenots had been befriended in many ways by subjects of the British Crown. Thereby they became debtors to the constituency of the Established Church, for with many in those days loyalty to the Established Church and allegiance to the Crown went hand in hand.[17] Owing to the very purpose of their flight from the primitive conditions in which they lived, and the absence of convenient means of communication and transportation, they were practically cut off from their native land. The Carolina Huguenots had begged the King of France, Louis XIV, for permission to settle in Louisiana, "for conscience sake".[18] This was denied them. Thereby the last tie that held them in affection to the mother

[16] See Good, *Swiss Reformed Church since the Reformation,* 123.
[17] *C. T. Yr. Bk.,* 1895, 347.
[18] Weiss, I. 302.

country was apparently cut. After this, though they still hoped to retrieve their lost fortunes in estates and treasures,[19] their faces were turned toward England rather than toward France.[20] The furnishings, books, papers, etc., that have survived the destruction of their institutions, show how closely they followed English thought and action. Their literature came from England. Their children were sent to school in the British Isles. In commerce and trade England was their customer.[21] There seems to have been little effort on the part of the Carolina French Protestants to perpetuate the remembrance of a distinct nationality.[22] Their children, except in the isolated sections, were not encouraged to speak French. Frequent interruptions in the conduct of the French churches, caused by the illness, death and resignations of French pastors, constantly afforded reason for their members to attend the services of churches other than their own. Owing to Dissenter antipathies the step to Anglicanism was sometimes made proportionately easy. By 1706, sufficient time had elapsed since the Revocation to give rise to a younger generation unsatisfied with the adherence to old French forms, a generation adverse to a language not in general use in the province, clamoring for the new and the popular. The rising generation could not be expected to feel the bitterness of the Revocation as did their parents. The children of many of the refugees were even ashamed to bear French names. The idea of remaining foreigners in a land in which they were born and reared was alien to their thought.[23] The establishment of the Church of England by

[19] MS Pr. Ct. Rcd., 1692-3, 377.

[20] *S. C. Gaz.*, June 8, 1734.

[21] MS list in the possession of Mrs. Josephine Jenkins, Adams Run, S. C. See also McCrady, *Hist. S. C.*, II. 475, note.

[22] Though the author knows of no direct evidence to induce him to believe that this condition prevailed in South Carolina, evidence is available to prove that the British government refused to allow the French Protestants at Manikintown, Virginia, many of whom moved to the Santee River, in South Carolina, even to call themselves a "French Colony", because it would give the impression of a distinct government. They were required to use the English language in all communications to the English authorities. See *Cal. St. Pa.* (*A. & W. Ind.*), 1702, 472.

[23] Smiles, *Huguenots*, 279 f.

law in the colony in 1700 welded these several links into a chain of necessity. The Bishop of London sagaciously supplied the Huguenots with a ministry of French nativity and Anglican ordination, men proficient in both the French language and the ritual of the Establishment.[24]

Not least important of all is the fact that there was no active mother church in France to nurture her child across the sea.

We have no accurate information of the extent to which the Huguenots of the tidewater section were incorporated into the Established Church immediately after 1706, nor how many affiliated with it prior to this important crisis. The extant church registers of St. Philip's date as far back as 1720. Records of death, marriages and births, and apparently even of baptisms prior to that time were voluntary, for it seems that no law requiring such records was enforced in the province before 1719.[25] Besides, the fact that deaths, marriages, births and baptisms of French persons were registered in St. Philip's records even after 1720, is not conclusive evidence that such persons were affiliated with St. Philip's Church. It indicates merely their residence within the limits of the parish, for the parish boundaries were political as well as ecclesiastical. The same pertains to other parishes. The vestry records of St. Philip's Church

[24] Not a few men born and reared in France served Anglican Churches in South Carolina. Among them are Le Jau, Pouderous, Varnod, Tissot, Coulet, DuPlessis, Durand, Tustian, Tourquand, De Richebourg, La Pierre, Bugnion, etc. (*Dalcho*, 269 and 297; *T. H. S. S. C.*, XIV. 23 note. MS Laurens Letter Bk., 1762-66, 43 and 56; Address of clergy of S. C. to King George on the death of his father, May 1727-8, in MS Col. Doc. S. C., XII. 13-15). Rev. John James Tissot was rector at St. Denis. He officiated in the French language and used the Durel translation. Francis Varnod, an Anglicanized Huguenot minister in St. George's Parish, Dorchester, 1723-36, was sent over by the S. P. G. See Humphreys, *S. P. G.*, 850. After the death of her husband, Mrs. Mary Varnod returned to England. See will in "Gleanings from England," *S. C. H. & G. Mag.*, IV. 237; See also Howe, *Hist. Presbyterian Church of S. C.* I. chap. 3.

[25] As early as 1683 regulations were made for registering births and marriages (Cooper, II. 14). By the Church Act of Nov. 30, 1706 a register of births, deaths and baptisms was provided for (Cooper, II. 15). The Act of March 16, 1695-6 required the registration of births and marriages (Cooper, II. 120). The regulations were apparently not enforced.

for the period prior to 1732 are not extant. Mrs. Woolford, in 1748, was blamed for their loss, but the charge was never proved and the records were never returned.[26] The register and vestry records of Christ Church parish reach back into the seventeenth century, their first date being 1694, but the early items are fragmentary. The parish was established in 1706. This was not a Huguenot stronghold. There are no records of St. James Santee parish before 1758. Those of St. John's Colleton and St. John's Berkeley are lost. There are no records of St. Stephen's before 1754. In St. James Goose Creek the situation is no better. On April 7, 1755, Zachariah Villepontoux, who had served as vestryman and as church warden for twenty years, declared under oath,[27] before Alexander Stewart, Esq., Justice of the Peace for Berkeley County, that no public register had been kept in the Parish of St. James Goose Creek for the past eighteen years. When these facts are remembered regarding records that were required by law, one need not marvel that extra-political organizations under no legal pressure did not keep complete accounts of their proceedings.

In 1725, when extant records of St. Philip's Church begin, we find French Protestants active in its life. The record of July 13, 1725, shows that Francis le Brasseur, recently deceased, was a church warden. There is evidence of very few pews owned or rented in St. Philip's by Huguenots after 1725. This however does not argue against the possibility of large numbers of them being affiliated with the church, for seats in the gallery were free to all and membership in the church did not necessitate the ownership nor the rental of a pew. In the years 1743-6, John Bonnetheau and John Neufville each rented a pew, for which each paid £7-10-0.[28] In 1743 Zachariah Brazier applied for a pew in the choir loft.[29] John Laurens in 1758 bought the pew owned

[26] MS Vestry Bk., 1732-56, entry Aug. 22, 1748.
[27] MS Pr. Ct. Rcd., 1754-58, 357; MS St. Philip's Vestry Bk.
[28] MS Vestry Bk., 1732-56, entry for Easter Monday of each year.
[29] MS Vestry Bk., 1732-56, March 19, 1743.

by Mr. Lloyd, of Goose Creek.[30] During the years 1749 and 1750 Peter Timothy, John Neufville and John Bonnetheau are among the pew holders.[31] The former paid £5-0-0 for his pew, the two others paid £7-10-0. each. At the same time Paul Grimke bought the pew which Mr. Welshuysen had owned.[32] After 1751 no French names except those of Peter Timothy,[33] in 1754 and 1767, Daniel Trezvant,[34] in 1767, and Isaac Huger,[35] appear on the records pertaining to pews.

In 1754, when the Rev. Alexander Garden, Rector of St. Philip's, resigned, the names of ten French Protestants appear with sixty-four others, subscribed to a letter that was given him at the time of his departure. These are the names in all probability of the male members of the church who were friendly to his ministry and may be a complete list of the male heads of families connected with the church, for Mr. Garden was a very popular man.[36]

A few French Protestants united with the so-called "Circular Church" of Charles Town, which was founded between 1680 and 1690.[37] Its membership consisted chiefly of Scotch and Irish Presbyterians and Congregationalists. No church records dated prior to 1724 are extant. Those embracing the period from 1724 to 1732 are included in the volume of records dated 1732-1796.[38] In 1724 no less than

[30] *Ibid.*, Dec. 29, 1746.

[31] *Ibid.*, Easter Monday, 1749-50. Persons owning pews were not required to pay rent. It is possible that a number of Huguenots were included in such a group and therefore secure no mention in the records after 1732.

[32] MS Vestry Bk., 1732-56, Oct. 9, 1749.

[33] *Ibid.*, Easter Monday, 1767.

[34] *Ibid.*

[35] *Ibid.*, 1768.

[36] *Ibid.*, April 10, 1754. John Neufville, H. Bérénger de Beaufain, Jacob Motte, Gabriel Manigault, John Guerrard, Benjamin d'Harriette, James Laurens, Paul Douxsaint, Henry Laurens.

[37] Ramsay, *Hist. of Indep. or Congregational Church of C. T.*, 3; Howe, *Hist. Presbyt. Church, S. C.*, I. 127.

[38] In the possession of Master Horace Mitchel, Charleston. The church which in its minutes is called "The Society or Church of Christian Protestant Dissenters of the Congregational or Presbyterial Form", was founded in Charles Town about 1685-90. This is shown in a letter in

HENRY LAURENS
1724-1792
President of Congress.
(From original in oil by Copley, in possession of Henry R. Laurens, Esq., Charleston, S. C.)

43 persons subscribed their names to a call extended to the Rev. Mr. Bassett, inviting him to become the pastor of the church. This list contains only three French names.[39] The extant minutes of the church date from 1732. In 1734 the list of pew holders included the following French: Solomon Legare, Jr., No. 11; Solomon Legare, Sr., No. 19; Henry Peronneau, Jr., No. 16; Henry Peronneau, Sr., No. 17; Alexander Peronneau, No. 34.[40]

In 1729, when proposals were made for a new church building, a number of French Protestants became subscribers to the project: "Henry Peronneau, Sr., £70; Henry Peronneau, (for a pew) £100; Solomon Legare, Jr., £40; Jacob Motte, 10m 4d. nails, [i.e.] £10; Gabriel Manigault, £10; Henry Peronneau, [Jr.], £60; Mathurin Boigard, £20; Benjamin d'Harriette, Jr., £20; Solomon Legare, £50, in lime; Peter Benoist, £10; John Laurens, £21; Elisha Prioleau, £10".[41]

The Peronneaus and the Legares seem to be the only ones of French nativity who were members of the church at this time for in the same year, when the pews were assigned, only these names appear in the list.[42] Furthermore they are the only French names on the records designated as members of the church. Then the name of Peter Benoist appears as one of those present at a business meeting of the church members and is later classed among the members.[43] In 1760 the name of Isaac Lesesne, who held pew No. 18, is added.[44] In that year he gave £100 to the church, probably for his pew. Charles Peronneau in his will bequeathed £1500 currency as an endowment fund, the interest of which should be used to support the "Independent Meeting House".[45]

the minutes, dated March 1, 1750. The church prior to 1750 was known as "The Brick Meeting of Charles Town". MS Minutes, pages 76, 80, and 85.

[39] Henry Peronneau, Solomon Legare, and Henry Varnon, *ibid.*
[40] *Ibid.*
[41] *Ibid.*, 20.
[42] *Ibid.*, 28.
[43] *Ibid.*, 86 and 88.
[44] *Ibid.*, 120.
[45] *Ibid.*, 72.

Isaac Mazÿck left to the poor of the church the sum of £25.[46] Mathurin Boigard, in his will, left the value of £4 proclamation money as an annual gift to the minister of the French Protestant Church of Charleston, but provided that during vacancies in the pastorates of the French Church the same amount be paid to the minister of the "New Brick Presbyterian Meeting House", in Charles Town.[47] This was the name sometimes applied to what was known as the Circular Church.[48]

But the absorption of the French was more extensive than a mere change in church forms. It extended to proper names, to language, to customs, and even to blood. It has become evident that for several reasons the Huguenots were regarded with disfavor before they were able to rise socially by the accumulation of wealth.[49] However unreasonable that circumstance may have been regarded it was nevertheless a fact and became very unpleasant. Out of it grew the desire to become anglicized. A French name was constantly a bid to disfavor. Therefore some people changed their names completely, others modified them, still others accepted the English equivalent. Jacque Serrurier easily became Smith;[50] for convenience Pasquereau degenerated into Packerow;[51] Villepontoux became Pontoux;[52] Lewis Janvier, a goldsmith, became Louis Jennings;[53] Timotheé[54] was anglicized to Timothy;[55] and Isaac Amyrand, Clerk of the Assembly, abbreviated his name to Amy.[56] La Motte was changed to

[46] *Ibid.*, 65.
[47] *Ibid.*, 59. Marthurin Boigard received denization papers March 11, 1699-1700. See reprint in *Pub. H. Soc.*, London, XVIII. 315.
[48] MS Minutes, 76, 80, and 85.
[49] Gregg, *Old Cheraws.*
[50] After the change in the name occurred he was frequently designated by the double name: James Serrurier Smith, to distinguish him from other Smiths.
[51] *Ibid.*
[52] MS St. Philip's Register; *S. C. Gaz.*, Dec. 28, 1734.
[53] MS St. Stephen's Vestry Bk., 1754 et seq., Nov. 17, 1767.
[54] *S. C. Gaz.*, Dec. 28, 1734; Jan. 4, 1734-5.
[55] The change may be noted on the pages of the *S. C. Gaz.* In the early issues he designates himself Lewis Timotheé, while later he subscribes himself Louis Timothy.
[56] MS Col. Doc. S. C., XIX. 281 and 296.

Mott, De la Pierre to Pierre, and so on through a long list.[57] Thus with their English or German veneer many of the names are today hardly recognizable.[58]

As the French mingled with the English the use of the French language was gradually undermined.

The Orange Quarter was a striking exception to conditions found elsewhere. There the French held rigorously to their own language and forms beyond 1730,[59] due to the diminishing numbers of English inhabitants in the settlement, but the greatest reason for this was probably their isolation from almost everything French. They were forced to mingle with the English in business and social intercourse as well as in political and industrial life. This made a knowledge of the English language indispensable. In proportion to the extent of their isolation from strictly French influence came the rapidity of the undermining of the French language. Before 1700 a number of wills written in French were left on record. After 1720 there are practically none. There were few if any inducements except sentiment for preserving the French language, but many reasons for relinquishing it.

The registers of the several churches of the colonial period, the newspaper reports and the original marriage bonds are replete with evidence that the Huguenots began to intermarry with the British almost as soon as they reached Carolina, in fact some of them had married English wives during their short sojourn in the British Isles. This intermarriage continued throughout the colonial period and be-

[57] Instances are numerous in the records of the Probate Court. The La, De, and Le are frequently dropped.

[58] The process of anglicizing names had been begun in England long before. An examination of the Parish Registers and their comparison with the registration in French congregations show many bearing English names to be of French descent. A few examples are: Andrier—Andrew; De la mere—Dalimer; De la Motte—Dalimote; De la Pierre—Peters; De Lespine—Lespine; Dubois—Wood; Du Boys—Boyce; DuForest—Forest; Oliviere—Oliver (*Pub. H. Soc. London,* XV. 216 and Rawlinson MSS, no. 271, folio 9, Library of Congress).

[59] See the chapter on churches.

came so general that by 1776 there was little if any pure French blood in the province.[60]

[60] The Charleston Library Society possesses the only known series of extant marriage bonds of the colonial period of South Carolina. See also MS Turquand Family Records, in possession of Mrs. Louisa Smythe, of Charleston. In 1754-5 the Rev. Mr. Garden wrote to the S. P. G., in London, that the French Protestants were quite generally intermarried with the English. Humphreys, *S. P. G.*, 1754-5, 56.

CHAPTER V

THE DISSENTER FIGHT OR THE RELIGIOUS AND POLITICAL STRUGGLE 1682-1706

Though information on local politics in South Carolina during the colonial period is now both meagre and unsatisfactory, from scattered sources the facts can be pieced together to show that rival factions began to appear and take definite shape rather early in the history of the Province. This is not surprising, for from the beginning differences of opinion might be expected in a population made up of different nationalities among whom were varying interests and points of view and diversified trades. It is not hard to understand why public questions in South Carolina should bring about a classification of people along religious alignments, when we recall that the same issues that divided people into groups in England were the principal topics of discussion and the main reasons for divisions in that Province. For our purposes it is convenient to divide them into five classes or groups.

1. South Carolina, being an English province and both at first and during many of the later years the largest, was the Church of England group, composed of such loyal British subjects as sympathized with the Anglican Church in England. They were either members of it, or in sympathy with its polity and doctrines, and are here sometimes called the "High Church" faction. In England allegiance to the government was practically identical with allegiance to the Established Church. In South Carolina the men who identified themselves with the Established Church embraced in the very nature of the case the officers of the government, clerks, secretaries, assistants, public officers of various kinds, and others whose living was obtained from the public treasury. Some families of French nativity by virtue of their contact with English churches in the British Isles identified them-

selves with this group and were members of the Anglican Church. Some of these were denizened in England, or even naturalized subjects and Anglicans when they reached South Carolina. The term *anti-dissenter* is sometimes applied to them in this chapter.[1]

2. The enumerations of population down to the middle of the eighteenth century leave the impression that English dissenters were given their regular classification in the thought of the people and that they were numerous enough in the province to attract attention and make an impression in elections and other public activities. They went to Carolina to escape religious and political restrictions in England and were opposed to Anglicanism on both religious and political grounds. Not a few people of French nativity found in them a bond of sympathy and some evidently voted with this group in contests of wide public interest.

3. There is no uniformity of classification of religious and political groups in the enumerations of population that one finds in the extant records. Classified under the term "dissenters" may be found Presbyterians, Quakers, and others. Nevertheless one can not escape the conviction that in the alignment people of various nationalities and religious persuasions, having political convictions similar to those of the English Dissenters, were sometimes separately classified, simply because, strictly speaking, they could not be called English Dissenters. Among them were Quakers, Lutherans, some Scotch Irish Presbyterians, and others who had come over to Carolina from provinces lying to the north, because South Carolina was offering greater encouragement than others in the form of bounties. They too had suffered for the sake of their religion and found a bond of sympathy in the Dissenter point of view.

The Huguenots, being an established group early in the history of Charles Town and Santee, warmly welcomed the

[1] *Cal. State Pa. (Am. & W. Ind.)*, 1696-7, 420; Ramsay, *S. C.*, I. 5-9; *Pro. Hug. Soc.* London. With reference to Locke's Constitution, these may be called strict constructionists.

Dissenters in South Carolina. Both had suffered by the narrowness of intolerance at home and both had found in South Carolina a place of refuge. But both were to be confronted there with difficulties and threats similar to those which they had encountered at home.

Though French Protestants who remained aloof from the Established Church were neither Non-Conformists nor Dissenters, strictly speaking, in the sense in which these terms are used in England, but Calvinistic in doctrine and polity, they were often classed with the Dissenters in the enumerations of population and in other contemporaneous literature. This was the case more particularly of members of the Charles Town Huguenot Church, who naturally did not travel politically with the Anglicans.[2]

4. As early as 1690-92 the French Protestants found reasons for a separate group alignment, distinct from the three just described. They differed in church polity and doctrine as well as in political interests and nationality. Though they were not numerous, and consequently their weight in elections ordinarily not important, politically they become probably the most feared group. This was because the weight of their influence at elections was great enough to determine issues between fairly evenly balanced voting groups. How mischievous a minor party can become in politics is strikingly illustrated here. The two leading groups were as a rule fairly well matched, so nearly so in fact that contests were very close indeed. Consequently success was assured to which ever side the French Protestants would give the weight of their influence and their ballots. The men who directed the movements of the French Protestants were sagacious enough to see that in order to obtain recognition for public offices and get a place in the councils of the province, with a view to the protection of their own interests, they would best cast their lot with the English Church party. This they frequently did.[3]

[2] Rawlinson MSS C. 943, Bodleian, Oxford; Fulham Palace MSS.

[3] Rawlinson MSS; Fulham Palace MSS, S. C.; Ramsay, *Hist of S. C.*, II. 121-2. Articles 96 and 101 of Locke's Constitutions were especially in point.

5. Besides these there was that uncertain, shifting, fluid mass made up of unclassified citizens, each of whom, after his kind, could be persuaded according to the issues and the seasons to support the major groups in their various contests for leadership. It cannot be counted on with any degree of certainty.

Here then is the basis for an interesting politico-religious and racial cross-rivalry. It can readily be seen that native Frenchmen who were members of the Anglican Church would easily combine their political and social interests by affiliating with the English members of the Anglican Church. But a similar union between English Dissenters and such Huguenots as turned from the Anglican allegiance is not so easy of accomplishment. Some of the Frenchmen, therefore, chose to associate with the Dissenters on political grounds.

There were among the French Protestants quite a number of men who were qualified for leadership, and though driven from their native home and aliens in Carolina, had enough courage to look after their own interests. But we have no reason to suppose that the Huguenots as such held together constantly in one group for the purpose of self protection. Their political strength was consequently greatly reduced. On the other hand there is abundant evidence to show that the very terms Huguenot and French Protestant carried with them unfavorable allusions and even ridicule. For this condition the Huguenots were not entirely blameless, as we shall see.

The anti-Huguenot feeling was caused mainly by two things: the political status of the refugees and their religious or doctrinal inclinations. The basis of the strife was not a matter of race prejudice primarily. Much more vital was the question whether an unnaturalized man could vote and hold office, and whether a person holding to the Calvinistic faith and with membership in a strictly Huguenot church in a province where the Church of England was established and the only legalized religion, could take part in the government at all or not.[4]

[4] MS Sec'y. Rcds., 1685-1712, 151.

Almost immediately after their arrival in noticeable numbers the Huguenots were drawn into the conflicts of provincial politics. It seems like a jest of fate that refugees, driven from France by political dissensions, should in their new home be forced to face the political turmoil of an undeveloped provincial government. While in the main the policy of the British government itself was friendly toward the French refugees, they met with considerable antipathy among members of the English Established Church. Even though policies indicating a tolerant attitude may have been adopted in the mother country, their practice often came into use only slowly and reluctantly in distant colonies.

The anti-Huguenot strife, as we have seen, centered on two things: the political status of the refugees, and their alleged ability and effort to control the political situation in the province.[5] In 1682 the Proprietors had ordered the territory divided into three counties. Berkeley County was to include Charles Town and extended from the Sewee on the north to Stone Creek, which separates James Island from John's Island, on the south. Craven County joined it immediately on the north, while Colleton lay to the south. Each county should extend thirty-five miles inland from the coastline. Roughly speaking then, the dissenters lived on the Edisto River in Colleton County. The strength of the anti-Dissenter party lay in Charles Town along the Cooper and Ashley Rivers in Berkeley County and part of Colleton, while the Huguenots were on the Santee, in Craven County, and in and about Charles Town. Colleton and Berkeley were allowed ten members each[6] in the biennial meetings of the so-called "Lower House of Assembly", but Craven County, which soon became a Huguenot stronghold, then too thinly populated, had no representation. It was given, however, a sheriff and four justices of the peace like the rest.[7] In 1691 Berkeley County was allowed seven members,[8] Colleton seven

[5] Rivers, *Sketch,* 134-5; MS Sec'y. Rcds., 1685-1712, 151.
[6] MS House Jrnl., 1692, 1.
[7] MS House Jrnl., 1692, 1.
[8] MS Assembly Jrnl., 1692, 1.

and Craven six, in order to adjust the unequal representation occasioned by the fact that Colleton County, though sparsely settled, had formerly enjoyed the privilege of ten representatives in the assembly.[9] Though Craven County was given six representatives it was necessary for the Craven County French voters to go to Charles Town to elect them,[10] which in those days was no small hardship. After the Revocation of the Edict of Nantes the French poured into Carolina in such numbers, especially around 1690, that steps were taken to check their increasing power.[11]

Writers on the subject have so far naturally sympathized in the main with the Dissenters, chiefly because practically the only sources used were partisan accounts, notably Defoe's *Case of the Dissenters,* published in London in 1705, after several attempts on the part of Ash and Boone (both Dissenters) to get the ear of the proprietors in England, and Oldmixon's account, published in London in 1708. Defoe's discussion of the case is based entirely on the statements of the displeased Dissenters. He had never lived in the province and hence had no first-hand knowledge of the facts. Oldmixon was naturally a Dissenter, for he was a tutor in Governor Blake's family.[12]

That the main legal issue in the Dissenter controversy up to 1706, as far as the French are concerned, centered on the fact that many of the French Protestants, who were not fully naturalized before going to Carolina, had been denizened in England, while few had been actually naturalized, has evidently been overlooked.[13]

[9] MS Col. Doc. S. C., II. 32; McCrady, *Hist. S. C.*, I. 198.

[10] Rivers, *Sketch,* chap. 7.

[11] By the "increasing power" is not meant necessarily their influence at the polls, for at the time of their arrival that was slight. As they became naturalized it was more evident. Throughout, however, as is evidenced in the several attempts to prosecute alleged illegal voting by French Protestants, the latter were influential as agitators and propagandists.

[12] McCrady, *Hist. S. C.*, I. 378.

[13] The distinction is made in the colonial manuscript material of Carolina continually. See MS London Tr., III. 166; IV. 135, etc.; MS Sec'y. Rcds., 1685-1712, 122-3.

There was a current recognized distinction between naturalization and denization.[14] Carolina was an English province and was governed by English law in accordance with the principle that allegiance is coterminous with dominion. The throngs of French Protestants that poured into the British Isles between 1670 and 1690 made necessary a complete recasting of the English naturalization and denization laws. The Huguenots, denizened in England, who went to Carolina during those years were neither aliens nor full-fledged English subjects from the standpoint of the English law. They were as a rule fractional subjects, or perhaps better, subjects with fractional privileges.[15] From the time when the first known instance of converting a foreigner into an English subject, the case of Élias Danbury in 1295,[16] who to all intents and purposes was regarded as an English subject; until 1603, apparently no distinction was made between naturalization and denization. Thereafter the distinction that arises finds its origin in the clauses of limitations in the grants themselves. Some of these grants confer full rights of citizenship, others only limited rights, but in the main the power to grant or to restrict lay with the English Executive. This change in the aspect of the subject was accomplished[17] in the Tudor period. The English Crown was in the habit of changing aliens into natives by letters patent, not by an act of Parliament, and the grants thus given by the Executive almost uniformly contained the clause regarding the payment of customs as required of aliens. Toward the end of Elizabeth's reign a revival of the power of Parliament occurs in this direction, but thereby the Crown is not necessarily shorn of the power it had possessed under the Tudor

[14] MS Col. Doc. S. C., III. 166; MS Sec'y. Rcds., 1685-1712, 122.

[15] A reprint of the denizations and naturalizations from 1602 to 1700 is found in the *Publications of the Huguenot Society of London,* vol. XVIII.

[16] 23 Edw. I. *Pro. H. Soc. London,* XVIII. p. iii; Pollock and Maitland, *Hist. of English Law,* I. 447.

[17] *Rolls of Parl.,* III. 590, 600, 748. Henry IV. 1406. See reprint of denizations and naturalizations, 1509-1603 in *P. H. Soc. London.* vol. VIII.

regime, but whereas, under the latter, a single type of grant was conferred there is now a double act performed and a two-fold grant conferred, the one by the Crown granting denization, the other by Parliament, granting naturalization. All through the Tudor period the grants of letters patent by the King to foreigners are numerous, but the parliamentary acts are few.[18]

It is well known that for naturalized subjects, duties were reduced one-half. This materially clipped the purse of the Crown and therefore denization was resorted to as it gave the subject the right, as a rule, to hold land and transfer it, but left the customs duties the same as those of aliens.

The nature of the distinction between the two (i.e., between naturalization and denization), involving the points at issue[19] in the Dissenter fight in Carolina before 1706, is vital. If they are distinguished at all, the usual explanation given is that naturalization conferred complete rights,[20] including those of purchasing, holding and transferring land, while denization was only a sort of half way covenant, conferring limited rights. This explanation not only does not hold in the Tudor period, but is untrue altogether for our purposes and in fact does not cover the most essential feature of distinction between them. After the two forms became fixed the real distinction was that grants of denization originated with the Crown and were not merely an act of the legislative department. The fact that denization conferred limited rights and naturalization full rights was purely accidental due to the unfettered nature of the power of the Crown, which could put into the grant any limitations of liberties it desired. Thereby denizens could be forced to pay alien's duties; they could be permitted to hold and transfer land,[21] or that right could be withheld. Residence could be insisted on[22] or dispensed with. They could be given the

[18] Agnew, *Protestant Exiles from France,* I. 36 f.

[19] MS Col. Doc. S. C., III. 166 f.

[20] Judicial and Statutory Definitions of Words and Phrases, *Naturalization and Denizenation. Pro. Hug. Soc. London,* XVIII, p. vi.

[21] MS Pr. Ct. Rcds., 1694-1704, 150 and 177.

[22] *Ibid.*

right to be shipmasters or not, as the Crown chose. The motive, thus to guard the Crown's customs, revenues, or some trade prejudices, was unchallenged. The tendency was to allow the action of the Executive to become less fettered than that of the legislative department, resulting in the latter becoming stereotyped while the former remained elastic.

There was great reluctance on the part of Great Britain to pass a general act of Parliament for the naturalization of French Protestants.[23] Repeatedly, between 1660 and 1710 efforts had been made without success.[24] In 1681 Charles II undertook to suggest the step to Parliament, but law-makers were deaf to his plea.[25] The Englishman regarded it as flinging away precious wealth, the restrictions of foreigners being regarded as providential blessings for Englishmen. But between 1660 and 1720, while naturalization was very unpopular, the old practice of denization was kept up as a beckoning hand to French Protestants on the one hand and in order on the other hand to satisfy the scruples of the English subject, while naturalization was doled out to a few by letters patent.[26] It becomes evident that while the legislative power became narrow, the executive power showed itself liberal. Not until 1708, after the Dissenter fight in Carolina had culminated in the Act of 1706, did Great Britain pass a general naturalization law.[27]

The period of greatest Huguenot immigration into England,[28] if the records of denization are an indication, was between July, 1681 and August, 1688. On July 28, 1681 the British Council granted leave to relax the red tape in denization procedure and wholesale grants of denization were made without even the requirement of fees. Between these two dates therefore there is a double series of denizations, viz., those made under the order of Council of July 28, 1681 and

[23] Agnew, *Protestant Exiles from France.* I. 36.
[24] *Ibid.*
[25] *Ibid.*
[26] *Ibid.*, 25 f.
[27] 7 Ann c 2.
[28] See lists of denizations and naturalizations, *Pub. H. Soc. London,* XVIII. 124 f.

the ordinary series entered as usual in docket books, privy seals and patent rolls. The former contain long lists of names of persecuted French, who emigrated to Carolina. It seems that the denizened Huguenots going there had in the main the privileges of buying, holding, and transferring land, but did not have the right to vote, hold office and serve on juries.[29] However it appears that, whenever proper application was made, the British Government granted naturalization to those who legally sought it.[30]

One of the chief difficulties then in Carolina lay in the close construction interpretation of the English law by the Dissenter party, while the French Protestants based their claims to the rights of citizenship and the ballot on the insufficiently authenticated word of the proprietors and the spirit of the English law in the light of the interpretation of the Stuart period. The great injustice that the French had to endure lay in the fact that they had to suffer the limitations made centuries before and passed not for them, but for alien French merchants, who for decades had sought the English markets only for the right to trade. The law of 1485 was passed because these merchants wanted naturalization for no other reason than for business privileges and the British Government, though willing to make them citizens, also

[29] MS Pr. Ct. Rcd., 1694-1704, 150, 177, 209.

[30] The naturalization papers of A. Bounin, filed Jan. 19, 1687-8, stipulate his right to pay customs duties only as natives do. (MS Pr. Ct. Rcd., 1694-1704, 149.) Bounin had been denizened in London by the King, Jan. 5, of the same year. Isaac Mazÿck was denizened April 15 and naturalized on the 26th of April, 1687. These were not recorded in Charles Town until May 3, 1699. (MS Pr. Ct. Rcd., 1694-1704, 177.) James Serurier was naturalized in Charles Town by Governor Blake, April 17, 1697. (*Ibid.*, 83.) The naturalization papers of Thomas St. Leger, Joseph de Lancey, Alexander de Roquett, *et al.*, do not stipulate immunity from customs duties (*ibid.*, 1694-1704, 371), while those of A. Bounin, Isaac Mazÿck and Stephen and Oree Perdriau state that they are to pay customs duties "only as natives do", i.e., as English-born subjects. (See *Ibid.*, 1694-1704, 149, 177.) James Dufay (alias Faye) petitioned with James Serurier and others for naturalization in 1685. This petition was granted and a record sent to the South Carolina Record Office, but the names of James Dufay and Suzanna his wife are found in the list of denizations of March 25, 1688. (MS Pr. Ct. Rcd., 1694-1704, 209; *Pub. H. Soc. London,* XVIII. 170.)

exacted aliens' customs fees from them.[31] At this time no distinction was made[32] between denization and naturalization. But numerous French merchants abused the privileges of their citizenship and violated the English laws to a sufficient degree to cause the enactment of a new law in 1657-8,[33] providing for the cancellation of the privileges granted in denization in cases of flagrant abuse. Under this trade odium the French refugees entered Great Britain even after the Revocation of the Nantes decree and under this trade prejudice against French subjects in general they went to Carolina. In its atmosphere they had to live in their provincial home.

Though the English formed the parent community in and about Charles Town, the Dissenters were in a majority, with the anti-dissenter,[34] Church of England party, a close second. But when the nationalities are considered the French were easily second to the English in numbers. The possibility of the impending disaster which might occur if the balance of power should be thrown on the side of the anti-Dissenter party caused the Dissenter party to fear the result.[35] Estimating the white population in 1700 as 6,000 and accepting Nairn's[36] statement as true that the Dissenters constituted fifty-seven and one-half per cent of the population and the English party forty-two and one-half per cent, we figure that there were approximately 3,450 Dissenters and 2,550 of the English party in the province. But Nairn, in accord with the current custom, classed the Huguenots with the dissenters. There were about 500 French Protestants in the province at

[31] 1 Henry VII c 2. 11 Henry VII c 14.
[32] Pollock and Maitland, *Hist. of Eng. Law,* I. 447.
[33] 3 & 4 Phil. & Mary c 5.
[34] Carroll, *Collections* I. 133; Nairn, *Letter from S. C.,* (1710) 41, 44. Nairn wrote in 1710 that the Presbyterians, "including those of the French who retain their own Discipline constitute 45% of the white population." See Nairn, p. 46. Hewat (I. 167) wrote that the Dissenters represent two-thirds of the inhabitants of the province.
[35] Mills, *Statistics,* 177, gives 7,000; Humphreys, *S. P. G.* 25, gives 7,000; Carroll, *Collec.* I. 132, gives 5-6,000; Drayton, *View,* 103, gives 5,500; Rivers, *Sketch,* 443, gives 1,100 families of English and French.
[36] Nairn, p. 46.

the time.[37] If the 500 were to throw their influence on the side of the anti-Dissenter party, it would leave the Dissenter party, even if thoroughly united, a minority.[38] The denizened French were thus a central party, not a leading group, between the Dissenter party and the anti-Dissenter party and chose for policy's sake to ally themselves with the latter.

It leaps to view also that the Dissenters refused to espouse the cause of the Church of England party because of their refusal to sanction Locke's Constitutions. In Governor Sayle's commission, which bears the date, July 26, 1669, his authority is restricted by the Proprietors' instructions and the *Fundamental Constitutions.* These of course are the first set of Constitutions, of July 21, 1669, erroneously called by Chalmers: "A rough sketch." In the letter to Sothel, of the probable date of 1690-1, there is the statement that the *Fundamental Constitutions* were engrossed on parchment and signed and sealed and that several hundred people swore allegiance to them.[39] An old odd leaf bound out of place in a record book in the Charles Town probate court corroborates this.[40] On this page are the signatures of some thirty persons

[37] *Cal. St. Pa.,* 1699: no. 183 gives 438. This is the Girard enumeration, but to this must be added 10 families on the West Branch of the Cooper River (see *S. C. H. & G. Mag.,* IX. 222). It enumerates the membership of the several Huguenot churches, but does not account for the Huguenots who were members of the Established Church in the several communities nor for those affiliated with no church at all. The total number of names of Huguenot families recorded in the Gaillard and Ravenel lists is 582. No doubt a number of these names had become extinct on account of the small-pox and fever epidemics that had made their fatal inroads into the colony. If the enumerations, such as the Girard, may be regarded as representing families instead of individuals, the argument presented here is even more important.

[38] This is figured on the assumed basis that the number of voters in each party was proportionate to the number of persons represented in the party. Of course it is safe to believe that families were divided as was the Pasquereau family and that the actual figures were not worked out exactly, though in the main the general deduction is correct.

[39] *Coll. S. C. Hist. Soc.,* V. 117; Chalmers, *Pol. Annals,* in Carroll, *Collec.,* II. 331; MS *Pr. Ct. Rcds.,* 1692-3, 347; MS Letters, Shaftsbury Papers, in N. Y. Public Library, Rivers to Bancroft.

[40] MS Pr. Ct. Rcd., 1792-3, 347. Cooper errs in inserting in the *Statutes at Large of S. C.,* (I, 43) the second set of Constitutions under the name "First Set." This mistake is also made in Carroll's *Collections,* which also omits two important lines, (¶53) which show by what authority money might be drawn from the treasury. Rivers, *Sketch,* 138f.

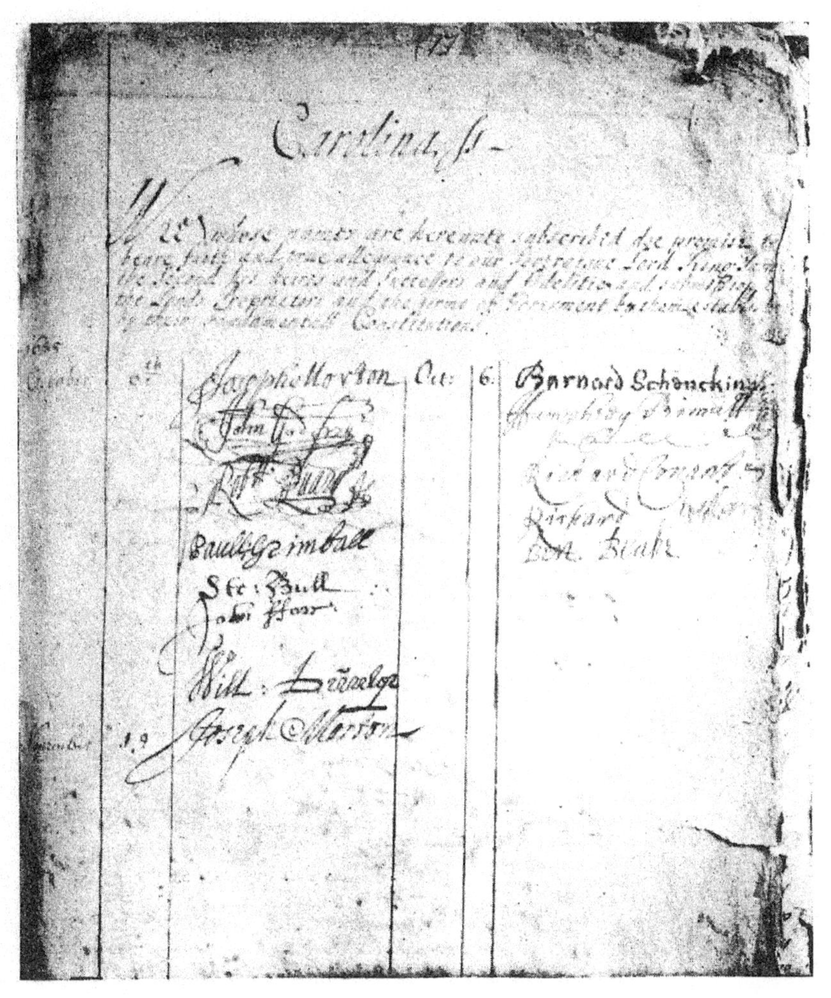

ODD LEAF BOUND OUT OF PLACE IN AN OLD RECORD BOOK IN THE PROBATE COURT, CHARLESTON

written in 1685 and the following years, subscribing their allegiance to King James II and their submission to the Constitutions of July 21, 1669, although several other sets had been sent out in the meantime by the proprietors. But both the assembly and the council had refused the second set of the Constitutions, because the people had all sworn to the first set. They were no doubt led to do so in order to secure the tenure of their lands, for subscription to the Constitutions was necessary to the validity of their claims. Others no doubt signed, because by doing so a foreigner could become naturalized. There are several reasons why the first set was prepared in spite of the declaration of the proprietors that each successive set was more favorable to the people and more restrictive of the powers of the proprietors. The first set, that of July 21, 1669, is without the clause relating to the introduction of religious worship according to the usages of the Church of England, which seems to have been retained in the other sets. Again, the second set omits the provision that where there is a registered contract or agreement between the tenant and lord of any manor, etc., the tenant might bring an action against the lord in the county court.

Among the signatures mentioned above are a number of French names, which without commentary reveal an important phase of their part in the party conflict that shook Carolina to the center.

The French, as far as we know, made no demonstrative fight for their rights before 1692-3, after their disheartening experience of yielding to the promises of their friends, the Dissenters, who were using them as a device to accomplish their own purpose. But now they again began to gird their loins against their opponents. In this their first significant effort to secure their rights they chose seven leading Huguenots to champion their cause and plead their case before the proprietors. They were the Rev. Francis Trouillard, Minis-

Original MS of Locke's first set of Constitutions, bearing his signature, in Charleston Library Society collection. MS Col. Doc. S. C., XX. 321.

ter of the Charles Town Huguenot church, MM. Buretal, Serrurier and Couran, Elders in the same church and MM. DeVervant, DeLisle, Cramahé, and Dugué, prominent Huguenot business men and planters in and about Charles Town. They dared to carry their grievances before the proprietors in London by a letter, and we have the proprietors' answer[41] which was made in writing on April 12, 1693, to the effect that the grievances had occurred against the will and desire of the proprietors and that the grievances had been provided against in the fourth set of the Constitutions.[42] In this reply the proprietors imply that at least part of the annoyance brought on the French was due to their own shortcomings. It appears that up to this time the French were uncertain as to which side to take in political matters for they pleaded their case singlehanded and alone, which is not true later, when they got the support of the Church of England party.[43]

So aggressive did the opposition against the Huguenots become that use was made of every possible pretext. The

[41] Letter of the proprietors to the French Protestants in South Carolina, April 12, 1693 (MS Col. Doc. S. C., III. 103).

[42] "Now what hand yo^{e} yor selves had in rejecting the wholesome provisions Wee had made against all oppressions whatsoever on yor selves or other Forraigners and all other Inhabitants of Our Province you best know and we heartely wish you may never feel any Inconvenience by hearkening to those that misled you and who in the bottom love you not."

[43] After May, 1696, there was little excuse for any Frenchman not embracing the privileges offered for naturalization, except his adherence to his Huguenot faith. The law passed then was for the express purpose of naturalizing French and Swiss refugees and made it so easy that practically nothing except inability to pay the customary fee of "seven pence half penny" or unwillingness to subscribe to the oath of allegiance stood in the way. There were of course obligations, such as registering with the Secretary of the Province, within six months of the passage of the Act. This was both an advantage and a disadvantage, for before 1693 the election laws had been so loose that they had provoked comment from the proprietors, who said that as the law stood (with only a property qualification) all of the pirates plundering ships in the Red Sea could vote for representatives in Carolina. Before 1696 the French taking the Act of 1691 in good faith, as enacted, depended on its presumed validity. But the proprietors nullified it, because it was not ratified by Parliament. More of the Huguenots were persecuted than was necessary, for it is evident that the special objects of attack among the French were those who were not naturalized. MS *Col. Doc. S. C.* III. 103; MS Sec'y. Rcds., 1685-1712, 93 f.

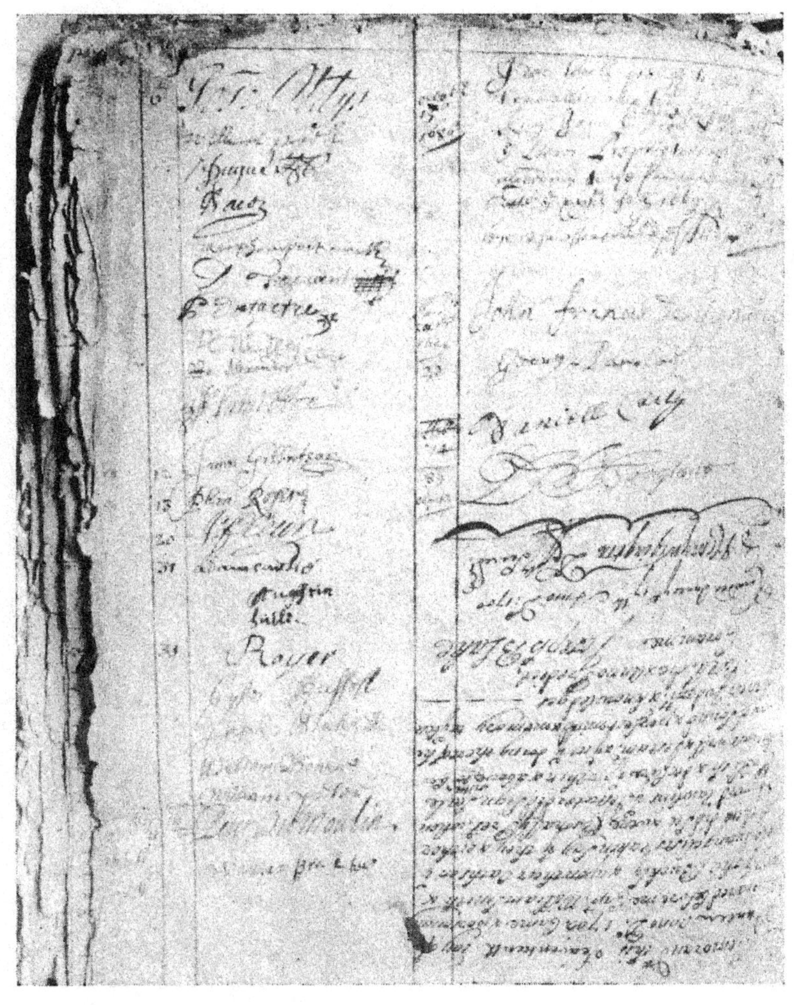

ODD LEAF BOUND OUT OF PLACE IN AN OLD RECORD BOOK IN THE PROBATE COURT, CHARLESTON

sacredness and validity of their marriages, the sufficiency of their ministry, and the legitimacy of their children were all challenged by the Dissenter party, because the Huguenots were not naturalized.[44] To annoy them, even the hour of their Sabbath service was interfered with. On June, 1692, the Grand Council ordered that they must have services in the Huguenot Church at nine in the morning and at two in the afternoon, instead of fixing the hour from time to time to conform with the tides for the accommodation of those who lived up the Cooper River and along the coast.[45] The proprietors forced the withdrawal of the order, however, when appealed to by the French.[46]

The Dissenters by 1693 became so powerful, that by their persistent complaints they forced Governor Smith to resign and then demanded a new incumbent.[47] Archdale, a Quaker, was sent over with instructions to pacify the parties.[48] The Huguenots, seeing this opportunity in the joy of Archdale's arrival to make a dash to secure their rights,[49] prepared a petition for their naturalization, probably late in the year 1695.[50] Archdale saw, however, what he supposed to be a necessity of catering to the majority. He therefore publicly cast his lot with the Dissenter group at once by signing a petition with Blake, Bull, Grimbal, More, Carey and others,[51] in opposition to the admission of French Protestants to the Assembly. This petition he sent to the proprietors. As this was less than two months after his arrival in the province, it settled at once for all time his attitude toward the Huguenots. Then as a proposal of peace to the other sections he excluded the French in Craven County from the following election. Thereupon he called a conven-

[44] MS Sec'y. Rcds., 1685-1712, 93f.; Rivers, *Sketch,* 455; Carroll, *Collections,* I. 103.

[45] *Council Jrnl.,* (Salley) 1692, 44.

[46] Letter, Proprietors to the Governor, April 10, 1693, MS Assembly Jrnl., 1693, 31.

[47] Hewat, *S. C.,* 128.

[48] MS Col. Doc. S. C., III. 139.

[49] Carroll, *Collections,* II. 426 f.

[50] It is supposed that the St. Julien list was composed at this time.

[51] MS Sec'y. Rcds., 1685-1712, 120; date, Oct. 2, 1695.

tion of all the "King's Liedge Subjects" to meet in Charles Town, December 19, 1695.[52] At this meeting, in which feeling was at its highest pitch, thirty representatives for four years were sought and as many more as might from time to time be necessary, and a bill was introduced accordingly.[53] Each county was to be given ten representatives, all to be elected in Charles Town except those of Colleton County, who were to be elected at Captain Bristow's plantation. The petition of Isaac Caillabaeuf[54] stating that Jonas Bonhoste, a wheelwright and James Lassade,[55] gentleman (all Huguenots) offered their votes on January 16, in the Berkeley County election and that Robert Gibbs, the sheriff, refused to take them unless they could show letters either of denization or naturalization, shows how the matter stood early in 1696. As both acknowledged they had not such letters, the ballot was denied them.

In the January election of 1695-6 the French lost so completely that only one of their number was elected to the house, viz., Henry Le Noble, who was returned from Berkeley County, but the anti-Dissenter party had carried the naturalization bill of 1691 in their behalf.[56] Thus the immediate fight culminated in the passage of the act of 1696,[57] entitled: *An act for the Making Aliens Free of this Part of the Province and for Granting Liberty of Conscience to all Protestants.* The act names sixty-three men, of whom sixty are French Protestants, who were thereby naturalized and constituted citizens. Next to the Act of May 1, 1691,[58] soon

[52] MS House Jrnl., 1692-1701, I. 89, 93, 103, 113; MS Assembly Jrnl., 1696, 1.

[53] MS Assembly Jrnl., 1692-1701, bill no. 65. See also pages 113 and 117.

[54] Gaillard MS.

[55] It should also be noted that in October 1695 the Council had sent word to the proprietors that they had discontinued writs of election to Craven County as the inhabitants were all French. MS Sec'y. Rcds., 1685-1712, 122 f.

[56] MS Assembly Jrnl.. 1796, 4.

[57] Cooper, *Statutes,* II. 131.

[58] *Ibid.,* II. 58; MS Pr. Ct. Rcd., 1694-1704, 53. A petition of persons "alien born" and dated March 30, 1696, as the date of record, sets forth that the undersigned had been encouraged to go to England and later to South Carolina and that they now seek naturalization in order that

after its passage disallowed by the proprietors and nullified, the Act of 1696 was for the French the most important passed before 1697. The list included only those who had not been naturalized previously, but it contains also many who had been denizened in England.[59] In the winter election of 1696 by means of an underhand gerrymander the Huguenots were again not represented and they therefore renewed their fight for their alleged rights. The Governor in issuing the writs for elections left out the French of Craven County, contrary to the instructions of the proprietors. The election returns show ten men elected from that county, but there are no Huguenots on the list.[60] After Archdale's governorship, matters quieted down for a little while. In May, 1699, the Council in a letter to the proprietors set forth that "the French here ever since Mr. Archdale laid down the government have been not differenced from the English in any manner of usage or concern, public or private, except being of the Assembly here, which the Act of their naturalization hath not given them and their being jurymen in tryals, which concern his Majesty's revenue or his customs . . . all aliens by an Act in England are made unqualified for."[61] But in April, 1702, they wrote once more to the proprietors saying that the Assembly was again in "violent heats" about the election, that two members from Colleton were challenged and that debate had put the House in the "same ferment as before", concluding their complaint with

their lands already bought may "be secured to them and their heirs". The list contains the following French names: Noah Royer, Jonas Bonhost, Pierre Poinsett, Jr., Pierre Poinsett, Sr., Jourdain Colliandeau, [Elisha] Poinsett, James Dugue, James Dubose, James Lardine, Daniel Bonell, Jean le Birt, Abraham Le Sueur, Louis Tibou, A. Bonneau, Jean Girardeau, Peter Gaillard, Peter Colloando (Couillinado), Ann Vinne, [Londonderry] Corquett, Dan'l Duraso (DuRousseau); Mathu Garin, Paul Borquett, Noah Sere, John Potine, Philip Norman, James Serau, Augustin Varry, John Potell.

[59] Compare with the lists in *P. H. Soc. London*, XVIII. Berkeley County on the northeast extended to within a few miles of the Santee. The French were settled chiefly on the land butting immediately on both sides of the Santee. This excluded them from participation in the elections. Carroll, *Collec.*, II. 426 f.

[60] MS Assembly Jrnl., 1696, 4.

[61] MS Sec'y. Rcds., 1685-1712, 151, May 12, 1699.

the assertion: "The two contending parties are so equal that we have little hopes it will be ended soon."[62]

In 1701, the Colleton Dissenters, constantly carrying their grievance about, again came forward declaring that the Governor had carried the election by fraud with the intention of capturing free Indians and monopolizing the fur trade.[63] The Colleton faction resorted to extreme methods to prevent an assembly quorum by withdrawing from the room when measures obnoxious to them were proposed. A riot ensued. The Assembly was evenly divided, fifteen for the Governor, fifteen against, but as the courts were on the side of the administration,[64] the malcontents could get no protection against the town mob. The struggle became so acute that, when in 1703 by alleged fraud and violence the Anglican party gained ascendency, they disqualified all Dissenters from sitting in the Assembly. A clause was inserted to protect the Huguenots in the Church of England party. It read: "excepting such as can declare on oath that they have not received the sacrament in a dissenting church for one year past".[65] They secured the French Protestant vote by putting a Frenchman on their ticket. That year Joseph Boone, accompanied by Robert Fenwick and John Crosskeys led the fight in attempting to prosecute the French for alleged illegal voting and thereby returning three members to the legislature. This matter, then, with the contention over the St. Augustine Expedition, brought things to an issue in

[62] *Ibid.*, 194. The Dissenter party renewed the fight now, reënforced by the recent law passed in England in their favor, though it was not meant to include the Huguenots. The "Act of Succession" (12 & 13 Wm. III. c 2.) provided that no person born out of England, Ireland and Scotland, although naturalized, or made a citizen, should be capable of sitting on the Council or of holding an office of trust under the Crown. This Act, directed against William's Dutch followers and when reënacted (1 Geo. I. statute 2, c 4.) directed against the Hanoverian followers of George, was by the Dissenter party in Carolina made to apply to their French Protestant enemies and was made a political document of no small influence, because in order to keep the Act inviolate it was prescribed that it must be inserted in all bills of naturalization.

[63] Carroll, *Collec.*, II. 417-22.

[64] Schaper, *Sectionalism*, 341.

[65] Rivers, *Sketch*, 226; Carroll, *Collec.*, II. 441; MS Sec'y. Rcds., 1685-1712, 115 f. and 151.

Governor James Moore's administration. To make matters worse for the French, county was allied against county, Colleton against Berkeley, and both Colleton and Berkeley at times combined against Craven. The subject of county representation had been brought to the attention of the proprietors, not as a strictly anti-Huguenot measure, but as an objectionable feature as early as 1684, before the Revocation of the Edict of Nantes and before the French had settled in Carolina in large numbers. The objection then was directed against unequal representation in proportion to county population. The proprietors[66] at the time took the position that representation should not be based on population, but on territorial divisions.

The Dissenter fight in 1702 and thereafter was no longer being waged primarily along the lines of religious conviction. It had become an almost purely political contest except that the entire series of rivalries culminated in what is known as the *Church Act of 1706*. In 1702, when the Huguenots were summoned for alleged illegal voting, it was voted in a purely Dissenter-party assembly (for the Church party had withdrawn)[67] that those not registered with the Secretary of the Province had voted illegally and in the same meeting the same members of the Assembly went on record in declaring that even a Roman Catholic if he had registered, voted according to law.[68]

Again and again the Dissenter party sought to bring their opponents to trial. Political astuteness on the part of the Governor and others was each time displayed in sufficient measure to prevent this. Indian wars, public defense, and other serious questions, played their part in crowding the prosecution of the Huguenots into the background, so that as far as we know their case was never brought into court.[69]

[66] Letter, Proprietors to Governor and Council, Mar. 13, 1684-5, MS Col. Doc. S. C., II. 32.

[67] MS Assembly Jrnl., 1682-1701, 469.

[68] Herein the sense of provincial sentiment and law are totally ignored, but it shows at least the Dissenter legalistic tendency.

[69] MS Assembly Jrnl., 1702-6, 12 f.; 1692-1701, 80 and 471. Following are lists of Frenchmen accused of illegal voting. Lists found *ibid.*, pp.

Another phase of this party antipathy is seen in the records of repeated arrests of French Protestant navigators on the Atlantic after 1693. So bent were the members of the Dissenter party on crushing out Huguenot prestige that every available pretext was sought and every slender pretense used. In August, 1694, the *Blue Star,* a vessel operated by a denizened Frenchman was seized off the Carolina coast on the charge that it was illegally manned.[70] Colonel Bull, a dissenter, heard the case when it was tried, and Ferdinando Gorges, the Attorney General,[71] questioning the King's authority in the denization, was sustained. This was not the only case of similar injustice, for the proprietors, in their letter of January 29, 1695, to the Governor and Council boldly pronounced against the practice of injustice against

471-7. *List 1:* Mathew Guerin, John Bonneau, Peter Mailliet, Abraham Dupont, Isaac La Pierre, John Serau, Paul La Roche, Abr. Lesueur, Nicholas Longuemar, Peter Collineau. *List 2:* John Deveaux, John Juine, James Dumoe, Nicholas Boneil, Samuel Dugue, Peter Dutart (Dutarre); Peter Poitevine, Monsr. Morbeuff, Peter Filleaux, Peter Gideau, Benj. Marion. *List 3:* Mathew Guerin, John Bonneau, Peter Maillett, Abraham Juijon, Paul La Roche, Abraham Lesurier (Le Serrurier); Paul Battoane, Elias Verbans, Nicholas Languemar, Salloman Legare. *List 4:* John Deveaux, James Dunoe, Nicholas Boneil, Samuel Dugue, Peter Dutart, Peter Poitvine, Monsr. Marbeuff, Peter Villepontoux, Peter Videau, Benj. Marion, Peter Lesau, Sr., Anthony Poitvine, Ja. Lasad, Gideon Lisile [or Soule], Sam'l Lisle, Wm. Rouser (Rousourier).

[70] MS Col. Doc. S. C., III. 166; "London, January ye 20th, 1695/6. Gentlemen We have now before us yo[r] Letter of ye 20th of August and Likewise one from ye Governor wherein he takes notice of y[e] Condemnation of a french sloope sayled by French Denizen[d] Protestants, & allsoe a Complaint of great Injustice done in the condemnation of a former sloop called ye blew starr when Coll[o] Bull sate as Judge Edward Bellinger as Attorney General for that time his Brother Richard Bellinger and Tho. Rose Clearks of ye Court the Informers, that y[e] Court would not allow any of y[e] Kings Denizations And y[e] Attorney General questioned y[e] Kings Authority of Denizeing. This matter you ought strictly to inquire into, and transmitt to Us y[e] particulars of that Court w[ch] was held y[e] 21st of Febr. 1694 that if you will not take care to punish such people as Despise the Kings Authority We may be Enabled to doe it here. We find some of those persons names to that Unreasonable Address ag[t] y[e] French that came Inclosed in yo[r] letter that were Managers of that Tryall and doubt not but y[e] People who are misled by them who haveing a Desire to Cover their Injustice against ye vessels of y[e] French Protestants of New York Incite y[e] people to fall upon y[e] French with you."

[71] *Coll. S. C. Hist. Soc.* I. 140.

the vessels of French Protestants.[72] Only a few weeks later the authorities went so far as to strain the navigation laws almost to the verge of breaking by detaining a ship because a negro cook was on board and served in the crew, thereby not complying to the full letter of the law.[73] In 1697 the vessel of one George Harris, a free denizen, born in St. Martins,[74] France, was seized and his case presented to the Board of Trade in London by Peter Renné,[75] after the Carolina Court had decided against him. Harris showed that he was made a denizen in 1694, and hence was entitled to damages.[76]

These seizures were in part an effort to enrich the purses of the provincial officers, lustful for prize, and at the same time an attempt to assert the Dissenter antipathy against the French. Governor Blake, a Dissenter, according to a letter by Edward Randolph to the proprietors, dated May 27, 1700, was reaping a lucrative harvest[77] by seizing and condemning ships. Whether the vessel was condemned as prize or not, he was almost certain to be the gainer, "having the judge always on his side and his creatures at his back to appraise the ships and their loadings sometimes at not one-half their original cost".[78] The game was a shrewd though cruel one. The money thus secured was perhaps tainted, but the stain was washed off in foreign waters. If the seized vessel was not condemned as prize, the Governor was sure of his customary fees and almost sure of a chance to buy the illfated vessel and sell it again at a profit, while the provincial treasury had to return but little, due to the low appraisement placed on the vessel. If the vessel was condemned he was certain of his one-third of the booty, according to the English

[72] MS Col. Doc. S. C., IV. 59.

[73] *Ibid.*, III. 169. The master and three-fourths of the crew must be English, 12 Chas. II. c 18, 1.

[74] MS Col. Doc. S. C., IV. 76.

[75] *Ibid.*, IV. 53.

[76] *Ibid.*, IV. 55.

[77] *Ibid.*, IV. 165.

[78] *Ibid.*

law, in addition to profits by its sale.[79] He had all of his men well coached. Even one Lewis Pasquereau, a Huguenot refugee, living in Governor Blake's house (if the letter of Trott can be credited with truth) and acting as a clerk to the Governor, was enlisted in the greedy game.[80] George Morton, brother-in-law of Blake sat in the Admiralty Court, while George Logan, Lewis Pasquereau and James Stanyan, a planter, were the official appraisers.[81] The following will serve as an example. The "cole and Bean" galley cost £1200 sterling, in London, including the cost of fitting her out. Her cargo cost £2700 sterling. She was seized in Charles Town and appraised at £755 Carolina money, by George Logan, one of Blake's Dissenter co-workers and the vessel bought by him for Blake at the appraised value.[82] The cargo was appraised at £1740-19-3½, Carolina money. Blake sent her to the Bay of Campechy to load logwood with the intention of selling her and her cargo at Curacao. In this particular case Governor Blake, according to Trott's letter, allowed Judge Morton £136-15-6 as his share of the plunder.[83]

Trott, the Attorney General and Naval Officer, alleges that while this case was being tried[84] he made remonstrances, seeing that Morton was bound to condemn the ship, but that he could get no hearing and was even denied an appeal to England. Blake died before the matter was finally settled by the proprietors.[85]

The Dissenters brought their contest to a debatable public issue by the proposed act of May 6, 1704, entitled:[86] *An Act for the more Effectual Preservation of the Govern-*

[79] The English law in the colonial period allowed one-third to the King, one-third to the Governor of the province, and one-third to the informer. (6 Geo. II. c 31.) See also Gray vs. Paxton, in Quincy's Reports, I. 541 and MS Col. Doc. S. C., III. 169 and IV. 59.
[80] MS Col. Doc. S. C., IV. 166.
[81] *Ibid.*
[82] *Ibid.*
[83] Letter, Trott to Proprietors, Apr. 7, 1702, MS Col. Doc. S. C., V. 49.
[84] Trott was suspended from both offices for insulting Blake in a committee meeting and not on account of partiality as a naval officer, as is often supposed; see Rivers, *Sketch,* 192 and McCrady, I. 372.
[85] Rivers, *Sketch,* 192.
[86] Cooper, *Statutes,* II. 232.

ment, etc. It was launched by the special May Assembly of 1704, which the Colleton County Dissenters claimed was "irregularly and scandalously" elected by "Jews, strangers, sailors, servants, negroes and almost every Frenchman in Berkeley and Craven Counties,[87] coming down to vote," of which Job Howes[88] was Speaker. This was at a time when there was but one Anglican Church in the province of about 6,000 white inhabitants and when the Dissenters had four[89] churches in Charles Town alone and at least three organized congregations in the country.[90] This bill, though nullified, by opposition in England and Carolina alike, in which the Society for the Propagation of the Gospel took active part, was a forerunner for the Church Act of 1706,[91] which made the Church of England the Established Church of the province.

The anti-Dissenters had carefully prepared their plans. Nathaniel Johnson, a member of the anti-Dissenter party, was Governor and in open assembly had pledged himself to support the repeal of the Act of 1704[92] as soon as the assembly would pass an act securing the Church of England in the province.[93] He took sides with the assembly, which made his continuance in office so essential to the continuance of the Established Church that they made a most extraordinary provision against his removal by death or otherwise; viz., the Act of March 23, 1705-6.[94] This provided that the present assembly should not determine to be, and could not be, dissolved by any person or power at any time within two years, nor in the case of a change in the government necessitated by the death of the present governor or the accession

[87] Carroll, *Collec.,* II. 429.
[88] McCrady, I. 406.
[89] Crisp Map, Library of Congress.
[90] *C. T. Yr. Bk.,* 1898, 328. The country churches were French. The word Dissenter is used here not in the sense of the exclusive or partisan content given it in England, but rather to designate the class in South Carolina that dissented from the forms of the Anglican Church.
[91] Cooper, *Statutes,* II. 282.
[92] Hewat (chapter 4) is clearly wrong in stating that the appointment of Johnson was adverse to Huguenot interest.
[93] Rivers, *Sketch,* 229.
[94] Cooper, *Statutes,* II. 266.

of another, until eighteen months from date, thus guaranteeing the prevailing order of administration. This bill having passed both houses, its logical successor, the Church Act of 1706, was introduced and passed.[95]

It was to a large extent the opposition of the Dissenter party against the Huguenots of Carolina that brought about the passage of the Church Act of 1706. Thus the Church of England was established by law through the bitter struggle of the proprietors and their followers, aided by the French vote, against a stronger, non-aristocratic Dissenter group in spite of the fact that a majority of the white inhabitants were in religious conviction dissenters.[96] The Huguenots thus directly or indirectly accomplished the passage of the Church Act of 1706. Henry Le Noble gave it his support in the Council,[97] not as an enemy of the French colonists, but as a pro-Huguenot advocate. The act was not anti-Huguenot, but pro-Huguenot. In support of this contention let it be observed that everything points to the fact that the Dissenters made the Huguenots the objects of attack after 1692 and perhaps before. The French therefore at least had the sympathy of the anti-Dissenter party, and after their decision to unite with that party they had the support of the adherents of the Church of England. Such facts necessitated their favoring the Act. Moreover, we find nowhere a recorded complaint registered by the Huguenots as a class against the Act. By this time the French were there in sufficient numbers to make a decided showing in a protest. They had done so when the legality of their land claims and the legitimacy of their children were challenged and also when they were denied the ballot. If they were seriously opposed to the Act, why did they not at least complain to the proprietors? Besides, the presence of four representative Huguenot leaders: Henry Le Noble, John Abraham Motte, René Ravenel, and Philip Gendron,[98] on the board of Commissioners

[95] *Ibid.*, II. 282.
[96] Rivers, *Sketch*, 217.
[97] Cooper, *Statutes*, II. 282 and 294.
[98] *Ibid.*, II. 288.

for the enforcement of the Act, as well as the appointment of James le Serrurier (Smith) a Commissioner of the Church Act of 1704,[99] its forerunner, argues in the same direction. So far as we know the Huguenots did not even make an objection to the Act of 1698, which settled £150 annually on the Rector of St. Philip's Church. Yet for the French to remain isolated meant that they must help support the Established Church by continuous taxation and at the same time maintain the churches of their own polity by subscription. Their indigent circumstances before 1707 made this impossible. Another thing that must not be overlooked is the fact that eight months before the passage of the Church Act of 1706, the French settlers of the Santee section petitioned the Assembly[100] to make Craven County a parish, and to give the French minister the same allowance received by the clergy of other parishes. In other words, they requested the establishment of the Church of England in the most thickly populated territory outside of Charles Town. Thereupon Ralph Izard and Lewis Pasquereau, the latter a Huguenot, were commissioned to draw up a bill to that end.[101] This bill became a law April 9, 1706, seven months before the Church Act of 1706 became a law. Thereby Craven County, the stronghold of French Protestantism in Carolina, became an Anglican parish.[102] The Act provided that all ecclesiastical rites and services could be conducted in the French language, provided the John Durrel translation of the Book of Common Prayer be used.[103] The Santee settlers did not seek "erection into a parish" in order to have the county represented in the Assembly. That they already had. It was a purely ecclesiastical measure.

In line with the movement of the Santee settlers, the French Protestants of Orange Quarter, the second largest

[99] *Ibid.*, II. 241; Nairn, 45.
[100] MS Assembly Jrnl., 1702-6, 496.
[101] *Ibid.*, 524.
[102] Cooper, *Statutes*, II. 268-9.
[103] *Ibid.*

Huguenot settlement outside of Charles Town, settled almost exclusively by French,[104] a settlement which by 1730 had not come in contact with the English[105] enough to learn the language, were at their own request "erected into a parish" and conformed to the Established Church.[106] They likewise were given the privilege of holding services in the French language.

It was therefore not the Church of England that was persecuting the Huguenots as is often supposed.[107] It was the very group one would expect to sympathize with them on religious grounds, that broke away on almost purely political grounds. On the contrary, the Established Church was catering to the French Protestants in every reasonable way and was seeking to win their support and allegiance to accomplish this by distributing public offices to the French. Can these reasons not be registered as important elements to show why the Huguenots, Calvinistic and Presbyterian in polity and doctrine, later turned directly against the Presbyterian Church in Carolina and became adherents of the Church of England? This becomes still more emphatic when it is remembered that the large colony of French Protestants who settled in Hillsboro Township, in 1764, untrammeled by political, social or ecclesiastical domination, at once organized a French Church, with Calvinistic doctrine and polity. They saw what the Dissenter party did not seem to see, viz., that the continuous immigration from France was almost sure to give support to the party that won the allegiance of the French then in the province. In this way they were working in harmony with the pleasure of the proprietors, who throughout the proprietary period were friendly toward the French.[108] This explains too, how Henry Le Noble could

[104] The largest number of Huguenots in one place was Charles Town, where in 1699 the Huguenot Church had a membership of 195. These resided in town and in the immediate vicinity.

[105] Humphreys, *S. P. G.*, 84.

[106] Cooper, *Statutes*, II. 288; *C. T. Yr. Bk.*, 1895, 352.

[107] See Howe, *Hist. Presbyt. Ch. S. C.*, I. 154. Howe classes the Huguenots with the Dissenters.

[108] MS Assembly Jrnl., 1693, 31; MS Sec'y. Rcds., 1685-1712, 97; MS Col. Doc. S. C., III. 195-6; IV. 59, and 100; Commission, MS Sec'y.

secure a place on the Council,[109] as a representative of Proprietor Lord Ashley as early as 1697-8 and could remain there through the hottest of the Dissenter fight and immediately thereafter and during the intervals before hold his seat in the Assembly, until his death about 1712. Naturalized in England, June 27, 1695, he went to Carolina vested with all the rights of an English subject and must have been a man of more than ordinary political ability. Political preferment, through wealth, cannot be used as an argument in his favor. There is no evidence that he had wealth when he arrived. He came as did many of his class and received a grant of land, 350 acres, for "bringing himself", his wife Catherine, and five negroes.[110] The presence of other Huguenots on the Governor's Council in the Assembly and in other prominent places of trust is equally significant. Witness, for example, Alexander Thesèe Chastaigner, John Boyd, Paul Bruneau, René Ravenel, John Gendron, James Le Bas, Lewis Pasquereau, Lewis de St. Julien (De Malacar), and James le Serrurier, in the Assembly; George Muschamp, First Collector of Customs; Henry Auguste Chastaigner, High Sheriff; and Peter Jacob Guerrard, Register of the Province, etc.

The results of the Dissenter fight and the Act of 1706 are important: (1) To a large extent the Church Act subdued, if it did not pacify the hostile, anti-Huguenot factions, for no marked outbreak is known against the French for more than a decade. (2) It gave them the desired hold on

Rcds., 1685-1712, 143, 196; MS Assembly Jrnl., 1692-1701, 397-8; 1702-6, 202.

[109] Commission, MS Sec'y. Rcds., 1685-1712, 143 and 196; MS Assembly Jrnl., 1692-1701, 397-8; 1702-6, 202; MS Col. Doc. S. C., V. 61, 70. See also Cooper, *Statutes*, subscription to the several acts of the period. The author has found no evidence to show that Henry Le Noble died in 1712, yet there is little or no evidence to indicate that he was in South Carolina after that. His wife, Katherine, remained in St. John's district a number of years later. Her will is dated Jan. 25, 1725-6; see MS *Pr. Ct.* Rcd., 1671-1727, 243; MS Assembly Jrnl., 1707-12, 1, 84, 220, 298, 325; 1712-16, 360; Pro. Hug. Soc., London, XVIII, 172.

[110] MS Land War., 1692-1711, 88; MS Council Jrnl., 1671-1727, 88; MS Assembly Jrnl., 1702-6, 247, 440-1; 1706 f., 183; 1692-1711, 1; 1693, 1; MS *Col. Doc. S. C.*, II. 194; Carroll, *Collec.*, II. 342; MS Assembly Jrnl., 1692, 1.

political positions, for there is not a year from 1706 to the American Revolution, when they were not conspicuous in the governmental bodies, on committees and other public activities as represented in important commissions. (3) To an extent at least, though exact computation is impossible, by their added influence thus acquired, the Huguenots helped dilute the high-church polity and kept the Established Church in South Carolina low-church until the Revolution. It has been low-church ever since. (4) It guaranteed, from the political standpoint, the absorption of the French into the Established Church, though from the standpoint of language and church polity it was not completed for more than two decades.

CHAPTER VI

POLITICAL AND RELIGIOUS RIVALRIES AFTER 1706

The Church of England was now established by law. The minority Church of England party, with the support of the French Protestants, had taken the laurels. The church acts passed since 1697 had been repealed and the new Church Act launched on its uncertain course. It remained in force as long as the province was dependent on Great Britain. Intolerance toward other churches subsided to some extent, except the opposition to Roman Catholics. The animosity against them was constant during the entire colonial period.[1] But the victory of the Establishment gained under such strained conditions left hard feelings among covertly and openly hostile groups, who were inclined to grasp every opportunity to make inroads into the "canons and rubrick" to which Anglican clergy held with such unswerving loyalty. These disquieted minorities found many opportunities to use luke-warm French Protestant clergymen in Anglican orders to advance their interests.

Though the Act of 1706 pleased the proprietors, the Dissenters were so disturbed by it that numbers of them moved to Pennsylvania, "in order to sit down under Penn's free and indulgent government". Many of those who remained in Carolina were content to acquiesce in the mandates of the Establishment, but others, insurgents of a more insistent type championed by Joseph Boone, renewed the struggle for control. They succeeded in temporarily gaining the ascendency in the Assembly, no doubt aided by the fact that Charles Craven, who sided with the Dissenters, was governor from 1712 to 1716.[2] Before 1706 the geographic divisions were designated by counties. The Act of 1706 created

[1] Cooper, *Statutes,* II. 281 f.; Rivers, *Sketch,* 230; MS Col. Doc. S. C., XXVII 57 f., 126 f.; MS St. Stephen's Vestry Rcd., 1756; MS St. Philips Vestry Book, 1756-76, 1756 f.; *Coll. S. C. Hist. Soc.*, I. 199.

[2] Hewat, I. 166; McCrady, *Hist. S. C.,* I. 453; Howe, *Hist. Presbyt. Ch. S. C.,* I. 161 f.

parishes, but only roughly defined their limits. In each of these parishes Huguenot families are found, at least through the period covered by extant parish records, public documents and newspapers. The Church Act of 1706 secured with such arduous effort was destined to test the strength of the ablest leaders of the Established Church and to try the patience of the most valiant supporters of her doctrines and polity. It is not to be assumed that the new law at once quieted in the Huguenots of the Province all opposition to Anglican Church forms. The very opposite is true of some parts of Carolina. They had hardly recovered from the conflict of feelings occasioned by the encroachment of Anglicanism into their ranks and their surrender to its demands, which culminated in the Act of 1706, when they were forced into another decade or two of strife over the demands of the Anglican leaders that the French-Anglican ministers, serving French congregations, must conform strictly to the *forms* of the Establishment in every detail. Commissary Johnston, obeying instructions from London, held unrelentingly to the letter of the law and forced even a more rigorous observance than was required in England, where Huguenot clergymen who served French-Anglican churches were permitted considerable latitude in the administration of the sacraments.[3] The French of Orange Quarter and the adjoining St. John's district were the least willing to relinquish their cherished practices for the sake of which they had fled from France that they might have more favorable environment in which to nurture their faith. The hundreds of letters, found in London archives, written by Commissary Johnston, his wife, Paul L'Escot, John La Pierre, Francis Le Jau and others are the principal sources for our information on this phase of the subject.[4] They show that as long as the Orange Quarter was able, even beyond 1730, they kept the issues active. It should be noted, however, that the quarrel after 1706 was not one to force loyalty to the Anglican

[3] MS Rawlinson, C. 943, Bodleian, Oxford.

[4] MS Rawlinson, C. 943, Bodleian, Oxford; MS S. P. G. Transcripts, Library of Congress; S. C. Letters, Fulham Palace.

doctrines—therein the French had acquiesced—but rather to enforce conformity to the Anglican *polity* and a strict adherence to prescribed forms. Some of the anglicized French Protestant ministers claimed the right to administer the sacraments in the form in which they desired. Nor were they the only ones who sinned in this regard. Mr. Thomas, an Anglican clergyman and an Englishman, had begun the practice. So some of the French-Anglican clergymen, particularly Gignilliat, La Pierre and De Richebourg, unwilling after 1706 to accommodate themselves to the Anglican forms, continued to baptize without the sign of the cross and without godfathers or godmothers, and administered the communion kneeling, sitting or standing, as the people might desire.[5] Thomas had done these things in an attempt to ingratiate himself with the lukewarm churchmen and the half-hostile Dissenters. Gignilliat, La Pierre and Richebourg did them to win favor with the newly acquired French Protestant constituency and at the same time to lure back to the Established Church the large number of scattered Dissenters who had forsaken it.[6]

In 1712 Philip Richebourg moved part of a French colony from Mannikintown, Virginia, to St. James Santee, in Carolina and became minister of the French at Santee. Being a Frenchman by birth and an Anglican by adoption, with the bitter memories of the Mannikintown experiences fresh in his mind, he continued in Carolina to take liberties with the "canons and rubrick" of the Establishment.[7] Whether to win favor in St. John's, in the hope of recruiting the scattered Huguenots, or merely to please the ardent French petitioners of that parish is not known now, but he consented to visit St. John's and administer the sacrament, using the French language.[8] As we have seen, Mr. Trouillard, the French minister of St. John's, died in March or April, 1712. On his death the Huguenots of his congregation decided to

[5] MS Rawlinson, C. 943, Bodleian, Oxford.
[6] *Ibid.*
[7] *Ibid.*
[8] *Ibid.*

unite as a body with the English-speaking Anglican Church of that parish, of which Mr. Maule was rector. It was Mr. Richebourg's interference at this point that incensed the Anglicans and renewed the already old quarrel between the French and Anglican factions. Mr. Richebourg visited St. John's and though an Anglican clergyman, administered the sacrament in the form of the French Protestant polity, broke his promises to Mr. Maule to observe the rites of the Established Church and so completely turned the heads of the Huguenots of the community that for the time being they abandoned their plans to unite as a body with the English-speaking Anglican Church of the vicinity.[9] Severely taken to task by the Anglican clergy, Mr. Richebourg confessed his error and promised never to commit it again. But later accusations from the pen of Commissary Johnston, asking for the cancellation of his license and his removal from the province, indicate that he continued his practices. Nor did the bitterness in the conflict abate until in the heat of their passions, as a climax of their divisions and quarrels, swords were drawn at the church door in defense of their claims. The patient and kindly Francis Le Jau, rector at Goose Creek, tried to pacify the parties. The Bishop of London was appealed to, but died before a settlement was made. Commissary Johnston threatened that he would deprive Richebourg of his cure and his salary and remove him from the province unless he desisted. Humiliated and conquered, he at length temporarily submitted.[10]

Mr. John La Pierre, rector in Orange Quarter (St. Denis), then the most thoroughly French section in Carolina, though in Anglican orders, insisted on administering the sacraments according to Calvinistic usage, citing English practice as the foundation for his claim. His church in St. Denis, in asking Sir Nathaniel Johnson to write to the Bishop of London for a clergyman, insisted that they must be permitted to receive the communion in the Calvinistic

[9] *Ibid.*
[10] *Ibid.*, MS S. C. Letters, Fulham.

form and unless this would be granted them no minister need be sent. Whether or not Governor Johnson made the promise to grant the request is an unsettled matter, but the French of that region understood that in view of the fact that a clergyman had been sent them, he came with that stipulation. John La Pierre was the incumbent and found it very hard to satisfy both a clamouring Calvinistic French population—members of the Anglican Church with whose forms and practices they were not satisfied—on the one hand, and the strict demands of Commissary Johnston on the other. Several times La Pierre was reprimanded and threatened with expulsion from his curé. Apparently he had never been completely won over to the Anglican side, but like others of his nativity had been coerced into a half-hearted allegiance to the Establishment in order to secure the support needed for a living.[11] No wonder then that Commissary Johnston wrote in 1713, addressing the Bishop of London: "Tis possible the French Clergy of our Church are not so much in love with our Constitution, as not to have a much greater fondness for their own old way; And perhaps an affected Moderation, & the desire of consolidation & uniting those of their nation among us in matters of religion might tempt them to take liberties, which was never given them."[12] Imprecations were hurled against La Pierre. He was admonished by the Bishop of London from time to time and finally in 1728 moved to Cape Fear.[13]

But his Orange Quarter parishioners, unable to move the British authorities to consent to their wishes, had in 1713 appealed to Paul L'Escot, pastor of the Huguenot Church of Charles Town, to be admitted to the communion in his church. His balance of mind and judgment are evidenced in his reply that "his Conscience being better inform'd than theirs did not permit him to admit to the Sacrament Persons out of Charity, as they are, not only with their Minister but

[11] *Ibid.* Before his Anglican ordination in 1707 he had served French Churches.

[12] MS Rawlinson C. 943, Bodleian, Oxford.

[13] Dalcho errs (p. 289) in stating that La Pierre died in 1728.

even with their Church, nor to separate any lawful Assembly of Christians, particularly of a Church which tolerates him (L'Escot) & his flock with so much Charity." His remonstrances and entreaties to them to return in peaceable demeanor to their church indicate that he was not a party to their actions. The French Protestant Church in Charles Town, being now the only Huguenot Church in the province and composed mainly of the few loyal Calvinists of French extraction who were unwilling to relinquish their faith in the Genevan religion, was forced into a delicate and most uncomfortable position by the struggles that followed the Act of 1706. Paul L'Escot had been its minister in the six years' stress period prior to the passage of the Church Act and was to remain in that capacity for twelve years to come. It was not so much his wise guidance and piety as it was the staunch loyalty of his congregation to Huguenot principles that saved this congregation from the dissolution to which every other French church of the community had been forced to yield and bore it safely across one of the most difficult periods of its history. Its position as we have seen was made more difficult because a number of French clergymen, ordained in the Anglican Church, were his associates in Charles Town churches and the country parishes. So strong was the Anglican feeling in the community that at times it seemed as though even Paul L'Escot would turn Anglican. Commissary Johnston, ever proud of his ability to proselyte, wrote home to the Bishop of London in 1713 that L'Escot had stated repeatedly in his presence that he would not be content to "live a day without Episcopal Ordination, could he bring his People to it, & heartyly wish'd that all his countrymen were so wise, as to lay aside their groundless prejudices, & once forever to join in full & perfect communion with the Church of England".[14] In the quarrels of the Anglican clergy with the dissenters over church forms L'Escot played continually into the hands of the Anglican party, at times even openly opposing the uncanonical actions

[14] MS Rawlinson C. 943, Bodleian, Oxford.

of his own countrymen who had been ordained to the Anglican priesthood. During the troublesome times over La Pierre's infidelity to the forms of the Church of England L'Escot and his congregation addressed several letters to him, denouncing his conduct and suggesting that he depart from the province. His attitude toward Richebourg was the same. His motive for this policy is hinted at in a letter of Mrs. Johnston to her husband, the Commissary, during his visit to England in 1712 as being that of gratitude to the church that tolerated him and his flock with so much charity.[15] L'Escot was broad enough in his sympathies to realize the necessity of every church organization clinging to its own prescribed forms. At least he was not willing to take sides against the Establishment, but used his influence to heal the dissensions and restore peace and order. He was one of the most respected clergymen in the province, loved by members of the Anglican and the French Protestant churches alike. The Commissary's letters as well as those of his wife are full of praises for his conduct, spirit and ability.[16]

The dissenter fight and the triumph of the English-Church Party did not entirely cast aside the odium attached to those of French descent, for we find hints of it after 1706.

But the period after 1706, fraught as it was with serious religious problems, was not exclusively ecclesiastical in its interests nor were the French Protestants in this period found to be active only in matters of religion. They engaged freely in the public political debates and as we shall see gave hearty support to a number of the most important political campaigns of the period. Their strength of leadership in several very important matters is revealing.

The too widely prevalent notion that the Huguenot settlers of South Carolina were during the first half-century of their residence in America an uninfluential folk is clearly refuted in the public records. There were of course many reasons why they might be expected to remain unobserved

[15] *Ibid.*
[16] *Ibid.*, MS S. C. Letters, Fulham Palace.

publicly. They were foreigners of a race other than that of the most numerous class in the community and spoke a language not only very different than that in general use in the province, but also held in contempt outside of English court circles. They came in want from a country that for centuries had been the political enemy of Great Britain. They were religious refugees and ardent advocates of a faith dissimilar to Anglicanism. Yet despite these facts some of their number entered public life almost as soon as they reached Carolina. Nor did the Huguenots as a class modestly decline public office. They were like other men of their time. Some of them clamoured for public distinction as did Gabriel Manigault.[17] Others refused to serve for various reasons. Instances of imposed fines for refusing to serve are not rare.[18]

It must again be borne in mind at this juncture that as the years move on toward 1750, the Huguenots were gradually and in some parts of the province rapidly losing class distinction and taking rank with the Established Church constituency.[19] This was especially true in Charles Town. In Orange Quarter it was not true, but the Frenchmen of Orange Quarter did not figure to any great extent in the provincial politics nor in public life. That is to say, as the middle of the eighteenth century is approached, both the interest in and the antipathy towards the Huguenots as a class diminishes. It was becoming apparent that if a person was pushed into the lime-light of public approval by election to an important position, or if he was relegated to the rear, it was because of personal qualities, party affiliation or other considerations and not because he was of French decent.

[17] *S. C. Gaz.*, March 17, 1732-3: "To the several Worthy Electors of Members of Assembly, for the Parish of St. Philips, Charles Town, Gentlemen, Your votes and Interest are humbly desire for Gab. Manigault, of Charles Town, Merchant to be your Representative in Assembly in the room of Robert Hume Esq; who has gone off the province. Gabriel Manigault.
N. B. The Poll will be opened and begun to be taken on Tuesday the 20th Inst at 10 o'clock in the Forenoon, at the Parish Church."

[18] *S. C. Gaz.*, Oct. 16, 1740.

[19] See above, Chapter V.

While before 1706 in Carolina public issues were fought out principally along the line of English political and ecclesiastical conviction, after 1719 crucial campaigns were waged along other lines. The Revolution of 1719 had swept away the authority of the proprietors by the establishment of the Royal government, but that fact did not forbid a departure from former lines. For example, the contentions over the passage of new money bills in 1722-24 marshalled the Charles Town merchants against the country planters. Apparently old party lines and religious factions were almost completely ignored by both sides. Within the scope of this chapter it will be impossible to make a complete survey of the field. All we can hope to do is to indicate a few examples of the part the French Protestants played.

If the anti-Huguenot agitators assumed that the Church Act of 1706 would push aside the French Protestant element, they were greatly mistaken. While there was a partial relapse in the years immediately following 1706, a number of French names are conspicuous soon after. Then they appear regularly in practically all public offices and official positions except that of Governor.[20]

There were two warm contests in 1722-3 on the issue of paper money, in which the Huguenots and Anglicans of Charles Town and vicinity were matched against the Dissenters and others of the country. They, however, are strictly economic contests and fail entirely to challenge the religious convictions of the opponents. The public faith in the sincerity of the mother country and in the trustworthiness of the officers of the province had been shaken.[21] Money appropriated for the expedition against St. Augustine and for the North Carolina expedition had been used for other purposes and to make matters take a still more serious turn, in blunt opposition to the local laws, paper money was poured on the public in such quantities as to cause its marked depreciation. The printing of paper money (bills of credit)

[20] See above, Chapter V.
[21] MS Col. Doc. S. C., IX. 179.

was thought to be the easiest way out of financial troubles, so the Assembly founded a provincial bank and forthwith issued £48,000 in bills, called bank bills. This money was to be loaned at 12% interest, on proper security and the debt was to be liquidated at the rate of about £4,000 a year. It brought the two leading classes of the community, the planters and the merchants, to their feet at once, to express their opposite views on the proposition. As a rule a planter either borrowed from the merchant if he had to borrow money or else he ran an account.[22] The proposed bill was a good thing for the debtor, but hard on the creditor. Fully one-half of the value of the current debts was thereby lost, because by the act of February 13, 1719-20, debtors were allowed to pay obligations in rice, at 40 shillings per cwt. and in pitch at 40 shillings per barrel.[23] This was over two times their market value in the case of rice and five times the value of pitch. That the French Protestants were inveterate moneylenders,[24] will be shown later. It is not surprising, therefore, that in this case again they made a dash for their financial safety. In fact they became the aggressors in a protest against the proposed changes. By the regulations enumerated above, money had depreciated to a ratio of 6 to 1, by 1722.[25] Besides, by this time as a rule it was easy for the near-by country constituency to outvote the city population, for the former represented easily the majority of the inhabitants of the province, in 1720. To force the issue, the party in power had passed two more acts, one for the issuance of £15,000 and the other for £19,000, a total of £34,000 in paper money.[26] These were called rice bills and were to be paid and cancelled in rice at the rate of 30 shillings per cwt. A more unjust law could hardly be imagined. The money being local, its inflation naturally drained off the gold and silver and left an almost worthless paper currency

[22] Carroll, *Collec.*, I. 180-1.
[23] MS Col. Doc. S. C., IX. 179, 182.
[24] See below, pp. 188 f.
[25] MS Col. Doc. S. C., IX. 179 f.
[26] *Ibid.*

behind. In proportion as it decreased in value it raised the price of local commodities. And though it depreciated 50% in a year and was a good thing for the debtor, the inevitable effect was that soon even the debtor would be forced to accept the same depreciated currency for the commodities he would sell. Another feature of injustice lay in the fact that with the rate of interest on the bills fixed at 12%, many persons not foreseeing the possibility of their depreciation, eagerly bought them in the hope of reaping a rich harvest. But in a few years the Assembly passed a law to the effect that the bills should be redeemed at face value. The absurdity of trying to legislate against an economic law is apparent.[27] In order to protest against these issues and to rebuke the leaders who had introduced a measure asking for another issue of £120,000, a petition was sent to the British government, contending that since the annual produce did not amount to more than £300,000, that £86,000 was sufficient currency to meet the needs of the province. The petition protested against the inflation of the currency and its attendant evils. Then as if to make certain of winning the ear of the English government, it clinched its appeal by the statement that the results of the inflation would be disastrous to England as well as to Carolina, for it would deter English merchants from trading with them for fear of the passage of other laws in favor of the debtor and the possible ruin of the creditor. The first six signers of this petition were French Protestants: Isaac Mazÿck, James St. Julien, James Dupois Dor (Dupois d'or), Paul Douxsaint, Elias Foissin, and Henry Peronneau.[28] They were evidently the leaders and called to their assistance four more of their nativity, namely Benjamin Godin, Isaac Mazÿck, Jr., John La Roche,

[27] The South Carolina currency usually ranged between one and seven, computed in sterling exchange. In 1706, £1,500 currency was worth £1,000 sterling. In 1721-2, it required £6 currency to equal £1 sterling. After 1730 for over 30 years as a rule £1 sterling was equal to £7 currency. See Anderson, *Commerce,* III. 227; MS Col. Doc. S. C., XXIII. 66; *S. C. Gaz.*, Aug. 13, 1744; *Letter from South Carolina,* written by "A Swiss Gentleman", published in 1732.

[28] MS Col. Doc. S. C., IX. 185-90; MS Assembly Jrnl., 1722-24, 118.

and Francis Le Brasseure. These ten Frenchmen and eighteen others, merchants and traders in and about Charleston, are represented then in the signature attached to the petition. To these were added the support of the English Lords, Westmorland, Dominique, Bladen, and Plumer, in a letter sent by them to the Lords Justices in Council, on July 24, 1723.[29] But the October grand jury of 1724, made up principally of country gentlemen and planters, having a French Protestant foreman and eighteen other members, of whom four were French,[30] after an investigation, published these findings: that the paper money issued from time to time has been the result of necessity; that it in no wise was the cause of the rise in the cost of produce as was the case in 1717, when rice advanced to £4 per cwt. and pitch to £4 per barrel, because the large amount of money was withdrawn. Two months later the Wando grand jurors, also a country body, sent a letter to Governor Francis Nicholson saying that the petition of the Charles Town merchants should be regarded as worthless, because it was based on imagination rather than truth. This letter was signed by seventeen men of whom six were French. It was clearly a case of the country pitted against the city. That there were others of the French Protestants who favored the opposition is shown in the letter of Governor Nicholson to the Board of Trade,[31] in which he mentions Jacob Satur, a Charles Town merchant, and Benjamin Conseillere, a London Merchant, vigorous opponents to the new money measures then before the Legislature. A letter from London and American merchants, dated October 16, 1724, in protest against the same measures, contains the names Stephen Godin, Jacob Satur, David Godin and Isaac Prior, all of them French.[32]

[29] MS Col. Doc. S. C., X. 125.

[30] Daniel Huger, foreman, Noah Serre, Elisha Prioleau, Peter Villepontoux, Anthony Bonneau (*ibid.*, XI. 221), Anthony Bonneau, Lawrence Coulliette, Clerk of County.

[31] *Ibid.*, XI. 371 f., Nov. 12, 1723. Lewis Dutart, James Levons, Isaac Lassene, James Sauineau, Jacque Boisseau.

[32] MS Col. Doc. S. C., XI. 235.

In South Carolina, the petition sent by the Charles Town merchants raised a storm of indignation. The Assembly insisted that it had been insulted by the petition and demanded and accomplished the arrest of the memorialists.[33] This may have been a shrewd manoeuvre on the part of the opposition to prevent the lobbying privileges of the opponents of the money bills, for, languishing in prison, they sent a letter to the Governor, stating that they were in confinement and were prevented from being heard. They requested that they at least be given the privilege of presenting their side of the case in the memorial. This letter is signed by all of the petitioners.[34] Its date is December 12, 1722. Thereupon it was ordered by the Governor and Council that these men be allowed to present their side on the following day.[35] When the instructions were not observed because the Assembly ordered that the petitioners must remain in the custody of the Messenger of the House, the memorialists demanded release. For two days, the 13th and 14th of December, they continued to petition without avail. Reply was made by the Assembly that the release could be secured only after the payment of 20 shillings for commitment and discharge fees and £1 for clerk and messenger fees, by each prisoner. Benjamin Godin was the first to pay this amount, and was released.[36] Francis le Brasseur paid his fees and was released. The others stubbornly held out against the payment. To force matters, the Assembly on the 14th of December ordered that the amount be raised to 40 shillings for commitment and discharge and that the messenger fees be raised to £4, for each person. Whether or not the persons secured their release by paying the sums demanded, does not appear in the records, but they did succeed in repealing the bills by continued attacks on the clause providing for the sinking of the paper currency debt.[37] This much is certain

[33] MS Col. Doc. S. C., IX. 192 f.; MS Assembly Jrnl., 1722-4, 277 f.
[34] *Ibid.*, 193.
[35] *Ibid.*, 196.
[36] *Ibid.*, 203; MS Assembly Jrnl., 1722-24, 285.
[37] MS Col. Doc. S. C., XI. 19 f. and 190.

then: the French merchants of Charles Town and vicinity were powerful enough to ally with themselves enough Englishmen to accomplish the repeal of two of the most important acts presented to the law-making bodies in that decade,[38] for the opposition, unwilling to be outdone,[39] had appealed to the Privy Council who, on August 27, 1723, disallowed the Act passed February 23, 1722, providing for an issue of £40,000 in bills of credit.[40]

The controversy opened an old sore, long ago supposed to have been healed. It raised the question again as to which of the French Protestants could vote. The question was referred to the British authorities, who on the basis of the settlement of the question as far back as 1706, made reply in May, 1723 that only such French Protestants as were not naturalized or who always had been excluded from "acting in the magistracy" in any capacity "as well in Great Britain as elsewhere" could be denied the ballot.[41] It is probable that the serious Indian troubles, which for a number of months after May 1723, were uppermost in the public mind were the most important factor in preventing at this stage a repetition of the heated controversy of the earlier years regarding the ability of the French in South Carolina to vote and hold office.[42] By November these matters had been disposed of and the way was clear again for taking up the former grievances. Governor Francis Nicholson cast his lot against the Charles Town merchants and stubbornly resisted their efforts to thwart the success of the bill. His reason for doing it could not have been a purely anti-Huguenot policy, for he had a larger number of country Frenchmen to support his position than are found in the list of the Charles Town opponents to the bill. He was the avowed enemy of the French Protestants, however, as we shall see.

[38] *Ibid.*, X. 221.
[39] *Ibid.*, X. 206.
[40] Trott, *Laws of S. C.*, p. 405 and no. 499.
[41] MS Col. Doc. S. C., X. 106.
[42] MS Col. Doc. S. C., X. 180.

Benjamin Godin, a merchant, and Benjamin Conseillere, a member of the Council, under the firm name of Godin & Conseillere were wholesale and retail merchants in Charles Town. They were staunch opponents of the new rice bills. They owned the frigate *Carolina* and carried on trade with northern American ports, the West Indies, Great Britain and some of the French possessions.[43] It was on account of their trade relations with the French possessions that the advocates of the money bills secured the opportunity to seek revenge.[44] Godin & Conseillere were American correspondents for several English firms. Among them was Stephen Godin, a brother of Benjamin Godin, the Charles Town merchant, and Jacob Satur, a broker. Satur, denizened in London[45] in 1685, was one of the Huguenots who went to Carolina after 1685 a very poor man. By 1722 he was reputed to be wealthy.[46] He and Godin had associated themselves with Samuel Buck, an Englishman, in London.[47] Both Godin and Satur had business offices in London and Charles Town.[48] Francis Nicholson now set into motion the machinery necessary to put them out of business. They were importing from New England iron and manufactured goods and returning lumber for them.[49] With an exchange of molasses from the West Indies and the manufacture of rum out of it and the importation of quantities of liquor from Surinam, the French Islands and Cape François, they must have carried on quite an extensive commerce.[50] At Cape François, a Frenchman whose name was Detchegoyen was their representative. Detchegoyen made frequent trips to Charles Town, where he was regarded as a solicitor and a spy[51] and while

[43] *Ibid.*, XI. 66 f.
[44] *Ibid.*
[45] Pub. *H. S. London*, XVIII. 180.
[46] MS Col. Doc. S. C., X. 195 f. Letter, Fr. Nicholson to Lords [of Trade], Nov. 12, 1723.
[47] MS Col. Doc. S. C., XI. 66 and 75.
[48] *Ibid.*, XI. 66 f.
[49] MS Col. Doc. S. C., XI. 75.
[50] *Ibid.*, XI. 67.
[51] *Ibid.*

there lodged with Mr. Lamand at Peter Manigault's.[52] What the ultimate outcome of Governor Nicholson's initiatory act in prosecuting these Frenchmen for their violation of English precedent may have been cannot be learned from extant material. The prosecution was based on the proposed English law of 1719, forbidding the manufacture in the American colonies of any "iron goods of whatever kind". Under its provisions no smith would have been able to make so much as a bolt or nail. No forge could be erected.[53] So great was the opposition to this bill that it was disallowed, but duties were imposed on all American iron imported into England. The charges against Benjamin Conseillere were apparently not sustained or else not prosecuted, for he remained on the Council until 1732. After that he was on the Commission of the Peace until 1737, when he was made Judge of the Court of Common Pleas.[54] Stephen Godin kept his name free from public stigma too, for in 1729 he was appointed the London Agent for the Province of South Carolina.[55]

It was but the beginning of a darkening storm that before long was again to threaten the security of the provincial government and throw the inhabitants into a political ferment, in which seduction, persuasion and bribery were freely employed in removing French Protestants from their political positions. As the dark of the storm was approaching, strategem and high-handed bribery were employed to remove Lawrence Couiliette, since 1724 Clerk of the Crown, Clerk of the Peace, and Clerk of the Supreme and General Pleas Courts of Charles Town.[56] Kilpatrick, an Englishman, had been notified that Couiliette's office would be disposed of and that if Kilpatrick could offer £300 he would

[52] *Ibid.*, XI. 72.
[53] McPherson, *Commerce,* III. 72.
[54] MS Col. Doc. S. C., XV. 227; *S. C. Gaz.*, Apr. 2, 1737; MS Commis. Inst. 1732-42, 236.
[55] MS Col. Doc. S. C., XIII. 238 f.
[56] MS Col. Doc. S. C., XII. 12; MS Commission, in MS Pr. Ct. Rcd., 1722-28, 116.

be "preferred".[57] But when Kilpatrick said that he did not have that much money, another trick was employed to keep the value of the office up. Captain Childermas Croft was directed to procure a complaint against Couiliette from the Judge of the Court and then petition him for the office. This Croft did, but either as the mere tool of wary politicians he was not properly coached in the matter, or else misunderstood the whole scheme, for in making his application for the office he did not accompany it with any cash. Kilpatrick (hearing of Croft's attempt and finding beside him another applicant for the position, a Mr. Pickering, who in the absence of ready cash offered a bond in purchase of the office) brought £200, which he had secured in ready cash, and thus obtained the office.[58]

Not quite so much ceremony was employed in the removal of the vendue master, a nominee of the Governor and the appointee of the Crown.[59] Croft, unable to secure the clerkship, was regarded as a more deserving incumbent for the office of vendue master, because he was able to hand over £100 in cash.[60] At the same time the office of provost marshall was offered at £400.[61] Couiliette, in his appeal to the Assembly, made vigorous but futile protest against the treatment he had received, stamping it as a "heinous offense" in the light of both common and statute law. He demanded that in justice the malefactors should be rendered incapable of holding office and be otherwise severely punished. He cited as authority the case of Peers of Great Britain vs. Lord Macclesfield, High Chancellor of England, the latter of whom was fined £30,000 sterling and committed to the Tower until it was paid.[62]

We have observed that though the Dissenter fight modified and to some extent mollified the hostile anti-Huguenot factions, it did not completely pacify them. Subdued by the

[57] MS Col. Doc. S. C., XII. 2.
[58] *Ibid.*
[59] Cooper, *Statutes,* II. 348; MS Col. Doc. S. C., XXIII. 178.
[60] MS Col. Doc. S. C., XII. 3.
[61] *Ibid.*
[62] *Ibid.*, XII. 12-13.

signal triumph of their political enemies, they did not come forward again in a strictly anti-Huguenot fight until 1723. The contention over the money bills had renewed an old question as to whether the French Protestants were eligible to the franchise. While the fight over the money bills was provincial, i.e., it claimed the interest and attention of the entire settled area of South Carolina, the contention we are now to discuss was confined to Charles Town. It was municipal and involved primarily only the questions concerning the government of Charles Town. The enemies of the French, by secret manoeuvres and by disguising their intentions under the title: *An Act for the Better Government of Charles Town,* sought to eliminate the Huguenots by law from local affairs.[63] The bill provided for a life-term for the mayor, aldermen, and common council, and made these officers a "closed corporation" for filling vacancies. If successful, the bill would preclude the possibility of the French Protestants of Charles Town ever exercising the functions of freemen, though at this time they constituted one-fifth of the Charles Town population and paid proportionately of the taxes of the community.[64] A heated protest was made against it by one hundred and eleven signers of a petition, twenty-seven of whom were Huguenots. In this case as in the cases of the money bills Francis Nicholson took sides against the Charles Town merchants.[65] Again, as was the case in the Dissenter fight of 1706, Indian wars, foreign trade, political astuteness, and the removal of Governor Nicholson, all helped to postpone the prosecution of these serious grievances.

So black did the situation become that Governor Nicholson, with ill health as an excuse, sailed for England.[66]

[63] MS Col. Doc. S. C., X. 82 f.

[64] *Ibid.*

[65] MS Col. Doc. S. C., X. 219, letter, Francis Nicholson to Chas. de la Faye, Dec. 4, 1723, "What you were pleased to write concerning the Merchants is very surprising to most People here that they should have the Impudence to say such things to their Excellencys the Lords Justices. I find they will lye most notoriously when they think anything will make for their Interest."

[66] *Ibid.*, XII. 70 f.

Though the chain of evidence for this conclusion is not complete in the documents that have been preserved, the disconnected links that are found indicate that the sentiment was abroad and was even expressed, that if Nicholson returned to South Carolina, the Swiss French who were already making arrangements to go to South Carolina would be prevented from going, because Nicholson was the avowed enemy of the French Protestants,[67] and that the French Protestants then in the province would be forced to go to other parts of America. Peter Purry at this time was working in France and Switzerland, promoting the interests of the colony of South Carolina and rallying the scattered forces of French refugees for emigration to what he was pleased to call the garden spot of the world.[68] In fact this very year he had led several hundred to the Atlantic shores in Europe and because the British authorities failed to carry out their side of the contract the colonists were compelled to go back.[69] There is no evidence so far as we know to warrant any conclusion, but it may well be asked here whether it is not probable that Nicholson on his return to England took steps to frustrate the plans of the Swiss French Protestants to go to South Carolina. When one remembers how anxious the British authorities were to send desirable gardeners to South Carolina it is hardly conceivable that anything except a drastic interference on the part of some powerful person could have prevented them from keeping their agreements. In South Carolina Benjamin Whitaker and Captain Henry Nichols had introduced a bill June 11, 1724, which, if passed would have enabled Protestant Dissenters to qualify for office according to the form of their own religious profession.[70] This would have thrown the gates open to Quakers, Presbyterians, Huguenots and all, without requiring subscription to the Established Church and its form of sacrament. Under the English law all persons

[67] *Ibid.*
[68] MS Col. Doc. S. C., XI. 132-3, XIX. 45.
[69] *Ibid.*
[70] MS Col. Doc. S. C., X. 45-8.

taking the oath of office had to express belief in the Established Church doctrines, "that there is not any transubstantiation in the Supper".[71] Governor Nicholson had vetoed the bill; endorsing on it the following comment:[72]

"June 14, 1724: The Commons desired the Governor's leave and has had the presumption to send it before they obtained it, which is taken to be very arbitrary.

Fr. Nicholson."

The political aspects regarding these matters here enumerated were so grievous that if a letter sent from Charles Town to London in 1727 can be credited with truth the people were taking steps to organize associations, the purpose of which was to inaugurate a movement to induce objectors to refuse to pay taxes.[73] The next step would be the refusal to pay debts. Mob riot reigned again. This "considerable merchant," apparently aroused to the pitch of hopelessness, wrote in his letter that for his part, he intended to pack up books, bonds, papers, etc., and send them on board the man-of-war. The conditions that he foresaw came to pass, for the courts of justice were closed four years, between 1727 and 1731, and during the same period no taxes were collected.[74] Trade was seriously affected by the feuds and dissensions.[75]

In 1733, again to make matters worse for the French Protestants, the now old question of qualifications for the franchise was revived. Huguenots had learned the grievous lesson years before, so now only a few were caught in the dragnet set for unqualified voters. It is perfectly evident however that the inquisition against illegal voting in 1733 was not directed merely against the French Protestants on account of local animosities, but was an attempt to eradicate

[71] *Ibid.*
[72] MS Council Jrnl., 1722-24, 276.
[73] MS Col. Doc. S. C., XII. 201. "Letter from a considerable merchant in Charles Town to a considerable merchant in London", April 25, 1727.
[74] MS Col. Doc. S. C., XV. 52.
[75] Address, Francis Yonge to Council, *S. C. Gaz.*, Apr. 21, 1733.

illegal voting of all kinds. This seems to be true of the entire period hereafter to the Revolution, for as late as 1773, Isaac Huger, of Charles Town, and Tacitus Gaillard, both of French lineage, were rival candidates for office in the parish of St. Matthews. Apparently fraud, superinduced by the indignation of an overzealous Huguenot, crept into the election, for in his complaint to the South Carolina Assembly Mr. Huger alleged that public notice of the election according to law was not given; that at two P. M. when the box containing the ballots was produced, two of the seals were torn off; that unwarranted methods were used by the friends of Mr. Gaillard to secure his election; that several persons whose votes were refused when they expressed on the first day of the election their favor for Mr. Huger were admitted to the ballot on the second day when they offered their votes to Mr. Gaillard; and that persons under age, and without property, and even several mulattoes were given the franchise.[76]

In 1733, out of a list of fifteen challenged votes only four were from French Protestants, Isaac Porcher, Peter Porcher, Francis Cordes and Peter Coutrier.[77] On a reconsideration, after a hearing of the accused persons, the number was reduced to two out of fourteen, Francis Cordes and Paul Marion,[78] both of whom were Frenchmen. It was claimed and proof was submitted that François Cordes had voted in St. James Goose Creek before voting in St. John's.[79]

The outcome of these struggles was not uncertain. The power was wrested from the hands of the overzealous ruling upper class, for the didactic Governor Glen, who was able to bombard the British Secretaries of State with Latin quotations and long legal opinions, declared that "little by little the people have got the whole administration in their hands . . . almost all of the places of profit or trust are disposed by the assembly. The Treasurer the person that receives and pays away all the public moneys is named by them and can-

[76] MS Assembly Jrnl., 1772-5, 16 f.
[77] *Ibid.*, 1733-8, 34; MS Col. Doc. S. C.
[78] *Ibid.*, 35.
[79] *Ibid.*

not be displaced but by them". The Assembly controlled all of the "livings" and the Governor found himself, as Egerton says, in the predicament of not being prayed for in church, while the Assembly was.[80]

[80] MS Col. Doc. S. C., XXI. 405; Rawlinson MSS., Library of Congress; Egerton's *Brit. Col. Policy,* 159.

CHAPTER VII

THE FRENCH PROTESTANTS AND CULTURE

For information concerning Huguenot influence on education and culture in South Carolina we are again forced to rely upon the scattered evidence left in newspaper advertisements, wills, mortgages, letters, inventories of property, etc. The Huguenots and their French Protestant descendants, so far as is known, created no distinct educational movement in Carolina. In fact, a distinct educational movement among them is hardly to be expected. They became a part of the English constituency so early that their educational efforts were naturally united with theirs and in only a few particular instances are they found among the leaders in intellectual uplift and educational enterprises. If culture is to be measured only in academic degrees, probably comparatively few of the early Huguenots aside from the clergy were highly educated. In 1712 there were twelve Anglican ministers in Carolina and seven serving other churches. Of this total of nineteen, five were French. Two of the five had academic degrees, Francis Le Jau, D.D., and John La Pierre, A.M.[1] But all of them took genuine interest in the mental improvement, of not only those of their own nationality, but of the negroes and Indians as well. According to the Crown instructions no one was permitted to teach without a license issued by either the Bishop of London or the governor of the province.[2] This restriction tended to keep educational leadership in Carolina in the hands of those who advocated the principles and practices of the Established Church. Natu-

[1] MS Rawlinson C. 943, Bodleian, Oxford; MS British Transcripts, S. P. G. Series A. Vol. III. no. 152, Chief Justice Nicholas Trott to Secretary of the S. P. G., Sept. 13, 1707.

Concerning Mr. Guerrard, Nicholas Trott says: "He is a very good Linguist being not only very well skilled in the Greek and Latin as a Scholar but having spent a great part of his life in Travelling he is a perfect Master of the Italian and Spanish and very well Skilled in the French and so much knowledge in the Dutch as to read and Translate from it".

[2] MS Col. Doc. S. C., VIII. p. 132 and no. 79.

rally the French ministers took a lively interest in intellectual pursuits. The faithful Francis Le Jau was a recognized leader in the education of negroes and Indians.[3] From 1710 to 1712 he was a commissioner of the free schools at Goose Creek. In 1733 Anthony Bonneau, Thomas Cordes, and others are found in similar positions. In 1734 Rev. Francis Varnod was made commissioner for Dorchester.[4]

With these facts before us it is perhaps not necessary to remind the reader that the French Protestants of Carolina, though they went to a wilderness in which the native Indian was still uncivilized, came from the heart of European civilization and culture. They were there educated to the extent to which the middle class of France, who had been the hope of the French nation in wealth and culture, was educated. Their problem then in South Carolina was the application of a European civilization to an American environment, or more particularly, a French civilization to a Carolinian environment. They were a people thoroughly imbued with French manners and traditions and with Protestant sentiments, though most of them had had opportunity to absorb the refinements of English life before embarking for South Carolina. The Huguenots of early Carolina history were therefore not grossly ignorant people. Some of them had been reared in plenty in France and had had educational advantages. Though religious zeal may have cooled the ardour of their intellectual pursuits they seem to have carried to the American shores at least some of the refinements of their earlier and better days. And in spite of the fact that most of their time at first was consumed in making a living, the mention of libraries in wills of the later period and lists of books in the inventories of property bears witness to their culture. Few of the wills of the early period have been preserved, so there is not much evidence of private libraries during this time, but after 1730 a number of in-

[3] MS Rawlinson, C. 943, Bodleian, Oxford; Le Jau letters to Bishop of London, S. C. Letters, Fulham; Carroll, *Coll.* II. 540; *S. P. G. Abs.,* 1701-10 to 1710-11, 39; Cooper, *Statutes*, II. 390.

[4] Cooper, *Statutes*, II. 342 and 390; *T. H. S. S. C.*, IV. 35.

stances of good private libraries are found. For example, take the case of James le Chantre, who died in August, 1732.[5] Among his books were two large French Bibles, ten volumes of Saurin's sermons, ten volumes of Seyserville's sermons, seven psalm books of the new version, and two volumes of Lamott's and Basson's sermons. The inventory of the property of René Ravenel includes a library of books valued at £32.[6] James Bonhoste's library consisted of two commentaries on the Bible, and other books.[7] Mme. D'Harriette's books, valued at £87, were found in various parts of her residence, indicating a home of culture and refinement.[8] The appraiser's second-hand valuation of Ann le Brasseurs' library was £30.[9] John Peter Purry left a "large French bible & other Pious books".[10] The only books Peter Benoist possessed were a "very good folio bible", bound in silver mountings, valued at £40, together with the works of John Bunyan and Erskine's sermons.[11] Many other examples might be cited to bear witness that the homes of many of the French Protestants, and their descendants who have left records, contained some books. On the other hand no doubt there were others who had none at all.

The foregoing examples are found among the laity. We may of course suppose that as a rule the clergy had larger libraries. The inventory of Rev. James Tissot's property is preserved. It contains books of various kinds valued at £200, one of the assets of his earlier years.[12] At the time of his death he was a planter. Francis Le Jau owned books valued

[5] MS Pr. Ct. Rcd., 1732-6, 82. Mme. Jean duPre's inventory contains the following books: Burnett's *Explanation*, one large folio Bible, one *Duty of Man*, three prayer books, a number of theological works, and a number of French psalm books. See MS Pr. Ct. Rcd., 1748-51, 230. Anthony Bonneau's inventory shows the following: three Bibles, Rapin's *History of England*, *Whole Duty of Man*, and four law books. See MS Pr. Ct. Rcd., 1739-43, 395.

[6] MS Pr. Ct. Rcd., 1763-67, 210.

[7] *Ibid.*, 1739-43, 243.

[8] *Ibid.*, 1758-61, 314.

[9] *Ibid.*, 1741-43, 169.

[10] *Ibid.*, 1736-9, 65.

[11] *Ibid.*, 1758-61, 225.

[12] *Ibid.*, 1761-3, 521 f.

at £100.[13] In 1750 the Rev. Samuel Quincy, Rector of St. Philip's Church, Charles Town, published a volume of twenty sermons. The publication was sold by subscription and contained the list of subscribers. In the Charles Town list are twelve French names.[14]

Though the emigrant Huguenots were naturally educated to the extent that the middle class of France were educated, their children in Carolina were as a rule not so fortunate. Being required upon their arrival immediately to clear the soil and make a living, the emigrants were unable to make provision for the education of their children. Tangible evidence of this is found in subscription crosses and other marks in substitution for signatures in various legal documents.[15] While this may not be conclusive evidence in every case it is at least indicative of a general condition. The second generation of children fared better. By that time much of the soil was under cultivation, many of the parents had become well-to-do and could hire private tutors and send their children to private schools, or to Europe, for their education.

As early as 1706-7 we find private tutors and boarding-school teachers appearing in the province. The first boarding-school among the French as far as is known was conducted by the Rev. Francis Le Jau, D.D. He and his wife were the teachers.[16] Unable to subsist on the meagre income from his ministry they opened a school of French and music. The school did not succeed, however, because the amount charged for instruction and board was not sufficient to defray expenses. Though direct evidence is wanting, it seems reasonable to suppose that a number of these schools existed prior to 1730, for as soon as the *South Carolina Gazette*

[13] *Ibid.*, 1758-61, 132.

[14] Anthony Bonneau, Wm. Baudoin, Jas. Boutineau, merchant; Rev. Levi Durand; John Dutarque; Rev. Levi Guichard, minister of the French Church; John Guerard, merchant; Gabriel Manigault; Jacob Motte; Mrs. Jane Mellichamp; John Neufville; Chas. Purry, merchant; Paul Simons.

[15] MS Pr. Ct. Rcd., 1694-1704, 53 f.

[16] MS Rawlinson C. 943, Bodleian, Oxford.

appears it contains advertisements of a number of French teachers opening schools.

In conducting private schools in Carolina the French Protestants were easily among the leaders. For some reason there seems to have been considerable demand for instruction in French as a cultural branch. The middle of the eighteenth century marks a revival in the interest in the French language, for the text books of the French scholar, John Palairet, teacher in English court circles, were used in Charles Town by French teachers.[17] The stigma that in the early years attached to the French Protestant was being removed because he was becoming wealthy and naturally some of the French inhabitants and others who were arriving from France from time to time, still clung to the French language.

Peter Précour, A.M., was one of the first to advertise his art.[18] His specialties were French and Latin, while his wife painted and mounted fans and taught drawing. They lived on the Green, in Dock Street. The year following advertisements appear regarding Adam Battin, in Church Street, who had taught English, French, Latin, "vulgar and decimal Arithmetic" and writing.[19] Mme. Delamère, who lived on Broad Street, conducted a school in which all of the mathematical and engineering subjects were taught. Her assistant was John Miller.[20] A private "Art School" was conducted by Mme. Varnod, widow of the Rev. Varnod.[21] This school was opened as early as 1734 in the home of Mme. Douxsaint, on Church Street, near the French Church. She called it a "French School for Young Ladies". All kinds of needle work were taught. These were the pioneers.

With the plantations far apart and many of the country places difficult of access, a public school system on the New

[17] *S. C. Gaz.*, Sept. 22, 27, 1746.

[18] *S. C. Gaz.*, Mch. 7, 1732-3: "Peter Precour, Master of Arts, is arrived in the Province but a Small Time and willing to acquaint the Publick that he will teach the French Latin Tongues; and his Spouse Mounts and paints Fans and will learn to Draw; they living on the Green at the house of Mr. Thomas Farless in Dock Street."

[19] *S. C. Gaz.*, July 14, 1733.

[20] *Ibid.*, May 19, 1733.

[21] *Ibid.*, May 18, 1734.

England plan was out of the question. But from all appearances private teachers fared well. In 1736 David de L'Escure advertised his ability to teach French and English.[22] His charges were £3 per quarter and he gave instruction either in his home on King Street or at the home of his patrons. He was at the same time reader in the French Church of Charles Town.[23] A combination day and evening school was operated by John Fouquet, teacher of French, English, arithmetic, and writing. His charges were 40 shillings a month.[24] Mark Anthony Besseleu, an enterprising merchant of Charles Town conducted a French school in addition to his store. He kept a stock of general merchandise at his house on Broad Street and in the same building maintained a school in which both he and his wife were teachers.[25] Evening school was reserved for instruction in French, while the day-school branches were those ordinarily taught. The hours were as follows: 9 to 11 a. m., 1:30 to 4 and 6 to 8 p. m. Martha Besseleu taught sewing, spinning and housekeeping.[26] She also took orders for all kinds of needlework and spinning. So successful was this institution in Charles Town that during the summer of 1754 it opened a branch school on James Island.[27] The branch, however, did not prove sufficiently remunerative to warrant its continuance. As did his predecessor, David de L'Escure, so did Francis Varambant combine the office of reader in the French Church of Charles Town with that of private French teacher.[28] The leading competitor of these men was Charles Walker Fortesque, who taught both in Charles Town and in the country. His wide range of subjects—Latin, Greek, rhetoric, logic, natural philosophy, geometry, trigonometry, chronology, astronomy, surveying, and mensuration—made his school a valuable addition to Charles Town educational

[22] *Ibid.*, July 3, 1735-6.
[23] *Ibid.*, Jan. 17, 1735-6.
[24] *Ibid.*, Nov. 5, 1744.
[25] *Ibid.*, July 20, 1747.
[26] *Ibid.*, Nov. 16, 1747; Feb. 6, 1755.
[27] *Ibid.*, Oct. 10, 1754.
[28] *Ibid.*, May 22, 1742.

MRS. SAMUEL PRIOLEAU
Née Catherine Cordes.
1745-1832

facilities. His wife, through the *Gazette,* solicited "business in mantua making", in which gentlemen were "served in the most elegant, new and modish manner".[29] This school no doubt enjoyed a splendid patronage, for two years later Fortesque advertised for a teacher of ability to take the elementary work so that he could devote all of his time to the advanced subjects.[30] Evidently Charles Faucheraud also conducted a combination industrial and educational institution, for in 1755 he advertised for a woman who could teach reading and all kinds of needle work, emphasizing that none under twenty nor anyone that "had passed her grand climacteric" need apply.[31] In the home of Peter Bouquet, on Broad Street, a French school was conducted by A. d'Ellient.[32]

A number of dancing schools were opened by French Protestants. One of the first was started by James Cliquet. He taught ladies and gentlemen at the home of Mary Roschelins, on the Bay.[33] The school was open three days each week for instruction in dancing and three other days were devoted to teaching gentlemen the "art of defence". On March 2, 1762, M. Valois, a dancing master, introduced himself to Charles Town by giving a ball at the home of Robert Dillon. This list of teachers is all that a careful perusal of the *South Carolina Gazettes* from 1731 to 1765 reveals. It is not a large one. The Huguenots as a class were not given over to educational activities. Their greater interest lay in industrial pursuits.

There are, as we have seen, many external evidences of the growing prosperity of the French of the tidewater areas. Among them is the tendency to send their sons abroad for their educational training. This was particularly true of those who were preparing for the legal profession. Though most of the direct evidences covering the earlier period are

[29] *Ibid.,* Nov. 30, 1747.
[30] *Ibid.,* Jan. 2, 1749.
[31] *Ibid.,* Sept. 11, 1755.
[32] *Ibid.,* May 7, 1763.
[33] *Ibid.,* Aug. 7, 1749.

lost, one occasionally comes upon hints pertaining to the later period. The Manigault collection of manuscript material contains a list of American students resident in London law schools, between 1759 and 1786, the quarter century before and during the American Revolution.[34] Out of a total of forty-eight from South Carolina twelve were of Huguenot descent. Forty-one per cent of the entire number were sent by South Carolina.

There is further evidence of the general fact in expressions and instructions in wills and other legal papers. For example, the will of Daniel Huger, drawn in 1754, provides that his sons should attend school until they were nineteen years of age and should be given as liberal an education as the province could furnish.[35] The will of Gabriel Manigault, while indicating an interest in education, provides against the needless squandering of money in securing it. He sets aside funds sufficient for a liberal education for each of his children, but designated that his sons be educated in America until eighteen and then sent to England for the completion of their training.[36] Gideon Couturier left money at interest for the education of his daughter Esther. Her education should continue until she was twenty-one, when the principal, it was stipulated, should go to her.[37] Among others who provided for the education of their children was Samuel Peronneau.[38]

In the person of Mme. Anthony Gabeau, who wrote a volume of interesting reminiscences for her grandchildren, we have an example of the special cultural interest some-

[34] The list of names is published in McCrady, *Hist. S. C.* II. 475, note. This list shows how fashionable it was in the American Colonies to send students to England. It shows:

77 at Middle Temple, of whom	39	were from South Carolina
24 at Inner Temple, of whom	2	were from South Carolina
15 at Lincoln's Inn, of whom	7	were from South Carolnia
116	48	

[35] MS Pr. Ct. Rcd., 1752-6, 282 f.

[36] *Ibid.*, 1774-8, 16 f.

[37] *Ibid.*, 1752-6, 528 f.

[38] *Ibid.*, 425 f.

ELIZABETH BACOT
Daughter of the emigrant Pierre Bacot.

times manifested among the French Protestants of South Carolina.[39]

In 1699 a public movement was started for the founding of a provincial library in Charles Town.[40] What part the Huguenots had in it is not known, but the books were purchased from Mr. Robert Clavill, a bookdealer in London.[41] On November 11, 1700, the bill that was introduced November 16, 1699, became a law establishing a public library in Charles Town.[42] Owing to the fact that most of the books that it contained were written by Anglican clergymen[43] and were naturally anti-Dissenter in spirit and furthermore because the library was in the custody of the rector of St. Philip's in Charles Town, its extensive influence in the community was impossible. Though its life was short this library was the forerunner of the Charles Town Library Society, founded in 1748, though there is, so far as is known, no organic connection between the two.[44] The list of members in 1750 totaled 125, of whom 10 were French.[45] The name Hon. Hector Bérénger de Beaufain heads the list, followed by those of Rev. Levi Durand, Paul Douxsaint, Elias Foissin, Henry Laurens, Gabriel Manigault, Jacob Motte, John Mayrant, David Montaigut, and John Neufville. Among its librarians was Philip Prioleau, 1787-1790. Gabriel Manigault was its president, 1753-56 and 1778-80. For twenty-one years he housed the library free of charge in one of his buildings, near Kinlock Court, and prepared the rooms at his own expense.[46] Henry Laurens was vice-president in 1768[47] and Gabriel Manigault from 1769 until 1771.[48]

[39] *T. H. S. S. C.*, XIII. 86.
[40] MS Sec'y. Rcds., 1685-1712, 176.
[41] MS Assembly Jrnl., 1692-1701, 265-6.
[42] *Ibid.*, 351.
[43] Hewat, in Carroll, *Coll.*, I. 132.
[44] The original list of members consisted of 19 men, two of whom, Paul Douxsaint and John Neufville, were French Protestants. See *Pub. C. T. Library Society*, series 5, volume V, p. 7: address by James Petigru, June 13, 1848.
[45] *S. C. Gaz.*, Apr. 23, 1750.
[46] Catalogue, C. T. Library Soc. 1876, preface, p. v.
[47] *S. C. Gaz.*, Jan. 25, 1768.
[48] *Ibid.*, Oct. 5, 1769; Jan. 11, 1770; June 10, 1771.

The original portraits of French Protestants done in oil and pastel as well as copies of the originals indicate that a number of the homes of Huguenots of Charles Town and vicinity were adorned with first-class pieces. These were the creation of artists in England and America. After the first years of hardship had passed, their patronage of the æsthetic arts offers repeated evidence of their finer tastes. There seems to have been a resident portrait painter in Charles Town early in the eighteenth century, for the portrait of Sir Nathaniel Johnson bears an inscription and the date 1705. But English artists figure more prominently in Carolina's early art than do resident painters. A miniature of Isaac Mazÿck was painted before 1700. The artist is unknown.[49] At Pinopolis, South Carolina, are preserved the original portraits in oil of Catherine Le Noble, wife of Henry Le Noble and the daughter of James and Elizabeth Le Serrurier, being one of the most perfectly preserved paintings in the state;[50] of Stephen Mazÿck, son of the emigrant and Susanne Mazÿck, daughter of René Louis Ravenel; and of Mme. René Louis Ravenel. These with several others of the later period in the possession of the Ravenels, Macbeths, Porchers, and Dwights, constitute the best collections of French Protestant portraits in South Carolina. Henrietta Johnson, who died in 1728-9, left a number of good pieces, notably those of Mademoiselle Cramahé, 1711, Mrs. Robert Taylor, née Catherine Le Noble, Mme. René Louis Ravenel, widow of Alexander Chastaigner, Mme. Daniel Ravenel, Elizabeth de St. Julien, Mme. Paul Mazÿck, Rev. Élias Prioleau, Mme. Élias Prioleau, née Jeanne Bouregeaud; all of them of Huguenot families.[51] The inventory of the estate of Catherine de St. Julien, widow of Paul de St. Julien, mentions eighteen paintings and six engravings of Don Quixote, framed.[52] The same

[49] The author is indebted for several of these facts to the article by Robt. Wilson, D.D., in the *Charleston Year Book,* 1899.

[50] In possession of Mrs. R. Y. Dwight.

[51] *C. T. Yr. Bk.,* 1899, 137 f.

[52] *Ibid., Ravenel Records,* 125. The will is dated 1742.

MARIE PERONNEAU
1700-1778
Wife of Pierre Bacot, 2nd.
(Original in possession of Mrs. Richard Caldwell, Mount Pleasant, S. C.)

articles appear in the inventory of James St. Julien in 1740.[53] Madam La Mere is said to have painted the portraits of Jacques Le Serrurier and Elizabeth his wife, the parents of Susanne Le Noble.[54] The hand of Jeremiah Theus executed a number of good pieces, notably those of Jacob Motte; Gabriel Manigault and his wife, Ann Ashby; Peter Porcher; Mrs. Thomas Cordes, née Ann Ravenel; and Mme. Samuel Prioleau, née Catherine Cordes.[55] The pastels of Rev. Élias Prioleau and his wife are probably copies of lost portraits, for both persons died before 1715.[56] These are examples enough to indicate at least the disposition of some of the richer French Protestants to secure the best portraits obtainable. In his will Peter Manigault bequeathed all his pictures, done in oil, to his son, Gabriel.[57] The portrait of Peter Manigault, Speaker of the Assembly, 1765 to 1773, is still in existence.[58] It was painted by Ramsay, Court Painter, London. The portrait of the Rev. Francis Le Jau, D.D., has been retained in the family of the Frosts. From the original, which was destroyed, was made a copy which is still in good condition.[59] The original portraits of James Le Serrurier, the emigrant, and that of his wife, Elizabeth Leger, are now in Charleston.[60] The portrait of Elizabeth Bacot, daughter of the emigrant, Pierre Bacot, and sister of Marie Peronneau, done in pastel by Flagg, who made a copy of the original, is also still preserved; while the portrait of Pierre Bacot, born in France in 1684, the son of the emigrant, Pierre Bacot, and the portrait of Marie Peronneau, his wife, born in 1700, are all still extant. The likeness of Marianna Le Serrurier Mazÿck, wife of the emigrant Isaac Mazÿck, Sr.,

[53] *C. T. Yr. Bk.,* 1899, 137 f.
[54] *Ibid.* In possession of Mrs. Maria R. Gaillard, Charleston, and Rowena D. Ravenel, Charleston.
[55] *Ibid.*
[56] *Ibid.*
[57] MS Pr. Ct. Rcd., 1774-8, 16.
[58] Jenkins home, Adams Run, S. C.
[59] In the possession of the Rev. Francis Le Jau Frost, of West New Brighton, N. J.
[60] In the possession of Mrs. Maria R. Gaillard and Miss Rowena D. Ravenel, Charleston.

is in Charleston, where that of her husband hangs beside it.[61] An original oil portrait of René Louis Ravenel (1694 f.) son of the emigrant, is owned by Mrs. René Ravenel, Charleston.[62]

The Huguenots in Carolina were not without refining influences. Without doubt some of them brought books from abroad. These scattered fragments were supplemented by the libraries sent over by the Society for the Propagation of the Gospel and the public library opened in 1700. They had British newspapers and London periodicals at intervals and a local press regularly after 1730. There was also a theatre in Charles Town. There were concerts, lectures on electricity and kindred topics, as well as other public uplifting influences.[63] Advertisements in the *Gazettes,* the diary of Mme. Manigault and other evidences show that the Huguenots and their descendants were active in all of these enterprises. Admissions to the theatre ranged in price from eighteen to fifty shillings.[64] The entertainments were usually held at six o'clock in the evening and a ball was often the closing feature.

The instances cited above do not represent the Huguenots as leaders in the several cultural activities. Before the Revolutionary war they were inclined to turn their attention more to the industrial than to the æsthetic, but this fact does not permit the conclusion that they totally neglected the cultural. As we have seen, many of their homes were adorned with the materials and equipment of refinement and culture.

[61] In the possession of Arthur Mazÿck, Esq., Charleston.

[62] The original portrait of Mrs. René Louis Ravenel, daughter of Henry and Catherine Le Noble is now in the possession of Stephen D. Ravenel, Esq., Cordele, Ga.

[63] *S. C. Gaz.,* Oct. 28, 1732; Sept. 30, 1732; Jan. 25, 1734-5; Dec. 11, 1736; Oct. 31, 1748; May 4, 1765; Mme. Manigault's diary.

[64] *S. C. Gaz.,* Oct. 21, 1732.

CHAPTER VIII

THE ECONOMIC SUCCESS OF THE HUGUENOTS IN SOUTH CAROLINA

Though the French Protestants went to Carolina at the request of the British government, with the intention of raising commodities that were staple in France and with which they were familiar, they soon learned the futility of such a plan. They learned that products easily gotten in England and France were unsuited to the soil and climate of their new home.

At first the proprietors had contemplated an experiment station in Carolina, with a probable extension as time passed.[1] They planned to put trained agents into the field. To this end they encouraged persons of skill in various pursuits to settle in the new province.[2] In conjunction with these facts they saw the necessity of a sufficient food supply for the inhabitants and had in mind the discovery of a staple easily salable in French markets, yet easily and cheaply producable in Carolina.[3] The proprietors hoped that after the first year the colonists would raise their own food supply, and thereafter by successful organization and effort produce a salable staple for England's profit.[4] The economic history as well as the material and industrial success of the Huguenots is very closely connected with England's economic policy.

In the first place England was making an economic ventrue in sending the French Protestants to Carolina. While, it is true that they were refugees from France for conscience' sake, there were other reasons for their emigration from England to America. Pouring their eager multitudes into

[1] Rivers, *Sketch*, Appendix; *Cal. St. Pa. (Col.)*, 1669-74, 86.
[2] MS Col. Doc. S. C., II. 284; IV. 117 and 189-90; VI. 172. *Cal. St. Pa (Am. & W. Ind.)*, 1669-74, 86.
[3] England's policy for centuries had been to favor certain "preferred products", as silk, olives, indigo, wine, and naval stores. See MS Col. Doc. S. C., I. 59; II. 43 f.; *Cal. St. Pa. (Col.)*, 1675-76, 240 f.
[4] *Ibid.*

England, the French Protestants were thereby at the same time both enriching and impoverishing their welcoming hostess; enriching her by their genius and skill, impoverishing her by displacing English labor, by sapping the poor-fund of its accumulations, by driving high the prices of the necessities of life because of the increased demand, and by reducing the prices of manufactured articles below the line of profit because of the increased production in the skilled trades. They had arrived in England in numbers too great to permit an equally ready absorption. The point of diminishing returns had been reached. Thus the eagerly sought and welcomed became before long a bane instead of a blessing.

The problem then of Great Britain was how to keep these efficient folk and at the same time rid herself of them. The answer was found in one word: colonization. Thereby they could at least produce the means of subsistence and perhaps more, while at the same time they would be kept dependent on Great Britain for all manufactured articles. Great Britain's motive in sending the Huguenots to South Carolina was a mixture of Christian benevolence and economic shrewdness. Apparently it was not so much the benevolent spirit of Charles II, as it was the economic policy of a great government that prompted him to charter vessels and transport these skilled Frenchmen to the shores of a British colony.[5]

Already it was dimly recognized that colonies are sometimes the foundations of great commonwealths. It had been estimated that by the lowest computation each laboring person sent to Carolina added annually an average of £5 sterling to the wealth of Great Britain.[6] She could, therefore, well afford by "Royal Bounty"[7] to pay the passage of

[5] *Coll. S. C. Hist. Soc.*, II. 90.

[6] Nairn, 59. Mr. Wood's letter, which was received in London, July 3, 1735, gives the impression that the alleged benevolence claimed for the British government was a "mere grimace". See MS Col. Doc. S. C., XVII. 388.

[7] The bounty was called "Royal" but the term is a misnomer. It was called "Royal" because the King's letter or brief was required in order

STEPHEN MAZŸCK
1718-1770
Son of the emigrant Isaac Mazÿck.
(From an oil painting in the possession of Thomas P. Ravenel,
Pinopolis, S. C.)

hundreds of Protestants, impoverished by persecution. In all the dealings of Great Britain with the Huguenots, during the colonial period, her policy is clearly marked and at times very prominent. The economic phase was constantly kept in the foreground. It was the keynote in petitions for permission to settle, for grants of land, for bounties of various sorts, for special privileges, and the enactment of laws. It was the argument repeatedly used in the appeals to the Lords of Trade, the Commissioners of Trade and Plantations and the King's cabinet. "The benefit Great Britain will derive therefrom" is a stereotyped phase in the English colonial records.[8] Contemporaries contend that it was a period of that mediocre spirit of commerce that wished to govern the colonies on maxims of the bargain counter. To this end the British government made every effort to keep manufactures out of the colony. Again and again inquiries were directed to the colonists regarding what was being manufactured, and each time the reassuring reply was returned that beyond a few articles of necessity nothing was being manufactured.[9] This is true until eventually silk factories were erected.[10] They were, however, for the purpose of spinning silk, not for weaving it. Thereby Great Britain stimulated her own foreign commerce without discouraging in the province the production of raw material in demand on foreign markets. These facts have not been sufficiently emphasized and appreciated in reference to the French. Skilled in nearly every industry to which France laid proud claim, they swarmed across Europe and the British Isles to make their deposit of economic and industrial skill wherever they went. Those going to Carolina included vinedressers, weavers, wheelwrights, saddlers, hatmakers, coopers, leatherdressers, joyn-

to sanction the appointment of a collector in the churches and the Lord Chancellor, as the keeper of the King's conscience, had to sign the brief. The funds came from the people. (See Agnew (2 ed.), I. 59.)

[8] MS Col. Doc. S. C., I. 65, 71, 73, 78-9, 95; Anderson, *Commerce,* III. 31. Preamble, 7 Anne c. 5.

[9] MS Col. Doc. S. C., VIII. 62-3.

[10] MS Assembly Jrnl., 1765-8, 146, 177, 180, 194, 195, 374, 659; 1769-71, 12.

ers, gunsmiths, sailmakers, braziers, gold and silversmiths, silk and cocoon specialists, planters, apothecaries, blacksmiths, etc.[11]

The Huguenots were Frenchmen of remarkable economic ability. By the uniform testimony of unprejudiced writers the Protestants of France were her strength in agriculture, manufacturing and commerce. No less can be said of the Huguenots of South Carolina. These strong, virile, industrious, sturdy and conscientious people left France under persecution. The exceptionally strong forsook the mother country. Persecution and close surveillance had developed their economic perception into one of peculiar quality. Does not persecution beget foresight? Its physical asset is endurance; its resultant economic return is prosperity. The proprietors endeavored to secure only the best quality of emigrants. They had been forced to acknowledge their miscalculation in regard to the possible numbers who could be induced to go. Therefore they urged their agents, that since more were willing to go than was expected, they "should encourage only the better sorte, substantial men and their families", who would stock the country with horses, cattle, negroes, etc., whereas the "poorer sorte" would have to rely on and be fed by the proprietors.[12] They proposed to search the world systematically for a suitable people, skilled in the production of English staples. In this way South Carolina was to be populated by scientific methods.[13] This sturdy Huguenot character, this virile life that successfully rode the tides of persecution, was the very element needed to colonize the new province. They became the gentle though profitable strangers who should introduce the culture of the vine and the olive tree.[14] Thus this numerous throng, entering Great Britain by every avenue of transit, could easily be utilized in realizing her plans beyond the sea. It is not surprising when these things are known that the Lords of Trade could

[11] Cooper, *Statutes*, II. 132.
[12] *Cal. St. Pa. (Col.)*, 1669-74, no. 694.
[13] *Ibid.*, p. 240.
[14] MS. Col. Doc. S. C., II. 284; IV. 117 and 190; VI. 172.

SUSANNE MAZŸCK

Wife of Stephen Mazÿck and daughter of René Louis Ravenel. (From original oil painting by Theus, in the possession of Thomas P. Ravenel, Pinopolis, S. C.)

write to the officials of Carolina: "By this [ship] comes Mr. Baille, a Frenchman skilled in all those things of Merchandise the Soyle of Carolina is proper for. Wherefore I desire you will give him all manner of Incouragement for he perfectly well understands Silke, wine and oyle."[15]

The colony needed such men. Sobriety coupled with earnest labor brought the destitute exiles competence and accumulated comforts.[16] Some of them had been in Holland, Germany, Switzerland, and the British Isles long enough to earn and save some money, and being frugal by nature were able to place it to good financial advantage.[17] Others succeeded in converting their French estates into money before leaving. But the great mass left their native shores without money and lived for months on the benevolence of the territories into which they emigrated. The fact that some of the Huguenots fleeing to Carolina were so poor that they were forced to receive material aid from the British government, is not to be denied. The Rawlinson Manuscripts[18] contain the lists of such persons and the amounts received by them. Still, some reached South Carolina with considerable money in addition to the stock they held in commercial enterprises. A number bought indented servants before leaving England, while others purchased land and negroes in Carolina upon their arrival. Those who were fortunate enough to bring property in the form of money or other valuables usually invested it in land and slaves. They were soon surrounded with plenty on their fertile plantations. Few failed to acquire independence. Many fortunes, large for those days, were made.[19]

[15] MS Col. Doc. S. C., I. 306, letter, dated June 28, 1684.

[16] Rivers, *Sketch*, 175.

[17] Owing to crowded conditions in Switzerland and the fact that little of the rural territory in France was unoccupied, and further because of the drain on the public purse, numbers of Huguenots emigrated to Ireland. See "Projets de Colonization en Irlande", par la Baronne Alexandre de Chambrier, in *Pr. H. Soc. London*, VI. 383-4 and 415.

[18] Rawlinson MSS A. Bodleian Library, Oxford, Transcripts, no. 271, folio 7, Library of Congress. Date probably about 1698.

[19] Dubose, *Reminiscences*, 6-7.

South Carolina profited materially by giving the thrifty French Protestants a home on her soil. Men, women and children labored almost unceasingly to build up their patrimony. Magnificent plantations were established along the banks of the principal streams. In 1685 the Huguenot as a rule owned a little hut, log-hewn, crude, and primitive. Its furnishings perhaps were cruder still. In 1735 his home was as a rule crowded with comforts; in addition there were frequently many luxuries.[20] Mahogany furniture, manufactured in Europe, was common,[21] solid silver services were found in many of the homes,[22] elaborate wardrobes, expensive coaches and ornamental jewelry were not the exception.[23] John Pettineau's will indicates how a man of the artisan class, a weaver, could by toil and thrift become the possessor of extensive fields and a large amount of personal property,[24] while the property inventory of Mrs. D'Harriette shows that she possessed one of the most elaborately furnished homes in the province.[25] The Huguenots materially increased the aggregate wealth of the province besides furnishing a constituency that was industrious, able, and more than ordinarily productive in material wealth.

The phrase "rich as a Huguenot" had European origin and was frequently applied there to the "landed" and industrially rich. It found root in Carolina nomenclature also and proved to be no misnomer. What was the basis of their economic success in this province? Numbers of them died in the possession of abundance, many were rich. Some had great wealth.

Aside from merchandise and trade the basis of their wealth lay in two things, land and negroes. Land naturally appreciated in value as the inhabited area was improved. Negroes, by their natural increase, aside from an increased

[20] MS Pr. Ct. Rcd., 1761-63, 50; 1758-61, 225; 1763-7, 221.
[21] *Ibid.*, 1758-61, 10; 1741-3, 169-76; 1758-61, 314.
[22] *Ibid.*, 1758-61, 314.
[23] *Ibid.*, 1741-3, 169 f.
[24] MS Pr. Ct. Rcd., Bundle C. C. no. 23, printed in *T. H. S. S. C.*, XIII. 20-1.
[25] MS Pr. Ct. Rcd., 1758-61, 314.

RENÉ LOUIS RAVENEL
1694-?
Son of the emigrant René Ravenel.
(Original portrait in possession of Mrs. René Ravenel,
Charleston, S. C.)

value, made many slave owners wealthy.[26] The rich soil of the tide-water was the basic element. Negroes imported by the thousand supplied the labor, supplemented by that of Indian slaves, white servants and other whites. These with their necessary complements, skillful economy and shrewd business management, produced wealth.

The Huguenots obtained land in three ways: (1) by gift outright from the authorities in England or their agents in Carolina, for contributing to the industrial welfare of the colony or its success in some special way, thus securing the favor of the proprietors; (2) by purchase;[27] and (3) by the head-right system, i.e., by meriting grants for bringing colonists, either slaves, white servants or free persons to settle on the land.[28]

In the first class a number of French Protestants are found. For example, on January 26, 1685-6 Arnold Bruneau,[29] "having merited well" received from the proprietors a grant of 3,000 acres for "contributing to the well settlement of Our Province".[30] With the grant went the privilege of having it created into a manor if he chose. This was a "free gift" and "without rent". M. Charasse, on October 23, 1684, "being a person well skilled in Drugs & divers other secrets of nature" deserving of the encouragement the proprietors were willing to give to a "man of his worth"

[26] See chapters 9, 10, 11.

[27] It is possible that some of the Carolina French Protestants recovered part or all of the property they forsook in France, though there is little evidence to lead to the conclusion that recoveries were numerous.

[28] The first settlers received land according to the provisions made Aug. 25, 1663, under the head-right system, each head receiving 100 acres. (Rivers, *Sketch*, 335.) In the first set of constitutions and agrarian laws provision was made for holding land at one penny per acre quit rent, "or the value thereof". This was made the principal inducement to many persons going to Carolina. In 1684 this was changed. Lands must be held by indenture only and the clause "or the value thereof" was stricken out. A reservation clause was added requiring re-entry on the failure to pay the quit rent. This operated against many who had settled there in the early period and who, on account of poverty and other reasons, had not secured an official conveyance of lands to which they were entitled. (Rivers, *Sketch*, 139 f.)

[29] This grant is mentioned in his will. MS Pr. Ct. Rcd., 1692-3, 172; 1671-1727, 275, reprint *T. H. S. S. C.*, X. 39.

[30] MS Col. Doc. S. C., II. 120. MS Sec'y. Rcds., 1685-1712, 13 and 66.

and ability to become an inhabitant of Carolina, received a gift of 3,000 acres, likewise "without rent". With it was given the option of having it converted into a manor. The holder also had the right to maintain courts thereon according to the provisions of the fundamental constitutions.[31] Mr. Francis Derowsery, "having with great Industry aplyed himself to ye propogation of Wine and other usefull things" in Carolina, received from the proprietors on March 29, 1683, 800 acres without being required to comply with the regulation of bringing servants or other persons for the same.[32] A warrant to "Jean Lewis de Genillat" is dated July 14, 1687, for 3,000 acres, is also a "free gift and without rent".[33] In July, 1685, Jean Francis Genillat, a Frenchman and doubtless one of the refugees to Switzerland, "being the First of his Nation that hath made knowne his designs of settling in Carolina And having showed Testimonyes of his Honourable Extraction", received 3,000 acres. James Boyd "having been very Instrumentall in ye Settlement of ye French Protestants in Carolina in endeavoring the establishment of a vintage and several considerable Productions" and having contributed in a considerable measure in other ways was given a manor of 4,000 acres.[34] Numerous other cases are on record.[35] Herein lay at least one factor in the economic success of the Huguenots of the succeeding generation. A rich soil given in generous and multiplied grants, well stocked with negroes, plus the willingness and ability to work it, created wealth and produced success.

While the bulk of the French Protestants who went to South Carolina were poor, many had the means for buying land, either in London from the proprietors directly, or from agents in Carolina. A few cases will suffice to illustrate. On

[31] MS Col. Doc. S. C., I. 312.
[32] *Ibid.*, I. 238.
[33] *Ibid.*, II. 209-10.
[34] *Ibid.*, II. 81. MS Sec'y. Rcds., 1685-1712, 66; MS Col. Doc. S. C., I. 96.
[35] MS Col. Doc. S. C. III. 150. René Petit and Jacob Guerard were each given a manor of 4,000 acres. See *Cal. St. Pa. (Am. & W. Ind.)*, 1677-80, no. 1233.

MRS. RENÉ LOUIS RAVENEL

Daughter of Henry and Catherine Le Noble.

(From the original portrait in pastel in possession of Mr. Stephen D Ravenel, Cordele, Ga.)

September 28, 1683, the Lords of Trade and Plantations wrote to Governor Joseph Moreton:[36] "Whereas We have sold unto Robert Stevens and Bartholomew le Roux 350 Akers of land for which wee have Reced ye sum of £17-10-0 you are to lay out the same" and they are sending in this ship five persons "by which 250 Akers more" are due them, for which they are to pay rent. "You are to lay out the whole 600 acres within the town precinct if they desire it." Arnaud Bruneau Chabociere, in 1688, bought 5,300 acres for cash.[37] Likewise on April 14, 1685, James Dugue bought 500 acres in London for £25.[38] A day later Isaac Lejay and Magdalen Fleury (alias Lejay) his wife, bought 500 acres, at the same price.[39] Charles Franchomine and Mary Baulier, his wife, on April 16, 1685, paid cash for 500 acres.[40] Some of the tracts thus purchased were sold on credit. For example, 3,000 acres were bought by James Le Bas on September 26, 1685, for £150. He paid £90 in cash and gave a mortgage for the unpaid £60.[41] There are records of the sale of no less than 33,000 acres of land to French Protestants in Carolina prior to the year 1698. Most of this was paid for in cash.[42] With few exceptions the rate at which it was purchased was £5 sterling per 100 acres. Even before the Revocation of the Edict of Nantes land was selling in Carolina at that price.

By far the largest number of Huguenots in South Carolina receiving land from the proprietors or the British government, secured it under the head-right system. It was in a sense the easiest way of securing land immediately, though it was not the cheapest way in the end, especially if the

[36] MS Col. Doc. S. C., I. 249.
[37] *Land War.* (Salley), 1680-92, 197.
[38] MS Col. Doc. S. C., II. 50.
[39] *Ibid.*, II. 55.
[40] *Ibid.*, II. 53.
[41] *Ibid.*, II. 6, 96.
[42] MS Register Rcd. Bk. D. 1696-1703, 199 and 200; Bk. 1675-96, 221-2 and 494; MS Sec'y. Rcds., 1685-1712, 68, 69; 100-1, 145; MS Col. Doc. S. C., II. 141-2, 165, 172, 174-5, 207, 216, 275, 277, 287, 222-7; XVI., 107; MS Land War., 1692-1711, 69, 75, 97, 219, 22-3, 26, 52; MS Grant Bk. no. 8, 1694-1739, 86, etc.

recipient paid the passage of the person upon whose arrival the grant was based. To persons who were willing to pay the regulation one-penny per acre rent annually and transport servants, slaves or other persons to the province the land was granted without purchase money. Hundreds of warrants and grants were issued to French Protestants on this basis. For example, Richard Deyos,[43] on December 7, 1672, secured 300 acres in consideration of the transportation of himself and one servant. Among the earliest grantees were Joan Bayly,[44] John Bullen (Bullein),[45] John Bazant and wife,[46] Lydia Barnott,[47] Peter Bodit,[48] Richard Gaillard,[49] and Thomas Fluelline.[50] With land as the basis of wealth, the Huguenots soon learned that the slave, negro or Indian, was his next best asset, though use was also made of the limited servant class. The French Protestants went to Carolina unfettered by prejudice against labor. In France the mass of them had been of the middle class, tillers of the soil, artisans, laborers, etc. A few were merchants. In Carolina it became necessary to reduce the forest and extensive swamp lands to cultivation, erect houses and build defences against the Indian enemy. With Charles Town during the early years as the only source of supplies, their hardships were not few. Judith (Manigault) Giton wrote that they encountered every affliction, disease, pestilence, poverty and hard labor and that in six months she had not tasted bread. Men and their wives worked together at the whip saw, in building houses, making fences and felling trees.[51] Thus they laid the foundation for their future fortunes.

The lands they received were worth little without applied labor. Indented servants were not numerous and were hard

[43] *Land War.*, (Salley), 1672-79, 55.
[44] *Ibid.*, 114.
[45] *Ibid.*, 153, 193, 139, March and August 1677 and Jan. 1678.
[46] *T. H. S. C. C.*, V. 9, Sept. 1678.
[47] *Land War.*, (Salley), 1672-9, 176, Sept. 1678.
[48] *Ibid.*, 167, July, 1678.
[49] *Ibid.*, 186, Nov. 1678.
[50] *Ibid.*, 134, 137, 46, 98, Apr. and June, 1677.
[51] Letter of Judith (Manigault) Giton to her brother, reprinted in Baird, *Huguenots in America*, II. Appendix.

PIERRE BACOT, 2ND
Son of the emigrant Pierre Bacot.

to secure. The Indian was shrewd, lazy, and deceptive, hence disqualified to be a desirable slave. This made the negro the superior in desirability. Moreover, the servitude of the white servant was temporary, that of the slave was permanent. Control over the servant was limited, over the slave it was practically absolute. In physical endurance the black slave was far superior to the white servant. Negro slaves were being brought into the harbor in large numbers, while Indians, though they proved to be poor slaves, could be bought in the markets or captured in the numerous Indian wars. The Huguenots owned both negro and Indian slaves;[52] some had brought negroes with them to Carolina,[53] others spent their ready cash in purchasing them, while still others used the ever ready credit system as a means of securing them. Had land yielded no profit at all most of the planters could have made fortunes by the natural increase of their slaves.[54] A number of Huguenots made traffic in them their principal occupation,[55] others made it a secondary line.[56] With the

[52] *Council Jrnl.* (Salley), 1692, 31; MS Pr. Ct. Rcd., 1671-1727, 167; 1722-26, 285. René Peyre owned an Indian wench 50 years old *(S. C. Gaz.,* Jan. 2, 1744). David Peyre owned one valued at £130 (MS *Pr. Ct. Rcd.,* 1732-6, 165). The inventory of the property of John Gendron shows that the law governing Indian slaves was not observed. In 1725 he owned four Indian slaves, of whom one was a shoemaker. In addition he owned eighty-three negro slaves, ranging in value from £30 to £800 each, of whom two were shoemakers and one a tanner (MS *Pr. Ct. Rcd.,* 1722-27, 285). Though Indian slaves were found among the families of French Protestants, the French were among the first to protest against their enslavement. In a letter, dated October 27, 1720, signed by sixteen prominent men of the community, of whom five were French Protestants (Stephen Godin, J. Godin, Jacob Guerrard, Allard Belin, and Paul Douxsaint) suggestions were made for strengthening the frontier, for increasing the number of inhabitants and for stimulating trade. It was advocated that the enslavement of Indians be prohibited. See MS Col. Doc. S. C., VIII. 226.

[53] Gabriel Manigault brought one, Henry Le Noble, five; see MS Land War., 1692-1711, 86, 88.

[54] Porcher, *Reminiscences,* 77; McCrady, *Royal Gov't.,* 403. In 1790 evidence was submitted to a committee of the House of Commons, in England, appointed for the purpose of investigating the treatment of slaves in British Colonies, to the effect that in thirty-eight years a part of the slaves of Gabriel Manigault, Jr., had increased in the South Carolina low country, from eighty-six to two hundred and seven without any aid from purchases other than the replacement of twelve or fourteen old slaves by a number of young ones.

[55] *S. C. Gaz.,* May 11, 1752; Dec. 16, 1732; Aug. 21, 1736.

[56] *Ibid.,* Nov. 4, 1732; July 15, 1732.

extension of the inhabited area into the back country new land in abundance was being opened. This necessitated a proportionate increase in labor. By 1735-1740 slaves were imported at the rate of 3,000 to 5,000 a year to supply the demand and were increasing in numbers much faster than was the white population. Negro importation became so excessive that public fear was expressed regarding its possible evil effects.[57] It was bound to increase the number of "bad paymasters" and to decrease the amount of money in the province.[58] Under the illusion of eighteen months credit a great many had been tempted to buy more than they could be expected to pay for in three years.[59] The duty on slaves imported between 1720 and 1735 was more than enough to sink the debt of the whole paper currency, or the whole provincial debt owing in 1723.

There can be no doubt that many of the French Protestants were drawn into the stream of slave-hungry purchasers. The wills and property inventories are full of indications as to the large number of slaves owned by these people.[60] In fact it is safe to say that more than one-half of the personal property owned by the Huguenots of the tidewater consisted of slaves. With some, slaves constituted nearly all of the personal property wealth.[61] So numerous had slaves become in Carolina by 1735 that planters in stocking new plantations were no longer forced to depend on slave brokers for a supply. They could be secured from the numerous auction sales and by private transfer.[62] The healthy normal slave was as good an asset as any other form of salable property. Continuous immigration resulting in the

[57] *Ibid.*, Apr. 2, 1737.
[58] *Ibid.*
[59] *Ibid.*, March 2, 1738.
[60] At the death of property holders, a committee was appointed to appraise all of the personal property owned by the deceased. The records of these inventories are preserved in the offices of the Probate Court in Charleston. Nearly every French Protestant whose inventory of property appears in the records owned slaves. They are often listed by name.
[61] Letter, Bull to Commissioners of Trade and Plantations, May 25, 1738. MS Col. Doc. S. C., XIX. 117.
[62] *S. C. Gaz.*, May 15, 1736; Apr. 12, 1736; July 2, 1753.

opening of large quantities of new land and the attendant demand for labor kept the price of slaves steadily on the increase.[63]

The appended table will indicate the interest of French Protestants in slave holdings:

Name	*Total personal property*	*Value of slaves*	*Number of slaves*
Ann LeGrand[64]	£ 3,403-10-3	£ 3,160-00-0	14
John Postell[65]	5,420-00-0	4,225-00-0	22
Ann le Brasseur[66]	2,566-16-4½	190-00-0	3
Peter Pury[67]	3,612-10-0	1,020-00-0	6
René Ravenel[68]	3,747-12-3	1,940-00-0	12
Martha d'Harriette[69]	29,450-00-0	1,602-00-0	10
Rose la Roche[70]	337-03-0	50-00-0	1
Peter de Plessis[71]	3,473-00-0	2,245-00-0	12
Peter de St. Julien[72]	11,893-10-0	10,440-00-0	67
Jonas Bonhoste[73]	*2,125-00-0	1,840-00-0	11
John Richebourg[74]	1,181-15-0	700-00-0	5
James Richebourg[75]	642-15-0	540-00-0	3
Caleb Avant[76]	3,837,00-0	3,030-00-0	19
Anthony Bonneau[77]	6,505-00-0	4,990-00-0	23
Benj. Bonneau[78]	12,094-00-0	9,605-00-0	35
Benj. Avant[79]	3,042-00-0	1,850-00-0	12
Peter Bacot[80]	3,762-05-0	2,800-00-0	26
Isaac Porcher[81]	10,225-05-0	*9,000-00-0	75
James Lardant[82]	3,764-00-0	2,965-00-0	22
Samuel Legare[83]	616-00-0	195-00-0	2
Mary Laroche[84]	4,699-04-0	3,905-00-0	19
Solomon Legare[85]	18,580-05-1	650-00-0	3

* Approximately.

[63] *S. C. Gaz.*, Aug. 20, 1772.
[64] MS Pr. Ct. Rcd., 1741-3, 215.
[65] *Ibid.*, 1736-9, 166.
[66] *Ibid.*, 1741-3, 169-76.
[67] *Ibid.*, 1736-9, 65.
[68] *Ibid.*, 1763-7, 210.
[69] *Ibid.*, 1758-61, 314.
[70] *Ibid.*, 1739-43, 131.
[71] *Ibid.*, 210.
[72] *Ibid.*, 277.
[73] *Ibid.*, 243.
[74] *Ibid.*, 386.
[75] *Ibid.*, 388.
[76] *Ibid.*, 279.
[77] *Ibid.*, 395.
[78] *Ibid.*, 1761-3, 50.
[79] *Ibid.*, 1739-43, 237.
[80] *Ibid.*, 1732-6, 179.
[81] MS Pr. Ct. Rcd., 1739-43, 256.
[82] *Ibid.*, 240.
[83] *Ibid.*, 1751-53, 419.
[84] *Ibid.*, 1758-61, 282.
[85] *Ibid.*, 493.

Francis Lejau[86]	16,456-06-9	11,831-00-0	70
Mary Marion[87]	263-17-6	210-00-0	2
Stephen Mazÿck[88]	47,073-00-0	34,842-00-0	108
Suzanne Mazÿck[89]	9,979-17-6	6,795-00-0	40
John Postell[90]	9,027-00-0	8,600-00-0	65
Benj. Perdriau[91]	1,194-00-0	980-00-0	3
Col. Samuel Prioleau[92]	7,011-14-4	4,760-00-0	11
René Ravenel[93]	3,227-10-0	2,950-00-0	17
Jacob Satur[94]	4,806-09-9½	1,515-00-0	11
Peter Simons[95]	7,573-10-0	5,880-00-0	36
Noah Serre[96]	10,528-19-10½	6,980-00-0	40
Rev. James Tissot[97]	1,417-00-0	620-00-0	4
Daniel Huger[98]	119,501-05-8	104,550-00-0	452
John Benoist[99]	2,404-10-0	2,230-00-0	8
Peter Benoist[100]	8,649-16-0	2,630-00-0	8
David Boisseau[101]	70,240-00-0	5,840-00-0	28
Paul Bruneau[102]	4,500-00-0	3,620-00-0	19
Jacob Bonnet[103]	242-00-0	200-00-0	1
Susanne Cordes[104]	3,828-04-5½	2,500-00-0	21
Andrew Dupuy[105]	1,750-00-0	1,350-00-0	5
Henry de Saussure[106]	10,400-00-0	6,670-00-0	39
Mrs. Jean du Pré[107]	1,388-16-6	1,070-00-0	6
Capt. John Dutarque[108]	30,675-00-0	19,420-00-0	63
Theo. Gourdin[109]	89,632-00-0	37,460-00-0	173
John Gendron[110]	21,018-10-0	19,850-00-0	83
Mary Jourdine[111]	3,748-07-6	3,365-00-0	17
Magdalen Deleisseline[112]	895-00-0	850-00-0	3
George Delebere[113]	1,584-05-0	1,500-00-0	6
Abraham Dupont[114]	24,121-19-8	19,010-00-0	78
John Gignilliat[115]	6,294-07-0	4,870-00-0	28
David Peyre[116]	*4,000-00-0	3,540-00-0	21

* Approximately.

[86] *Ibid.*, 132.
[87] *Ibid.*, 1748-51, 351.
[88] *Ibid.*, 1771-4, 101.
[89] *Ibid.*, 1732-9, 103.
[90] *Ibid.*, 1732-46, 188.
[91] *Ibid.*, 1763-7, 99.
[92] *Ibid.*, 1751-3, 415.
[93] *Ibid.*, 1748-51, 344.
[94] *Ibid.*, 1732-6, 47.
[95] *Ibid.*, 1748-51, 81.
[96] *Ibid.*, 1729-31, 136.
[97] *Ibid.*, 1761-3, 521.
[98] *Ibid.*, 1758-61, 598.
[99] *Ibid.*, 1763-7, 173.
[100] *Ibid.*, 1758-61, 225.
[101] *Ibid.*, 203.
[102] *Ibid.*, 78.
[103] *Ibid.*, 49.
[104] *Ibid.*, 1739-43, 251.
[105] *Ibid.*, 331.
[106] *Ibid.*, 1761-3, 186.
[107] *Ibid.*, 1748-51, 230.
[108] *Ibid.*, 1763-7, 378.
[109] *Ibid.*, 1771-4, 521.
[110] *Ibid.*, 1722-6, 285.
[111] *Ibid.*, 1758-61, 304.
[112] *Ibid.*, 184.
[113] *Ibid.*, 624.
[114] *Ibid.*, 544.
[115] *Ibid.*, 1748-51, 285.
[116] *Ibid.*, 1732-6, 165.

White servitude in Carolina was coeval with the period of the first permanent settlement. The vessel manned by William Sayle brought at least sixty-three servants, of whom several were French Protestants.[117] There is, however, no evidence that a large number of Huguenots went to Carolina as servants, though there are indications that some were in the province as such and that a number were owned by Huguenots. For example, the volume of manuscript land-warrants, 1680-1692, bears record of the following, who brought servants with them:

Anthony Boureau, one, October, 1686;[118] one, November 29, 1686.
M. de la Plaine, four, April, 1680.[119]
M. de Russeree, one, November, 1683.[120]
Jacob Guerrard, six: Peter Oliver, Charles Fromagett,[121] John Carier, Ann Lafelleine, Mary Fortress, and one other, Feb. 1680.
John Harris, six, February, 1683-4.[122]
Benj. Marion, three, March, 1693-4.[123]
Lewis Tibou, two, April 1680.[124]

Daniel Leger owned John Fryer;[125] Paul Trézvant owned Paul Floyd.[126] Daniel Huger brought several over in 1686.[127] In 1735-6 Louis Timothy advertised for sale the time of a Swiss servant, who still had three years to serve.[128] Isaac Chardon's servant, James Craddock,[129] in 1737, embezzled money and sundry other goods from him.[130] John Guerrard owned two servants who were coopers.[131] To John Laurens, a saddler, a five-year-old child, Thomas Miller, was bound out to serve until of age and was to be taught the saddlers' trade.[132] François Macaire owned François Bonnet.[133]

The following French Protestants are among those who have been found in South Carolina in the state of white servitude:

[117] *Coll. S. C. Hist. Soc.*, V. 134.
[118] *Ibid.*, I; MS Council Jrnl., 1671-1721, 98.
[119] *Ibid.*, 107.
[120] *Ibid.*, 106.
[121] *Ibid.*, 31.
[122] *Ibid.*, 138.
[123] MS Land War., 1692-1711, 12.
[124] Land War. (Salley), 1680-92, 138.
[125] MS St. Phillip's Vestry Bk., 1755-76.
[126] MS St. Phillip's Ch. W. Acct. Bk., 1725-52, entry, May 29, 1750.
[127] MS Land War., 1692-1711, 45.
[128] *S. C. Gaz.*, Jan. 17, 1735-6.
[129] Craddock, not French.
[130] *Ibid.*, Jan. 1, 1737.
[131] *Ibid.*, Apr. 9, 1737.
[132] MS St. Phillip's Vestry Bk., 1732-56, entry Nov. 5, 1740.
[133] *S. C. H. & G. Mag.*, V. 225.

Name	*Arrival*	*Owned by*
Francis Bonnet[134]		Francis Macaire
Peter Bovet[135]		Peter Pury
Madalean Bullivat[136]	Mar. 1693	Benjamin Marion
John Carrier[137]	Feb. 1680	Jacob Guerrard
Andrew Deleau[138]	Mar. 1693	Benjamin Marion
Robert Done[139]		
Charles Fromaget[140]	Feb. 1680	Jacob Guerrard
Thomas Gourdin[141]		
Josias Dupré[142]	late in 1686	Isaac Varry
John Fougasse[143]		Joseph Child
Mellicent Howe[144]		
Ann Lafelleine[145]	Feb. 1680	Jacob Guerrard
Albert leNud[146]	born at French Santee	John Laurens
Lewis Naudin[147]		Anthony Boureau
Charlotte Phillips[148]		daughter of Pierre and Jeanne Phillips — apprenticed to René and Charlotte Ravenel.
Abraham Phillips[149]		
Peter Poinsett[150]		John Legare
Ann Rebaulda[151]		Daniel Huger
Unnamed French girl[152]		Eliz. Heduits

It is lamentable that so little can be learned regarding ing the extent to which the individual French Protestants were engaged in planting and stock-raising. From a careful study of the records preserved in the inventories of property

[134] *S. C. H. & G. Mag.*, V. 225.
[135] *S. C. Gaz.*, Dec. 23, 1732.
[136] MS Land War., 1692-1711, 12.
[137] *Ibid.*
[138] MS Land War., 1692-1711, 12.
[139] MS Council Jrnl., 1671-80, 7.
[140] Land War., (Salley), 1680-92, 31.
[141] *Ibid.*
[142] MS Land War., 1692-1711, 26.
[143] *Ibid.*, Jan. 29, 1750. "John Fougasse, a Frenchman, born in Beaurdeaux aged 33 years, tall and well made, with his own hair, of a chestnut or reddish colour, and indented servant to the subscriber, having absented himself from his Master's plantation on Ashley River, all persons are hereby forbid to harbour, entertain or employ him, on pain of being prosecuted with the utmost rigour; and a reward of FIVE POUNDS (besides all lawful charges) is hereby offered to any person that takes up and secures him in the work-house, giving notice thereof to

Joseph Child."

[144] *Coll. S. C. Hist. Soc.*, V. 134.
[145] *Ibid.*
[146] *S. C. Gaz.*, Jan. 11, 1746.
[147] MS Land War., 1672-92, 1.
[148] MS Reg. Rcd., 1675-96, 536.
[149] *Ibid.*
[150] *S. C. Gaz.*, Feb. 16, 1738.
[151] MS Land War., 1692-1711, 45.
[152] *S. C. Gaz.*, March 6, 1735-6.

we gather that in stock-raising they were quite extensively engaged. These inventories are a catalogue of the possessions of a given individual at the time of his death. Though they are a list of his possessions at only one period of his life, they at least indicate his pursuits and his possessions at that time. The following list gleaned from inventories, is of course abridged, but it contains material of some interest:

Benj. Avant[152a]	live stock value £806
Caleb Avant[153]	52 cattle 45 hogs
	8 oxen 24 sheep
Mme. Margaret H. Bonneau[154]	16 cattle 19 sheep
Francis Coutourier[155]	46 cows 34 hogs
	22 sheep 12 oxen
Benj. d'Harriette[156]	75 cattle 17 horses
	10 oxen on John's Island
Isaac Dubose[157]	52 cattle 17 mares and yearlings
Abraham Dupont[158]	168 cattle 41 hogs
	15 horses 8 sheep and lambs
John Gendron[159]	106 neat cattle
	76 sheep
Theodore Gourdin[160]	7 oxen 60 hogs
	63 black cattle
	10 horses
Wm. Gourdin[161]	18 cattle
Mary Jourdin[162]	10 hogs 5 horses
	25 black cattle
James Lardant[163]	75 cattle 7 hogs
	8 horses
Francis Lejau[164]	15 work oxen
	71 cattle 17 hogs
	18 sheep 14 horses
Peter De St. Julien[165]	113 cattle 24 oxen
	20 horses
Susanne Mayrant[166]	59 neat cattle

152a MS Pr. Ct. Rcd., 1739-43, 237.

153 MS Land War., 237; MS Reg. Rcd., 1739-43, 279.

154 MS Land War., 1761-3, 9.

155 *Ibid.*, 1758-61, 10.

156 *Ibid.*, 1753-56, 445 f.

157 *Ibid.*, 1739-43, 220.

158 *Ibid.*, 1758-61, 544.

159 *Ibid.*, 1722-8, 285.

160 *Ibid.*, 1771-4, 521.

161 *Ibid.*, 1758-61, 493.

162 *Ibid.*, 304.

163 *Ibid.*, 1739-43, 240.

164 *Ibid.*, 1758-61, 132.

165 *Ibid.*, 1739-43, 277.

166 *Ibid.*, 1732-9, 103.

Stephen Macÿck[167]	21 horses 34 oxen 57 cows and calves 13 hogs 61 sheep
Lewis Mouzon[168]	12 oxen 30 hogs 21 black cattle 18 sheep 10 horses
Benj. Perdriau[169]	27 cattle worth £5 each
David Peyre[170]	190 cattle 16 hogs
Isaac Porcher[171]	123 cattle 50 sheep 30 hogs 23 oxen
John Postell, Sr.[172]	79 cattle 12 hogs 8 work oxen
John Postell, Jr.[173]	71 cattle worth £426 hogs worth £50 4 oxen worth £60
René Ravenel[174]	17 black cattle worth £185
Peter Simons[175]	25 sheep worth £37 15 oxen 40 cattle 36 hogs 4 horses

The French raised horses both for sport and for profit. By nature they were lovers of the turf. With increased prosperity and wealth they indulged in fine coach horses and chariots, trained their racers on the running courses and became leaders in the production of a fine breed of stock.[176] Fairs were conducted and race tracks were maintained on the plantations of some of the wealthy.[177]

As long as stock raisers were forced to allow their horses to run at large in the woods it was not profitable to devote much attention to fine breeding, for the best stock would degenerate by the exigencies of promiscuity as well as by the precariousness of subsistence in the forests.[178] Quantities of horses of low breed had been brought over from

[167] *Ibid.*, 1771-4, 101.
[168] *Ibid.*, 1748-51, 50.
[169] *Ibid.*, 1763-7, 99.
[170] *Ibid.*, 1732-6, 165.
[171] *Ibid.*, 256.
[172] *Ibid.*, 1732-46, 188.
[173] *Ibid.*, 1736-9, 166.
[174] *Ibid.*, 1763-7, 210.
[175] *Ibid.*, 1748-51, 81.
[176] *S. C. Gaz.*, Dec. 14, 1734.
[177] *S. C. Gaz.*, Oct. 5, 1731; Apr. 27, 1747.
[178] Cooper, *Statutes*, II. 164-5. Preamble.

Virginia and other northern colonies before 1700.[179] To prevent this an act was passed making it finable to the extent of £5 to bring horses to South Carolina by land.[180] The best horses therefore that were owned by the Huguenots were not secured from the northern colonies, but from abroad. Numerous horses were imported from England, Arabia, Barbadoes and other places.[181] The special interest in blooded stock must have taken its rise about 1730. In 1734 the first races were run in Charles Town.[182] The prize was a saddle and bridle valued at £20. The race was run on the first Tuesday in February, there were four entries, mile heats and white riders. The horses carried ten stones. Elaborate in display and consuming in interest, these races were observed year after year. Prizes in the form of silver punch bowls valued as high as £90 for the three best heats, French embroidered waistcoats valued at £90 and silver mugs valued at £30 were offered.[183] Before 1747 there were not many full-blood horses in the province, but soon after a number of splendid specimens of horses and mares were brought from England. [184] Among the French in South Carolina, Abraham Dupont is one of the first to be found in the possession of standard stock. In 1739 he advertised for sale a good pacing stallion.[185] Isaac Dubose at the time of his death was greatly interested in pedigreed horses. The property inventory shows a number of them, among which was a bay stallion.[186] Andrew Deveaux owned a pacer that won recognition.[187] *Starling* was an imported English horse. He covered in St. John's Parish from 1767 to 1772 at £35 currency.[188] *Flimnap* became the fastest horse in South Carolina. On March 16, 1773, he beat *Little David,* running the first four miles in four minutes and seventeen seconds. £2,-000 was won and lost at this race and *Flimnap* was sold at

[179] *Ibid.*
[180] *Ibid.*
[181] Irving, *Turf*, 5, 6, 7, 39.
[182] *S. C. Gaz.*, Feb. 1, 1733-4.
[183] *S. C. Gaz.*, Oct. 10, 1743.
[184] *Ibid.*, Feb. 12, 1763. Irving, *Turf*, 34.
[185] *S. C. Gaz.*, May 19, 1739.
[186] MS Pr. Ct. Rcd., 1739-43, 220.
[187] *S. C. Gaz.*, Aug. 6, 1753.
[188] Irving, *Turf*, 40.

auction the same day for £300 sterling.[189] Frank Huger, also in St. John's Parish, on Midway plantation owned and sold many fine horses. He was said by Nicholas Harleston to be "the most magnificent horseman" he ever saw. He was an importer of the best Arabian stock, the most notable among which was his celebrated Arabian horse *Abdallah,*[190] sixteen hands high which had never been ridden before reaching South Carolina. John Huger owned the Hagan plantation, a large stock farm and a rendezvous of the best horsemen in the province. He is credited with owning nineteen pedigreed horses at one time.[191] Interest in race and riding horses continued to increase after 1750. Races are announced to take place in various parts of the tide-water, at Jacksonborough, Ferguson's Ferry, at Goose Creek on Isaac Peronneau's plantation, at Childsbury, Georgetown and Charles Town. In St. John's Parish in fact, where many rich Huguenots lived, interest did not abate until long after the Revolution though the legislature put a check on racing during the war. Jacob Bonhoste's horse, *Prince,* was advertised by the *Gazette* to serve at Daniel Huger's plantation for the season of 1762,[192] while the same issue announces that *Nonpareil* would serve at the same place. The rate for *Prince* was £10, for *Nonpareil* £20, for James Postell's *Friar,* which served at Dorchester, £30.[193] Daniel Horry's English bred chestnut horse, *Sprightly,* was entered in the races at Georgetown on January 5, 1768.[194] At the Strawberry races, on the 19th, James Ravenel's filly took first, and Paul Mazÿck's colt, *Starling,* second.[195] The day following, Daniel Horry's filly, *Cherry,* took first, and Daniel Ravenel's colt took third. James Ravenel's bay colt, *True Blue,* was entered for the February races in 1768.[196]

The first contest to attract general attention and to cause almost universal excitement was that of March 2, 1768, at

[189] *Journal of Josiah Quincy,* March 16, 1773.
[190] Irving, *Turf,* 39.
[191] *Ibid.,* 45.
[192] *S. C. Gaz.,* March 6, 1762.
[193] *Ibid.,* Jan. 19, 1767.
[194] *Ibid.,* Jan. 25, 1768.
[195] *Ibid.*
[196] *Ibid.,* Feb. 1, 1768.

New Market.[197] A race was run between Daniel Horry's horse, *Sprightly,* and Benjamin Huger's *Crocus,* both horses five years old, for £300 currency. The race was won by the former, *Crocus* having thrown his rider in the first heat.[198] James Ravenel's *Friar*[199] and Daniel Horry's *Maks* were among the prominent leaders during the 70's.[200] In 1779 John Gaillard's horse *Centinel* is advertised. This horse was imported from England and bred by *Duke of Ancaster.* In 1767 he was brought to South Carolina and his owner backed him against any horse in the province.[201] In Goose Creek Parish Isaac Peronneau built a course on his own plantation and equipped it for races.[202] Fairs and races were held here during much of the colonial period.[203] When the British overran St. Stephen's Parish during the early days of the Revolutionary War, they confiscated more than forty horses, mostly brood mares, belonging to Peter Sinkler.[204]

Mr. Daniel Ravenel raised many fine horses on his plantation, known as *Wantoot,*[205] in St. John's Parish. His principal brood mares were: *Gray Pleasant, Lucretia, Rose,* and *Moll-Slammokin.* His most distinguished colts and fillies were: *Fox Hunter,* out of *Gray Pleasant* and sired by William Harleston's bay horse *Prince,* and a bay filly called *Lucy,* out of *Rose* and sired by the imported horse *Friar.* Mr. Ravenel kept up his stock farm until 1785. His most distinguished imported stallions were *Brutus, Friar, Spotless, Flimnap, and Starling.*[206]

Of horses, South Carolina produced the best. It would be difficult to over-estimate the value of this fact in the results of the Revolutionary War. The cavalry of Francis Marion, the "Swamp Fox", was little less famous than that of Forrest.

In the foregoing pages we have attempted to present some of the activities of the French Protestants in agricultural

[197] *Ibid.,* March 2, 1768.
[198] *Ibid.,* March 7, 1768.
[199] *Ibid.,* March 14, 1771.
[200] *Ibid.,* Apr. 2, 1772.
[201] Irving, *Turf,* 36-7.
[202] *S. C. Gaz.,* Apr. 27, 1747.
[203] *Ibid.,* March 11, 1756.
[204] Dubose, *Reminiscences,* 29.
[205] Irving, *Turf,* 35.
[206] *Ibid.*

pursuits. There were other avenues as well in which they found opportunity to show their skill. Merchandise and trade were among the foundation stones on which were built some of the great fortunes of South Carolina Frenchmen. Though they were usually not among the largest shippers, in fact, in the main, among the least prominent in this particular pursuit, they played an important part in the colonial commercial development. Now and then a Huguenot commercial leader looms up above the rest, but the majority of those engaged in trade were active only in a limited coastal trade or inter-provincial commerce, ranging from Savannah, on the south, to New York, on the north. Occasionally they are found engaging in English commerce, or with the West Indies. These forms of traffic, petty in detail, nevertheless had extensive results and, in the final estimate were not unimportant. The preserved records are scarce and scanty; still the occasional glimpses are interesting hints of the extent and character of its wider scope.

The eighteenth century was perhaps not the first period in modern history when the destinies of mankind were shaped by commerce and the industries dependent on it, but during it French and English commercial companies were contending for the monopoly of trade, while both war and peace tended to create new commercial desires. The main drift of the historic current in Europe and America in this century was in the play of this new commercial life. This the Huguenots of South Carolina were not slow to see. Accordingly they seized the opportunities opened to them. Still, though they had inherent adaptabilities to commercial enterprises by their inherited trade tendencies they were hampered at every turn from becoming leaders in maritime trade.[207] In addition to being retarded by the trade prejudice against their nation, owing to the violations of the English navigation laws by unscrupulous French merchants in earlier periods, the Huguenots had to suffer by the resultant restrictive laws. Before the passage of the Naturalization Act of 1696 most

[207] Burke, *Account of European Settlements in America,* II. 41.

of them then in South Carolina,[208] even if they had money, were virtually excluded from a commercial livelihood by the rigid English laws.[209] Complaint against their restrictions was made by the French Protestants in 1699,[210] when they allege that they are not permitted to become owners and masters of vessels even though they have been in the province a long time and in spite of the fact that many of them had been made denizens. In spite of these exigencies a number of them were engaged in the maritime occupations and some of them, as we shall see, became wealthy thereby. The prominence of the Huguenots in commerce cannot be argued from large numbers of extant records, but in newspapers, wills, indentures, mortgages, etc., are found hints indicating their trade interests on land and sea. Lewis Perdriau in 1694-5 wrote in his will: "Intending to leave for New York in my ship and considering the great dangers and many accidents that may happen, . . . I make my will."[211] George Baudoin,[212] in his will and Daniel leGendre[213] disposed of money they were expecting for consignments of goods sent to England and from England. The firm of Godin & Conseillere and Daniel leGendre were shipping brokers. Lewis Pasquereau was a shipper and merchant.[214] Mr. Godin laid the foundation for his fortune in Charles Town and then moved to London, where he continued to do an extensive business with Charles Town merchants.[215] Ebenezer Simons owned the sloop *Madera*.[216] Godin & Conseillere owned the frigate *Carolina*[217] and carried on trade with northern American ports, the West Indies, the British Isles, and some of the French possessions. They were American

[208] Cooper, *Statutes*, II. 131.
[209] *Cal. St. Pa. (Am. & W. Ind.)*, 1699, no. 183.
[210] Rivers, *Sketch*, chap. 8.
[211] MS Pr. Ct. Rcd., 1692-3, 18.
[212] *Ibid.*, 1671-1727, 49 and 78.
[213] *Ibid.*, 78.
[214] *Ibid.*
[215] MS Col. Doc. S. C., V. 37; MS Pr. Ct. Rcd., 1671-1727, 155.
[216] MS Col. Doc. S. C., XVIII. 193-4. MS Letter, Blondel to Godin, Sept. 16, 1726, in S. C. MSS, folio 33, 1700-1732, Library of Congress.
[217] MS Col. Doc. S. C., XI. 66.

correspondents for several English firms.[218] In 1755 David Godin advertised for sale an 80-ton vessel.[219]

Credit played a leading part in the financial development of the province of South Carolina. The Huguenots by their wealth, financial skill and integrity played an important part in this development. Planters as well as merchants were continually deep in debt.[220] Money was borrowed not only to buy land and slaves, but also to establish commercial houses.[221] Frenzied finance on slave margins led to the financial ruin of many colonists. Slaves were bought by rich and poor alike, mainly on credit, in quantities so large that purchasers were unable to pay for them. The financial stability of the colony was thereby threatened.[222] Still, in spite of it all, people were prospering, crops were good, finery was being imported in great quantities, and luxuries were indulged in by persons of practically all classes. Here the Huguenots found a ready market for their accumulated savings.[223] The inventories of property of deceased French Protestants, the mortgages, bonds, indentures, wills and other legal instruments on record in the Mesne Conveyance Office in Charleston and in the Probate Court in Charleston as well as in the office of the Historical Commission in Columbia, bear abundant evidence of these facts. It is true that most of these are but shafts of light thrown on an otherwise dark page, but they are expressive of the unrevealed full page. Large amounts were borrowed from private parties in Carolina, though some, of course, came from English brokers. And though a bank was established in Charles Town as early as 1712 the Huguenots continued to loan large amounts.[224] In 1691 the rate of interest had been fixed by law at 10%.[225] This rate was renewed in the Act of

[218] *Ibid.*, X. 195 f.

[219] *S. C. Gaz.*, Aug. 14, 1755.

[220] *S. C. Gaz.*, Apr. 2, 1737; March 2, 1738; MS Col. Doc. S. C., XV. 74; XXII. 273.

[221] *Ibid.*

[222] *S. C. Gaz.*, Apr. 2, 1737.

[223] *Ibid.*

[224] Brevard, *Digest*, Intr. p. 11.

[225] Cooper, *Statutes*, II. 62.

1719,[225a] and the Act of 1721.[226] In 1748 the rate was reduced from 10% to 8%[227] and the Act of 1777 reduced it to 7%.[228] Money was well worth 10% if invested in negroes and its increment was easily three times that if the negroes were placed on rice or indigo land.[229] Both European and American money was hard to secure; therefore credit was not only a convenient, but also a necessary form of exchange. The advertisements in the *South Carolina Gazette,* begging, pleading with, and threatening creditors are a weary monotony. Gold and silver were being drained off by the petty traders from the northern colonies, who dealt in beer, apples, chestnuts, and other similar goods, and who picked up all the metal money obtainable by paying a little more for it in trade than market values quoted.[230] Though there is now no way of ascertaining the extent to which the Frenchmen of the province were engaged in the loan business, the sources quoted at least indicate that it was one of the leading as well as most favored methods of making money.[231] For example, the inventory of the personal property of Solomon Legare shows that out of a total value of £18,580-05-1 in personal property, £17,628-10-1 was at the time of his death in the form of credit obligations, such as notes, bonds, mortgages, etc.[232] The following table is evidence of a number of important factors:

Name	*Amount Loaned*	*Total Estate*
Peter Benoist[233]	£ 5,446-10-0	
Francis Courtourier[234]	100-00-0	
Benj. d'Harriette[235]	33,413-06-5	including book accounts
Martha d'Harriette[236]	18,603-13-10½	

[225a] *Ibid.,* III. 104.
[226] *Ibid.,* III. 133.
[227] MS Col. Doc. S. C., XXIII. 228.
[228] Cooper, *Statutes,* IV. 363.
[229] MS Col. Doc. S. C., XXIII. 230.
[230] *S. C., Gaz.,* Dec. 11, 1749.
[231] See table appended.
[232] MS Pr. Ct. Rcd., 1758-61, 493.
[233] MS Pr. Ct. Rcd., 1761-3, 134.
[234] *Ibid.,* 1758-61, 10.
[235] *Ibid.,* 1753-6, 445 f.
[236] *Ibid.,* 1758-61, 314 f.

Abraham Dupont[237]	863-11-6	
Elias Foissin[238]	300-00-0	
Theodore Gourdin[239]	11,273-18-11	
Daniel Huger[240]	3,994-17-8	
Ann le Brasseur[241]	3,471-12-6	
	325-07-1 sterl.	
Solomon Legare[242]	17,628-10-0	18,580-15-1
Ann le Grand[243]	35-00-0	3,403-10-0
Isaac Lesesne[244]	5,270-00-7	22,142-15-0
Paul Mazÿck[245]	33,712-10-5	50,720-18-5
Stephen Mazÿck[246]	6,691-00-0	
Jacob Motte[247]	188,589-12-9	228,301-00-0
Elisha Prioleau[248]	12,297-00-0	12,995-00-0
Peter Purry[249]	1,443-00-0	

Mortgage to Cornelius and Gideon Dupont[250] for £10,000.....................by Benjamin Villepontoux
Mortgage to Solomon Legare[251] for£44........by John Bonneteau
Mortgage to James Laurens[252] for £400...........by John Robert
Mortgage to Peter Birot[253] for £300..........by Joseph Dolorme
Mortgage to Henry Peronneau[254] for £428...........by R. Rivers

Peter Manigault, according to his advertisements in the *South Carolina Gazette* loaned thousands of pounds.[255] Several thousand pounds, belonging to the children of Daniel Huger, deceased, were advertised to be loaned.[256] Hundreds of other cases are on record in the form of mortagages, notes, and other obligations, indicating the use made of this method of earning money.

Everywhere the factor has been a necessary complement to the machinery of commerce. He has been the indispensable medium between producer and consumer. In Europe he had a function distinct from that of the broker and the storekeeper, but his business partook of the nature of both. The English factorage business then became closely identified with handling the leading agricultural staples which were

[237] *Ibid.*, 544.
[238] *Ibid.*, 1739-43, 87.
[239] *Ibid.*, 1771-74, 521.
[240] *Ibid.*, 1758-61, 598.
[241] *Ibid.*, 1741-43, 169 f.
[242] *Ibid.*, 1758-61, 493.
[243] *Ibid.*, 1741-3, 215.
[244] *Ibid.*, 248.
[245] *Ibid.*, 1748-51, 297.
[246] *Ibid.*, 1771-4, 101.
[247] *Ibid.*, 27.
[248] *Ibid.*, 1732-46, 252.
[249] *Ibid.*, 1736-9, 65.
[250] *Ibid.*, 1767-71, 371.
[251] *Ibid.*, 1722-6, 221.
[252] *Ibid.*, 195.
[253] *Ibid.*, 1729-31, 222.
[254] *Ibid.*, 110.
[255] *S. C. Gaz.*, Dec. 8, 1758.
[256] *Ibid.*, Sept. 8, 1756.

grown in the colonies for export to the British Isles. In South Carolina the factor functioned in the colonial period as a creditor, but the balance on his books was seldom in the planter's favor. He was the "go-between" for the London "principals" and the South Carolina planter. The first crop was often "pitched" on capital borrowed at a high rate of interest with the expectation on the part of the planter that the profits of the first year would liquidate the obligation. However that may have been, the outcome was usually the same. The planter usually either renewed his obligation by reason of a failure in his hopes or, in order to enlarge his operations, made a new loan even if he paid his first one. This of course always meant an increased hazard. Then if misfortune found him, he was financially ruined, by the possible foreclosure on his entire estate. With the numerous profits accruing to the factor his income was practically guaranteed. He not only received interest on the money he loaned, but charged a commission both on the goods he sold for the planter and on the goods bought by the British merchant or his agent. These, supplemented by charges for insurance, storage, and handling of the goods, gave him an enviable income from business of even a limited amount.[257] The factorage business grew to large proportions before the American Revolution, though it was not entirely in the hands of the French Protestants. The navigation laws required that the factor must be a native or a naturalized English subject. The person to whom the goods were consigned from abroad was not infrequently a merchant who owned a share in them and who therefore in handling them acted both as a partner and as a go-between. But, as a rule, the factor had no pecuniary interest in the cargo itself, except his commissions and fees.

In Carolina, however, the factorage business was not restricted to foreign trade. Factors bought country produce in the Charles Town markets and disposed of it at once in

[257] MS Col. Doc. S. C., XXII. 272. *The South in the Building of the Nation*, V. 398.

Charles Town, or shipped it to Philadelphia, New York, Barbadoes and England.[258] Peter Leger, a French Protestant, was in this business in 1754, connected with the firm of Milner & Leger.[259] After the copartnership contract expired in 1756 both men pursued the business independently.[260] Leger's specialty was country produce.[261] After 1764 the firm of Waldron & Bounetheau was engaged in the business.[262] Benjamin Villepontoux advertised his business in 1772.[263]

Another phase of the factorage business was the Indian trade carried on between whites and the several Indian nations of the back-country. Foreign manufactured products were hauled inland by the use of wagons and water conveyances and exchanged for skins, furs, meats, etc. By 1735 this traffic was extensive enough to require 800 horses, besides all of the canoes, boats, vessels and other means of conveyance.[264] The principal basis for the great profits that the exchange in furs poured into the lap of trade lay in the natural results of exchanges between the agents of two very different civilizations, having entirely different standards of value. Furs and skins could be procured by the natives in the back-country for little or no outlay. In England they had great value. The factor and the trader were the medium between these two standards,—and their skill and ingenuity brought them rich harvests in return. The ignorance of the Indian combined with his propensity to drink and his love for display delivered him over to a greater or less degree to the greed of the white man. While on the war path and in ambush he was able to wield weapons of defense and exercise unusual skill, as a trader he was usually defenseless in the presence of the cupidity of the agents of civilization. But Indian trade was tenaciously retained in South Carolina

[258] *S. C. Gaz.*, Sept. 19, 1755.
[259] *Ibid.*, Oct. 17, 1754.
[260] *Ibid.*, Sept. 16, 1756.
[261] *Ibid.*, Nov. 13, 1755.
[262] *Ibid.*, Nov. 19, 1764. Supplement.
[263] *Ibid.*, Sept. 10, 1772.
[264] MS Col. Doc. S. C., XVII. 412.

not merely on the basis of money profits, but because it kept the Indians dependent on Charles Town for numerous articles that otherwise would have cost them more if purchased from the Spanish in other ports and because the presence of Indians tended to keep the rapidly increasing number of negro slaves along the frontier in awe and subjection.[265]

A number of cases are on record of whites in South Carolina taking Indians for slaves and mistresses, but perhaps at no time except immediately after a massacre or Indian war was it customary in general to hold them in prolonged captivity.[266] In South Carolina to take captive an Indian from a tribe in amity with the inhabitants of the province was a violation of law.[267] There seems to have been little or no disposition on the part of the provincial government to allow the enslaving of Indians, except temporarily after military engagements, when it seemed necessary. Then the Public Receiver was empowered to send Indian captives to the West Indies to be sold there and a penalty of £200 was threatened on offenders who disposed of Indian slaves in South Carolina or in the provinces of the north.[268] In 1707 there was a penalty of £60 in addition to forfeiture on persons trading among the Indians who were convicted of selling a free Indian as a slave. Though, as a rule, the French Protestants are said to have treated the Indians with kindness and consideration, in this regard at least they seem to have followed the tendencies of their English neighbors. In 1710 Phillip Gilliard, it was alleged, took a young Indian against her will.[269] In 1713 complaint was made to the Board of Indian Commissioners that two Indian women, of the Cherokee nation, were being detained as slaves at the home of M. de St. Julien.[270] When the defendant was summoned to appear before the Board in Charles Town he was exonerated by the

[265] MS Col. Doc. S. C., XVII. 412; MS Indian Bk., I. 19.
[266] MS Indian Bk., I. 12, 38, 67.
[267] *Ibid.*, I. 49-50.
[268] Cooper, *Statutes*, II. 321-2.
[269] MS Indian Bk., I. 2.
[270] *Ibid.*, I. 79, 93.

Governor on the ground that he had held them to justify a grievance and was dismissed. Though the instances are not numerous, there are in the later period a number of cases in which French Protestants owned and sold Indian slaves whether in violation of law or not. In 1695 a Commission for settling disputes between whites and Indians was provided by law.[271] As early as 1710 Indian trade became extensive enough and abuses frequent enough to call for a permanent Commission to regulate and direct it.[272]

The French Protestants were not so active in this pursuit as one might expect. They are represented on the Commission almost continuously, but few of them appear on the lists of licensed traders.[273] In the reports of the Commissioners of Indian Affairs, in 1710, out of a list of twenty-one applicants, only one Huguenot name appears, that of John Frazier.[274] But Phillip Gilliard is also an Indian trader according to the Journal of the Council.[275] In 1711-12, nineteen applications were answered with licenses, two of whom, John Gilliard and Barnabas Gilliard, were French Protestants.[276] In 1714, Cornelius La Motte is the only French Protestant in a list of twenty-six.[277] The later period records the names of such men as Jerome Courtonne, trader among the Chickasaws, Gabriel Manigault, Isaac Motte, of New Windsor, and others.[278] A much larger list of French Protestant merchants appears in the records as recipients of public money for consignments of goods sold to the Indians or to the Indian agents.[279]

Among the French Protestants, who served on the Board of Commissioners of Indian Affairs are William John

[271] Cooper, *Statutes,* II. 322.
[272] MS Indian Bk., I. 1.
[273] MS Indian Bk., I. 6, 26, 76, 101.
[274] *Ibid.,* I. 10.
[275] MS Council Jrnl., 1707-12, 211.
[276] MS Indian Bk., I. 25.
[277] *Ibid.,* 107.
[278] MS Council Jrnl., 1757-8, 9; *S. C. Gaz.,* Sept. 8, 1739.
[279] MS Indian Bk., I. 2, 18, 4, 19, 23. Isaac Mazÿck, Satur & Wragg, Godin & Conseilliere, Bartholomew Gaillard, Elias Foissin, Elisha Prioleau.

Guerrard, who was on the first list.[280] In 1711, John Motte was added. In 1714, on the death of John Guerrard, Benjamin Godin was chosen to fill the vacancy. Gabriel Manigault served after 1765. In 1752 Peter Mercier was Indian Agent at the Congaree fort.[281] Other prominent Indian traders among the French Protestants were Peter Horry, Benjamin Godin, Gabriel Escott, and William La Serre.[282]

The most thickly settled Huguenot section outside of Charles Town in the early part of the eighteenth century, was on the Santee River in and about Jamestown. Here the Indians were also numerous, as they were likely to be along most of the far-reaching frontier. In 1716, Barthelemy Gaillard, then still a resident at Santee, seeing the advantage of Indian trade, and aware of the check the presence of Indians in the Santee community would be on the conduct of negro slaves, suggested to the Board of Commissioners that a factorage be established on the Santee in order to retain the Indians by Indian trade.[283] Acting on his suggestion a trading post was erected there, owned and financed by the provincial government, and Mr. Gaillard the same year was constituted the superintending factor.[284] It is interesting to note that his instructions recite that all trade should be carried on with the Indians on the basis of a minimum of 100% profit and that if he received any gifts from the Indians, other gifts should be made in return, not to exceed one-half the value of these received from the Indians.[285]

[280] MS Indian Bk., I. 101.
[281] *S. C. Gaz.*, July 20, 1765.
[282] MS letter, Indian Bk., II. 235.
[283] MS Indian Bk., I. 19.
[284] *Ibid.*, 19 and 58.
[285] *Ibid.*, 66 f.

CHAPTER IX

RURAL INDUSTRIES IN WHICH HUGUENOTS ENGAGED EXTENSIVELY

One of the primary purposes for which each of the groups of French Protestants was sent to Carolina was to raise silk, and they pursued the industry at intervals for more than a hundred years, with varying success. To this end the *Richmond* was commissioned in 1680 by the British government and loaded with Huguenots, who brought eggs of the silk worm with them.[1] But owing to the delays in the voyage, the eggs were hatched at sea and the worms perished for want of proper food.[2] Thus was frustrated at this early date the plan to establish a silk manufactory in Carolina. According to the expert testimony of Jean Lewis Gibert no country in the world was better fitted by nature for the cultivation of silk.[3] The mulberry trees on which the silk-worm fed grew native and were easily cultivated. In addition large groves of mulberry trees were planted by the French for their purposes in both the tide-water and the back country.[4] With the possibility of a double or triple crop each year,[5] as far as natural adaptability was concerned, little or nothing seemed to stand in the way of its success. Not only the British government,[6] the proprietors in England, and the several South Carolina agents resident in London, but also the Governor and the Council of the province gave it every encouragement. The British government had long envied France her possession of the silk industry.[7] In the reigns of both Elizabeth and James I, attempts were made to intro-

[1] Chalmers, *Pol. Annals,* in Carroll, *Collections,* II. 312.

[2] Thomas Ash, in Salley *Doc. of Early Carolina,* 143; Rivers, *Sketch,* 174.

[3] Letter, Gibert to Governor and Council, MS Assembly Jrnl., 1765-8, 177.

[4] MS Col. Doc., S. C., XVII. 178-80.

[5] *Ibid.,* V. 152.

[6] *Ibid.,* XXIV. 158, letter Halifax to Glen.

[7] Smiles, *Huguenots,* 258.

duce it into England. In 1607,[8] James I issued orders requiring land owners to plant mulberry trees to guarantee the food for the production of silk worms. At the same time William Stallings secured a license covering twenty-one years to print a book of instructions, entitled: *Instructions for the planting and increase of mulberry trees, breeding of silk worms and making of silk,* for their guidance.[9] By 1699 in South Carolina, with Governor Archdale's encouragement the industry had become extensive enough to warrant a gift of silk to the proprietors in England.[10] Repeated experiments and tests were made[11] on scientific principles by experts, while specialists were sent to England and France to confer with leaders in the industry.[12] They pronounced the South Carolina product as good as the Piedmont silk. Benjamin Godin, in 1716, reported that he had sold several bales of silk at 33 shillings a pound.[13] Mr. Beresford imported twenty pounds at twenty-four shillings per pound. In 1722 the English silk-bounty act was passed providing for the following bounties on silk, designed especially to encourage its culture in the colonies:[14]

Ribbons and stuffs of silk, each lb. £0-3-0
Silk and ribbons of silk, mixed with gold or silver. . . .£0-1-0
Silks mixed with "uncle" or cotton. £0-1-0
Stuffs of silk or worsted. £0-0-6

Silk was raised by the French in and about Charles Town,[15] in Purrysburg Township[16] and with particular suc-

[8] *Cal. St. Pa. (Dom.),* 1598-1601, 500.
[9] *Domestic Papers,* Jas. I, Jan. 5, 1607.
[10] MS Col. Doc. S. C., IV. 117; Carroll, *Collections,* II. 118. Archdale in his *Description of S. C.* wrote in 1707: "Silk is come into great improvement, some families making 40 lb. or 50 lb. a Year and their plantations not neglected; little negro children being serviceable in Feeding the silk worms. The inhabitants work the silk into Druggets, mixed with wool."
[11] *S. C. Gaz.,* Sept. 19, 1755.
[12] MS Col. Doc. S. C., XVII. 178, report to Lords of Trade, Nov. 9, 1734.
[13] *Ibid.,* 6, 286.
[14] 8 Geo. I. chap. 15; Anderson, *Commerce,* III. 130.
[15] In and about Charles Town, Benj. Godin, Hercules Coyte and Lewis Poyas plied the industry. See *S. C. Gaz.,* Dec. 11, 1736; MS *Assembly*

cess in the Hillsboro section; in the latter place under the direction of Louis Gibert.[17] If any lull occurred in the interest for silk culture, it was revived by the anticipated arrival of the Swiss and French bound for Purrysburg. Their principal purpose in settling there was to raise silk. Hopes ran so high that it was estimated that the colonies of South Carolina and Georgia[18] would be able to raise 200,000 pounds of raw silk annually, thereby entirely displacing the Piedmont silk export to Great Britain.

By 1738 the private experimental stage had been passed and the provincial government felt safe in proposing to make the industry a public enterprise. The French were naturally looked to as leaders in the project of establishing a provincial silk station, operated and maintained by the government. Isaac Mazÿck, one of Charles Town's most successful business men and commercial leaders was appointed a commissioner to encourage the growth of silk in South Carolina.[19] The commission, after careful inquiry learned that worms hatched in April would spin their balls and lay eggs that could be hatched in June, and that the first crop of worms thus produced would begin to spin in six weeks from the time it was hatched, and the second crop the month following; that six persons on the average, were able to gather the leaves and feed the worms from 15 to 20 ounces of seed; that from one ounce of seed 7 or 8 pounds of raw silk could be expected; that one person could ordinarily draw 70 or 80 pounds of "organzine" silk and a proportionately larger amount of coarser silk. It was computed that as the crop required only about five months, April to August, and that with "organzine" silk at 18 shillings sterling, per pound, one manager and six negroes could make £65 sterling in a sea-

Jrnl., 1737-41, 94; 1733-8, 281 and 287. Mr. Amatis, agent for the Georgia trustees for the encouragement of silk culture in Carolina, made frequent trips to Charles Town. See *S. C. Gaz.*, May 12, 1733; May 11, 1767; MS Sec'y. Rcds., 1732-42, 207.

[16] *S. C. Gaz.*, May 11, 1767; Ramsay, *Hist. S. C.*, II. 221.

[17] *S. C. Gaz.*, May 11, 1767.

[18] *Ibid.*, Dec. 9, 1732.

[19] Cooper, *Statutes*, III. 487; *S. C. Gaz.*, Feb. 15, 1739.

son.[20] On this computation the commission made the following recommendation: That John Lewis Poyas, a Frenchman, should be employed for a period of seven years at the rate of £100 sterling, cash salary; that six negroes be purchased at once and that the Poyas family and the negroes be maintained the first year at public expense; that all profits arising from the business be placed in the public treasury. Three plantations on which to establish this silk project were offered to the commission. One of 80 acres, five miles from Charles Town, sufficiently supplied with mulberry trees and good buildings, owned by the Hon. Joseph Wragg, was offered at £100 per annum. Isaac Mazÿck, one of the members of the commission, offered his plantation adjoining Bonneau's, in St. John's Berkeley, gratis, for seven years, while Captain Morris proposed that his farm of 100 acres, twelve miles from Goose Creek, should be selected. His offer was that at the end of seven years he would reimburse the value then placed on the improvements that had been made on the property in the meantime.[21] The debate in the house on the report of the commission clearly indicates that the representatives of the people were not hasty to venture the public money on a new enterprise. It was urged that the selected plantation be made a training station for teaching a number of persons each year the art of raising silk, thereby not only perpetuating its economic success, but also giving the public ample opportunity to examine the product in its various stages of development.[22] Poyas was finally employed for a period of seven years with the understanding that he remain during the entire period, whether the enterprise under his management should prosper or not. He was to receive £100 annually the first three years in addition to the necessities of living for himself and family.[23] Six negroes should be supplied him for the seven years. After the first three years he should receive all accruing

[20] MS Assembly Jrnl., Col. Doc. S. C., 1733-8, 281.
[21] *Ibid.*
[22] *Ibid.*, 287.
[23] *Ibid.*, 303. Cooper. *Statutes*, III. 487.

profits in lieu of salary.[24] But none of the three plantations that were offered was accepted. The station was placed on the plantation of M. Cattell. Here a training school was opened where apprentices to the number of ten, coming from any of the townships, were maintained at public expense and were taught the art.[25] No record of the success or failure of this venture has been found. In 1741 Poyas advertised his bid for silk worms at £4 per bushel[26] and the year following he advertised for 4,000 bushels of worms, but did not specify how much money was offered.[27]

Silk culture was not profitable enough for self maintenance. Repeatedly stimulants had to be applied in the form of bounties and other forms of encouragement. In order to urge its growth the Assembly on May 29, 1744 empowered the commissioners for five years to pay the following prices for silk products:[28]

15 shillings per bushel for merchantable silk balls;
8 shillings per bushel for inferior balls, so-called "knubs";
40 shillings per bushel for best "organized" silk.

Governor Glenn, in a speech on Tuesday,[29] November 21, 1749, declared: "Our silk is as good a quality as that of any other country." He made a plea for its more extensive production. Ten thousand pounds of raw silk was raised in South Carolina in 1759.[30] Two years later John Lewis Poyas advertised that he had just received by importation a large consignment of goods including black padusoy, made of Carolina silk.[31] The raw silk was raised in Carolina, shipped to England, there manufactured into cloth and finally returned to Carolina. This roundabout method in the productive process was required by the British trade policy.

[24] MS Assembly Jrnl., Col. Doc. S. C., 1731-47, 59, 94, 99, 105.
[25] *S. C. Gaz.*, Feb. 15, 1739.
[26] *Ibid.*, May 7, 1741.
[27] *Ibid.*, Apr. 10, 1742.
[28] MS Assembly Jrnl., 1733-8, 282, 288, 303, 320; 1740, 388-9; *S. C. Gaz.*, Apr. 1, 1745.
[29] *S. C. Gaz.*, Nov. 27, 1749.
[30] Mills, *Statistics of S. C.*, 155; Anderson, *Commerce*, III. 309.
[31] *S. C. Gaz.*, Nov. 13, 1752.

So extensive and successful did the silk enterprise become in South Carolina that public comment was excited in Europe regarding its quality.[32]

Silk culture reached its highest development both in quality and quantity after the Hillsboro settlement of French Protestants was completed. These people came almost directly from the gardens of France and were well qualified to produce the best. It was largely through the efforts of John Lewis Gibert that the industry was promoted there. By stimulating the interest of Gabriel Manigault in his work, he secured funds and the necessary encouragement.[33] During the first year after his arrival, he raised 620 pounds of cocoons on Manigault's plantation, *Silk Hope,* out of which he secured 50 pounds of drawn silk.[34] That year he went to England with both the silk and the two boxes of cocoons in order to show them to experts in London and to solicit the financial aid of English capitalists in building factories in South Carolina.[35] This aid, apparently willingly given, was withdrawn as soon as the rumblings of the approaching Revolution were heard.[36] It was due largely to this achievement at *Silk Hope* and the success in Hillsboro Township that a factory for spinning silk was opened in Charles Town in 1766 or 1767 and one in Hillsboro Township the same year. Parliament in England forsook former policies long enough not only to remove the duties from silk but also to place a bounty on its production in the colonies and on its exportation to England.[37] After sending to southern France for three experts to assist him in the manufacture of silk,[38] Louis Gibert was employed by the provincial government to teach the winding of silk and to

[32] Anderson, *Commerce,* III. 309.
[33] MS Assembly Jrnl., 1765-8, 177, letter, Jean Gibert to Governor and Council.
[34] *S. C. Gaz.,* Aug. 3, 1765. *Silk Hope* was originally owned by Sir Nathaniel Johnson. See *S. C. H. & G. Mag.,* XII. 112.
[35] *Ibid.,* Aug. 3, 1765. MS Assembly Jrnl., 1765-7, 177.
[36] *Ibid.*
[37] MS Assembly Jrnl., 1769-71, 12.
[38] *Ibid.,* 1765-8, 177.

superintend the plant. He established quarters in the old free school house in Charles Town, near the barracks,[39] where his work was open to public inspection. £1,000 was appropriated annually for the extension of the work in Charles Town and in New Bordeaux. In 1768,[40] £4,000 was appropriated for the erection of a filiature for winding silk at Purryburg.[41] John Delabère, a French Protestant, in London, represented the colony in the export of silk from South Carolina.[42] In 1769, 300 pounds of silk was shipped to him from the Charles Town factory for which £2,173-5-4 currency was received.[43] This money was turned back into the treasury for the purpose of extending the enterprise.[44] In January 1770, 240 pounds was shipped to M. Delabère from Charles Town. The total amount raised for export and shipped from the province during the previous season was the

[39] *S. C. Gaz.*, May 11, 1767. "We have the pleasure to acquaint the public that the successful introduction of the SILK MANUFACTURE in this province bears a promising aspect as we hear there are great quantities of silk worms raised in almost every family in Purryburg parish and some by the French of Hillsborough and the English and Germans near Long Canes; and that several gentlemen and ladies near Charles Town will make the private amusement of raising silk worms, tend to the public benefit by showing how easily the knowledge thereof is to be acquired and that small labour is necessary in the management of them. Mr. John Lewis Gibert, a native of France, who is employed by the gentlemen concerned on behalf of the public in the encouragement of this manufacture, to wind and teach the winding of silk has now a considerable number of silk worms, in the old school house near the barracks where gentlemen who are desirous of seeing them either through curiosity or inclination to promote so valuable a branch of trade may at one and the same time view them in the various stages of life, some young, some full grown and some spinning their balls or cocoons. The Librarian of the Charles Town Library Society also raises a few in the lobby of the library room where gentlemen who are not willing to go as far as Mr. Gibert's may satisfy their curiosity. Workmen are now employed in building an oven for curing the cocoons, erecting four machines and all other necessaries for winding silk with all expedition, in rooms adjoining Mr. Gibert's in order that the filiature may be set to work as soon as the cocoons are fit, which may be in about three weeks."

[40] MS Assembly Jrnl., 1765-8, 183 and 194.

[41] *Ibid.*, 247.

[42] *Ibid.*, 1769-71, 116-7.

[43] *Ibid.*

[44] *Ibid.*

first consignment from the American colonies to receive the benefit of the Royal bounty.[45]

The project thus safely launched, with all its promise of success, was defeated by a combination of economic forces in conjunction with the litigations attending the rapidly approaching Revolutionary war, though in Hillsboro Township and in Charles Town Mr. Gibert continued his silk culture until the opening years of the nineteenth century.[46]

The cultivation of silk was never a financial success in South Carolina. Either the proprietors or the provincial government, or both, with each newly arrived colony of French, repeated their proposals for silk culture, basing them on the theory of cheap labor among the female portion of the newcomers. They advanced the claim that the women and girls could do the work necessary to keep the worms cared for in addition to their regular routine work on the plantations. But each group soon learned that more money could be made with equal labor in other pursuits.[47] For this reason the early arrivals of Huguenots laid it aside when rice was introduced. They even stopped raising it for their own use because by their profits from rice they could buy more silk than they could raise with an equal amount of labor.[48] These conditions drove the industry into the hands of the well-to-do and the extremely wealthy classes. They could afford to raise silk for the sake of enjoying a pastime and the love of novelty, and not, as the poor were forced to do, as an economic venture. This is why it was pursued almost continuously until after the American Revolution. Charles Pinckney, a wealthy

[45] MS Col. Doc. S. C., XXXII. 160, Bull to Hillsboro.

[46] *Ibid.*, 21, 404.

[47] MS Col. Doc. S. C., XXXII. 396-8.

[48] MS Col. Doc. S. C., XXXII. 396, Wm. Bull to Earl of Hillsborough, Charles Town, Nov. 30, 1770. "Silk is a very flattering article as it is of great value. It is raised here of the finest sort with great ease and in great perfection. The only objection which occurs to me against its being carried to such a degree as will render it a considerable branch of commerce, is as singular as it is true, viz. the great prosperity of our Province. If we turn our eyes to those countries where it is made in abundance, Spain, the South of France, Italy, Turkey, China, there labour is very cheap, in our Province it is very dear."

planter and a member of the Council, in 1755 presented to the Prince of Wales at Leicester House a piece of silk damask, the raw silk of which was raised on his own plantation, and dyed with indigo raised in South Carolina.[49] Gabriel Manigault never lost his interest in silk.

The British government was certainly aware of the tendency to drop silk from the list of industries in this southern province, for repeatedly new encouragement was offered to revive it. In 1749, after continued urging,[50] the duty on raw silk was removed.[51] In 1755, the "Society of London for the encouragement of Arts, Manufactures and Commerce" offered a prize of ten pounds sterling to the person who would plant and properly fence the largest number of white mulberry trees on his own plantation in South Carolina, before March 1, 1756. The second and third prizes were five and three pounds respectively. To the advertisement in the South Carolina *Gazette,* Hector Bérénger de Beaufain, perhaps the foremost merchant and planter of Purryburg, subscribed his name.[52] After Georgia began silk culture in earnest she was held up as an example to South Carolina planters of the possibilities of the industry, it being shown that in the year of 1758 Georgia was able to raise 7,040 pounds of the raw product. Savannah, the central market, received 10,000 pounds for export annually.[53] By mixing wool with silk in the manufacture of shawls and rugs, the Huguenots in South Carolina attracted attention abroad. Their cloth factory was known widely enough to receive mention in such French literature as Dumont's *History of Commerce.*[54] The factory was evidently suppressed by the

[49] London letter in *S. C. Gaz.,* Apr. 10, 1755.
[50] MS Col. Doc. S. C., VI. 289-90.
[51] *Ibid.,* 24, 158.
[52] *S. C. Gaz.,* Sept. 19, 1755.
[53] *Ibid.,* June 9, 1759; Anderson, *Commerce,* III. 309.
[54] See Georges Marie Butel Dumont: *Histoire et Commerce des Colonies Anglaises dans L'Amerique Septentrionale,* Nouvelle édition, A la Haye, 1755, 292-3.

"Quelques familles s'y sont addonées à élever des vers à soye. Les profits qui ont été faits dans cette partie de l'économie rurale n'ont pas jus qu'a' ici invité le plus grandnombre á les imiter. Il y en a pourtant

mother country, for not until late in the eighteenth century did the British authorities become willing to submit to a radical reversal of policy and allow a factory for spinning silk to be erected in Charles Town. And then it was with the evident motive of reëncouraging the production of a commodity continually prone to be driven into the background by economic reversals. In spite of the great importation of negroes, the price of labor was kept above the point where silk culture would pay adequate returns. In 1769 Parliament placed a bounty on silk production[55] in South Carolina, but it was too late. As a leading industry in the province it was doomed.

From the earliest history of Carolina the Huguenots displayed a lively interest in the production of wine.

Though the grape grew wild there its artificial culture was begun by the Huguenots during the early years of the life of the province, its cultivation being made the reason for one of the first bounties recorded by the proprietors in London.[56] Namely, on March 29, 1683, Francis Derowsery received a gift of 800 acres of land "because he had with great industry applied himself to the propagation of wine and other things in Carolina".[57] This was a gift outright from the proprietors. Likewise James Boyd had planted a large vineyard in Carolina before December, 1694, for on the twenty-seventh the proprietors granted him 3,000 acres "because he had been at great charges in endeavoring the establishment of a vintage and several considerable productions".[58] By this time the transplanting of native grapevines

qui en ont jusqu' à 40 & 50 livres sterling (920 & 1,150 livres tournois) de la récolte de leurs soyes, sans que leurs autres travaux en ayent souffert, parce qu'on occupe au government des vers les Négrillons & Négrites qui seroient incapables de foire rien de plus profitable. Cette soye s'employe dans le pays mêlée avec de la laine. On en fait des droguets. Outre cette manufacture, les habitans de la Caroline ont une fabrique de toiles que les Protestans François qui s'y sont réfugiés y ont portée."

[55] Governor Johnson's speech to Assembly, MS Assembly Jrnl., 1769-71, 12.

[56] MS Col. Doc. S. C., I. 238.

[57] *Ibid.*

[58] *Ibid.*, III. 150.

had already been begun by the Huguenots, whose vineyards had contained the "noblest and excellentest vines of Europe".[59] There is, however, little evidence that they took much interest in it after 1700 until the arrival of Lewis Gervais and Lewis St. Pierre, who planted extensive wine gardens in the back country. St. Pierre returned to England and France to secure the best plants that the market afforded and to hire specialists in vine culture for his grape farms on the Savannah River.[60] Here the growth of the vine reached its greatest success.

Lewis Gervais, after six years of industry and painstaking effort is reported to have cultivated a vine that needed no supports, neither of sticks nor frames. It was wound on the ground and piled up in such a way as to form a close bower, or as the French called it a chapele, whereunder it shaded its own ground and thereby retained the moisture.[61] By this method, according to DeBrahm,[62] who was British Surveyor for the southern district of North America, the blossom of the grapes was shielded from vernal frost and the grapes were guarded against violent summer heat. He says that by the method formerly in vogue "the vine was winded on sticks or frames and deprived the soil of its moisture so that the stoks of the grapes withered and consequently shut the channels of the sap, which after the next rain, rising found no passage into the wine berries, they of course separated from their stoks and dropped off for which disorder of the vine no remedy could be prescribed in former times, so that New Bordeaux is justly intitl'd to that merit, which much be allowed a great acquisition in the culture of wine upon that extensive continent of America, where a 60 years experimental inquiry has met with no more discovery than to condemn America as not possessed with the faculty to produce wine."

[59] Rivers, *Sketch*, 174.
[60] Weston, *Doc.*, 167.
[61] *Ibid.*
[62] *Ibid.*

In Hillsboro Township St. Pierre hoped to exploit the most extensive vineyard scheme in America. In addition to his own large holdings he wanted every planter to have at least one-half acre of grape vines. With this in mind he petitioned the Governor and Assembly of South Carolina for an appropriation.[63] A committee, after examining his proposals recommended their adoption, but the Assembly, though anxious to encourage the work already begun by Pierre, refused to appropriate the necessary funds. Eighteen months later Pierre secured 3,000 plants from abroad, but 2,000 of them died before reaching their destination. From the Island of Madeira he received 1574 plants, all of which thrived.[64] Encouraged by the success of a neighboring German settler, who made 80 gallons of wine for which he received a prize of 50 guineas from the *London Society for the Encouragement of Arts, Agriculture and Commerce* and by a gold medal given to St. Pierre himself by the same society for his skill in making wine and by the fact that the climate of New Bordeaux was about the same as at Marseilles with a soil "infinitely superior",[65] St. Pierre felt that the success of the vine in South Carolina was guaranteed. Certain of success he bargained for 160,000 plants from French gardens and then, having spent his entire fortune in the project, except a patrimony in Normandy, and finding himself embarrassed on account of lack of funds, he sought aid from the British government to the extent of £40,000.[66] In his petition "to the public" he expressed his willingness to mortgage all his lands and chattels in South Carolina; proposed the incorporation of a joint-stock company which should sell shares at £50 each with a guaranteed interest at 6%; and agreed, when the required £40,000 were forth-

[63] MS copy of St. Pierre's Plan for the Cultivation of the Vine, etc., at New Bordeaux, written in 1771. Library of Congress. This is probably a copy of either a printed poster circulated in England or a newspaper account, done on English paper and with great care.

[64] *Ibid.*

[65] *Ibid.*

[66] *Ibid.*, and MS Col. Doc. S. C., XXX. 101 f.

coming, to purchase the negroes, machinery, and other things necessary for the success of the enterprise. To strengthen his appeal he secured the support of the Earl of Hillsborough and other men of influence in England.

In reading the narrative in the government documents and in the accounts of contemporary travelers of the events just outlined, one can hardly refrain from marveling that wine culture failed so signally in South Carolina. In the case of silk it was clearly a case of the interference of economic laws operating against the success of silk. That was not true in the case of wine. In trying to find the reason for the failure, one looks in vain in contemporary accounts; futile search is made in the records of travelers. Still it is hard to dismiss the subject from the mind with the supposition that the oncoming war was a determining factor or that the business methods of St. Pierre were unproductive of results. We cannot dispute the fact that St. Pierre failed to secure the necessary financial aid from English capitalists and the British Government. He returned to South Carolina late in 1772, after associating himself with one Cluny. A disagreement between them before leaving England resulted in a separation, and though Cluny and St. Pierre both returned to Charles Town, Cluny forsook the vintage proposition to accept the post of Lieutenant in a small fort in the back country at a salary of £30 a year.[67] But these things do not explain why the vine project failed there. As far as extant published or written material is concerned only one clue has been found. It is in a brief public statement made several decades after St. Pierre's fruitless attempts. The author of the statement attributed it to the persistent interference by the French government both by bribery and persuasion. The statements were made in an address by a now unknown author, before the Agricultural Society of South Carolina, at its annual meeting held November 7, 1798.[68] The speaker

[67] *Ibid.* See also Memorial on *Practicability of growing Vineyards in S. C.*, etc., 1798. Library Pa. Hist. Society, and *C. T. Library Soc. Pamphlets*, vol. XIX.

[68] *Ibid.*, "Memorial."

discussed the practicability of growing vineyards in the state of South Carolina. He quoted the expert opinions of prominent Frenchmen, such as Raynal and the Marquis Chastellux, who had visited America and had declared conditions in South Carolina to be equally favorable with those of France. But the French government long before having felt the sting of England's colonial encroachments on her industries and doubly humiliated because the very ones she once had nursed at the mother-breast were now beyond the seas carrying on activities that threatened the industrial life of France, bitterly resented these conditions. Raynal, a French journalist, writing before the American Revolution protested strongly against England's intentions to introduce the vine into Carolina, declaring that the field should be left to France alone. That is not all. The French government interfered, for Brissot,[69] in an account of his travels in America states that he had visited the vineyards of M. Legaux, a Frenchman and a refugee for conscience' sake, who had been absent from France for a number of years. This published information alarmed the French government. Orders in secret were dispatched to the French minister, then resident in Philadelphia, to take action in the matter. Legaux, by his flight from France, according to the French laws, forfeited his citizenship and his property and ordinarily could not return to France without risking his life. Instructions were sent to the French minister in Philadelphia that if Legaux would destroy all of the vineyards he had planted and return to France, the French government would restore his citizenship, return all of his confiscated property, defray the expenses necessary for his return to France and make him a present of $3,500.[70] Besides it was reported in South Carolina that Lord Hillsborough, then "British Minister to the American Department", who had so graciously aided St. Pierre in the early part of his attempts, was induced by the

[69] Chapter 19, quoted in *Ibid.*, p. 6. See also *Broadsides,* VI. no. 799 and no. 821; Map Of. 6976, in Pennsylvania Hist. Soc.
[70] *Ibid.*

French Government for a consideration of £50,000 to withdraw his support from St. Pierre and to discountenance his efforts.[71]

If these allegations are true it is not strange that a single Frenchman, with this overwhelming opposition, was unable to make his project succeed. It is possible, however, that in spite of these adverse conditions, with the assistance of Lewis Gervais, Pierre's equal, if not his superior in vine culture, South Carolina would have become rich in grape gardens had not the untimely death of St. Pierre, who was killed in an engagement against the Indians, brought an end to the entire affair.

Thus it is seen that the alleged reason for the failure of the vine in South Carolina among the French Protestants lies in the interference of France.

So great was the promise of grape cultivation that it pushed to the rear the possibilities of the olive oil enterprise. Olive trees were imported from the West Indies and grew luxuriously, but this new possibility was also displaced by more profitable employments.[72]

The successful staple triumvirate among the Huguenots was rice, indigo, and cotton, not silk, wine, and oil, as the proprietors had planned. Each in its turn claimed the field. Rice was introduced first. Indigo by 1750 became its rival and to a large extent displaced it. Indigo held the place of ascendency, until finally, coeval with the American Revolution, cotton became foremost. To what extent the French Protestants pursued these industries is of course unknown, but on entering the colony they seem to have begun the culture of rice, at least on a small scale, for the wills and other records in the probate court of Charleston contain many references to the facts.[73] Rice was grown there as early as 1684. The warrants of land show that Landgrave Smith

[71] *Ibid.*
[72] Rivers, *Sketch,* 174.
[73] The plantation of Daniel Huger was named *Rice Hope.* See his will in MS Pr. Ct. Rcd., 1752-56, 282.

arrived in the colony on the tenth of July of that year and that at that time rice was already being grown in Carolina.[74] These facts indicate that the stories that have gone their perennial rounds with reference to the introduction of rice about 1702 are principally myths.[75]

The Huguenots were brought into the limelight in the very beginning by the invention of the "Pendulum Engine" by Peter Jacob Guerrard, one of their number. During the first decade the expense of threshing, winnowing and husking rice was one of the principal barriers to its success.[76] By the old method the grain was beaten from the straw by the use of a flail and with a fork the straw was drawn aside. Finally the adhesive husk was removed from the kernel by the use of a mortar and pestle—the mortar as a rule a hollow stump, the pestle a wooden club. This laborious and expensive process, according to Ramsay, often crippled the strength of the men and destroyed the fertility of the women therein employed, resulting in disease and death. All this was revolutionized by the use of the Guerrard machine.[77] The Act of September 26, 1691 conferred honors on Guerrard and gave him the exclusive right to its manufacture and sale, because as the act recites,[78] "It doth much better and in lesse time and labour huske rice than any other hertofore hath been used in the province". The Guerrard machine, though crude and clumsy, served its day and purpose by forming the mechanical basis for later inventions and improvements, notably those of Peter Villepontoux, DeNeale,[78a] Francis Gracia[79] and George Veitch.[80] Peter Villepontoux introduced his machine to the public in 1732[81] and

[74] Salley, *Nar. and Doc. of Early Carolina*, 69.
[75] Ramsay, *Hist. S. C.*, II. 200; Anderson, *Commerce*, III. 15.
[76] MS Col. Doc. S. C., XX. 338. Richard West's letter to the Commissioners of Trade and Plantations, Oct. 25, 1722.
[77] *S. C. Gaz.*, July 21, 1733; Ramsay, *Hist. S. C.*, II. 207. Ramsay's statements are probably overdrawn.
[78] Cooper, *Statutes*, II. 63.
[78a] Ramsay, *Hist. S. C.*, II. 207.
[79] MS Assembly Jrnl., MS Col. Doc. S. C., 1728-33, 1043.
[80] MS Col. Doc. S. C., XXXII. 33.
[81] MS Council Jrnl., 1730-4, 246; MS Assembly Jrnl., 1728-33, 888.

the year following received a patent from the Assembly[82] which in 1736 was renewed for seven years.[83] He took into partnership with himself one Samuel Holmes, to whom was assigned the major part of the work of building the machines.[84] The details of the mechanical construction are not known today beyond the bare facts presented in the advertisements in the *South Carolina Gazette,* in which the inventor sets forth that the following amount of lumber was necessary for the construction of each machine:[85]

> "Oak plank, 100 feet, 5 inches thick
> 4 pieces pine, 12 feet long, 6 inches square
> 12 pieces pine 7 feet long, 22 x 18 inches
> 2 pieces pine 30 feet long 7 x 5 inches
> middle post 8 feet long and 18 inches in diameter."

This consignment of lumber had to be provided by the person purchasing a machine. Villepontoux then supplied the iron work and the skill in erecting it. His regular price was £60.[86] Though with the aid of four horses it cleaned 2,000 pounds of rice a day, the machine was hard to sell. The inventor was a persistent advertiser and at certain seasons of the year offered it at half price.[87] In May, 1734, two years after its introduction, there was only one of Villepontoux manufacture in use in the tide-water section and it was on James Island.[88] Its price was against it; £60 even in 1734 was not a small sum for a planter to pay. Besides, it could easily be copied and rebuilt as much less cost.[89] By September, 1734, the original machine had been so greatly improved

[82] *S. C. Gaz.,* July 21, 1733.
[83] *Ibid.,* Aug. 21, 1736.
[84] *Ibid.*
[85] *S. C. Gaz.,* May 18, 1734.
[86] *Ibid.*
[87] *Ibid.,* May 18, 1734.
[88] *Ibid.,* May 18, 1734. This conclusion is reached by the fact that Mr. Villepontoux states in his advertisement that there is a machine in operation for inspection on James Island. Had there been one in or about Charles Town, he would not have failed to mention it, for James Island was inconvenient to reach and inaccessible except by boat across the Ashley River.
[89] *S. C. Gaz.,* Aug. 21, 1736.

that 5,000 pounds could be cleaned with ease in a working day by the use of two horses, and much better than with mortar and pestle,[90] while if four horses were employed the machine would turn out 1,000 pounds an hour without breaking the rice.[91]

Rice was a profitable staple. It was in great demand in Europe and in America.[92] It yielded as high as 50 bushels to the acre even in the early years. By 1748, in spite of the crude methods of agriculture and rice harvesting and the close rivalry indigo was offering as a competitor, rice-land was doubling in value every three or four years.[93] With the use of slaves, 2,200 pounds per hand could be raised in a season in addition to the necessary provisions and the fodder for the plantation.[94] At that time the fields were weeded by slaves who were compelled to stand in a stooping position in pools of stagnant water.

This part of the rice culture was revolutionized by Gideon Dupont, also a French Protestant, of Goose Creek, who about the time of the American Revolution discovered the water-culture method of tending rice.[95] In 1783 he asked for a patent on his discovery.[96] Rice culture had been in a state of constant improvement. First came its transfer from the highlands to the swamps,[97] which gave utility and therefore value to thousands of lowland areas theretofore valueless. Then came the water culture of the grain. It is well known that the very conditions that are favorable to rice growth also favor the growth of water grass and weeds. These, until the Dupont method was introduced, were destroyed by slaves standing sometimes loin-deep in water. Gideon Dupont pointed out that by overflowing the fields at

[90] *S. C. Gaz.*, Sept. 14, 1734.
[91] *Ibid.*
[92] Ramsay, *Hist. S. C.*, 205.
[93] MS Col. Doc. S. C., XXIII. 211 f.
[94] *Ibid.*, IV. 189; XXIII. 341; IX. 89 f.
[95] Ramsay, *Hist. S. C.*, II. 206.
[96] *Ibid.*
[97] Ford (Americanus), *The Constitutionalist*, etc., C. T. Library Society Miscel. Tracts, no. 4 and no. 8, p. 23.

stated seasons of the year the grass and weeds were killed, while at the same time the rice flourished thereby. Owing to the practicability of the method it sprang into general use at once.

Reports in 1744 show that rice was in a measure falling from favor, because it was becoming unprofitable. Numerous planters, ruined by the low price of rice,[98] were turning with hope to indigo and silk.[99] This decline was due to the high freight rates, expensive insurance and other excessive charges in trade, occasioned in part by foreign war and not necessarily by domestic conditions.[100] Indigo and rice were the chief sources from which were poured the streams of wealth into the pockets of French planters during the prosperous period, 1745 to 1775. Indigo was quickly seized upon by the Huguenots when introduced as a commodity for export,[101] as is shown by the numerous advertisements in the *Gazette* of the period and the inventories of property.[102] It was due partly to the fact that indigo was favored in trade by Great Britain much more than were rice and silk. She used it in large quantities in her textile industries. Besides, France, her commercial rival, to whom she was paying £200,000 sterling a year for indigo, had a monopoly of its production in the West Indies.[103]

Ramsay attributes the introduction of indigo into South Carolina to Eliza Lucas,[104] the mother of Major General Charles C. Pinckney. But Governor West's instructions (1674) included detailed stipulations for the introduction of indigo in South Carolina from Barbadoes. It was not introduced until much later as a commodity of general

[98] MS Col. Doc. S. C., XXII. 273.

[99] Letter to Committee on Trade in Assembly, Dec. 8, 1744, *S. C. Gaz.*, Dec. 10, 1744.

[100] *S. C. Gaz.*, Dec. 10, 1744.

[101] Indigo for home use had been made in S. C. as early as 1682. See Wilson's *Account*.

[102] *Canadian Archives*, II. 1202; MS Ravenel Rcd. Bks.; *S. C. Gaz.*, Feb. 6, 1755; Oct. 22, 1753; Aug. 25, 1757.

[103] Schaper, *Sectionalism in S. C.*, 291.

[104] Ramsay, *Hist. S. C.*, II. 209; Holbrook (Editor), *Journal and Letters of Eliza Lucas*, 1850. Library of Congress.

promise.[105] If Eliza Lucas gave the first impulse to its general introduction, Andrew Deveaux, a Frenchman, supplied the original skill and industry. Indigo grew wild in South Carolina.[106] Miss Lucas observing that and, having raised some of it on her father's plantation, sent to Montserrat, through her father, for an expert. This expert, Cromwell by name, repenting of his bargain to go to Carolina for fear that he would thereby hurt his own industry in the Indies, though he was paid a large bonus, deceived his mistress by using too much lime in his experiments,[107] thereby spoiling the results. Miss Lucas, suspicious of his conduct, employed Andrew Deveaux,[108] who discovered Cromwell's duplicity and aided in perfecting the process. It seems that Deveaux, either by virtue of previous experiments in this line in South Carolina, or in France, had gained a knowledge of the art. With the aid of his French associates he made the Carolina indigo, much to the satisfaction of the proprietors, the rival of indigo raised in France. Deveaux thereby became the provincial expert and trainer in the art of raising and extracting indigo.[109] In 1747-8, the export product amounted to 134,118 pounds.[109a] In 1754, it reached 216,924 pounds.[110] The product, in 1774, amounted to about a million pounds, worth £250,000 sterling.[111] Indigo became a general favorite among the French planters. Fortunes were rapidly made by its cultivation.[112] The British Government soon put a bounty upon it to encourage its exportation, and Moses Lindo, a London Jew, went to Charles Town with the express purpose of buying it directly from the planters and merchants. He made large consignments to London

[105] Cooper, *Statutes,* II. 78.
[106] Holmes, *American Annals* (1748), II. 167; (Wilson's *Account*).
[107] Ramsay, *Hist. S. C.,* II. 210.
[108] See Lucas, Letter; Philips, Industrial Hist. Doc., I. 165, MS in S. C. Library Society Coll. Journal and Letters of Eliza Lucas.
[109] *S. C. Gaz.,* Dec. 2, 1745.
[109a] Wm. DeBrahm, in Weston's *Doc.,* p. 88.
[110] Holmes, *American Annals,* II. 204.
[111] MS Col. Doc. S. C., XXXIV. 204.
[112] Gregg, *Old Cheraws,* 112.

brokers.[113] Lindo invested £120,000 currency in the business in South Carolina, besides £30,000 in prize goods and other commodities. By Thomas Boone in 1762, he was appointed "Surveyor and Inspector General of Indigo in South Carolina."[114] The principal men among the South Carolina Frenchmen with whom he did business were: Thomas Legare, James Laurens, Abraham Michau, Henry Bourquin, Peter Legare, Jr., Richard Benison, Jacob Motte, Jr., John and Edward Neufville, Boyd and Brailsford,[115] Arthur Peronneau, and Benjamin Guerrard. In St. Stephen's Parish the Biggin Swamp land was occupied early by the St. Juliens, Marions, Mazÿcks, Ravenels and others who grew rich in the cultivation of indigo, while in Santee and other sections Arthur Peronneau, Francis de la Gras,[116] John Guerrard, Thomas Legare, Abraham Michau, Henry Bourquin, Peter Legare, Jacob Motte and others became the leading planters and merchants who raised or exported it.[117]

As in the case of rice, silk and cotton, samples of indigo were sent to London for expert examination, where in 1745 it was pronounced as good as that grown in France.[118] Planters doubled their capital every three or four years on indigo. It proved a greater financial benefit to South Carolina than did the mines of Mexico and Peru to their owners.[119]

Less than a score of years after its introduction as a profitable industry, Thomas Mellichamp, a prominent Swiss-French planter revolutionized the culture of indigo by the introduction of his new method of the growth and extraction of the dye stuff, for the discovery of which the Assembly made him a special gift of £1,000 currency.[120]

[113] *S. C. Gaz.*, Dec. 16, 1756.
[114] Commission, MS Pr. Ct. Rcd., 1763-7, 120.
[115] *Ibid.*, Dec. 24, 1772.
[116] *Ibid.*, Feb. 7, 1746.
[117] *Ibid.*, Dec. 24, 1772. In 1748 Great Britain placed a bounty of 6d per pound on indigo exported directly to England. (Holmes, *Am. Annals*, II. 178.)
[118] *S. C. Gaz.*, Apr. 1, 1745.
[119] McCrady, *Hist. S. C.*, 1719-1776, 270.
[120] *S. C. Gaz.*, Aug. 23, 1760; *S. C. & Ga. Almanac* (Tobler), 1776.

While at the same time the back country was being developed in 1761, some of the rich tidewater planters made plans to extend the great indigo plantation system into the newly opened region. Henry Laurens and John Lewis Gervais, both of Huguenot descent, obtained 13,200 acres of land, near Ninety-Six, where they planned to lay out a great indigo plantation. The introduction of chemical dyes on the European market, however, in addition to a combination of other economic and political factors, forced indigo from the center of the stage and made cotton the leading staple during the years that follow.[121] Rice and indigo claimed the ascendency until a short time before the Revolution. Cotton then made its appearance and took its place as a profitable staple.[122] The several causes that coöperated to accomplish cotton's supremacy over indigo were: (1) The loss of the English bounty on indigo. (2) The development of the cotton gin, which stimulated cotton culture and introduced a formidable rival to indigo. (3) The fact that to place a bale of cotton on the market was much easier than to ship a barrel of indigo. (4) The fact that indigo required skilled and technical oversight and an ever-vigilant care, while cotton did not. (5) The fact that in the process of extracting the dye stuff from the indigo, vapors, injurious to the health of the planters, rose from the vats and drying sheds. (6) The introduction of chemical dyes into European markets.

Though the export of indigo in 1775 was 1,150,662 pounds, cotton became the leading staple after the war.[123]

[121] See D. D. Wallace, in *The South in the Building of the Nation,* V. 181.

[122] Seabrook, *Memoirs on Cotton.* An item in the contemporaneous press presents an illustration of the rapid development of cotton manufacturing in S. C. "We are well informed that a planter to the Southward who 3 months ago had not a negro that could either spin or weave has now 30 hands constantly employed from whom he gets 120 yards of good wearable stuff made of woolen and cotton every week. He had only one white woman to instruct the negroes in spinning and one white man to instruct in weaving. Soon he will clothe all of his own negroes and supply neighbors. This is a most effectual way of lessening the present exhorbitant prices of cloth." *S. C. American General Gazette,* Jan. 30, 1777.

[123] Wallace, in *The South in the Building of the Nation,* V. 181.

CHAPTER X

EMINENT AND THRIFTY HUGUENOT FAMILIES

That the original Huguenots and their French Protestant descendants were aggressive and thrifty industrial leaders can not be disputed. Enough has been said to substantiate this, but a number of other examples claim fuller attention in this connection. In some cases it is difficult to classify their activities, since they frequently made ventures in several directions as did Gabriel Manigault, who was a merchant, a trader, a broker, a brewer, a mechanic, and a factor.

Posterity need not deceive itself concerning the greatness of such a name as Hector Bérénger de Beaufain. He went to South Carolina probably with the Purry group, but settled in Charles Town after a few years' residence in Granville County. He was born in Orange, France, in 1697 and arrived in South Carolina in 1733. There he lived until his death in 1766.[1] For twenty-four years he was Collector of Customs in South Carolina, to which office he was commissioned in 1742.[2] In 1747 he was appointed to membership in the Governor's Council, but resigned in the thick of the political disturbances of 1756.[3] He was a Fellow of the Royal Society of London, and though a foreigner, was "master of learned languages" and a profound critic of the English language, a man of unshaken integrity and of benevolent disposition.[4] In 1740 he was admitted to membership in St. Andrew's Society of Charles Town, a fraternal, mutual organization, founded by the Huguenots and others to relieve the suffering and distress of the poor.[5] In 1753 he advanced £2,500 for the relief of poor Protestants then arriving in South Carolina in large numbers.[6] His public

[1] *S. C. Gaz.*, Oct. 31, 1766.
[2] Commission, MS Council Jrnl., 1741-9, 19.
[3] MS Col. Doc. S. C., XXVII. 151; XXII. 250.
[4] *S. C. Gaz.*, Dec. 13, 1773.
[5] List of members, MS Records, St. Andrew's Society.
[6] Cooper, *Statutes*, IV. 5.

spirit and his interest in religious education are manifest in patronage by subscription of the two-volume set of published sermons by the Rev. Richard Clark.[7] He was an honored member and patron of the Charles Town Library Society until his death.[8] His will bequeaths the income from his pew in St. Michael's to the use of the poor. To the poor he also left £500 currency, together with his house and its furnishings. How extensive his wealth was, is not known, but his will disposes of £2,600, a library, a home and its furnishings, unspecified amounts of land, an annuity of £50 to the mother of his nephew, [——] de Beaufain, and an annuity to his sister, Clodre de Beaufain, also possessions in England and in South Carolina.[9]

George Baudoin was an example of thrifty Huguenot blood. He died shortly after reaching Carolina, but left property in England and in America.[10]

Arnaud Bruneau Escuyer Sieur de la Chabocière was one of the early settlers at Wanthee, near Jamestown, on the Santee. At the time of his death, in 1694, he owned more than 3,000 acres of land in addition to large quantities of personal property. There, with his son, Paul Bruneau Sieur de Revedoux and his grandson, Henry Bruneau, he had settled in 1690. These were persons "of quality" who were driven from their rich estates ten miles from Poitiers, in France, probably carrying with them some wealth.[11] The 3,000 acres mentioned in his will were granted to Arnaud Bruneau in recognition of services rendered to the proprietors and for recognized merits.[12] But other property was also owned by the father. Like others of his associates at this early period he expressed in his will the hope of a restoration of the Reformed religion in France.[13]

[7] List of subscribers at £2-3-0 per set, in *S. C. Gaz.*, Dec. 8, 1759.
[8] *S. C. Gaz.*, Apr. 23, 1750, *passim*.
[9] Will, "Gleanings from England", *S. C. H. & G. Mag.*, XI. 132. Grants of land to him total 2,800 acres in Granville County alone. See MS *Grants*, II. 41, 42, 213, 252.
[10] MS Pr. Ct. Rcd., 1671-1727, 49.
[11] MS Pr. Ct. Rcd., 1671-1727.
[12] MS Col. Doc. S. C., II. 120. Ms Sec'y. Rcds., 1685-1712, 13 and 18.
[13] Will, MS Pr. Ct. Rcd., 1671-1727, 275. MS Pr. Ct. Rcd., 1692-3, 172.

Another family, in interest similar to the St. Julien's,[14] deserves attention here. It is the family of de Chastaigner Seigneurs de Cramahé (or Cramahais) and de Lisle, also of the nobility. Their prominence in the Huguenot colony in Dublin is shown in nearly fifty entries in the nonconformist registers of that place.[15] In the register of the Peter Street Church, Mademoiselle Charlotte Chastaigner de Cramahé is noted as godmother to a child of M. Daniel Belrieu, Baron de Virazel. Three brothers, Cramahé, De L'Isle, and Des Roches, arranged to escape from France at the repeal of the Nantes Edict. The two former succeeded and settled in England, but Des Roches was detected, seized, flogged, mistreated, plundered, and cast into prison. After twenty-seven months of confinement he was banished. Two other brothers, Henry Augustus Sieur de Cramahé and Alexandre Thésée, Sieur de Lisle, went to South Carolina. They were the sons of Roche Chastaigner de Cramahé of the ancestral chateau, five miles from La Rochelle.[16] Henry Augustus was denizened in London, April 9, 1767, and is listed as Henry Augustus Chastaigne de Cramahé.[17] Alexander Thésée Sieur de Lisle (alias Thésée Castaigner) was denizened March 5, 1685-6.[18] He is found in London as early as 1681.[19] In South Carolina these gentlemen immediately took conspicuous positions in provincial business affairs and politics. Alexander is found in the Assembly[20] as early as 1693 and Henry Augustus appears on the Governor's Council.[21] The name of an elder brother, Hector, was in 1698 on the list of applications for naturalization in Dublin.[22]

[14] See Index.

[15] *Pub. H. S. London.*

[16] *T. H. S. S. C.*, XII. 29.

[17] *Pub. H. S. London*, XVIII. 177 and 184. Alexander Thésée de Chastaigner, Sieur de Lisle and his wife, Elizabeth Buretel, went to Carolina in 1685. He was denizened in March of the same year and must have been naturalized in Carolina, for in 1693 he was a member of the Assembly. He died in 1707. See *Coll. S. C. Hist. Soc.*, I. 114-9. MS Assembly Jrnl., 1693; Archives, Colonial Dames, nos. 62 and 114.

[18] *Ibid.*, XVIII. 184.

[19] *Ibid.*, XVIII. 177.

[20] Cooper, *List of French Protestants in England*, 40.

[21] MS Assembly Jrnl., 1692, 3.

[22] *Pub. H. S. London*, XVIII. 350.

It is proper that special mention be made of Benjamin d'Harriette, a French Protestant merchant, and his relation to South Carolina history.[23] The editor of the *South Carolina Gazette* styled him "an eminent merchant". The home of his widow in 1760 was one of the most elaborately furnished houses in South Carolina.[24] Benjamin d'Harriette was one of the refugees who went to South Carolina from New York early in the eighteenth century. The will of Mrs. Phoebe Outman shows that her daughter Ann was then (1732) the wife of Benjamin d'Harriette, of Charles Town, formerly of New York.[25] The will of Benjamin d'Harriette, Sr., a New York merchant, shows him to have been a man of wealth and refinement. Much of the large estate in the possession of Benjamin d'Harriette, Jr., while resident in Charles Town, was inherited from his father.[26] His former wife, Ann Smith, died on July 12, 1754.[27] On October 16, of the same year, he was married to Mrs. Martha Fowler, the widow of James Fowler.[28] Mr. d'Harriette was probably in Charles Town as early as 1726, at least a bill of sale to him of a negro boy is recorded March 1, 1726.[29] In 1736 an advertisement appears in the *Gazette* stating that he desires an overseer for his plantation on John's Island.[30] The will of his father mentions him as being in Charles Town then, that is, in 1741.[31] His advertisements in the *Gazette* in 1739 show that he was then a merchant on Union Street.[32] In 1752 he was in partnership with John McCall, engaged in the business of importing white servants and slaves of all sorts.[33] Benjamin d'Harriette died in February, 1756.[34] On

[23] *Coll. N. Y. Hist. Soc.,* (Wills) I. 346.
[24] MS Pr. Ct. Rcd., 1758-61, 314.
[25] *Coll. N. Y. Hist. Soc.,* (Wills) III. 55 and 331.
[26] *Ibid.,* III. 331.
[27] Tomb Stone, St. Philip's Church-Yard, Charleston.
[28] *S. C. Gaz.,* Oct. 23, 1755.
[29] MS Pr. Ct. Rcd., 1726-7, 240.
[30] *S. C. Gaz.,* Dec. 18, 1736.
[31] *Coll. N. Y. Hist. Soc.,* (Wills) III. 331.
[32] *S. C. Gaz.,* May 26, 1739.
[33] *S. C. Gaz.,* Oct. 3, 1752.
[34] His tomb-stone has Feb. 17. The *S. C. Gaz.,* Feb. 19, 1756, has Feb. 15.

February 26, 1756, his executors, Gabriel Manigault,[35] Alexander Broughton, and Peter Manigault, advertised for sale at auction part of the estate of the deceased, including 1,070 acres of land on John's Island, twelve miles from Charles Town, hogs, cattle, tools, etc. On March 31 were sold a lot in Charles Town, on the corner of Meeting and Queen Streets, 200 x 150 feet, with two houses on it, a lot on the Bay, 25 x 25 feet, and a lot on Union Street, 44 x 205 feet.[36] Mr. d'Harriette left a considerable estate of personal property.[37] His codicil provides that his wife Martha, be given the household furniture, a suit of mourning, seven negroes, and £10,000 currency in addition to undivided portions of the estate. Among the French Protestants of South Carolina he was one of the most generous contributors to benevolent causes. The following amounts are bequeathed in his will: £1,000 to the French Protestant Church of Charles Town; £500 to the "Brick Meeting House"; £500 to the Baptist Society of Protestant Dissenters; £3,000 to the South Carolina Society; £1,000 to the Church Wardens and Vestry of St. Philip's; £1,000 to the French Protestant Society of New York City. To friends and relatives he bequeathed no less than £24,000. Among them he remembered his friend Gabriel Manigault with £100; and the Rev. Richard Clarke, Rector of St. Philip's, and the Rev. John Tetard, Minister of the French Protestant Church, of Charles Town, with £100 each. To Thomas Grimball he bequeathed his wearing apparel, gold watch, silver-hilted sword, his gun, and all of his French books. His humane sympathies are evidenced in the fact that he also made provision for the freedom of four of his faithful slaves and the care of a number of others. Though a public spirited man, aggressive and able, he was apparently not a money hoarder nor a grasping money maker. The *South Carolina Gazette* was in its obituary comments usually conservative and not given to flattery. As a

[35] *S. C. Gaz.*, Feb. 26, 1756.
[36] *Ibid.*
[37] MS Pr. Ct. Rcd., 1753-56, 445; *S. C. Gaz.*, Feb. 19, 1756.

rule it selected a leading trait of the deceased and commented briefly on it. With reference to Benjamin d'Harriette its brief though striking comment is included in these few lines: "On Sunday died Suddenly Mr. Benjamin d'Harriette, formerly an eminent Merchant of this Town, but had retired from Business some years—Knowing when he had enough".

The De Saussure family in South Carolina dates from about 1730, when Henri arrived in Charles Town from Lausanne, Switzerland and settled in the Beaufort district.[38] A grant of land to Henry De Saussure is dated March 6, 1732-3. The land was located in Purryburg, Granville County, on the Savannah River and contained 690 acres.[39] In Europe the family history dates back several centuries in Switzerland and France, where the name is prominent in Metz, Strassburg, Geneva, and Neufchatel.[40] The name is intimately bound up with the experiences of the Huguenots on both sides of the sea. Antoine de Saussure took bold and active part in the Reformation at these places. From Neufchatel the Charles Town French Church received its liturgical service. In South Carolina those bearing the name remained faithful to the doctrines and polity of the Reformed religion.

Henry De Saussure died in 1761, highly esteemed and respected. His four sons and a grandson took active part in the Revolutionary War. Louis and Thomas died on battlefields, Henry from disease. Daniel was a member of the Provincial Congress in 1775.[41] He was captured in 1778, but was exchanged. He served in the defense of Charles Town in April and May, 1780 and on the capture of the city was exiled with the St. Augustine expedition, and released in 1781. After the war, he became president of the

[38] MS Hist. De Saussure Family, by Wilmot G. De Saussure and Henry A. De Saussure, joint authors. MS in possession of Mrs. Martha De Saussure, Charleston.

[39] See MS Public Records, I. 279.

[40] *Ibid.*, Hist. De Saussure Family; Harper, Memoirs of Henry W. De Saussure. The name De Saussure is said to have been derived from the Duchy Saussure, formerly in possession of the family.

[41] MS Hist. De Saussure Family.

Charles Town Insurance Company and was a member of the Committee of Safety.[42] He served also on a commission to repair Fort Littleton.[43] He served as senator in the new government and in 1789-1790 was president of the senate.[44]

Daniel De Saussure, born April 10, 1736, at Purryburg, was one of the original trustees of Charleston College and was present at the first meeting of the Board in August, 1785.[45] He was a member of the Privy Council before the Revolution.[46] In commercial activities he was engaged forty-two years. He was respected for his industry, talents and moral integrity.[47]

Philip Gendron, though he went to South Carolina an unnaturalized alien, was popular enough there to be listed, together with two other Huguenots,[48] John A. Motte and René Ravenel, among the commissioners of the Church Act of 1706. Philip Gendron came to his new home from Marans near Rochelle, in France, about 1690, but must have been naturalized soon after reaching America. His wealth lay in fine stock, profits from which he reinvested in local commercial ventures.[49] Like many of his nationality, he was an inveterate money lender.[50] His will disposes of no land, but in it he bequeaths £10,700 to his near relatives. He left £10 to the poor of the French Church of Santee and the same amount to the poor of the French Church of Charles Town. The latter bequest was made on condition that the church remain true to the Reformed faith.[51]

Gabriel Guignard, the first of the name in Carolina, was born on the Isle of Oléron, France, in 1708. He is found

[42] Drayton, *Memoirs,* 75 and 86.
[43] *Coll. S. C. Hist. Soc.,* III. 61.
[44] MS Hist. De Saussure Family.
[45] *Catalogue of Charleston College,* 1900-1901, Historical Sketch, pp. 13-14.
[46] *S. C. Almanac,* 1785.
[47] MS Hist. De Saussure Family.
[48] Cooper, *Statutes,* II. 282 f.
[49] MS Pr. Ct. Rcd., 1722-24, 301.
[50] *T. H. S. S. C.,* XVI. 20.
[51] *Ibid.*

HENRY DE SAUSSURE
1763-1839
Director of the Mint, appointed by President George Washington. (Penned from a miniature by Fraser, in possession of Dr. Henry W. De Saussure, Charleston, S. C.)

in the South Carolina Assembly in 1737.[52] He must have accumulated considerable property, for, in accordance with a time honored custom, in recognition of those who had large accumulations of property, a street in Charles Town was named for him. In 1740 he married Frances de Liesseline. Their son, John Gabriel, was State Treasurer from 1790 to 1799. He also held the office of State Surveyor.[53]

Daniel Huger, the son of the emigrant by the same name, added to the land wealth of his father by the purchase of 4,564½ acres in several tracts, paying for them £4,693.[54] According to the inventory of his property made in 1754, he takes rank among the richest in the province, having a large estate in land, slaves, tools, etc. But his five sons were the best legacy he left. Daniel Huger, the third of the name, served as delegate to the Continental Congress, 1786-88, and was a representative at the Federal Congress, 1789-93. He died in 1761, leaving an estate of £119,501.[55] There were 452 slaves, all named in the lists. Isaac was a lieutenant in the Cherokee War and a lieutenant-colonel in 1776. In 1779 he was made a brigadier-general.[56] John, prior to the Declaration of Independence, was a member of the Assembly and after the war, Secretary of State in South Carolina. Benjamin was major of the First Regiment of riflemen and a member of the Provincial Congress. Francis was a captain in Moultrie's regiment and later a quartermaster general in the continental army.

The Legare family has several branches.[57] One appears in New England, another in South Carolina. The will of Francis Legare, of Braintree, Mass., is dated Feb. 3, 1710-11. It mentions his wife Ann and a son Solomon "now in Carolina" and a son Daniel.[58] Baird errs in his claim that

[52] *T. H. S. S. C.*, IV. 46.
[53] *Ibid.*
[54] *S. C. H. & G. Mag.*, XII. 6 f.
[55] MS Pr. Ct. Rcd., 1758-61, 598.
[56] MS Pr. Ct. Rcd., 1752-56, 282; *S. C. G. & H. Mag.*, XII. 7; Archives, Colonial Dames.
[57] *T. H. S. S. C.*, IV. 7.
[58] MS Pr. Doc. Mass., quoted in Baird, *Hug. in Am.*, II. 112.

he was one of the founders of the so-called Circular Church in Charles Town, a church of Congregational polity and Presbyterian doctrines, but independent in its life. Solomon Legare probably never lived in Charles Town. The South Carolina Solomon Legare died in November, 1774, at the age of seventy-one. The *South Carolina Gazette* and *Country Journal*[59] observed that he was a man of the "most remarkable integrity of character and undissembled piety". The burial services held in the Congregational (Circular) Church were remarkable for the fact that on this occasion for the first time the "non-consumption agreement" with reference to British goods was observed.[60] Neither gloves nor scarfs were furnished. Even the nearest relatives appeared in their usual dress with the exception that hat-bands of black ribbons were added.

Henry Le Noble was a conspicuous figure in the early political history of Carolina. Born in Paris, the son of John Le Noble and Susanna leMercier, he found it necessary to remove his ancestral limitations by becoming an English subject.[61] With his widowed mother and his three brothers, John, Peter, and James, and five sisters, Mary, Susanna, Magdalena, Charlotte, and Anne, he fled from France to England.[62] There he was naturalized June 27, 1685. So he went to Carolina vested with all of the powers of an English subject. He proved to be a man of more than ordinary powers of political leadership. Though naturalized in 1685, he does not seem to have gone to Carolina until several years later.[63] He and his wife, Katherine Le Serrurier, went to Charles Town, probably in the year 1694-5. At any rate July 13, 1695,[64] is the date of his land warrant for a 350 acre lot in Charles Town. In 1698, Lord Ashley, one of the Proprietors, residing in London, named Henry Le

[59] Nov. 22, 1774. *S. C. Gaz.*, Nov. 21, 1774.
[60] *S. C. Gaz.*, Nov. 21, 1774.
[61] *P. H. Soc. London*, XXVIII. 159-60, 172.
[62] *Ibid.*
[63] MS Council Jrnl., 1671-1721, 88; March 4.
[64] MS Land War., 1692-1712, 88.

BRIGADIER GENERAL ISAAC HUGER

1743-1797

One of the descendants of Huguenots.

(The original portrait is in the possession of John W. Huger, Esq., Montgomery, Alabama.)

Noble his Deputy in the province.[65] He was a member of the Governor's Council from 1698 to 1706. He was a Commissioner of the Church Act of 1706.[66] Like many of his French associates he anglicized his name to Noble, soon after his arrival.

Henry Le Noble was a large landowner in St. John's Berkeley and St. Stephen's.[67] but most of his life was spent in political activities in Charleston. His wife, after his death, retired to the estates in St. John's. A splendid original oil portrait of her, painted in the early part of the eighteenth century, represents her as a beautiful and fashionable woman of middle age.[68] Her will, dated January 25, 1725-6, disposes of two and one-third lots in Charles Town, several plantations, slaves, horses, promissory notes, bonds and money. How extensive the estate was cannot be gathered from the will.

In the political history of South Carolina the name Le Serrurier occupies a prominent position. James Le Serrurier, Sr., a wealthy Charles Town merchant, denizened in London, May 16, 1683,[69] soon after leaving France under persecution, emigrated to Carolina about 1685. James Le Serrurier, Jr., the son of James Le Serrurier, Sr., and Elizabeth Leger, his wife, was born in St. Quentin, France.[70] He was naturalized in England, June 27, 1685, and was naturalized again in South Carolina in 1699.[71] After a few years' sojourn in South Carolina the father, in 1701, returned to England, leaving his Carolina interests in the hands of his son, James, and Pierre de St. Julien.[72] This was not unusual among Huguenots who became wealthy. James Le Serrurier, Sr., remained until his death a firm advocate of the princi-

[65] MS Sec'y. Rcds., 1685-1712, 143.

[66] Cooper, *Statutes,* II. 288. MS Col. Dames Archives, no. 27; MS Assembly Jrnl., 1692-1701, 190.

[67] MS Sec'y. Rcds., 1685-1712, 153.

[68] In possession of Mrs. R. Y. Dwight, Pinopolis, S. C.

[69] *Pub. H. Soc. London,* XVIII. 162.

[70] MS Pr. Ct. Rcd., 1694-1704, 209.

[71] *Pub. H. Soc. London,* XVIII. 169-70; MS *Pr. Ct. Rcd.,* 1694-1704, 209.

[72] MS Pr. Ct. Rcd., 1694-1704, 366.

ples of the French Reformed Church and requested in his will that he be buried in the French church-yard of the place where he might happen to die.[73] His son, James, after the beginning of his public career in Charles Town, anglicized his name to Smith. In the public records he is referred to frequently as Le Serrurier Smith.[74] He was the brother-in-law of Henry Le Noble, probably the leading Huguenot politician in South Carolina in his generation. The year 1704 finds James Smith, alias Le Serrurier, a member of the Court of High Commission of Sir Nathaniel Johnson and one of the Commissioners of the Church Act of 1704. Whether the charge against him of having embezzled £1,000 from the "Scots Society", of London, was ever sustained, is not known. He remained one of the leading political and business figures in the province.[75]

The will of the widow of James Le Serrurier, Sr., was made September 26, 1721 and proved July 1, 1725.[76] Her bequests to English charities are small, but the will reveals possessions in England and in South Carolina as well as the hope of recovering estates formerly owned in France.

No name in South Carolina provincial history is better known than that of Manigault. Gabriel Manigault combined the labors of merchant, factor, trader, manufacturer and planter, but made large amounts of money in his foreign commercial enterprises as well. He was an excellent specimen of the resolute, self-possessed, thrifty business-man of French extraction. He owned a number of ships, among which were the *Neptune* and *Sweet Nelly,* and was in the habit of making frequent trips to England, Barbadoes or the northern American ports, in his own vessels. The *South Carolina Gazette* of the period contains a large number of advertisements giving evidence of his commercial interests. As colonial expansion continued and with it new opportunities presented themselves, he entered with zeal into the gen-

[73] Will, "Gleanings from England", in *S. C. H. & G. Mag.,* VII. 146.
[74] Cooper, *Statutes,* II. 241.
[75] *T. H. S. S. C.,* IV. 31.
[76] Will, "Gleanings from England", in *S. C. H. & G. Mag.,* IV. 294.

JAMES LE SERRURIER
The emigrant.
(From an original portrait in oil in the possession of Mrs. Maria R. Gaillard, Charleston, S. C.)

eral movement among American merchants to secure better equipment, more efficient vessels and larger ships. After reading the heart-rending letter of Judith Giton Manigault, replete with pathetic settings that reveal the hardships of exiles fleeing from a beloved fatherland and the privations endured on a strange soil, it is a wholesome antidote to read the will of Gabriel Manigault, at the time of his death one of the three richest men in America, and the inventory of his property and that of his brother Pierre.[77]

Judith Giton, better known as Judith Manigault, born in la Voulte, Languedoc, France, escaped from her native country in secret with her associates, one of whom was her mother.[78] Abandoning the house and its furnishings to the enemy, they reached England by way of Holland.[79] On her arrival in Carolina, penniless, she married Noe Royer,[80] a weaver, also a refugee for conscience' sake. She tells how with her husband she grubbed the land, helped fell the trees and with him operated the whip-saw. For periods of six months at a time they had no bread, in fact saw no bread. In this toil and hardship lay the foundation of what was to become one of the largest fortunes in America prior to the American Revolution. In the rich Santee soil they secured their start. On the death of her first husband, she married Pierre Manigault in 1699,[81] who with his brother Gabriel had emigrated to Carolina after the repeal of the Edict of Nantes. These two brothers brought money with them, but it was quite limited in amount. Pierre's first step on reaching Carolina was either to purchase or to rent a small property and take boarders and lodgers.[82] While his wife was occu-

[77] *S. C. Gaz.*, July 7, 1739; *T. H. S. S. C.*, IV. 54 f; *S. C. Gaz.*, Oct. 30, 1736; Sept. 6, 1735; Baird, *Hug. In America*, II. appendix; Ramsay, *Hist. S. C.*, 6; MS Pr. Ct. Rcd., 1783-86, 135; 1783-97, 434.

[78] Letter, Judith M. to brother in Germany, reprint in Baird, *Hug. in Am.*, II. appendix; or in Ramsay: *Hist. S. C.*, I. 6 f.

[79] *Ibid.*

[80] Baird, *Hug. in Am.*, II. 112.

[81] She died in 1711. In 1713 Pierre was married again, this time to Anne Reason, a woman of English parentage. She died in 1727. Pierre died in 1729. See *T. H. S. S. C.*, IV. 56 f.

[82] *Ibid.*

pied with the details of this part of their work, he built a distillery and a cooperage. Having become familiar in France with these industries he soon built up a good business and before long doubled his capacity in the erection of another distillery. From the earnings of these activities he set himself up in business, building massive warehouses in Charles Town harbor and retail stores on her principal streets. He was among the first refugees to prosper. When he died, in 1729, he left to his two heirs, a son Gabriel and a daughter, Mrs. Judith Banbury, several storehouses and warehouses, two distilleries, a city lot and dwelling as well as considerable other property, such as slaves, a cooperage, and ready cash.[83] Gabriel Manigault's share of the property thus accumulated by his father formed the basis for the fortune that Gabriel was to possess later. Like his father he maintained great warehouses and stores where a wholesale and retail business was carried on, principally with the West Indies, England, and La Rochelle, dealing in the main in negroes, liquors, clayed sugars, clothing, bricks, building material, and grain. In 1754, following the popular tide, he invested large amounts of money in indigo and rice plantations, in which, with large numbers of slaves to work the land, he became increasingly prosperous.[84] That he was also an inveterate money lender is evidenced in the advertisements of the *South Carolina Gazette,* as well as the numerous bonds and other commercial papers still in the possession of Mrs. Josephine Jenkins, of Adams Run, South Carolina. At the time of his death his estate was valued at $845,000.[85] His estate consisted of 47,532 acres of land, including the Johnson barony of 14,000 acres. There were 490 slaves, store houses in Charles Town, residences and vacant lots and large sums of money represented in notes, bonds, mortgages, etc.[86] Gabriel Manigault was all through his mature life a prominent figure in South Carolina. As a member of

[83] MS Pr. Ct. Rcd., 1671-1727, 216 f.
[84] *T. H. S. S. C.*, IV. 58.
[85] MS Pr. Ct. Rcd., 1783-97, 434; 1783-86, 424; *T. H. S. S. C.*, IV. 61-2.
[86] *T. H. S. S. C.*, IV. 63.

ELIZABETH LEGER

Emigrant. Wife of James Le Serrurier, the emigrant.
(From original portrait in oil in possession of Miss Rowena D. Ravenel.
Charleston, S. C.)

the Assembly, as Public Treasurer and Receiver General, as one of the founders of the Charles Town Library Society, and, as its Vice-President and President, he figured in no small way in the political and cultural as well as the financial development of the commonwealth. When in 1753 funds were necessary, he advanced £3,500 for the use of poor Protestants coming from Europe to settle in South Carolina.[87] In 1763 he was one of the five appointed to carry on trade with the Cherokee Indians[88] and two years later was made Commissioner of Indian Affairs.[89] He enlisted in the War of the Revolution at the age of seventy-five and made a loan of $220,000 to the government, of which only about $40,000 was ever recovered. Though he was not in the habit of courting favor, he was a general favorite, for in one of the contested elections in Charles Town, the mechanics walked in procession to the polls and by a unanimous ballot elected him.[90]

The manuscript extracts of the diary of Mrs. Gabriel Manigault throw a good deal of light upon their family history.[91] She was a connoisseur who entertained South Carolina Governors, members of the Council, wealthy sea captains and prominent merchants of two continents. She occupied a prominent place in the audiences of the sessions of the Assembly and made regular visits to the local theatre, mentioning in her diary the names of plays she attended and commenting on their merits.

Their son Peter, born in 1731, was educated in England and traveled extensively on the continent after his classical education was completed in Charles Town.[92] On his return to South Carolina he was elected to the Assembly in 1755

[87] MS Archives Colonial Dames S. C., no. 62; Ramsay, *Hist. S. C.* II. 501; *S. C. Gaz.*, Jan. 27, 1733; March 24, 1733; May 30, 1743; Jan. 2, 1775; Cooper, *Statutes*, IV. 5.

[88] *S. C. Gaz.*, June 4, 1763.

[89] *Ibid.*, July 20, 1765.

[90] *T. H. S. S. C.*, IV. 36; McCrady, *Royal Govt.*, 403.

[91] Preserved in the library of the South Carolina Historical Society is what is supposed to be a manuscript epitome of the original diary of Mrs. Gabriel Manigault.

[92] MS Letters in possession of the Misses Jervey, Charleston.

and retained his seat eighteen years. In 1765 he was elected Speaker of the House, being honored with the position three times. He opposed the enforcement of the Stamp Act in 1765. When Parliament repealed the Act he wrote a letter of appreciation to Charles Garth, his representative in London. Until 1773 he was engaged in a general legal practice and brokerage business in Charles Town, with branches in London.[93] Frail in body, he never became the great magnate that his father had been. He died in his forty-second year.

With the Manigaults we may in some respects rank the family of Mazÿcks. Isaac Mazÿck, the first one of the family to emigrate to America, began his commercial career in Charles Town in 1686,[94] according to the Mazÿck manuscript account.[95] The parents of Isaac Mazÿck, namely Paul Mazÿck and Helizabeth Van Wick, were Walloons of wealth, who went from Holland to France about 1685, following the Huguenot exodus of the Revocation.[96] Isaac Mazÿck, the emigrant to South Carolina, had £1,500 with which he purchased a cargo of goods in London and then sailed for his new home in America. This cargo of merchandise became the basis for his great fortune. In Charles Town he was intimately associated with Jacques Le Serrurier, Sr., his father-in-law, and James Le Serrurier, Jr., his wife's brother, with Pierre and Lewis Perdriau and with Pierre De St. Julien, all of whom were ship-owners and merchants.[97] With Charles Town as home port, and with Isaac Mazÿck as the leading figure in the firm, they operated a business here many years. Their transactions involved trade with Barbadoes, Portugal, Madeira, the West Indies and ports in North America.[98] They have been styled the first Huguenot syndicate in

[93] Col. Dames Archives, no. 62.

[94] *Council Jrnl.* (Salley), 1692, 61, states that Isaac Mazÿck (Massique) arrived in April, 1692, in the ship *Loyal Jamaica.* Daniel Horry, Peter Gerrard, Jr., Peter Gerrard, Sr., and Peter La Salle came in the same vessel.

[95] Mazÿck MS in possession of Mrs. Arthur Mazÿck, Charleston.

[96] *Ibid.*

[97] MS Pr. Ct. Rcd., 1694-1704, 366.

[98] Mazÿck MS.

America.[99] When Isaac Mazÿck landed in South Carolina in 1686, he encountered a civilization unique and alien to English and French experiences. The absence of social restraints on production and exchange were especially inviting to persons used to the customs of the old world. The province held numberless untested possibilities for the development of wealth, especially for men of financial skill. By his bold mercantile genius he became a "merchant prince", amassed a great fortune, and helped to lay the foundation of commercial prosperity in Carolina that gave her the great economic strength she possessed at the time of the American Revolution. His ships are said to have done the largest amount of commerce of any ships in the colony,[100] and he is said to have been the largest land owner in the province.[101] He was conspicuously active as a commissioner in the erection of the first Huguenot Church in Charles Town, in 1691, and liberally supported it during his life.[102] In his will he bequeathed £100 sterling for the maintenance of a minister of the Calvinistic faith in his beloved church.[103] Grave and careful, bold in speculation, yet exact and methodical in business affairs, he was considered a model merchant. Though wealthy, he took no active part in politics, but was a staunch adherent to the doctrines and practices of the Reformed Church of France. This fact probably helped to exclude him from prominence in matters of public politics, for the Established Church and local political affairs were closely related. His commercial interests and his importance in business affairs on both sides of the water are indicated in the extent of his land holdings, letters that are still preserved, mortgages, his will, his endorsement of extensive

[99] *T. H. S. S. C.*, XIV. 39.
[100] *Ibid.*, IV. 33.
[101] Mazÿck MS.
[102] MS Pr. Ct. Rcd., 1732-36, 397 f.
[103] *Ibid.* A group of beautiful miniatures of Stephen Mazÿck, Isaac Mazÿck, the immigrant, his son and his grandson, all three of the same name, done in oil on ivory, and mounted in gold, are in the possession of the family of the late Rev. Robert Wilson, D.D., of Charleston.

financial ventures, etc.[104] His will disposes of £44,800 and over 4,000 acres of land in addition to a large amount of personal property.[105]

His eldest son was born in Charles Town, March 6, 1700.[106] Unlike his father he entered actively into politics and was for thirty-seven years a prominent member of the Assembly.[107] In 1740 he was appointed Assistant Judge.[108] He died in July, 1770,[109] and was buried in the French Churchyard,[110] as was also his mother, who died in 1732.[111] The fact that both he and his mother were held in high esteem by the people of Charles Town and vicinity is shown in the fact that she was the only woman, except the wife of Governor Johnson, of the period, who was honored with an editorial obituary notice in the *South Carolina Gazette.* The notice states that her funeral was attended "by most of the chief Merchants and public officers of the Province that were then in town".[112] The marriage, birth and baptismal notices of the family, bearing date of 1694 and later, are found in the old family Bible.[113]

To the ravages of time and the elements are due the destruction of material that contained the secrets of a man well known in the province, but of whose life records few are preserved. This man was Jacob Motte, Register of the Province in the last half century of its history. At the time

[104] MS Letter, Blondel to Godin, Sept. 16, 1726. *S. C. MSS,* folio 33, 1700-1732, Library of Congress.

[105] MS Pr. Ct. Rcd., 1732-6, 397.

[106] Mazÿck MS.

[107] *S. C. Gaz.,* July 31, 1770: "Last Wednesday Morning departed this Life, after a lingering Indisposition, Isaac Mazÿck, Esq., aged 71 Years, and a Native of this Province, whose Death is much regretted by all who had the Pleasure of his Acquaintance. . . . He was descended from an ancient and respectable Family in the Isle of Rhe, that fled from the Persecutions in France and settled in this Country about the year 1685. . . . He had served Thirty-Seven Years as a Member of the Honourable the Commons House of Assembly of this Province."

[108] *Ibid.*

[109] *Ibid.*

[110] *Ibid.*

[111] Record in Mazÿck Bible, in possession of Mrs. Arthur Mazÿck, Charleston.

[112] *S. C. Gaz.,* Apr. 8, 1732.

[113] In possession of Mrs. Arthur Mazÿck, Charleston.

of his death his property was valued at £228,301, of which £188,000 was in the form of promissory notes, bonds, book accounts, and other debts due him. He was a confirmed money lender. His son's wife, Rebecca Brewton Motte, was one of the most beloved of the women of the province.[114] In the vestibule of St. Phillip's Church, Charleston, a marble slab is mounted in her honor. The Mottes are said to be descended from the Marquis de la Motte, who left France prior to the Revocation. They established residences in England and in Ireland. John Abraham de la Motte was one of the Dublin colony who moved to Charles Town about 1700. Jacob de la Motte was a Commissioner of the Church Act of 1706.[115]

Of the Peronneau family little is known, but it contained several men of leadership and high moral character. Henry Peronneau, the emigrant, reached Carolina in 1687, an unnaturalized and undenizened alien. His name does not appear in the 1696 list of naturalized foreigners, though he was then in Charles Town.[116] He was probably one of the number who chose rather to remain alien than to swear allegiance to the Anglican Church and take the sacrament according to the form prescribed by the Establishment, both of which were steps necessary in the routine of naturalization.[117] The *South Carolina Gazette* bears testimony to his fortune, his worth and "his fair character".[118]

The will of Henry Peronneau, third of the name, made in 1753 and proved August 9, 1755, disposes of £90,000 currency, several Charles Town lots and houses, plantations, negroes, four mourning rings and a suit valued at £175, together with other valuable property.[119]

[114] MS Pr. Ct. Rcd., 1771-4, 27.
[115] MS Archives, Colonial Dames, no. 21, p. 51; Cooper, *Statutes,* II. 288.
[116] *S. C. Gaz.,* June 6, 1743. Not listed in naturalization and denization lists in *Pub. H. S. London,* Vol. XVIII.
[117] Cooper, *Statutes,* II. 132. He died in 1743 at the age of 76 years, having lived in South Carolina 56 years.
[118] *S. C. Gaz.,* June 6, 1743.
[119] *S. C. H. & G. Mag.,* V. 218.

Mr. Isaac Porcher, born in the town of St. Severre, Berry, France, and his wife, Claude de Cherigny, a native of La Rochelle,[120] left France before the Revocation and emigrated to Carolina by way of the British Isles.[121] No record of their naturalization in England can be found. The will of George Baudoin mentions him as Mr. Isaac Porcher, Chirurgien.[122] The extent of his possessions is unknown, but the quality of his character is well attested. On the occasion of his wife's death, on August 10, 1726, he wrote in his family Bible: "God give grace to make an end as Christian as she has done."[123] They had lived together about forty-five years, having been married October 9, 1681. His son Isaac was a successful planter who at the time of his death, in 1743, owned 75 slaves, valued at £9,000, 30 hogs, 23 oxen, 123 cattle, 50 sheep, and other personal property.[124]

The will of Antoine Prudhomme, written in 1695, one of the first of the extant wills of South Carolina Huguenots, though it does not dispose of vast land areas and hoarded treasures, is one of the most interesting of the preserved documents.[125] It portrays a man thrifty, yet benevolent, possessing a plantation well stocked and successfully managed. It shows that as early as 1695 the Huguenots possessed the propensities that were so marked throughout the period of their activities in this province in the accumulations of land and money. In the will he bequeathed to the Goose Creek congregation a cow with a heifer following her and another heifer, to constitute a nucleus for a fund to help provide for the poor of the parish.

The name Ravenel in South Carolina has had a continuous existence from 1686 to the present time. Though most of the French branch of the family were Catholics, and some of those moving to England turned Anglican, the South

[120] MS *Pr. Ct. Rcd.*, 1671-1727, 275.

[121] Record in Porcher Bible, in possession of Mr. Isaac Porcher, Esq., Pinopolis, S. C.

[122] MS Pr. Ct. Rcd., 1671-1727, 49.

[123] Porcher Bible.

[124] MS Pr. Ct. Rcd., 1739-43, 256.

[125] MS Pr. Ct. Rcd., 1671-1727, 51; 1692-3, 227.

Carolina branch has remained until today among the staunchest adherents of the Huguenot faith. This may explain why René Ravenel, in emigrating to America in 1685, did not apply for naturalization in England, for naturalization then required allegiance to the Established Church. René Ravenel, the emigrant, after arriving in Carolina, married Charlotte de St. Julien, in 1686. She was the daughter of Pierre de St. Julien.[126]

Among the wealthiest and most interesting Huguenot families in South Carolina were the St. Juliens de Malacare. They were an old noble Breton family who took refuge under persecution on friendly American soil, after a sojourn in both England and Ireland. Peter de St. Julien and his wife, Jane Le Fèbvre, with their seven children, Peter, Lewis, Paul, Aymee, Carolina, Margaret, and Emilia were denizened in London, April 9, 1687.[127] The property, which in the flight from France was confiscated, amounted in value to £41,000.[128] The St. Juliens were among the families that tarried in Ireland prior to their residence in South Carolina. The non-conformist registers of the Dublin churches yield nearly all of the links to the family chain of the St. Juliens.[129] The register of the Church of La Patente, Spitalfields, London, entry for July 29, 1694, reveals the fact that the elder de Malacare was in London while his son in Carolina had taken his father's place in the business activities there.[130] In the record of his death in 1705, at the age of seventy-one, the elder St. Julien is named Pierre de Malacare St. Julien. The marriage certificate of René Ravenel and Charlotte de St. Julien, daughter of Pierre de St. Julien and Jeanne Le Fèbvre, married at Pomkin Hill, states that the groom was attended by Sieurs Josias du Pré and Nicholas

[126] No record of an application by René Ravenel is found. Samuel Ravenel was naturalized in 1685, Mary in 1694, and Daniel in 1698-9. The last named was born in Vitré, in Bretagne, and was the son of Daniel Ravenel and Émee le Febvre. See *Pub. H. S. London,* XVIII. 174, 237, 263; *T. H. S. S. C.,* VI. 42.

[127] *Pub. H. S. London,* XVIII. 188.

[128] *T. H. S. S. C.,* XI. 42.

[129] *Pub. H. S. London,* XIV.

[130] *T. H. S. S. C.,* XI. 42 f.

de Longuemare.[131] The wedding occurred October 24, 1687, in South Carolina. St. Pierre, Jr., here signs his name simply Pierre de St. Julien.

Nearly all of the land disposed of in the will of Peter de St. Julien, consisting of 8,800 acres and five Charles Town lots, had been purchased.[132] Pierre St. Julien de Malacare, who emigrated with the family to Carolina, became a member of the Governor's Council in 1717.[133] He married into the family of Serruriers. The son, Peter, born in 1699, married Damaris Elizabeth Le Serrurier.[134] By this marriage the political and financial interests of two of the most important Huguenot families of the South were united. He was a careful business man as his will proves. At the time of his death, 1743, he owned 67 slaves, valued at £10,440, 24 oxen, 113 cattle, 20 horses, including a fine stallion, as well as numerous other items of household and plantation assets. His personal property alone was valued at £11,893-10-0.[135] He was a member of the Council[136] from 1724 to 1725 and was a Justice of the Peace from 1730 to 1734.[137] Much of his wealth was apparently kept in the immediate family, for in 1753 Benjamin de St. Julien advertised for sale 3,734 acres of land in seven different tracts, most of which was in the Santee section.[138]

These are but a few examples out of a much larger number that might be cited to indicate the prominent leadership in some of the undertakings and political controversies in which the French Protestants took part and their general interest in public concerns of South Carolina as well as their share in general in the production of the material wealth of the community. There was hardly a public enterprise, a benevolent undertaking, a business project, or an ecclesiastical issue in which they were not participants.

[131] *Ibid.*
[132] MS Pr. Ct. Rcd., 1671-1729, 110.
[133] MS Archives S. C. Colonial Dames, nos. 112 and 144.
[134] St. Philip's Register; *T. H. S. S. C.*, XI. 42 f.
[135] MS Pr. Ct. Rcd., 1739-43, 277.
[136] *Coll. Hist. Soc. S. C.*, I. 284.
[137] MS Pr. Ct. Rcd., 1729-31, 315.
[138] *S. C. Gaz.*, June 18, 1753.

CHAPTER XI

SIDELIGHTS ON THE HUGUENOT INFLUENCE IN CHARLES TOWN LIFE

The newspaper, printing and book-binding business of South Carolina was in the hands of French Protestants almost exclusively from 1725 to 1765. Lewis Timothèe, a Protestant refugee, in 1733-4 bought the printing establishment formerly owned and edited by Mr. Whitmarsh and the *South Carolina Gazette,* which on account of the death of Mr. Whitmarsh had been discontinued after September 1733.[1] Timothy however made it the first permanent newspaper in the province. He was the son of French Protestant refugees.[2] On the tide of emigration from France after the repeal of the Edict of Nantes, he reached Holland, learned the printer's trade, and then embarked for America, where he is found in 1731[3] in the printing establishment of Benjamin Franklin, in Philadelphia.[4] Late in the same year he was appointed librarian for the Philadelphia Library Company, which was organized the year previous.[5] In 1733 he moved to Charles Town, bought the Whitmarsh printing establishment and revived the publication of the *South Caro-*

[1] Whitmarsh's *South Carolina Gazette* may not have been the first newspaper in South Carolina, for the provincial Assembly on Feb. 5, 1731, voted that the £500 appropriated to E. Philips in May, 1730, be paid. See MS Col. Doc. S. C. (Assembly Jrnl.), 1728-33, 841. As early as April 9, 1725, a bill of £50 was paid to Adam Beauchamp, press master. MS Col. Doc. S. C. (Council Jrnl.), 1721-25, 337-9. Eleazer Philips died in Charles Town, July 10, 1732, and on the 15th a notice appeared in the *Gazette* to that effect. But two years later his father, Eleazer Philips, Sr., a bookseller in Charles Town advertised in the *Gazette* for the settlement of all debts due him on the estate of his son, Eleazer, Jr., for *news, printing,* etc. Mention is also made of bills due for six months of the *Carolina Weekly Journal.*

[2] Thomas, *Hist. Printing,* II. 155.

[3] *Ibid.*

[4] The Timothy family arrived in Philadelphia in September, 1731, for the Col. Doc. S. C. (III. 414) contain a record of the arrival of Peter, Ludwig and Carl Timothée, on Sept. 21, 1731, all of them under 16 years of age. See also Rupp, 30,000 Names of German, Swiss and French in Pa. 1727-1776, 68-70.

[5] Thomas, *Hist. of Printing,* II. 155.

lina Gazette in February 1734 in his shop on Church Street, in Charles Town. This then, in addition to his public duties for the provincial government, constituted his principal occupation. In 1734 he printed the famous *Trott's Laws* and was in addition to the amount received for this work given other public encouragement in the form of bounties. In 1735-6 he received grants of land for 600 acres and one town lot in Charles Town.[6] It is not positively known when printing was introduced into Carolina, but it was prior to April 9, 1735, for the *Council Journal*[7] of that date contains a bill of £50 to Adam Beauchamp, Press Master. Beauchamp,[8] as his name indicates, was French. After forsaking the printing business he became a merchant in Charles Town.[9]

Whether or not Eleazer Philips, a printer, was a Frenchman has not been established. The name, though perhaps not purely French in that form, was not uncommon among the French Protestants.[10] He petitioned the Assembly for £1,000 as a bounty.[11] On May 21, 1730, the Assembly voted him £500 and gave him the promise of all of the public printing in the province as an encouragement to come to South Carolina and open a printing shop. Philips died before his plans were fully realized; in 1731 Whitmarsh entered the field, backed by the money voted him by both houses of the government.[12] In 1732, the father of Eleazer Philips, deceased, petitioned the Assembly for the bounty promised to his son, setting forth that he had been subjected to great expense in the importation of machinery and type and in getting the shop into order.[13]

[6] *S. C. Gaz.*, Feb. 2, 1733-4. Cooper, *Statutes,* III. 392. MS Public Land Rcds., III. 143 and 519.

[7] MS Council Jrnl., 1721-25, 339.

[8] *Pro. H. Soc.*, London, XVIII. 307.

[9] MS St. Philip's Church Wardens' Account Book, 1725-52, Dec. 7, 1739.

[10] See p. 9.

[11] MS Council Jrnl., 1730-4, 162.

[12] MS Council Jrnl., 1730-34, 165; MS Col. Doc. S. C. (Assembly Jrnl.), 1728-33, 841-2.

[13] MS Council Jrnl., 1730-34, 335.

Louis Timothy (alias Timothée) published the *South Carolina Gazette* until his accidental death in 1738.[14] He, with his fellow refugees, was quick to recognize the bid to disfavor which a French name bore with it even as late as this. Accordingly, after August 1734, his name appears in the anglicized form, Timothy, instead of Timothée, as formerly. After his death his widow, Elizabeth Timothy, with the aid of her son Peter, became editor and manager and remained in charge until Peter's majority.[15] He took independent charge of the business in 1741. Peter thus also succeeded his father as printer to the province and after the Declaration of Independence became State Printer.[16] Peter Timothy was one of the most widely known men of the South during his lifetime. He was not only editor and owner of the *Gazette,* but was active in all public affairs as well. His services to the province are hard to estimate. For years clerk of the Assembly, his signature appears on many of the public documents of the pre-Revolutionary and Revolutionary periods. He was a decided and aggressive friend of his country. When South Carolina became active in the cause of the colonies he was elected secretary of the "Associations". He was secretary of the Congress that drafted the Constitution for the new government in 1776. The *Gazette* espoused the cause of the Whigs and remained loyal to its position, though for a time it tried to remain neutral. During the siege of Charles Town, Timothy remained in town, was taken as a prisoner to St. Augustine, in 1780, and a year later was exchanged and sent to Philadelphia.[17] In trying to reach Antigua, where his widowed daughter, Mrs. Marchant, owned property, he perished on the vessel that foundered off the coast of Delaware.[18] Peter Timothy was made the first provincial post-master of South Carolina, in

[14] *S. C. Gaz.*, Jan. 4, 1739. Thomas, *Hist. of Printing,* II. 155.
[15] Elizabeth Timothy died in 1757. MS Pr. Ct. Rcd., 1756-58, 164.
[16] MS Assembly Jrnl., 1734, 186; MS Assembly Jrnl., 1772-5, 95.
[17] MS Letters and Papers on S. C., Folio no. 21, 1780-81, Library of Congress.
[18] Thomas, *Hist. of Printing,* II. 157.

1756, appointed by the Crown.[19] In 1766 he was appointed Post-Master General for the Southern District.[20]

Years before a regular government post-office was established in South Carolina the printing office of both Louis Timothy and Peter Timothy had been headquarters for the distribution of letters, packages and papers. A general post-office had been established in 1702[21] for receiving foreign letters and packages, but no provision had been made for the receipt and delivery of mail at the several points and centers of population lying outside of Charles Town, i.e., no provision had been made for the disposition of internal provincial mail. In 1737 Francis Sureau,[22] a French Protestant, appears as one of a number who undertook to establish an internal mail-route from Charles Town to Ashley Ferry, Dorchester, Stono, and Pon Pon. This successful attempt was extended in 1754 by an organization formed by about fifty gentlemen in and about Pon Pon, each of whom agreed to supply a boy in routine to carry the mail to and from Charles Town. The first mail from the north under this new arrangement reached Charles Town on Thursday, August 19, 1756.[23] In all of this development Peter Timothy was the impelling force and life. In 1756 the British government extended to Charles Town the mail route that before that time had reached no farther than Newbern, North Carolina. Prior thereto, since 1739, the South Carolina Assembly had appropriated £200 a year to carry mail north to connect with routes established there. This, in addition to what was subscribed by interested South Carolina people, financed a monthly trip for carrying mail to Cape Fear.[24] Peter Timothy was a fearless and outspoken advocate of honorable principles. He was frequently in

[19] *S. C. Gaz.*, Aug. 19, 1756; Aug. 26, 1756.
[20] *Ibid.*, Aug. 11, 1766.
[21] Cooper, *Statutes*, II. 188.
[22] *S. C. Gaz.*, Sept. 3, 1737.
[23] *S. C. Gaz.*, Aug. 26, 1756; May 3, 1739.
[24] *Ibid.*

debt,[25] perhaps not so much because of a lack of thrift as because his profession was one which in those days was hard to establish on a paying basis. Bills were exceedingly hard to collect. More than once the paper was temporarily discontinued as a threat and a possible leverage for collecting bills from delinquent debtors. But in spite of his financial reverses he made the paper remunerative and laid the foundations for its powerful public influence. To the Timothys belong the honor and credit of founding in South Carolina a permanent journalism and of maintaining an exemplary standard of business integrity. Ann Timothy, the widow of Peter Timothy, after the close of the Revolutionary War hostilities, revived the temporarily discontinued *Gazette.* She was appointed State Printer and retained the appointment until her death in 1792. Her shop was on the corner of Broad and King Streets.[26]

As far as is generally known the first fire-insurance company in America was founded in Charles Town, in November, 1735, with Huguenots among the leaders in its organization and support. It was a mutual company known as The Friendly Society. Owing to the frequency of fires and the attendant risk on property values, the Charles Town merchants had several years before this made the attempt to get London insurance companies to underwrite against the loss of property by fire.[27] To these solicitations the London insurance companies replied that they had received numerous applications from several of the American colonies, but that no encouragements had been given to the authors of such appeals because the charter privileges of the London insurance companies did not extend to America.[28] In November, 1735, then, a number of the citizens of Charles Town met and drew up papers for the formation

[25] MS St. Philip's' Vestry Bk., 1732-56, May 21, 1753; Aug. 20, 1751; Sept. 5, 1748.

[26] Thomas, *Hist. of Printing,* II. 158 and 255.

[27] Extract of London Letter in *S. C. Gaz.,* Jan. 22, 1731-2.

[28] *Ibid.*

of an insurance company.[29] Before January first about £100,000 was subscribed as capital.[30] Unfortunately the list of stockholders is not preserved, but from the scraps of information gathered here and there it can be shown that Jacob Motte, James Crockett, and Henry Peronneau, Jr., were selected as the first managers.[31] The first and last of this list were French Protestants. At a meeting held on February 3, 1735-6, Gabriel Manigault was elected treasurer, Jacob Motte, clerk, and Henry Peronneau, Jr., one of the five directors, all French Protestants;[32] John Laurens, also a French Protestant, was chosen one of two fire-masters.[33] Though regular business meetings were held and it seemed to be doing a flourishing business, this insurance company was short lived.[34] Organized shortly before the great fire of November 18-20, 1740, it was unable to ride the tide of that great financial loss which involved the destruction of more than £250,000 worth of property estimated in sterling.[35] In this fire the French Protestants were heavy losers, their loss of property aggregating £60,000.[36] Nothing is heard of the insurance company after the fire.

The pioneer salt manufacturing concern in South Carolina, and in fact of the lower South, was that of a French Protestant, William Mellichamp, who came to America from France by way of Switzerland and the British Isles. Salt making as a profitable industry in South Carolina at one time gave promise of considerable success. Salt was not only a scarce article, but it was also high priced.[37] It was a commodity of prime necessity, hence its production was a subject of grave concern. Fish abounded in the streams, and

[29] *S. C. Gaz.*, Nov. 15, 1735.
[30] *S. C. Gaz.*, Jan. 3, 1735-6.
[31] *Ibid.*, Nov. 15, 1735; Dec. 20, 1735; Dec. 27, 1735; Jan. 3 and 22, 1737; Feb. 7, 1736; Feb. 19, 1741.
[32] *Ibid.*, Feb. 7, 1735-6.
[33] *S. C. Gaz.*, Jan. 29, 1737; Jan. 26, 1740.
[34] MS Col. Doc. S. C., XX. 327 f.
[35] *Ibid.*
[36] *Ibid.*
[37] Cooper, *Statutes*, III. 247-8.

large quantities of beef and pork were raised by the planters of the country.[38] Besides, wild meat was abundant. The scarcity of salt precluded the possibility of extensive exportation of fish and other meat. In the earlier days the people were practically coast-bound on account of their need of salt. Governor Johnson had paid some attention to salt production before 1700 without success.[39] He named his plantation on Sewee Bay, *Salt Hope.* As late as 1752, it was the only seaport south of Bolings Point in Virginia, where salt could be procured.[40] In 1752 Bishop Spangenburg, who was then seeking lands for a colony in North Carolina, wrote:[41] "They will require salt and other necessities which they can neither manufacture nor raise. Either they must go to Charles Town, which is 300 miles distant . . . or to Bolings Point, in Virginia, which is also 300 miles away or else go down the Roanoke I don't know how many miles, where salt is brought up from Cape Feare." Annual pilgrimages were made to the coast for salt. Taking flocks, or furs, and produce, planters made their perennial tours to the sea for this necessity of life.

Here again the Huguenots take the initiative in the production of a staple article. William Mellichamp, a French refugee, in the spring of 1724, seeing possibilities in the manufacture of salt, petitioned the Governor's Council[42] for the exclusive right of salt manufacture in the province of South Carolina. In his petition he sets forth that he wishes to manufacture salt on the same general plan as that used in Great Britain, that the enterprise will not only bring profit to him, but will each year save from decay great quantities of commodities often thrown away on account of the need of salt and that it will increase trade with the

[38] *Ibid.*
[39] Bishop, *Hist. Manufactures,* 1608-1860, I. 287.
[40] *Col. Rcds. N. Carolina,* V. 3. A "salt works" had been set up at Cape Charles, on the east shore of Virginia, in 1620. See Beverley's *History of Virginia* (1705), 38.
[41] *Col. Rcds. N. Carolina,* V. 3.
[42] MS Col. Doc. S. C. (Council Jrnl.), 1721-25, 252.

province by increasing the quantities of provisions for export.[43]

The process of salt evaporation as it was operated in the British Isles at the time was very simple. Its manufacture had been carried on since the time of the Roman occupation and the method had undergone so little change that the plant then in use (1725) was practically the same as that which was used 1,400 years before. The salt brine was run into shallow pans and heated from below. At first the pans were made of lead.[44] In the seventeenth century iron pans were introduced and were larger, some being as large as 10 x 20 feet. By the use of evaporating basins and troughs, water was let in from the ocean by means of sluices and transferred from one basin to another as the various steps in the process were necessary, until the salt finally crystallized.[45] The crystal salt was shoveled into heaps to dry, after which it was crushed or pounded fine. The warm climate of South Carolina was peculiarly adapted to salt making.

Mr. Mellichamp's petition in its original form was objected to by Governor Nicholson, for, as a private bill, he contended that it should have contained a time limit and a clause stipulating that it should not take effect until the pleasure of the British Crown was known. In its amended form it passed both houses and became a law.[46] It went into effect April 17, 1725. Mr. Mellichamp was thereby granted a private monopoly on the manufacture of salt for a period of fourteen years and also a monopoly on the sale of all salt handled in the province. The act further grants that a bounty of twelve pence currency be given him for every bushel of salt he would produce as long as the price of salt did not exceed ten shillings per bushel. He was required to certify under oath as to the number of bushels he manu-

[43] *Ibid.*

[44] Thorpe, article "Sodium", in *Dictionary of Applied Science,* London, 1893, vol. III.

[45] *Louisiana Geological Report,* 1907, 227.

[46] MS Col. Doc. S. C. (Council Jrnl.), 1721-25, 305 f. Cooper, *Statutes,* III. 248.

factured and to begin the manufacture of salt within two years of the date of the passage of the act. In spite of the fact that the equipment that he ordered sent from England was greatly delayed in transit, and hurricanes and financial barriers hindered his work, he was able to report on July 8, 1731, that 14,000 bushels of salt had been manufactured.[47] It seems that Mr. Mellichamp either died soon after or was forced out of business by competitors. Either Croft and Peronneau or Henry and Alexander Peronneau or Thomas Bolton succeeded him in the business, for after February 10, 1732[48] they advertise salt at eight shillings per bushel. Nothing more is heard of William Mellichamp in connection with the salt business. In 1759 John Guerrard advertised salt for sale at 10 shillings per bushel.[49]

At the death of Benjamin d'Harriette, the accumulations of two generations of d'Harriettes in New York and South Carolina fell into the hands of Martha Fowler d'Harriette, widow of James Fowler, who had married Benjamin d'Harriette October 16, 1755. Benjamin d'Harriette survived the marriage but a short time.[50] The inventory of the property that Mme. d'Harriette owned at the time of her death in 1760 contains material of compelling interest.[51] The lists of mahogany furniture, china and glassware, silverware and wearing apparel rivalled the furnishings found in the homes of the English aristocracy. There were ten slaves, worth £1,602, probably all of them household servants, for the property on the plantations is not listed in the inventory. Owing to Indian massacres and a small-pox epidemic, the appraisers were unable to get to the personal property in the country. The mahogany furniture in the home at its second-hand value was appraised at £600, china and glassware at £129, bed and table linens at £301. Though there were costly articles like a mahogany couch and wrought

[47] MS Col. Doc. S. C. (Assembly Jrnl.), 1728-31, 734.
[48] See *S. C. Gaz.*, Jan. 13, 1732 *passim*.
[49] *S. C. Gaz.*, Jan. 12, 1759; Jan. 13, 1732.
[50] *S. C. Gaz.*, Feb. 26, 1756; Oct. 23, 1755.
[51] MS Pr. Ct. Rcd., 1758-61, 314.

cover, valued at £20, an eight-day clock valued at £40, a bureau with glass doors valued at £20, a Marseilles quilt worth £25, the affluence and luxury of the home do not appear in the house furniture so much as in the silverware and jewelry which Mme. d'Harriette owned. There was a gold snuff-box valued at £88 and one of silver valued at £6, a gold watch and its appurtenances, the second-hand value of which was £130. There were two stone buckles valued at £3, solid silver knives, forks and spoons, a solid gold girdle buckle weighing 14½ pwt., a silver tea-kettle and lamp weighing 65 2/3 pwt., valued at £164-7-6, a pearl necklace, five diamond rings valued at nearly £200, four mourning rings, one engraved "Beadon", a silver tea-pot valued at £50, a large silver tankard at £70-17-6, a pair of white stone sleeve-buttons valued at £8, a silver goblet at £15, a pair of gold shoe-buckles worth £32, a bodkin of gold, a silver milk-pot marked T. F. M., a silver tea-pot worth £32, a pair of silver cups weighing 17¾ ounces, bearing the coat of arms of the d'Harriettes. Ready money was found in the bed-chamber of the deceased as follows: 3 Spanish pistoles, 4 French guineas, a quantity of German money (unspecified amount), and British silver and paper money. In all, £180. In bonds, mortgages, book accounts, etc., principal and interest, there were due her at the time of her death nearly £20,-000. The list names many of her debtors, most of whom were Englishmen, who owed amounts ranging from £44 to £1,750 and interest. The libraries found in various parts of the house include the standard books of the day, such as Tillotson's Sermons, Bunyan, Foxe's *Book of Martyrs,* Dr. Gill on the Canticles, etc. There also was a Bible and sundry other books. How extensive her land possessions were at the time of her death is not known. Her husband received a grant of 1,450 acres in March, 1733, and one of 200 acres in June, 1734, both in Colleton County.[52]

Among the French Protestants probably the closest rival of Mme. d'Harriette in ostentatious display of wealth was

[52] MS Public Rcds., S. C., I. 427-9 (1733-4).

Mme. Ann le Brasseur, left a widow by the death of her husband Francis le Brasseur in 1737. She was a "gentlewoman of considerable fortune",[53] who had been profoundly stirred by the revival efforts of George Whitefield, who visited Charles Town a number of times amidst great excitement. The Huguenot Church of Charles Town was thrown open to his services.[54] The *South Carolina Gazette* of this period contains long and glowing accounts of his work.[55] Mme. le Brasseur became so enthusiastic a disciple of his that her reason was dethroned and in an evil hour she committed suicide with a pistol. In her expiring breath she professed full assurance of salvation and recommended her child to the care of the Reverend Mr. Garden. The inventory of her property[56] does not tally so high in aggregate amounts nor was her home so elaborately furnished as was that of Mme. d'Harriette, but in the amount and the cost of personal apparel she far outrivals her. Her wardrobe, described in the terms of commonplace male appraisers, seems like that of a European princess. In addition to the commonplace calico, muslin, and ordinary linen clothing and the "old red damask cloggs" contained in her boudoir, there were gold-laced "brocaded shoes", white "damask silver lace shoes", two pairs of "new green callimanco shoes", silver and gold lace, a pair of mittens valued at £2, one new ivory fan and five other fans, a brown "grograin gown" trimmed with gold lace and valued at £15, a "flowered brocaded night-gown" (evening dress), a white Persian quilted petticoat, valued at £7, a white "Padusoy petticoat" valued at £25, "a striped Lutestring woman's gown and coat" worth £15 and a "Gold Brocaded night-gown with a blew silk tail" worth £35. There were two pairs of silver buckles worth £5, a diamond ring valued at £60, a gold watch and appurtenances worth £90, two pictures set in gold, a pearl necklace, a gold thimble, lace, plain and fringed aprons, and a "Fustian

[53] *S. C. Gaz.*, June 21, 1742; March 26, 1737.
[54] *Ibid.*, Jan. 5, 1740.
[55] *Ibid.*, June 21, 1742; Jan. 5, 1740.
[56] MS Pr. Ct. Rcd., 1741-3, 169 f.

stomacher" worth £15. The list contains a black head dress with ruffles and a handkerchief of very fine lace which are appraised at £40, while a double-bordered head dress with ruffles and fringes was worth only £2. Another handkerchief, "laced around", of fine lace was valued at £15. There were masks, net and "gause" hoods, silk tippets, girdles and gloves—in fact practically everything necessary in those days for the wardrobe and dressing-table of the wealthy. It is amusingly noticeable that Mme. le Brasseur had only two pairs of silk stockings and eight pairs of worsted, but she had fourteen pairs of gloves, four pairs of which were new. She had twenty-two handkerchiefs, six of which were done in fancy and expensive laces. Though the facts in the case are not known today, it is easy to surmise that the bitter denunciations on the part of George Whitefield of all display and sumptuary clothing, and his insistence on an agonizing repentance and change in life and character worked seriously on her mind, resulting in the unbalancing of her reason. Mortgages, bonds, and other obligations due her at the time of her death amounted to more than £10,000 currency. She was the wife of Francis le Brasseur, a prominent merchant, politician and public spirited citizen of Charles Town.[57]

In unhappy contrast to the outlays of luxury described above, is the inventory of the possessions of Mme. Elizabeth Timothy, the sorrowing widow of Louis Timothy, the printer.[58] It bears with it a tale of solemn pathetic interest, for it contained little besides the bare necessities of life in a home. There was a "parcel of books" and two French Bibles, two old desks and some printing paper, a little china and thirty-eight ounces of old silver, six small pieces of jewelry, some old pewter, and a little furniture. The inventory mentions three grown negro slaves and two negro children. There was a marble-[covered] side-board, perhaps the heri-

[57] The *S. C. Gaz.*, of Feb. 3, 1732, announces that Francis le Brasseur has opened a store on Elliot Street.

[58] MS Pr. Ct. Rcd., 1756-58, 166.

COLONEL PETER HORRY
1747-1815
Buried in Trinity Churchyard, Columbia, S. C.

tage as well as the daily reminder of better days, for its value was £5. The list makes mention of some old dental tools ("a parcel of tooth Drours"), an old copper worth £5, a cross-cut saw, a few bottles, a spit, dogs and stand, a stone pot, an iron pot, a net, and a brass mortar and pestle. Its entire value was £25 currency, i.e. estimated in standard values, about $17.50. Here too are recorded some of the money debts that tardy debtors still owed her. Nor dare we look on the meagre remnants left to the widow Timothy by her honored and industrious husband as the result of reckless speculation or wanton neglect. He hazarded for others the enterprise which as a rule was one of the hardest to establish, especially in a new country and fought back again and again the encroaching poverty and despair that are incident to such heroic attempts at serving a public that was either ungrateful or else unable to give worthy support to a deserving educational force—the local newspaper.

Pathos finds a still more solemn note in the perusal of the possessions of Mary Marion, one of the ancestors of the illustrious "Swamp Fox", the fiery and far-famed Revolutionary hero, Francis Marion. Consider the list. It tells exactly what she owned, for all that she possessed is here recorded. What the list lacks is more conspicuous than what it contains. There was not one piece of furniture of any value. The nearest approach to it were a "little trunk" and two cedar boxes, valued at "29 shillings". She had only one book, a French prayerbook, perhaps her principal comfort and solace in her advancing age. Seven old napkins, two pillow cases, and a "sheat" were valued at £3. There was a "tea boyler" without a lid, valued at more than a pound. Her barnyard stock consisted of "7 ganders & 2 geese, one old grey horse & an old side saddle". The horse must have been very old and useless, for while the ganders and geese were appraised at 35 shillings, the side-saddle and the horse together were valued at only 20 shillings. Even her one ball of yarn is included in the list, three pairs of spectacles and a few buttons, knives, etc. Aside from two slaves, valued at £210, the item of largest value in her entire outfit was 17 ounces of old silver, valued at £29-15-0.[59]

The Huguenots that went to South Carolina were not as a class in the condition of abject destitution frequently found among the early immigrants to some of the American colonies. As early as 1700, when Lawson visited the Santee French settlement, he found some of the planters in a prosperous condition.[60] He mentions dwellings of brick and stone. These people were not a helpless horde, debilitated by poverty and incapacitated by privations. They were a thrifty, sturdy folk. They had an asset more valuable than mere money—they were money makers, they were wealth producers. The early part of the first decade among them represents a condition of general poverty and indescribable hardships, excessive labor and privation. Before the last years of the first generation were past, however, they showed signs of growing riches and of accumulating comforts. The fourth decade found them in a large part re-

[59] MS Pr. Ct. Rcd., 1748-51, 351. Property of Mary Marion, deceased; appraised Dec. 1, 1750.

"17 oz old silver @ 35 s per oz.	£29-15-0
a parcel stone buttons & false stones	5-0
3 pr. spectacles, 2 knives, a snuff box a grater, 2 pocket Bks a little trunk 25 sh. 2 pair stockings a ball of yarn, a small quantity of thread, a parcel of knitting needles a French prayerbook	1-10-0
7 old napkins, 2 old pillow cases & one sheat	3-00-0
1 old suit cotton curtains 22/6 2 cedar boxes 4 o/o	4-22-6
1 Tea boyler without a cover 25/ 1 bed bolster & one old blanket	11-05-0
7 ganders & 2 geese 35/	2-15-0
	53-17-6
one old negro man named Ienny	10-00-0
one woman named Lizette	200-00-0
	263-17-6"

[60] Lawson, *South Carolina,* 7-10.

covered from their poverty and moving onward slowly but surely toward financial prosperity and wealth. Where there was poverty it was usually the poverty of merit, not the poverty that bears with it a stigma. It was a poverty that represented only a transition between a period of great prosperity and comforts in France and a period of prosperity in America. It was a poverty that bore its first-fruits in reaccumulated treasures. When it is remembered that several great fires in Charles Town, Indian massacres in the country, pestilence in the form of smallpox and fever, as well as severe storms on land and sea, repeatedly put a damper on their progress, these facts bear still greater weight.[61]

So far as we know there was no pauper class among the Huguenots. It is true that most of the records covering the first decade or two have perished, but can we not infer that the presence of a pauper class in 1700 would mean a larger one in 1720? It is not customary for a pauper class to diminish; more regularly it increases. It is true that there were a few persons of French lineage who were very poor and occasionally one is in destitute circumstances, but they were not paupers. Almost without exception the cases of relief among French Protestants were after the fire of 1740, which burned nearly one-third of Charles Town and occasioned a loss of property amounting to about £250,000, sterling. Of this amount the French Protestants lost nearly £61,000 currency. Jacob Motte and Jacob Guerrard sustained the heaviest losses.[62]

[61] MS Col. Doc. S. C., XX. 301 f.

[62] See appendix for detailed schedule of losses. There is on record (MS Council Jrnl., 1725-6, 104), a petition presented to the council by Isaac Le Grand, John Deleisseline, and Peter Robert. It is dated Sept. 8, 1725, and sets forth that Isaac Le Grand had been a very poor man and that on account of sickness and infirmity his family were unable to go to Charles Town to have the will probated. The petition asks that a magistrate in the parish of St. James Santee be empowered to do so. In response Nicholas Mayrant was authorized to act. In this case there is no record of public financial aid. The instances of public aid in fact are rare. In the vestry and church wardens' records there are a few cases. For example, Mrs. Jourdine in 1732 received aid from the parish. She was evidently aged and sick, for there is one item of money for bandages, another for care and board, and she is referred to as "old Mrs. Jourdine".

The fire of 1697-8, which caused losses amounting to £30,000 sterling, burning the stores and dwellings of at least fifty families, and the smallpox, which so frequently made its fatal inroads into Charles Town and the vicinity, added grave burdens to the struggling inhabitants of this new community. The marvel is that in the midst of all of these exigencies there was no pauper class among the Huguenots. In the smallpox epidemic of 1697-1698 nearly three hundred people died in Charles Town. The epidemic of 1699-1700 claimed one hundred sixty victims.[63] During the epidemic of 1760, six thousand people in Charles Town alone had the disease.[64] Three hundred and eighty white persons died and three hundred and fifty negroes. One doctor alone, in this epidemic, had six hundred patients.[65] The fire of 1740 broke out at two o'clock in the afternoon of November 18th.[66] It destroyed all of the property of several of the French Protestants who were so unfortunate as to live or have property within the fire zone. Three hundred residences and a large number of business properties were given up to the flames. The estimated loss in merchandise alone was more than £200,000.[67] This calamity threw a number of French Protestants on the mercies of the local authorities and several

She died in January, 1732. Her period of aid covers only three months. (See MS St. Philip's Vestry Bk., 1732-6, November, December, January; MS Ch. Wardens Acct. Bk., 1725-52, Nov. to Jan.) According to MS St. Philip's Vestry Bk., 1725-52, under date, aid was given in November 1740 to Mrs. Leger, widow, who was burnt out, £20; to Wm. Bisoleonew, a sailor, £10; to Esther Laurens, widow, and her children, £20. In Jan. 1740-1, Mrs. Couliette and family received 1 bbl. rice and £20; Mrs. Dupré and family, £50; Samuel Leger, a hatter, £100; on Jan. 9, Mrs. Le Fountain received £10. In April Lucy Delescure was a beneficiary and in December Mrs. Filleaux received £20. The vestry lists of poor immediately prior to the fire contained no French names. Though no evidence seems to have been preserved regarding this, it is possible that French Protestants who were still affiliated with the Charles Town French Church received necessary aid from funds in its charge.

[63] MS letter to Lords Proprietors, March 12, 1697-8, in MS Sec'y. Rcds., 1685-1712, 130.

[64] Letter, Council to Proprs., *Ibid.*, 166.

[65] *S. C. Gaz.*, Apr. 19, 1760; Feb. 16, 1760.

[66] MS Col. Doc. S. C., XX. 327; *S. C. Gaz.*, Nov. 20, 1740. List of sufferers: MS Col. Doc. S. C., XX. 559 f.

[67] *Ibid.*, *S. C. Gaz.*, Nov. 20, 1740.

COLONEL JOHN LAURENS
1756-1782
Aid on Washington's Staff.
(From original portrait in oil by Copley, in possession of Henry R. Laurens, Esq., Charleston, S. C.)

became beneficiaries from the public parish funds. Jacob Motte sustained the heaviest losses. Practically all of his large stock of merchandise valued at £12,790 was burned.[68] Relief for all of the sufferers was solicited in each of the American colonies, in the West Indies and in England. Special Sundays were appointed in South Carolina for the purpose of raising relief money. On November 29 the collection received at the church door of St. Phillips amounted to £683-12-6.[69] In addition, the lodge of Free Masons contributed £50 and Mr. Benjamin d'Harriette is given special mention for a gift of £25.[70] The Quakers in and about Philadelphia collected about £500 proclamation money. In the Barbadoes £146-18-6½ sterling, was received. Here three Sundays were designated for public offerings, and the church wardens of each parish were sent from house to house to solicit funds. In England similar efforts were made, resulting in the bestowal of public and private gifts aggregating nearly £3,000 sterling to the French Protestants alone.[71]

In the things, then, cited above, as in other matters, the French Protestants of South Carolina aided materially in laying the foundations of American stability.

The following table shows some of the representative amounts owned by Huguenots at the time of their death.

It should be noted that the amounts appended do not represent the total value of property, but merely personal property such as furniture, slaves, cash, tools, etc. No land or other real estate values are included in this table.

Caleb Avant[72]	1743	£ 3,837
Benj. Avant[73]	1743	3,042
Peter Benoist[74]	1761	6,000

[68] *Ibid.*
[69] MS St. Philip's Vestry Bk., 1732-56, Nov. 26, 1740.
[70] Ibid.
[71] *S. C. Gaz.*, May 14, 1751; MS Col. Doc. S. C. (Council Jrnl.), 1741-43, 166; MS Col. Doc. S. C., XX. 327, 557 f.
[72] MS Pr. Ct. Rcd., 1739-43, 279.
[73] *Ibid.*, 237.
[74] *Ibid.*, 1761-63, 134.

Peter Benoist[75]	1758	8,649
David Boisseau[76]	1758	7,024
James Boisseau[77]	1750	5,000
Anthony Bonneau[78]	1744	6,500
Benj. Bonneau[79]	1763	12,094
Peter Bonneau[80]	1748	9,470
Henrietta C. Cordes[81]	1765	13,178
Francis Coutourier[82]	1758	9,210
Isaac Dubose[83]	1743	6,296
David Dupré[84]	1735	6,092
Capt. John Dutarque[85]	1767	30,675
John Gendron[86]	1725	21,018
Theo. Gourdin[87]	1774	89,632
Daniel Huger[88]	1761	119,501
Mary La Roche[89]	1760	4,699
Solomon Legare[90]	1761	18,580
Francis Le Jau[91]	1761	16,456
Gabriel Manigault[92]	1786	13,569
Suzanne Mayrant[93]	1736	9,979
Paul Mazÿck[94]	1750	50,720
Stephen Mazÿck[95]	1775	47,073
Elisha Prioleau[96]	1746	12,955
Samuel Prioleau[97]	1752	7,011
Paul Trapier[98]	1758	3,002

An admirable trait of the Huguenot, found in the rich and the poor alike, is his benevolence. Among those who lived in Carolina, gifts for worthy causes were so frequent that one hardly reads a will without expecting to find a clause bequeathing something to the French Church in Charles Town, or to St. Phillip's, or to the "poor of the parish", or to some other charitable purpose. It was a philanthropy which, if judged on modern standards, does not seem to have been liberal. Most of those who made such bequests did not give large amounts, compared with the aggregate

[75] MS Pr. Ct. Rcd., 1758-61, 225.
[76] *Ibid.*, 203.
[77] *Ibid.*, 1748-51, 417.
[78] *Ibid.*, 1739-43, 395.
[79] *Ibid.*, 1761-3, 50.
[80] *Ibid.*, 48.
[81] *Ibid.*, 1763-67, 22.
[82] *Ibid.*, 1758-61, 10.
[83] *Ibid.*, 1739-43, 220.
[84] *Ibid.*, 1732-6, 165.
[85] *Ibid.*, 1763-7, 378.
[86] *Ibid.*, 1722-8, 285.
[87] *Ibid.*, 1771-4, 521.
[88] *Ibid.*, 1758-61, 598.
[89] *Ibid.*, 282.
[90] *Ibid.*, 493.
[91] *Ibid.*, 132.
[92] *Ibid.*, 1782-97, 434.
[93] *Ibid.*, 1732-9, 103.
[94] *Ibid.*, 1748-51, 297.
[95] *Ibid.*, 1771-4, 101.
[96] *Ibid.*, 1732-46, 252.
[97] *Ibid.*, 1751-53, 415.
[98] *Ibid.*, 1756-58, 442.

amount of their possessions, but the poorest among them usually gave something. These French Protestants were religiously benevolent. It was a part of their Christianity.

One of the earliest examples is found in the will of Antoine Prudhomme,[99] who in order to create a fund for the relief of the poor bequeathed a cow and three heifers to the French congregation at Goose Creek. The will of Caesar Mozé,[100] giving thirty-seven pounds sterling for the construction of a church, antedates this by seven years, having been drawn up in June, 1687. By the will of George Baudoin, June 22, 1695.[101] June 22, 1695, fifty shillings was given to the poor French people of the country. In 1718 Pierre de St. Julien,[102] the younger, left £18 to the Charles Town French Church. Isaac Mazÿck, the emigrant, expressed in his will the deep feelings that characterized his life.[103] He left £50 currency to the French Church of Charles Town and to the poor of each of the Established Churches and to the poor of the Presbyterian Church he devoted £25. Item No. 18 of his will follows: "Since God has favored my leaving France and the New Babylon (without my bending my knees to the idol) to take refuge in a country where I have by the grace of God and of our good King William of blessed memory, and of our good King George, also of blessed memory, full liberty to exercise our good and holy religion, I have willed my executors to set aside seven hundred pounds, current money of Carolina as it is now, that is seven for one sterling, to put it at interest for the purpose of paying the interest to said minister each year, on condition that he deliver to us a sermon Sunday morning and after dinner, one sermon a fortnight, but if said minister shall give us only one sermon in the morning it will not be necessary to give him but fifty pounds. But the condition

[99] July 21, 1695. MS Pr. Ct. Rcd., 1671-1727, 51, 1692-3, 227.
[100] July 6, 1687. MS Rcds. Court of Ordinary, 1672-92, 282.
[101] MS Pr. Ct. Rcd., 1671-1727, 49; 1692-3, 226; *T. H. S. S. C.*, XI. 49.
[102] MS Pr. Ct. Rcd., 1671-1727, 110; *T. H. S. S. C.*, XI. 42.
[103] MS Pr. Ct. Rcd., 1732-7, 395.

of this is that the service shall be Calvinistic, like that of Holland."

Daniel Huger,[104] remembering the kindly treatment accorded him by the English people, gave the church of Shoredich Parish, near London, fifty pounds out of his South Sea annuities. This, his will states, should be added to the legacy founded by Mrs. Thomas Fairchild and appropriated to the same use, namely, that a sermon be preached each year on "The Wonderful Works of God in the Vegetable Creation".

James Le Bas,[105] of St. John's Berkeley, left £100 currency for purchasing a piece of silver plate for the use of the parish church.[106] William Franchomme, left to the poor of St. Phillip's parish, the sum of £10.[107] Jacob Dupont and Elisha Prioleau each bequeathed £50 for the same purpose. Levi Guichard[108] gave £100 to the needy of St. James, Goose Creek. Peter Manigault[109] showed his impartial benevolence by a gift in his will of £10 to the poor of the English Church of Charles Town and the same amount to the poor of the French Church of Charles Town. Francis Le Brasseur and Hector Bérénger de Beaufain gave in a number of worthy causes, in large and small amounts.[110] Pierre Perdriau[111] (1692) bequeathed £5 to the poor of the French Church of Charles Town and £8 sterling to M. Trouillard, its minister. Louis Perdriau[112] presented to the Charles Town French Church the sum of £4. Katherine Le Noble[113] in January 1725, in her will set aside £6 sterling for the poor of the French Church of Charles Town and the same amount for the poor of St. John's Parish. The

[104] Mch. 2, 1737. MS Pr. Ct. Rcd., 1752-56, 282.
[105] March 2, 1737. MS Pr. Ct. Rcd., 1736-40, 199.
[106] MS St. Philip's Ch. Warden's Acct. Bk., 1725-52, Apr. 11, 1726.
[107] *Ibid.*, Apr. 1727 and June 13, 1748.
[108] MS Pr. Ct. Rcd., 1729-31, 265.
[109] MS Pr. Ct. Rcd., 1671-1727, 216 f.
[110] Gleanings from England, *S. C. H. & G. Mag.*, XI. 132; MS St. Philip's Vestry Bk., 1732-56, Feb. 27, 1737.
[111] MS Pr. Ct. Rcd., 1692-3, 18; *T. H. S. S. C.*, X. 43.
[112] MS Pr. Ct. Rcd., 1692-3, 182; *T. H. S. S. C.*, X. 47.
[113] MS Pr. Ct. Rcd., 1671-1727, 243; *T. H. S. S. C.*, XIII. 27.

poor of the French Church of Jamestown profited by a legacy of £10 currency as did the poor of the French Church of Charles Town by a similar amount,[114] left by the will of Philip Gendron. Louis Poyas[115] left £20 currency to the poor of the French Church of Charles Town. Likewise Jacque La Sade,[116] in November, 1703 bequeathed £5 sterling to the poor of the Charles Town French Church and 50 shillings to the poor of the Charles Town Anglican Church. Noah Serre[117] was one of the few who were thoughtful enough to remember in his will the minister who would officiate at his funeral. He set aside £20 for him. Francis Macaire,[118] born in Pouten Royan, and a merchant in Lyons, before moving to Charles Town, in 1691 gave to the poor of the French Church of Charles Town the sum of £2. This is by no means a complete list of benefactions, but is sufficiently large to prove the prevalence of this trait in the character of the French Protestants of that period.

The French Protestants were intimately identified with the several organizations formed for the purpose of charitable assistance to the needy. They are found active as members and officers in a number of them, notably in the Masonic Lodges, the Ubiquarians, the Fellowship Society, the St. Andrew's Club, the Winyah Society, and the South Carolina Society.[119] Though organized some time before, the Winyah Society was not incorporated until 1757.[120] The identity of the French Protestants with the South Carolina Society was probably most noteworthy. Though the Society was not founded by Huguenots, its origin lay largely in the charitable activities and interests of the French refugees, who were members of the congregation of the Charles Town

[114] MS Pr. Ct. Rcd., 1722-24, 301 f; *T. H. S. S. C.*, XVI. 16.
[115] MS Pr. Ct. Rcd., 1752-56, 479.
[116] MS Pr. Ct. Rcd., 1671-1727, 75.
[117] MS Pr. Ct. Rcd., 1729-31, 88.
[118] *S. C. H. & G. Mag.*, V. 220.
[119] *S. C. Gaz.*, Jan. 2, 1742; Apr. 3, 1742; June 12, 1755; Oct. 9, 1755; Dec. 9, 1732; Apr. 4, 1771; MS Col. Doc. S. C., XXXII. 150 and 159; MS Records S. C. Society.
[120] Cooper, *Statutes*, VIII. 110.

French Church. The exact date of its origin is unknown, owing to the fact that in the fire of 1740 the journals of the Society covering the years prior to April 1738, were destroyed.[121] It was probably founded in 1736, or early in 1737. One of the members of the congregation, being in financial straits, had opened a small tavern in order to support himself and family. It was agreed by members of the congregation, that whenever there was business to transact, they would meet at the tavern and if there was no business to be considered they would meet there anyway several times a week in order to aid the proprietor. The organization was then known as the French Club. As the membership increased it was agreed that each one give fifteen pence at each meeting for the support of other members who might need assistance. From this fact the organization received the appellation, "The Twobit Club".

Owing to disputes and quarrels, by 1738 the Society was threatened with dissolution, but a revision of the regulations embracing a change in the name of the organization and a regulation that none but the English language be spoken, made possible its continuation. In 1738 there were forty-three members. In April, 1743, the general stock of the Society amounted to £2,366-12-6 currency. By 1770, it had increased to £52,686-01-1 currency. In 1777 it amounted to £72,530-11-7 currency. The largest bequests and gifts to the Society prior to the American Revolution were made by Hector Bérénger de Beaufain, Benjamin d'Harriette, and Gabriel Manigault. Benjamin d'Harriette in 1756 gave £3,000, Gabriel Manigault in 1781 gave £5,000. Hundreds of widows have been supported and thousands of children have been fed, clothed and educated by its charities. Many of the leading citizens became identified with it, among them the leading French merchants, philanthropists, and planters of the province. This vine planted by the French Protestants has continued to bless thousands of persons in its nearly two hundred years of continuous activity.

[121] MS Records, S. C. Society.

COLONEL SAMUEL PRIOLEAU, 2ND
1717-1792
Son of Colonel Samuel Prioleau. Clerk of the S. C. Society thirty-five years, 1740 and 1743 to 1777.

CHAPTER XII

CONCLUSION

Our study has brought us to its concluding section. There is little need of carrying the narrative farther. When Lafayette, intrepid adventurer, decided to leave his young wife in France to carry the flame of French devotion for liberty to America he was but typifying in a later age the same devotion of his countrymen who in earlier years were willing to die for freedom's cause. The *Victoire,* the vessel that bore him to America, landed off the coast of Georgetown, South Carolina in 1777. By that time the French Huguenots in Charles Town had become so completely a part of the province, sharing in its public offices and civic and economic responsibilities, as to become one with it. They were no longer a separate group, eager to retain their native tongue, nor even anxious to hold to their Calvinistic religion. Save for the small group who still worshipped in French in the little Huguenot church in Charles Town and a few stolid persons in the country, they were one with the English.

In an earlier age the Huguenots who left France under the extreme conditions of religious and political persecution, hoping to find refuge in alien lands, were by circumstances akin to fate forced to take shelter in the havens of a country for centuries the political enemy of their fatherland. England embraced them with open arms, making them the solicited and encouraged principals in her trade policy and transferring them to the American colonies for mutual advantage. In South Carolina their experiments and industry kept the stream of wealth to the British treasury constant in spite of the fact that political acrimony and class discriminations made them for years the object of the most bitter attacks on the part of both the hostile religious factions and the political opponents.

Their actual numbers and the percentage of their numbers compared with the rest of the population have never been established except in rare instances, for aside from the bare hints left by the Godin enumeration and the few indirect references placed now and then in public records, no statistics have been preserved. Still, judging from the representation of French names appended to petitions, public protests, lists of provincial officers, business directories, in the *South Carolina Gazette,* subscriptions to church buildings, books, etc., it seems to be fair to estimate that after 1700 they constituted no less than from one-tenth to one-fifth of the white population of the province. Edward Randolph, in March 1699, reported 1,500 males in the province between 16 and 65 years of age; 11,000 families of English and French and 5,000 slaves.[1] The Girard enumeration of the same date states that there were 438 French in the colony in addition to 10 families on the West Branch of the Cooper River.[2] This would make a total of about 500 French Protestants. If River's statement that there were 5,500 whites in South Carolina in 1699,[3] is correct, the Huguenots constituted about one-tenth of the population at that time. Commissary Johnston reported that in 1712-13 the French families in the four parishes of the province where they were most numerous constituted one-sixth of the total population of the province.[4] An address to the King dated Feb. 24, 1717-18 sent and signed by the leading inhabitants of the province, heads of families, has appended to it the signatures of 563 men;[5] 53 of these were French Protestants. In 1723, the French in the city of Charles Town constituted about one-fifth of the population and paid proportionately in taxes.[6] Whether or not the rural areas would show the same proportion throughout cannot be established, but in

[1] *Cal. St. Pa.,* 1699, no. 183.
[2] Rivers, *Sketch,* 447.
[3] *Ibid.,* 443.
[4] MS Rawlinson, C. 943. Bodleian Lib. MSS, Oxford.
[5] MS Col. Doc. S. C., VII. 88.
[6] *Ibid.,* X. 82 f.

1713 the French in the country constituted one-sixth of the rural population. In the year 1723, in a petition of the "major part of the inhabitants of Charles Town" to the Assembly, 113 names were appended of which 26 were French.[7] Taxable inhabitants in 1723-4 in South Carolina numbered 13,000.[8] In July, 1733, Rev. Bugnion reported that three-fourths of the inhabitants of Santee parish were French. Advertisements in newspapers leave a similar impression,[9] though of course no accurate and reliable deductions can be made from the facts at this distance.

Again, our study has indicated that of their life the two leading features of which we have knowledge were: their religious activities, and their economic importance. The fact that they emigrated from a French anti-Huguenot soil to an Anglican environment in the British Isles produced important results in the ecclesiastical and political history of Carolina. The first two decades of their new life were chiefly occupied in becoming established economically and in settling their political and ecclesiastical allegiance. In permanently and extensively transplanting and propagating their Calvinistic principles and churches they failed; in producing fortunes, in building the economic structure of the province, in developing the natural resources, they succeeded.

Distributing themselves along the tide-water area and later far into the back-country, principally on the frontier, often forced to accept the less desirable and the least protected tracts, they became an important factor in the industrial development of Carolina. Practically forced into allegiance with Anglicanism, they were rapidly absorbed ecclesiastically. The British interests and beliefs overcame those of the French. In rapidity, completeness and in the manner accomplished it is one of the most remarkable cases of absorption in history. On the contrary, however, in their

[7] *Ibid.*, MS Rawlinson, C. 943.

[8] MS Col. Doc. S. C., XI. 19; Drayton's *View*, 103, gives 14,000; Holmes, *Am. Annals*, II. 110, 14,000; Glen, *Descript. of S. C.*, in Caroll, II. 261, 14,000.

[9] Bugnion to Bishop of London, Fulham Palace MSS, S. C.

industrial life they overcame their British neighbors. Sent to Carolina by the English authorities for the purpose of producing wine, oil and silk, the victims of a bargain-counter colonial policy, they gradually abandoned their first purposes and their original trades to become specialists in raising horses, in brokerage, in rice and indigo culture, in stock raising, money lending, etc. Their inventions and discoveries and those of their descendants came into general use in the South. Skilled in nearly all of the industries of France, and of sturdy, industrious habits, they could not do otherwise than influence the economic activities of their environment. It cannot be disputed that they were people of unusual industrial ability. Emigrating in poverty, they soon became well-to-do and rich. A number of large fortunes were found among them. The second quarter of the eighteenth century beheld them as the lenders of large amounts to their numerous English neighbors. In Guerrard's "Pendulum Engine" for pounding rice, in the natural monopoly on the manufacture of salt, in the introduction of indigo and in the marked improvements in the growth of rice, silk, and wine, as well as in cultural endeavours, the French Protestants played an important part. As defenders of the frontier, as political leaders, as industrious builders of fortunes, as tillers of the soil, their influence on Carolina cannot be erased. Among their poor are found examples of the most heroic struggles against privation and poverty; among their wealthy, praiseworthy examples of benevolence. Their interests and affections, diverted from their native land by their exile and the attitude of the French government after their departure, were given over to the espousal of the claims of the country of their adoption. In the Revolutionary war, their descendants, with but few exceptions, were loyal supporters of the cause of the Colonies and with unalloyed devotion fought and died in the ranks that sought the overthrow of British rule.

BIBLIOGRAPHY

Manuscript Material

The manuscripts used in the preparation of this essay were, in the main, of the crudest sort. They comprise the almost complete set of written records of the province of South Carolina from 1669 to 1787, the great mass of original and copied wills, inventories, mortgages, indentures, church and parish registers, letters, etc. The journals of the Assembly and Council reveal the important positions held by French Protestants, their political and business interests and the vital part played by them in the several crises that shook the province to the center. With the exception of only a few incidents, the valuable transcripts of the British Record Office contained in the Colonial Records of South Carolina, also known as London Transcripts, are indispensable to this study. They reveal the large amount of correspondence carried on between the colonial officers, the emigrant Protestants, and the British authorities. They contain in tables, lists, and other form, valuable information regarding the industrial, social and ecclesiastical development of the colony. These together with the Land Warrants, Grant Books, Indian Books, Secretary's Records, and other public records described below, constitute an exceedingly valuable collection of manuscript material, most of which has not been published. Few, if any, are provided with reliable indexes, some are not paged.

Assembly Journals, in the Office of the Historical Commission, Columbia.

Sept. 20, 1692 to Aug. 28, 1701; original.
Aug. 24, 1702 to Apr. 9, 1706; original.
March 6, 1707 to July 17, 1707; original.
April 2, 1712 to Oct. 11, 1715; copy.
Feb. 28, 1716 to Aug. 15, 1721; copy.
July 31, 1716 to Dec. 17, 1720; original.
May 25, 1722 to Feb. 15, 1725; copy.
March 23, 1724 to Sept. 30, 1727; original.
Jan. 31, 1728 to July 22, 1728; London Transcripts.
Jan. 21, 1729 to Sept. 22, 1733; London Transcripts.
Feb. 7, 1734 to Sept. 6, 1735; original.
March 5, 1735 to March 5, 1738; London Transcripts.
Nov. 6, 1734 to May 29, 1736; original.
May 25, 1736 to March 1, 1737; original.

Mar. 1, 1737 to Mar. 15, 1739; original.
Mar. 15, 1739 to Feb. 27, 1740; original.
Feb. 27, 1740 to Sept. 19, 1740; original.
Nov. 18, 1740 to May 23, 1741; original.
May 23, 1741 to July 1, 1741; original.
July 1, 1741 to Jan. 28, 1742; original.
Jan. 28, 1742 to July 10, 1742; original.
Sept. 14, 1742 to May 7, 1743; original.
Oct. 4, 1743 to July 7, 1744; original.
Oct. 2, 1744 to May 25, 1745; original.
Sept. 10, 1745 to June 17, 1746; original.
Sept. 10, 1746 to June 13, 1747; original.
Jan. 19, 1748 to June 29, 1748; original.
Mar. 28, 1749 to Nov. 21, 1749; original.
Nov. 21, 1749 to May 31, 1750; original.
Nov. 13, 1750 to Aug. 31, 1751; original.
Nov. 14, 1751 to Oct. 7, 1752; original.
Nov. 21, 1752 to Aug. 25, 1753; original.
Jan. 8, 1754 to Sept. 6, 1754; original.
Nov. 12, 1754 to Sept. 23, 1755; original.
Nov. 20, 1755 to July 6, 1757; original.
Oct. 6, 1757 to April 7, 1759; original.
July 2, 1759 to Jan. 24, 1761; original.
March 26, 1761 to Dec. 24, 1761; original.
Feb. 6, 1762 to Sept. 13, 1762; original.
Jan. 24, 1763 to Oct. 6, 1764; original.
Jan. 8, 1765 to April 12, 1768; original.
March 14, 1769 to Nov. 5, 1771; original.
Oct. 8, 1772 to Aug. 30, 1775; original.

Bodleian Library MSS, Oxford. See Rawlinson MSS.

Bacot Papers, in possession of Thomas Wright Bacot, Esq., Charleston.

Book of Memorials of Deceased French Protestants, in French Protestant Church, Charleston.

British Colonial Papers, containing material relating to South Carolina, in the form of accounts, descriptions, instructions, orders, letters, etc., Library of Congress.

CHURCH, VESTRY, AND PARISH RECORDS

Christ Church Parish, Vestry Minutes, 1708-1847.

Christ Church Parish Register, 1694-1784. In possession of The Colonial Dames of South Carolina.

Circular Church Minutes, 1732-96, and Register, 1732-8, original in possession of the Church.

Prince Frederick Winyah (Winyaw) Register, 1713-78, copy in possession of Mr. J. Ioor Waring, Esq., Charleston.

St. Andrew's Church and Parish Register, 1714-1899, in possession of The Colonial Dames of South Carolina.

St. Helena's Parish Register, 1724 ff., in possession of The Colonial Dames of South Carolina.

Minute Book, 1706-1812, copy in possession of Mr. J. Ioor Waring, Esq., Charleston.

St. Michael's Church Vestry Book, 1759 ff.

St. James Santee Parish Register, 1758-88, in possession of The Colonial Dames of South Carolina.

St. James Colleton, Minutes, 1734-1817, in possession of The Colonial Dames of South Carolina.

St. Matthew's Parish Vestry Minutes, 1767-1838, in possession of The Colonial Dames of South Carolina.

Register of the Church of the Redeemer of Orangeburgh, South Carolina, Register of the First Episcopal Church, of Orangeburgh and Amelia Townships, 1744 f., certified copy in possession of Charleston Library Society.

St. Phillip's Church Wardens' Account Book, 1725-52,

St. Phillip's Church Wardens' Account Book, 1756-76,

St. Phillip's Church Register, 1720-58,

St. Phillip's Church Register, 1753-82,

St. Phillip's Church Vestry Books, 1732-55,

St. Phillip's Church Vestry Books, 1756-76, all in the archives of the church.

St. Stephen's Parish Vestry Book, 1754 ff., in possession of J. Ioor Waring, Charleston.

These show the distribution of the French Protestants over the province, indicate their church affiliation, marriages, dates of birth and death, and give lists of beneficiaries of poor relief, with some of their occupations, incumbencies of parish positions, etc.

OTHER RECORDS

Claims of South Carolina Loyalists in the American Revolution, taken from the set of 57 volumes of transcripts in the New York Public Library secured from the British Public Record Office. Only four of the South Carolina descendants of French Protestants appear in the list. Information of value and interest is found in these volumes, for example, the offices of public trust held by those included in the lists, the value of their personal property, and the losses they sustained.

Colonial Dames of South Carolina, Records. This is not always dependable material, though some things were found here not found elsewhere.

Colonial Documents of South Carolina, also known as London Transcripts, copies of a mass of records in the British Public Record Office relating to South Carolina, during its provincial history. 36 volumes.

Vol. 1. 1663-84.
2. 1685-90.
3. 1690-97.
4. 1698-1700.
5. 1701-10.
6. 1711-16.
7. 1717 to March 1720.
8. April 1720 to December 1720.
9. 1721-2.
10. 1723.
11. 1723-5.
12. 1725-7.
13. 1728-9.
14. 1730.
15. 1731-2.
16. 1732-4.
17. 1734-5.
18. 1736-7.
19. 1738.
20. 1739-42.
21. 1743-4.
22. 1745-7.
23. 1748-9.
24. 1750-1.
25. 1752-3.
26. 1754-5.
27. 1756-7.
28. 1758-60.
29. 1761-3.
30. 1764-5.
31. 1766-7.
32. 1768-70.
33. 1771-3.
34. 1774.
35. 1775.
36. 1776-82.

All in the Office of the Historical Commission of South Carolina, Columbia.

Commissions, Instructions, etc., 1732-42, Historical Commission, Columbia.

Council Journals:

Aug. 25, 1671-92, scattered records; original.
1696, original.
Aug. 12, 1717 to Oct. 3, 1717; copy.
June 28, 1721 to July 11, 1721; copy.
May 23, 1722 to Feb. 23, 1723; copy.
June 2, 1724 to June 17, 1724; copy.
May 17, 1725 to May 21, 1726; original.
June 14, 1727 to Sept. 30, 1727; original.
Dec. 18, 1727 to Feb. 21, 1729; original.
June 26, 1729 to Apr. 29, 1730; original.
Dec. 16, 1730 to Sept. 22, 1733; original.
Nov. 13, 1733 to May 31, 1734; original.
Nov. 7, 1734 to Oct. 7, 1737; original.

And all subsequent journals to and including 1776, all in the Office of the Historical Commission, Columbia.

Court of Ordinary, Records, Deeds, Grants, Bills, Bonds, Wills, etc.

Volumes: 1672-92.
Nov. 1675 to Oct. 1796.
1684-87.
Jan. 26, 1686 to May 5, 1714.
1710-14.
1692-1711.
May 12, 1712 to May 29, 1713.
June 23, 1707 to Sept. 20, 1711.
June 30, 1705 to Feb. 19, 1709.
Sept. 27, 1704 to April 18, 1709.
1709-11.

All in the Office of the Historical Commission of South Carolina, Columbia.

These records were kept by the Secretary of the Province and by the Governor, as Ordinary for the same. Other Ordinary Records are found in Charleston and are listed under the Probate Court Records of Charleston.

Crottet MSS, in 3 volumes, 1578 ff. Records of parishes and consistories in France; letters, accounts of personal visits to Huguenot prisoners in the galleys, confessions of faith, etc. Purchased by the Charleston Library Society from the widow of M. Crottet, a French Protestant, Pastor of Saintonge, France, who rescued them from an old dove-cote of the Château D'Uzes.

De Saussure Family History, by Wilmot De Saussure, in possession of Isabelle De Saussure, Charleston.

Fulham Palace MSS, London. Letters by Fr. Le Jau, John La Pierre, Joseph Bugnion, etc., illuminating the period 1706 ff.

Gaillard MSS, prepared in or about 1848 by Thomas Gaillard. This is a narrative of the lives of a number of Huguenots and their descendants, and of some of the Huguenot Churches of South Carolina. It quotes copiously from standard authors such as Dalcho, etc. Though it is faulty in some of its stated facts, parts are valuable because Mr. Gaillard had access to material that has since perished. The list of names the MS contains is not complete. It also contains some that evidently were not of French extraction (cf. Gaillard list of Huguenots of South Carolina, published 1848).

Grant Books, vols. F; no. 8 C; no. c., 1694-1739 and a number of other volumes of grant books were consulted. All in Office of Hist. Commission, Columbia; and Office of Secretary of State. Volumes: P. no. 3; A 12; B 14; A. A; F no. 10; all in Mesne Conveyance Office, Charleston.

Hazard Transcripts of South Carolina material in British Public Record Office. See South Carolina material, in Library of Congress.

Hayne Records, preserved by Colonel Isaac Hayne, who was executed by the British in 1781. Records of births, deaths, cattle marks, etc., apparently taken from newspaper reports, hearsay, etc. In possession of the South Carolina Historical Society.

Huguenot Society of South Carolina Minutes, 1885 ff.

Indian Books. These are the journals of the Commissioners of the Indian trade and other Indian affairs. 1710; 1716-18; 1716; Letters and documents concerning Indian affairs: 1752-3; 1753-4; 1754-7; 1757-60; 1749-62. Office Hist. Com., Columbia.

Land Plats, 20 volumes covering the years 1680 to 1776. In the Office of the Secretary of State.

Land Warrants, 2 volumes, 1672-92, 1692-1711. Contain lists of servants and slaves, names of emigrants, amounts of land allotted and for what purposes. In the office of the Hist. Com., Columbia.

Manigault Diary. Purports to be extracts from the original diary of Mrs. Ann Manigault, wife of Gabriel Manigault. The original has perished. In possession of the South Carolina Hist. Soc.

Manigault MSS, consisting of letters, accounts, bills, and miscellaneous matter, in possession of the South Carolina Hist. Society; of the Misses Jervey, Charleston; and of Mrs. Josephine Jenkins, Adams Run, South Carolina.

Marriage Bond Book. A volume of original marriage bonds, 1743-4. The only one known to be in existence. In possession of the Charleston Library Society.

Mazÿck Bible, containing the family register of a number of Mazÿcks. In possession of Mrs. Arthur Mazÿck, Charleston.

Memorial Books:

A. Vol. I, part 2, 1732-4.
A. Vol. I, part 3, 1732-7.
A. Vol. I, part 4, 1732-40.
B. Vol. II, 1733-42.
D. Vol. IV, 1732-63.
E.F. Vol. V, VI, 1761-2.
G. Vol. VII, 1762-5.
H. Vol. VIII, 1765-8.

K. Vol. X, 1769-71.
L. Vol. XI, 1771-2.
M. Vol. XII, 1772-4.
N. Vol. XIII, 1774-5.
O. Vol. XIV } 1672-92.
P. Vol. XV }

This set of Memorial Books was the result of the revolution in the record offices of the province about 1730-2. At this time an attempt was made to have all land and other titles recorded and restored. Many had been lost and the land office for years had been closed and at intervals had kept practically no records. These conditions endangered the validity of claims, so depositions and affidavits were taken and testimony heard from persons witnessing transactions. Rewards and bounties were offered to persons for information that would assist the authorities in restoring the records. The volumes contain, therefore, material contained elsewhere, but have also much that is found nowhere else. In the office Hist. Com. Columbia.

North American, Miscellaneous Papers. Instructions, Orders, etc., Am. Br., 1704, Library of Congress. Contain letters, orders, instructions, accounts relating to the colonial period in South Carolina.

New Castle Papers, Library of Congress, may be similarly described.

Pension Office Archives, Revolutionary War Department. Here are preserved the records of the number of descendants of Huguenots who engaged in militia service and were active in the Revolutionary War. Washington, D. C.

Porcher Bible, containing the family records, in possession of Mr. Isaac de C. Porcher, Pinopolis, S. C., originally owned by the emigrant, Isaac Porcher.

Pennsylvania Historical Society Manuscript Collection, containing valuable letters of South Carolina French Protestants, letters and orders of Francis Marion, letters of Peter Timothy, one volume of letters of Henry Laurens, the Boudinot papers, account books, etc. Philadelphia.

Probate Court Records, Charleston, South Carolina. (See also Records of the Court of Ordinary.)

Volumes: 1671-1727.
1672-92.
1687-1710.
1692-3.
1694-1704.
1711-18.
1714-17.
1716-31.
1721-31.
1720-1.
1720-2.
1722-4.
1724-5.
1722-8.
1722-6.
1726-27.

1727-9.	1756-61.
1729-31.	1758-61.
1731-6.	1758-63.
1736-40.	1761-3.
1736-9.	1763-7.
1739-43.	1761-77 R.R.
1740-6.	1765-9.
1746-9.	1761-7.
1748-51.	1767-71.
1749-51.	1771-5.
1751-4.	1774-9.
1752-8.	1782-97.
1754-8.	1783-86.

Ravenel MS, prepared by Daniel Ravenel. A history of the Huguenots of South Carolina. Draws copiously from standard authors, such as Dalcho, etc. Though not entirely reliable, it contains material that is valuable because based on observations and on material that has since been lost. *The Ravenel List of Huguenots,* better known as the *St. Julien List,* contains the names of 154 French Protestants of South Carolina. The MS list was found among the papers that had belonged to Mr. Henry de St. Julien, of St. Johns Berkley, who died in 1768-9 at the age of 70 years. It has been published in *The Southern Intelligencer,* 1822, and in pamphlet form by Mr. Theo. G. Thomas of New York.

Ravenel Record Books,
Record Book, 1741-87.
Ledger A, Jan. 1750 f.
Day Book, 1748 f.
These are valuable for the lists of names of persons in the St. John's district, who had accounts with the Ravenels at their plantation commissary. There are also lists of slaves, diary extracts, accounts, letters, etc. In possession of Mrs. H. F. Porcher and Mrs. R. Y. Dwight, Pinopolis.

Rawlinson MSS, Bodleian Library, Oxford. The appointment of the Rev. Albert Pouderous, the appointment of the Rev. Paul L'Escott, 1719, and the report of Commisary Johnson, on ecclesiastical affairs in South Carolina in 1713. The latter is the most valuable single document for the period 1706 ff. that the author has found. See appendix.

Register's Records, volumes: 1675-96.
1696-1703.
1704-8.
1707-11.

In the office of the Hist. Com., Columbia.

Royal Society (London), MSS. Moses Lindo's letter of description of his experiments with indigo in South Carolina.

Sainsbury Papers, descriptions, letters, accounts, transcripts from British Record Office, etc. New York Public Library.

Secretary's Records, volumes: 1685-1712.
1675-1696.
1704-8.
1703-9.
1709-11.

Contain lists of emigrants, land records, commissions, letters, accounts, etc. In the office of the Hist. Com., Columbia.

Society for the Propagation of the Gospel in Foreign Parts. Transcripts of records. About 150 volumes in Library of Congress.

South Carolina Papers, miscellaneous letters, papers, correspondence between Geo. Bancroft and Mr. Rivers, transcripts of British Record Office, accounts, etc., New York Public Library.

South Carolina Papers, miscellaneous as above, Library of Congress.

South Carolina Society, Records, 1739-76, Charleston. Valuable because this society was founded by Huguenots. The earliest records are lost, but the list of members, as restored, is thought to be complete, or nearly so.

Turquand Records. History and original documents relating to the activities of the Rev. Paul Turquand, in possession of Mrs. Louisa Smythe, Charleston. Valuable because they throw light on the activities of one of the clergymen of French extraction, who came to South Carolina late in the eighteenth century. There are three volumes of MS sermons, by Turquand, in the collection. Also the Pierce Family Records and the MS of David G. McCord, whose mother was one of the daughters of Paul Turquand.

Miscellaneous:

Numerous letters, muster books, papers of various kinds, in the possession of the Charleston Library Society.

Account books, letters, papers, receipts, etc., relating to the Laurens and Manigault families. In possession of the South Carolina Historical Society, Charleston.

Book of accounts with Indians, bills and letters, in the Ayer Collection, Newberry Library, Chicago.

Original land indentures, letters, receipts, etc., in the possession of Mrs. H. F. Porcher, and Mr. Isaac de C. Porcher, Pinopolis, South Carolina.

MAPS AND ATLASES

Original pen map of Hillsboro Township, by Patrick Calhoun. In the office of the Hist. Com., Columbia.

Original pen map of Purrysburg Township, by Hugh Bryan. In the office of the Hist. Com., Columbia.

Original pen map of the Southern Colonies, by Joseph Purcell, Newberry Library, Chicago.

Crisp Map, in Library of Congress, by E. Crisp. The date assigned to it is 1711. It is a map of South Carolina and contains two inserts, one of the town and harbour of Charleston, the other of the town and harbour of St. Augustine.

Mill's Atlas of South Carolina. Columbia. 1825.

Carte Particuliere de la Caroline, about 1700, by Pierre Mortier, Amsterdam.

The Moll Map of Carolina, 1706.

Map of South Carolina in Jeffreys' American Atlas, by Henry Mouzon, et al., 1776.

Map of South Carolina, by Jedediah Morse, in American Geography. London, 1794.

PRIMARY PUBLISHED MATERIAL

Almanacs and Registers of South Carolina, published by Wells and by Tobler, for 1762, 1763, 1765, 1770, 1774, 1776; in South Carolina Hist. Soc. Library, Charleston. For 1766, 1768, 1769, 1771, 1775, 1776, 1777, 1778, 1779; in possession of the Charleston Library Society. Almanacs of South Carolina and Georgia, 1766, 1767, 1768, 1770, 1782; South Carolina Hist. Soc. Library.

American Archives, (Force) 4th Series, 6 volumes.
5th Series, 3 volumes.
Washington, 1837 passim.

ARCHDALE, (JOHN) *Description of South Carolina.* London, 1707.

BLOME, R. *Present State of His Majesties Isles and Territories.* London, 1687.

BREVARD, JOS. *Digest of the Public Statute Laws of South Carolina.* 3 volumes, Charleston, 1810.

BURKE, E. *Account of the European Settlements in America.* London, 1757.

BURTON, ROBERT. *The English Empire in America.* London, 1739.

Calendar of State Papers:
Domestic Series, 1625-95, 61 volumes.
Colonial Series, 1574-1702, 30 volumes.

Canadian Archives. Second Report of the Bureau of Archives for the Province of Ontario. (Claims of Loyalists for property and other losses during the Revolutionary War.) Part II.

CARROLL, B. R. *Historical Collections of South Carolina.* 2 volumes, New York, 1836.

Charleston, Government of the French Church of. Charleston, 1845.

CLUTE, ROBERT. *St. Thomas and St. Denis Parish Registers,* 1680-1884; registers and a short history. Charleston, 1884.

Collections of the Historical Society of South Carolina. 5 volumes, Charleston, 1857 to 1897.

Collections and Publications of the Huguenot Society of America. 7 volumes.

Colonial Records of the State of Georgia, 1732-1776. Atlanta, 1904 passim.

COOPER, THOMAS. *Statutes at Large of South Carolina,* 1669 f. 6 volumes, Columbia, 1836 passim.

COOPER, WILLIAM DURANT. *List of Foreign Protestants and Aliens Resident in England,* 1618-88. Printed for the Camden Society, 1862.

[DEFOE, DANIEL.] *Case of the Protestant Dissenters in South Carolina.* London, 1706.

DE SAUSSURE, W. G. *Names of the Officers of South Carolina Regiments.* Columbia, 1886.

Discipline, Reformed Church of France. 1718.

Documents Chiefly Unpublished Relating to the Huguenot Emigration to Virginia. Brock, R. A., *Virginia Historical Collections.* Vol. V. Richmond.

DRAYTON, JOHN. *View of South Carolina.* Charleston, 1802.

FAUST, A. B., AND BRUMBAUGH, G. M. *Lists of Swiss Emigrants in the Eighteenth Century to the American Colonies.* 2 volumes. Washington, D. C., 1920-1925.

FORCE, PETER. *Tracts.* 4 volumes, Washington, 1836-46.

FOTHERGILL, GERALD. *List of Emigrant Ministers to America,* 1690-1811. London, 1904. Based on MSS in British Public Record Office. Contains a list of about 1,200 names of ministers and teachers who received Royal bounty for passage.

Gaillard List of Huguenots of South Carolina, prepared by Mr. Thomas Gaillard, Esq., of Mobile, Alabama, after years of search. It contains some names that are clearly not Huguenot, as Chicken, Christie, Coram, etc. Mr. Gaillard moved to Alabama in 1832. He completed his MS and list in 1848. See Gaillard MS.

GLEN, JAMES. *Description of South Carolina.* London, 1761.

HEITMAN, F. B. *Historical Register of Officers of the Continental Army during the War of the Revolution.* Washington, 1893.

HENING, WILLIAM WALLER. *A collection of all the Laws of Virginia.* (1619 f.), volume III. Philadelphia, 1823.

HOLMES, ABIEL. *American Annals,* 1669-1775. Cambridge, 1805.

HOLBROOK, E. *Journal and Letters of Eliza Lucas.* Wormsloe, 1850. Only 18 copies printed.

Huguenot Society of London, Publications and Proceedings of the. Contain valuable material in the form of church registers, lists of naturalized Frenchmen, beneficiaries, lists of ministers, etc. The records of some of the French churches of the British Isles have been lost. The congregations died out and the records, if any were kept, were lost. The registers of many of the most important ones, however, have been preserved. A Royal commission appointed for the purpose collected many of them and placed them in the custody of the Register General, at Somerset House. Most of them passed through the hands of Mr. J. S. Burn, Secretary of the Commission, who in 1846 published the results of his examination in his history entitled, *History of the French Protestants in England.* The registers are being printed in full by the Huguenot Society of London.

La Liturgie ou la maniere de celebrer Le Service Divine dans L'église de Geneva. Geneva and Paris, 1828.

LAWSON, JOHN. *Journal.* London, 1714; London, 1718.

Letter from a Swiss Gentleman to his Friend in Bern. London, 1732.

Liste des François et Suisses. Reprint from MSS. (See Ravenel List.) Charleston, 1868.

Liturgy of the French Protestant Church. Translated from the editions of 1737 and 1772, published at Neufchatel with additional prayers, arranged for the use of the French Church of Charleston, South Carolina. Charleston, 1836.

London Gazette, 1698 and 1699.

MCCORD, DAVID J. *Statutes at Large of South Carolina,* volumes 7-10. Columbia, 1841 passim.

MARTYN, BENJAMIN. *An Account Showing the Progress of the Colony of Georgia.* London, 1741. Martyn was Secretary of the Trustees of Georgia. The account shows the part that South Carolina residents played in the early settlement of Georgia.

PHILLIPS, U. B. *Documentary History of American Industrial Society,* volumes I and II. Cleveland, 1910. Contains some material relative to Huguenots of South Carolina.

Purry Memorial, Presented to His Grace the Duke of New Castle, etc., On the Present Condition of South Carolina, by Jean Pierre Purry, of Neufchatel, Switzerland. Reprinted by Col. C. C. Jones, Augusta, 1880.

NAIRN, THOMAS. *Letter from South Carolina.* London, 1710.

QUICK, JOHN. *Synodicon in Gallia Reformata, or Acts, Decisions, Decrees, and Canons of the Famous Councils of the Reformed Churches of France.* 2 volumes, London, 1692.

RAVENEL, HENRY E. *Ravenel Records.* Atlanta, 1898. Contains a history of the Ravenel Family in Europe and America and a number of reprints of original documents.

RIVERS, WILLIAM J. *Sketch of the History of South Carolina, to 1719.* Charleston, 1856. Appendix contains valuable source materials.

"The Carolinas," in Windsor's *Critical and Narrative History.*

A Chapter in the Early History of South Carolina, Charleston, 1874.

RUPP, DANIEL. *A Collection of 30,000 Names of Germans, Swiss, Dutch, and French, in Pennsylvania, 1727-1776.* Philadelphia, 1876. Contains names, later and earlier familiar in South Carolina.

St. Andrews Society of Charleston, Laws and List of Members, together with an historical sketch. Published by the Society.

SALLEY, ALEXANDER S., JR.:

Warrants for Land in South Carolina, 1672-79. Columbia, 1910.

Warrants for Land in South Carolina, 1680-92. Columbia, 1912.

Journal of the Grand Council of South Carolina, 1671-80. Columbia, 1907.

Journal of the Grand Council, Apr. to Sept. 1692. Columbia, 1907.

Journal of the Grand Council, 1693. Columbia, 1907.

Journal of the Commons House of Assembly, Sept. and Oct. 1692. Columbia, 1907.

Journal of the Commons House of Assembly, Jan. to Mch. 1696. Columbia, 1908.

Narratives of Early Carolina, 1650-1708. New York, 1912.

SAUNDERS, WILLIAM L. *Colonial Records of North Carolina.* Volume I. Raleigh, 1886.

Society for the Propagation of the Gospel, Digest of Records. 5th edition, London, 1895. Known in the body of this work as *S. P. G. Digest.*

Society for the Propagation of the Gospel, Society's abstracts of proceedings. For the years 1702 to 1788 inclusive, contained in the collection of the New York Public Library and of St. Phillip's Home, Charleston. Published in London by the Society. The Proceedings of each year are published separately and have appended the sermon preached at the annual meeting of the society. Known in the body of this work as *S. P. G. Abstracts.*

South Carolina Gazette, 1731-1776, edited and published in Charleston by Thomas Whitmarsh, and Lewis, Elizabeth, and Peter Timothy.

South Carolina Gazette and Country Journal, 1765 to 1775, edited by Charles Crouch and Mary Crouch.

Statutes of the Realm. 8 volumes, London, 1821.

Statutes at Large. (Danby Pickering) Cambridge, 1762.

TIMOTHY, PETER. *Extracts from Journals of the Provincial Congress of South Carolina, held in Charleston, November 1-24, 1775.*

THOMAS, ISAIAH. *History of Printing in America,* 2 volumes. Worcester, 1810.

TROTT, NICHOLAS. *Laws of South Carolina.* London, 1721.

Wells Register; see Almanacs.

WESTON, P. C. J. *Documents in Connection with the History of South Carolina.* London, 1856.

SEMI-SOURCE MATERIAL

(Material which because of the fact that it was written contemporaneously, or nearly contemporaneously, with the period in question, becomes practically primary source material, though not strictly so.)

ANDERSON, ADAM. *History and Chronological Deduction of the Origin of Commerce.* 4 volumes, London, 1801.

BEVERLEY, ROGER. *A History of the Present State of Virginia.* London, 1705.

BURN, J. S. *A History of the French Protestants in England.* London, 1846.

BURTON, ROBERT. *The English Empire in America.* 7th edition. London, 1739.

CLAUDE, F. *Short Account of the Complaints and Cruel Persecutions of the Protestants in the Kingdom of France.* London, 1707.

DALCHO, FREDERICK. *An Historical Account of the Protestant Episcopal Church in South Carolina.* Charleston, 1820. Remarkably free from error, and a mine of valuable information.

DRAYTON, JOHN. *View of South Carolina.* Charleston, 1802.

HEWAT, ALEXANDER. *History of South Carolina and Georgia.* 2 volumes, London, 1779.

HUMPHREYS, DAVID. *Historical Account of the Incorporated Society for the Propagation of the Gospel in Foreign Parts.* London, 1720. Also published in Carroll's Collections.

JAMES, WILLIAM D. *Life of Marion.* Charleston, 1820.

MCPHERSON, DAVID. *Annals of Commerce.* 4 volumes, London, 1805.

MILLS, ROBERT. *Statistics of South Carolina.* Charleston, 1826.

SIMPSON, WILLIAM. *Practical Justice of the Peace, of South Carolina.* Charleston, 1761.

SOULIER, PIERRE. *Histoire du Calvinisme.* Paris, 1686.

THOMAS, ISAIAH. *History of Printing in America.* 2 volumes, Worcester, Mass., 1810.

GENERAL WORKS

AGNEW, D. C. A. *Protestant Exiles from France.* 3 volumes, London, 1871.

ASHE, S. A. *History of North Carolina.* Greensboro, 1908.

ASTIE, J. F. *Histoire de la Republique Etats Unis.* 2 volumes, Paris, 1865.

BAIRD, HENRY. *Rise of the Huguenots in France.* New York, 1900.

BAIRD, CHARLES W. *The Huguenot Emigration to America.* 2 volumes, New York, 1895.

BISHOP, J. L. *History of American Manufactures,* 1608-1860. 3 volumes, Philadelphia, 1866.

BOSTAQUET, DUMONT DE. *Memoires inedits de Dumont de Bostaquet.* Paris, 1864.

BROWNING, W. S. *A History of the Huguenots.* 3 volumes, Paris and London, 1839.

BURN, J. S. *History of the French Protestants in England.* London, 1846.

CHAPMAN, JOHN A. *History of Edgefield County, South Carolina.* Newberry, 1897.

CLEMENT, PIERRE. *Lettres, Instructions and Memoires de Colbert.* 7 volumes, Paris, 1861-70-82.

COMBE, ERNEST. *Les refugiées de la revocation en Suisse*. Lausanne, 1885. English translation by Teofilo & Comba. London, 1889.

COURT, ANTOINE. *Mémoire historique de ce qui s'est passé de plus remarquable au sujet de la religion réformée en plusieurs provinces de France,* etc. Paris, 1876.

DEMAREST, DAVID D. *The Reformed Church in America.* 4th edition, New York, 1889.

DEWHURST, WILLIAM W. *History of St. Augustine, Florida.* New York, 1881.

DRAYTON, JOHN. *Memoirs of the American Revolution.* 2 volumes, Charleston, 1821.

DUMONT, GEORGES MARIE BUTEL. *Histoire et Commerce des Colonies Anglaises dans Amerique.* A la Haye, 1775.

FAIRBANKS, GEORGE R. *The Spaniards in Florida.* Jacksonville, 1868.

FLOQUET, AMABLE. *Histoire du Parlement de Normandie.* Rouen, 1840-2.

FONTAINE, PETER. *Memoirs of a Huguenot Family.* New York, 1892.

GRAYSON, WILLIAM J. *Life of James L. Petigru.* New York, 1866.

GREGG, ALEXANDER. *History of the Old Cheraws,* 1730-1810. New York, 1867.

HAAG, E. *Bulletin de la Societie du Protestantisme Français.* Paris, 1852-61.

HAWKS, FRANCIS L., AND PERRY, WILLIAM S. *Documentary History of the Protestant Episcopal Church of the United States of America.* New York, 1862.

HEWAT, ALEXANDER. *An Historical Account of the Rise and Progress of the Colonies of South Carolina and Georgia.* 2 volumes, London, 1779.

HOWE, GEORGE. *History of the Presbyterian Church of South Carolina.* Columbia, 1870. 2 volumes. Valuable and clear, though slightly partisan.

IRVING, L. *History of the Turf in South Carolina.* 1857. Not always reliable and accurate.

LEVASSEUR, EMILE. *Cours d'economie rurale.* Paris, 1876.

LOGAN, J. H. *History of the Upper Country of South Carolina.* Volume I, Columbia, 1859. Volume II, in MS in Wisconsin Historical Society Library, Madison.

MARTIN, FRANCIS XAVIER. *History of North Carolina.* 2 volumes, New Orleans, 1829.

McCRADY, EDWARD. *History of South Carolina, 1670 to 1860.* New York, 1897 *et seq.* 4 volumes.

MASSON, GUSTAV. *Huguenots, A Sketch of their History.* Cassell, 1881.

MOERIKOFER, J. C. *Geschichte der evangelischen Flüchtlinge in der Schweiz.* Leipzig, 1864.

MONTET, ALBERT DE. *Dictionnaire biographique des Genevois et des Vaudois qui se sont distingués dans leur pays ou à l'étranger par leurs talents, leurs actions, leurs oeuvres littéraires ou artistiques,* etc. Lausanne, G. Bridel, 1877-78. 2 v. [Full name: Emmanuel Charles Albert de Montet.]

MOULTRIE, WILLIAM. *Memoirs of the American Revolution.* N. Y., 1802.

O'NEAL, J. B. *Bench and Bar in South Carolina.* Charleston, 1859. Useful, though old.

POLLOCK AND MAITLAND. *History of English Law before Edward I.* Cambridge, 1895. 2 volumes.

RAMSAY, DAVID. *History of the Revolution in South Carolina.* Trenton, 1785. 2 volumes.

RAMSAY, DAVID. *History of South Carolina.* Charleston, 1808. 2 volumes. Reliable only on things that came under Ramsay's own observation. *History of the Independent Church of Charleston.* Philadelphia, 1850.

RIVERS, WILLIAM J. *A Chapter on the Colonial History of the Carolinas.* Baltimore, 1885.

A Sketch of the History of South Carolina to 1719. Charleston, 1859. Valuable and accurate.

SALLEY, ALEXANDER S., JR. *History of Orangeburg County, South Carolina.* Orangeburg, 1898.

SIMPSON, WILLIAM. *Practical Justice of the Peace and Parish Officer of South Carolina.* Charleston, 1761.

SMILES, SAMUEL. *The Huguenots.* New York, 1868.

VOLTAIRE, F. R. M. A. *Siècle de Louis* XIV. Paris, 1870.

WEISS, CHARLES. *History of the French Protestant Refugees.* Edinburgh and London, 1854.

COLLECTIONS AND TREATISES CONTAINING BOTH PRIMARY AND SECONDARY MATERIAL

Charleston Year Book: 1880-1892. Appendices contain interesting and valuable reproductions of source material and articles by prominent citizens.

Proceedings of the Huguenot Society of America. (See under primary material.)

Publications of the Huguenot Society of London. (See under primary material.)

South Carolina Historical and Genealogical Magazine. Volumes 1 to 14, published by the South Carolina Historical Society, Charleston.

Transactions of the Huguenot Society of South Carolina. 23 numbers published by the Society, Charleston.

The South in the Building of the Nation. New York, 1902.

In addition to the material enumerated above, a large quantity of manuscript and printed literature has been consulted, which contributed in no important degree to the finished product.

APPENDIX

The appendix contains a number of documents which, on account of their length cannot be brought into foot notes. In the main they consist of manuscript letters, etc., which have never been published heretofore and which should be studied in connection with the content of the several chapters of this volume.

British Transcripts, Library of Congress.

S. P. G. Series A vol. 3, No. CLII. 13 Sept. 1707. p. 3.

Chief Justice Trott to ye Society

S: Carolina
13th Sepr. 1707

He is a very good Linguist being not only very well skilled in the Greek and Latin as a Scholar but having spent a great part of his life in Travelling he is a perfect Master of the Italian and Spanish and very well Skilled in the French and so much knowledge in the Dutch as to be able to read and Translate from it. But notwithstanding these Accomplishments, his Delivery being something mean I fear his preaching will not much take with the people here. So I proposed to him if he wou'd be willing to live amongst the Jamasee Indians and Learn their Language & if he wou'd then preach to them and endeavour to convert them; and he is very willing to accept the same provided he cou'd have some support and he being a Person well Skilled in Languages and the Art of Grammar wou'd quickly be able in that Language to express and explain to them the Articles of the Christian Religion for these persons that Trade amongst those Indians tho' they can speak their Language so as to be able to Trade and hold Commerce with them yet being Ignorant of Grammer and the Nature of the Speech I never met with any one of them that cou'd Translate me the Lord's Prayer into that Language.

Now if your Honorable Society would please to allow M^r. Gerrard forty or fifty pounds P Ann Sterling Money to be paid to his Order in London for three Years and also the like Numb^r. of Books that you allow the other Missionaries for a Parochial Library I am very well Satisfyed that he wou'd undertake the Mission and with God's Blessing might have Success in it and after the Expiration of three Years I am in great hopes we shou'd be able to give him some support and Assistance from these parts.

I had Drawn an Act for the Establishing of a Society in this Province for the Propagation of the Gospel amongst the Indians wch. passed once in our House of Assembly, But that Assembly abruptly breaking up and being dissolved for reasons too long to trouble your Honours with the Account of them.

Upon the next Election some Seditious Designing Persons who called themselves of the Church of England but were really of no Religion; for their own Interest and to keep some places of Profit and get others made it their Business to divide the Interest of the Church of England and so strike in with the Dissenters Faction by means of which we lost that Election and the Dissenters are now in the Assembly and it is in vain to propose to them an Act for the Propagation of the Gospel which would be received by them with Scorne and Contempt, for they never were in the Assembly but they always opposed every thing that was good and would neither do any them selves and as near as they cou'd wou'd suffer no one else to do any; And if they cou'd have their Will we shou'd have neither Church nor Ministers but shou'd turn Heathens ourselves insted of Converting the Heathen.

And that was the reason why we passed the Act to exclude them from being chosen of the Assembly because they never did any good there nor never will do any. But that Act being now repealed in Obedience to the Orders we received from her Maj^ty^. and they having now by their Corrupting some of the Church of England for their Interest as before related and their Many falsities and Jealosies spread amongst the People (wch they are always ready at) procured themselves to be chosen of the Assembly, We must wait with patience for another Opportunity when we hope we shall be able to outvote them & get a Church of England Assembly; But in ye meantime if your Honble. Society wou'd please to give the proposed encouragement to *M^r^. Gerrard* to go amongst the Indians if it pleas'd God to give Success it wou'd be ye more encouragem^t^. to us to pass an Act for ye Establishing of a Society for ye Propagation of ye Gospel amongst the Indians.

I am

May it please Your Lops &c

Nicholas Trott

Since the writing of the above mentioned Letters of the 16th of *Decembr 1706,* sent your Honble. Society by ye Govr & Council there arrived here one M^r^. Richard Marsden a Divine that came from Maryland for ye present he Officiates in the Town and is very well liked there.

British Transcripts, Library of Congress.
S. P. G. Series A vol. 3. No. CLIII.

CLIII

The Governour and Council of
South Carolina to the Society

South Carolina
19th. Septr. 1707

May it please Your Lops and you
the Honble. Gentlemen of the Society &c

In our last Letters of the 16th of December 1706 We requested your Honble. Society to send us more Ministers for Carolina, and we take this Opportunity to renew that request to your Honours that if you have not already sent some that with all Expedition you will please to encourage some good Ministers to this place Our Pishes not being half provided.

By the same Opportunity we sent a Copy of our New Church Act which we hope hath been approved of by Your Honble. Society that Clause in the former Act that lodged a power in the Com^{rs}. to remove Scandalous (which was made to get rid of the Incendiaries and pest of the Church M^{r}. Marston) which we understood gave Offence being now Omitted. And in this new Act the Ministers' Sallary's after three years time from the ratifie Date thereof is Doubled so we hope this new Act will be fully approved by your Honorable Society and particularly by their Lordships the Bishops and that they and your Honorable Society will please to signify your Approbation of the same that so the Act may be ratifyed and Confirmed in England which is absolutely necessary to stop ye Insolence of the Dissenters Faction, who confidently give out that they Question not but that Act is by this time repealed in England as well as the former; For they give out amongst the people that by reason that in the Order of her Majesty in Council it is Ordered in General that the late Church Act shou'd be repealed therefore the Dissenters give out amongst the people that it was ye Intention of her Maj^{ty}. that we shou'd not at all Establish the Church of England in this province by an Act; and that there shou'd be no public Maintenance settled there by Law, A thing that no one but persons of their Confidence wou'd Assert as being not only expressly contrary to the known favour and Protection that upon all Occasions her Majesty hath been Graciously pleased to Shew the Church of England, but also in itself absurd and unreasonable to think that we that are Plantations belonging to the Crown of England shou'd forbid to Establish by Law here, that Church which is the Established National Church in England, And that we may fully satisfy your Honorable Society how the Dissenters here strike at our Church Act, We pray leave to inform your Honble. Society that by a Clause in our said Church Act in Order to Defray the parish Charges and to repair the Churches the Vestries of the Particular parishes have power to raise by Equal Assessments any Sum not exceeding One Hundred Pounds. Pursuant to that Clause the Vestry of S^{t}. Philips in Charles Town ordered an Assessment to be made accordingly.

We will not trouble your Honours with a Relation of the many Abuses the persons that Collected the said Assessm^{ts}. met with from the Faction, But will only give the Honorable Society an Account of one passage. The Collectors going to the House of Mr Boon the Dissenters Agent in England to demand of his wife the Sum assessed upon him, there was in Company wth her Landgrave Smith and his Brother George Smith two of the Ringleaders of the Faction of ye Dissenters and who by their factions false and Seditious Stories stir'd amongst the People procured themselves to be chosen

Members of the present Assembly since the Act that excluded them was repealed; Upon the Collectors coming to demand the Money of Mrs Boon Landgrave Smith asked them how they durst have the impudence to demand money by virtue of an Act that was repealed by Order of her Maj^ty. The Collectors replyed that they did not demand ye Money by virtue of that Act that was Ordered by her Maj^ty. to be Repealed, for that the same Act was repealed in Obedience to her Majesty's Order but they demanded the Assessm^t. by virtue of the New Church Act which was in force, he replyed he knew no Act we had, for that he was sure that Act was also now Repealed in England and his Bro^r. M^r. George Smith was pleased very Civilly to add, that as for the New Act he valued it not and that it was only fit to wipe his A-se wth. all, and further said that we of the Church of England often declared that we were not for Persecution, but if this was not Persecution he desired to know what was and that they had as good rob him as to demand the money of him and that if she did this was not the first time that she had been robbed in Carolina, And M^rs. Boon asked if Coll Rhett and M^r. Trott the Chief Justice had paid their parts? they told her, yes, they paid at first for a good Example to others she was pleased very civilly to reply that it was great pitty that M^r. Trott had not been hanged seven Years past and then they had had none of these things put upon them for that he had made all this disturbance.

From this Account out of the Many others that cou'd be given, your Honorable Society may be fully satisfyed of the Insolence and Malice of the Faction here and what it is they Complain of and call Persecution which is nothing else but the Establishing the Church of England though otherwise they have the full Liberty of their Consciences as they have in England & no one ever went about to take it from them.

And by this also your Honorable Society may see how those that have been Instrumental in Establishing the Church of England here are exposed to the Malice and Reproach of the Impudent Tongues of the Faction.

And from this may be seen the true reason why M^r. Boon the Dissenter Agent in England took so much pains to destroy the late Church Act which he pretended to do in Defence of the rights of the Clergy which he pretended was struck at by the above menconed power lodged in the Commissioners when the true reason (tho' he did not care to shew it) was because it Established the Church of England and this Province and settled a Maintenance on the Church Ministers, for tho' (as we are Credibly Informed) that now M^r. Boon is in England he pretends himself to be a Moderate Church of England Man; yet it is notoriously known here that he is a most rigid Dissenter, and hates the Church of England from which he hath Apostatised and is one of the Elders of the Dissenters Congregation in Carolina.

From this Account and much more that we cou'd write we hope your Honble. Society will be fully satisfyed of the Malice of the

Faction here against our Church Act and the Necessity there is to have it Ratifyed in England—And also the Great Necessity there for Ministers to keep the People firm to the Church of England, we dayly loosing some unsteddy people for want of Ministers to supply our Churches. Both which Matters we hope your Hon[ble]. Society will please to take into your serious Considerations. We are

May it please y[r]. Lopps
And you the Hon[ble]. Gent.
Your most Humble and
Obed[t]. Servants.

N. Johnson
Tho: Broughton
Nicholas Trott

P.S.
Some of the Members of the
Council being out of Town
was the reason there was no
more hands to this Letter.
Directed
To the Most Reverend the
Right Reverend and Right
Hon[ble]: the Lords and others
the Rev[d]. and Hon[ble]: Members
of the Society for the Propagation
of y[e] Gospel in Foreign Parts.

Letter to the Bishop of London. Original in Fulham Palace, London, *South Carolina Letters.*

South Carolina, Parish of St. James
Goose Creek, September 17. 1711.

My Lord,

The inhabitants of this Parish have charged me with the care of returning to your Lordship their most humble thanks for sending to us such an able schoolmaster as Mr. Dinnys. I acquit myself of that obligation with the most Profound Respect and Beseech your Goodness to accept our humble acknowledgement of your Paternal care and permit to us to beg the continuation of your Lordship's favour and protection with your Holy Blessing for ourselves and our families.

We shall endeavor to settle Mr. Dinny and his family as advantageously as our circumstances can afford.

I believe your Lordship has been informed by the Commissary of Mr. Marstons being gone to New York but I knew not whether he has mentioned the alteration in Mr. Gignilliat's condition who by marrying a rich French widow very ancient is become my Parishioner, but it seems he has a mind to return to Switzerland. Mr. Stevens is very hearty, when I waited upon him in obedience to your Lordship's command, he told me he had writ and sent a box with some of this country products by Capt. Belcher, directed to your Lordship. About six months ago that old gentleman had the courage to pull a rattle snake out of hole by the tail, he was bit in the thumb, but by eating presently after a piece of the broiled liver of the snake in a house that happened to be near, and supping up some broth made with the same snake and flesh he has recovered his life, and his health is grown stronger by degrees.

It is with abundance of grief that I must acquaint your Lordship with the too visible progress of Atheism Irreligion and Immorality in these parts. The Clergy do what they can to put a stop to it but Evil Spirits find means to get strange books containing Blasphemys that make one tremble to hear of, and the infection is spread. I humbly submit to your Lordship's wisdom as to the means how to repress the scandal, several zealous persons wish there was a Society erected here for the reformation of manners, but those persons have little Power. We emplore your Lordship's favor that through your authority the good work of a reformation may be carried on in this Province. I humbly presume to say my Duty and obedience to your Lordship whom I pray to Almighty God long to preserve and crave leave to subscribe myself with utmost veneration.

My Lord

Your Lordship's

Most humble and

most obedient servant

Francis Le Jau.

Letter to the Bishop of London. Original in Fulham Palace, London. South Carolina Letters.

My Lord,

The clergy of this province met about a month ago, Mr. Gignilliat excepted, who dos not come near any of us, I suppose because none of us dos approve his leaving his Parish, nor his inhuman usage to his wife. We joined together in an humble address to your Lordship which, I presume to affirm again, is most true and sincere in all it contains. Mr Taylor who was newly arrived did take notice with joy and admiration of our loving carriage towards one another. We hope that Good Gentleman will be admitted into the Parish he was recommended to by the Society. In obedience to Your Lordship's commands, and out of great affection I bear to him I will serve him to the best of my power. Since it is your Lordship's pleasure, I will speak concerning some important particulars with all Humility and submission to Your Lordship's Judgment. I don't hear of any design, nor indeed any inclination hitherto, that Missionaryes should be sent among our Indian neighbours; the Yamoussees have a great desire to have some Clergyman among them as I have been often informed, that nation has behaved herself very well in our late expedition against the Tuscaroras, who had murdered our Renoque neighbors and with whom peace was lately concluded; the General who commanded our forces, one Mr. Barnwell, is not yet returned. As his plantations and settlement borders upon the Yamoussees I intend as soon as he is come, to ask him what he thinks might be done for the entertainment of some clergymen in those parts. If he offers his house and service it will be in my humble judgment the best one can desire. I will not fail to inform Your Lordship of what I can hear and obtain. The Indian traders have always discouraged me by raising a world of difficultyes when I proposed anything to them relating to the conversion of the Indians. It appears they do not care to have Clergymen so near them who doubtless would never approve those perpetual wars they promote amongst the Indians for the onely reason of making slaves to pay for their trading goods; and what slaves? poor women and children; for the men taken prisoners are burnt almost barbarously. I am informed it was done so this last year, and the women and children were brought among us to be sold.

Permit to my zeal My Lord to implore your favour and charity in behalf of the poor slaves that live among us; they are suffered; some forced to work upon Sundays, having no other means to subsist; they are used very cruelly many of them, the Generality of the Masters oppose that they should know anything of Christianity. I earnestly beg that those evils may if possible, be remedyd but whether this be a proper time to desire such a Reformation, I humbly submit to your Lordship. In relation to the good understand of the clergy amongst themselves Mr. Commissary has, I hope, informed Your Lordship that since Mr. Marston went to New York, and God has removed Mr. Maitland out of this world our peace was not at all disturbed and I hope it will continue seeing the good and docile disposition of all my Brethren. It is with much sorrow I expected Mr. Gignilliat, I will advise with Mr. Comm^ry^ how we may bring him to live in better intelligence with his wife or at least to remove the scandal of their separation. The last thing your Lordship commands me to declare is concerning Mr. Marston's unsincere proceeding, in my humble judgment this is the ground of it, that Gentleman in my frequent conversing with him for near five years never did express a clear resolution to relinquish all pretentions to the living of Charlestown, I always perceived he entertained thoughts and hopes of possessing that place again, which made me judge from the beginning that any minister in Charlestown would be ever uneasy, had that Gentleman continued here. All the clergy fears his returning hither more than I can tell, and the Mr. Comm^ry^ has been wonderous kind and charitable to him, and is so to this very day, to his family, whom his strange temper has rendered very unfortunate; we foresee that if he should return and persist in his former mind he would be troublesome again.

Having thus endeavoured to obey your Lordship's commands I humbly beg your pardon for what may be amiss in my judgment so plainly declared. I crave your Lordship's blessing upon myself, my family and flock who most heartily join with me in praying for your health and preservation.

I know not how my small services are agreeable to the Society having heard nothing from that Honble Body this long. I entirely rely upon Your Lordship's favour and Protection which I shall always take pains to reserve to my perfect respect and obedience. Mr. Stevens is very well, his lady told me he had received your Lordship's letter. I am with all submission, My Lord, Your Lordship's Most dutiful, most humble, and most obedient servant,

Francis LeJau.

South Carolina, Parish of St. James, nr. Goose Creek,
May 27th 1712.

Letter to the Bishop of London. Original in Fulham Palace, London. South Carolina Letters.

South Carolina Parish of St. James
nr Goose Creek. Feb. 23, 17 12/13

My Lord,

I acknowledge with all humility Your Lordship's Great Goodness to me, and shall endeavour with the Grace of God not to prove unworthy of it, by my profound Respect and Perfect obedience to your Commands, and by acquitting myself of my duty in my Mission with all the Fidelity and diligence I am capable of.

Mr. Commissary seems resolved to go of in a short time. The clergy met a month ago and their Meeting was attended with great Unanimity and mutual Demonstrations of friendship. Mr. Osborn arrived at that time and makes the Eleventh of us, by the coming of that Gentleman all our parishes are provided.

We had the honour to write to Your Lordship a letter which we delivered to Mr. Commissary desiring him to give to Your Lordship an account of the condition we are in, and of some particular things wherein we humbly beg Your Lordship's instruction.

I crave leave to refer myself to the Information he will give, but if his intended voyage should be deferred too long I will give myself the Honour to declare with entire submission to Your Lordship's Judgment what in my humble opinion might be done for the good of many in this Province, and to prevent many sins and scandals; not doubting but that the Governor, who always expresses much kindness and affection to the Clergy when we wait upon him will do anything upon Your Lordship's Recommendation.

When your Lordship's letter to Mr. Gignilliat came to my hands he had actually sold all his wife's Estate in order to carry what he can to Europe allowing to the poor woman who stays here some small matter. However to try whether he would have any regard for Your Lordship's Charity. With the advice of Mr. Commissary I sent Your Lordship's letter to him, he did not come since near any of us, I hear he waits for an opportunity of going off very speedily, I suppose for London.

None of us has received any directions from the Society this considerable time. My Brethren Missionaryes have desired me humbly to ask the Continuation of Your Lordship's favour with them, as I presume to do for myself. They are very regular and exemplary in their lives and very zealous to promote the Kingdom of our Lord Jesus.

And as we are informed that the Society has augmented the Marks of their bounty to some Missionaryes, we humbly beg that through Your Lordship's Goodness our case may also be considered. We live in a place where everything necessary for life is sold much dearer than in London, our allowances and Perquisitees whatever the name may be, proves in effect very considerable and those that have familyes, far from saving anything are always behind hand tho they live but meanly. Which makes us humbly represent that some addition to our salaryes would be an act of Charity. Pardon, My Lord my importunity. I dayly pray for your preservation, and craving your Blessing for me and my family I subscribe myself with all veneration

My Lord
Your Lordship's
Most humble and most obedient
servant
Francis Le Jau.

Representations made by the Rev. Gideon Johnston, A.M., Commissary of the Bishop of London in the province of South Carolina, to Bishop Robinson and to the Society for the Propagation of the Gospel, on the state of ecclesiastical affairs there; together with instructions given to Commissary Johnston by the clergy respecting ten articles of complaint to be laid before the Bishop. Bodleian Library, Oxford, MS. Rawlinson C. 943 ff.

(The following is a summary of the contents, except where wider margins indicate that the complete text has been copied.)

The following are the ten articles, with a summary of Johnston's comments thereon. They are dated Charleston, March 4, $17^{12}/_{13}$ and are signed by:

Francis Lejau, D.D., Rector of St. James, Goose-Creek.
Robert Maule, A.M., Rector of St. John's.
Thomas Hasle, Rector of St. Thomas's.
John La Pierre, A.B., Chaplain of St. Denis's, in Orange Quart[r].
Gilbert Jones, A.M., Rector of Christ Church.
Eben Ezer Taylor, Rector of St. Andrews, formerly a Presbyterian teacher.
Philip de Richebourg, Rector of St. James's Santee, formerly a Roman.
William Tredwell Bull, A.M., Rector of St. Paul's.
Nathaniel Osborn, A.M., Rector of St. Bartholomew's.
William Guy, Rector of St. Helen's.
John Whitehead, A.M., Curate & Catechist of St. Philip's.
Gideon Johnston, A. M., Rector of St. Paul's.

This is an exact list of the present Clergy of South Carolina, and according to their Seigniority, the last excepted, who is the third in order: tho' only the first nine signed these instructions. The original is in the hand of Mr. Taylor, Secretary of the Society.

Article I. In the four Acts made of late in this Province, there are some particular Articles tending to lessen the Episcopal Authority and Jurisdiction of the Lord Bishop of London and the privileges of the Clergy.

There was formerly an Act in the Province which gave a certain number of Lay-Commissioners power to suspend and deprive Ministers for certain causes, but the Act gave great offence at home and was repealed. It was lately reassumed in another form under pretense of judging and determining the legality and validity of the Ministers' Elections. In short ordination and confirmation only are left to the Bishop, institution, induction, deprivation &c. being entirely in the hands of the Church Commissioners and people. Mr. Johnston, appointed vicar of St. Philips by the Bishop of London, met with much opposition. The scheme of Church Government is in many cases contrary to the Scriptures, and to the Union Act which establishes the Church of England in all dominions belonging to the crown of England. Affairs are as bad in Virginia and not much better in other Plantations.

Article II. The Clergy are much discouraged in their work by the masters of the slaves and by the laws of the place. Conversion of slaves is scarcely possible: Dr. Le Jau has made great efforts. The difficulties are that (1) slaves have no time to be instructed except on Sunday, when ministers have work enough with white folk; (2) slaves cannot be assembled because the plantations are so many and so remote, and if assembled they might be tempted to endeavour to regain their liberty; (3) the masters of slaves think that a slave grows worse by being a Christian; (4) the Legislature does not encourage the work; (5) many planters give their slaves one day a week to plant for themselves, and this day is often Sunday. The work cannot be carried on if the Legislature does not promote and encourage it by proper laws.

Article III. The manner of instituting and inducting ministers in the province, and also that of filling the places of Clerks and Sextons is contrary to the constitutions and practice of the Church of England. If a minister desires to be admitted into a parish he has to appear before a board of Church Commissioners, consisting of at least eleven members. If the Commissioners approve, they grant an order in the nature of a Congé d'etire to the parishioners of the parish. This order is read at Divine Service on two several Sundays. The parishioners then assemble, and as many as are Conformists have a right to vote for or against the Minister. The Electors must make a return to the Commissioners within two months or the election is void. If the Minister gives offence to any of the parishioners they complain of an undue election, and the minister is probably deprived. As to the choice of clerks and sextons the minister has no more to do with it than any other common vestryman: they are selected by a majority of the vestry. The Church and the Church yard are vested in the Clerk by law, and he has the fee for breaking up the ground in either place: though this is said to be due to a mistake or oversight in the Church Act.

Article IV. There are great abuses in granting licenses to marry people. The governors of provinces grant licenses and so, through carelessness, polygamy and incestuous marriages are often countenanced.

Article V. The money bills by which the salaries of ministers are paid have occasioned a rise in prices so that £100 of the province is hardly equal to £30 in London. All of the necessaries of life are dearer there (in Carolina) than in any part of the known world. Imported goods sell generally in the retailer's shop at 400 per cent. Prices of many commodities are given—e.g. Mutton 7½d., Lamb 12d. Butter 15d., Vinegar 2s. 6d. per quart, Ale 40s. to 50 s. per barrel, etc. Things cannot be otherwise till the current money be of the same kind or value as at home. It is impossible for the Clergy to live comfortably, far less provide for their children. It is suggested that the enumeration of rice be taken off, and Clergy paid in rice at the current price. Mr. Ketilbey, a member of the Society (S.P.G.) and Agent for South Carolina, has instructions to use his utmost endeavours to get the enumeration of rice taken off by Act of Parliament this session. But the American colonies are well able to provide for their clergy, though they say that they are but new settlements and cannot afford to maintain clergy. It is suggested that they should be obliged by law to do this, and that living in the Queen's gift at home be made possible for missionaries on their return.

Article VI. By the tenour of the Acts of this Province, the Minister of a parish has no negative in the vestry, and they pretend to make a vestry without him. The clergy have only the bare liberty of praying and preaching, of which they cannot be deprived. But even so they must be exceedingly cautious or the validity of their election will be questioned, and ten to one "out they goe".

Article VII. Ministers are confined and commanded to refund the money received upon their arrival, if by sickness or any other accident, they are obliged to leave within two years of their coming there. By an Act passed in June 1712 every clergyman sent thither by the Bishop of London or the Society was to have £25 of that country's money for the relief of his wants, until placed in some cure or parish. The Commissioners, having approved the Minister, give him an order for this amount and he has to sign a bond to refund the money if he leaves the country within two years.

Article VIII. That their election to a parish may be disputed whenever any troublesome person or persons have a fancy to it.

Article IX. That they, their widows or executors, upon removal by death or otherwise, are obliged to put their parsonage houses into good repair, which by reason of their insufficient salaries, is attended with great difficulties. The houses are so long a-building that the timber is spoiled before the house is finished, and a minister no sooner gets into a house but by the Act must repair it.

Article X. There should be more coöperation between the legislature and the clergy; at least some of the representatives of the Clergy should be consulted before Acts are passed that concern the church activities. At home the Bishops are an essential part of the legislature; it should be so in the provinces too. But in Carolina they are entirely excluded from the least share in the legislature, and do not know what passes in the Assembly with reference to ecclesiastical affairs, until the blow is struck, and past their power to oppose or prevent it. This is the reason why the Church is established there on so wrong a foundation.

To the above articles Mr. Johnston appends the following notes:

I desired to be appointed a Commissioner of the Indian trade, in order to find out the disposition of the Indians toward Christianity, and to report to the Bishop and to the Society. I asked that I might be debarred from all manner of business, except what directly concerned the propagation of the Gospel, thinking that this would take off the aversion they otherwise would have to a Clergyman meddling in secular affairs. But they were resolved that no minister should sit among them.

The Church wardens have taken the whole right of disposing of the offerings to themselves, and I have been so ill used by the people, when I have asserted my right, as minister, to dispose of the offerings, that I have laid this down as a rule, never to carry things further than they will bear.

> The last thing I shall take notice of, is the hard usage I have met with on the Account of my Clerk: it being I think my undoubted Right to order and direct all parts of the divine Service and worship in the Church, of which Psalmody is no inconsiderable Article, provided I transgress no Canon or Rubrick. But this Right, tho' one would imagin at first view, no Layman would contest with me, was nevertheless encroacht upon usurpt by a certain Gentleman and a Lady, that shall be nameless; For the Clerk was commanded to sing the Psalms as they woud have him, which he did; But when I found how the thing was, I ordered him at his Peril to go on in his old way, and he obey'd. This the Gentleman and Lady resented very ill, and threaten'd him severely, but he did not follow their directions; but the Clerk still stood his Ground. The Lady therefore thinking that a piece of money would make the

most powerful impression upon him, she gave him one if I mistake not, and made him large promises of future favors, if he woud but oblige her in singing after her way; which accordingly he did. Upon this I chid him severely and assur'd him he and I shoud part, if ever he did the like again; which he promis'd he never woud; and told me what arts and methods were made use of, to frighten and seduce him from his duty. The Gentleman and Lady nettled at the Clerk and the opposition I made them, brought the matter before the Vestry, as if it were their undoubted right to command the Clerk nay and the Minister too, in matters relating to the divine Service in the Church, and the Gentleman plainly told me, that "he woud make me know it was so whether I woud or not." To this I answered that this sort of procedure was contrary to the Canons and Rubrick; and that a Minister at this rate was but a meer nose of wax, a vile worthless thing, who was to be instructed every moment by his People what he shoud do, or how he shoud behave himself in the performance of his Duty. And I farther added that I was sure whatever his or other Peoples notions were of this thing, I was in the right, and that neither he nor the whole vestry put together shoud command either me or my Clerk in any thing that belong'd to the public Service in the Church. And I was certain that not only the Bishop of London, but the most Illustrious Society woud wonder that a Man of his figure and pretensions shoud be guilty of so great blunder. This provoked him to give me a great deal of ill Language, which I patiently bore, but woud by no means give up my right, which was the right of the whole Clergy in Effect. Nor indeed did one Man in the Vestry attempt to second that Gentleman; so that by that Stand I then resolutely made, I have hitherto secured my own and the Clergys Right in this matter.

These things I have mentioned more at large to shew what sort of People, we have sometimes to deal with; And how much they envy and malign us for the poor bread of carefulness we eat, and the least Priviledge that is left us. The Clergy were extremely well pleas'd with my conduct on this occasion; And I had their unanimous thanks for it at the following meeting. But as Doctor Le Jau was the next neighbouring Minister to me, so he expresst his particular satisfaction in a Letter which he writt to me, when this Accident happened, before the Clergy met, which Letter will not perhaps be unworthy his Lordships and the Societie's perusal, if they have time and leisure for it.

Parsonage near Goose-Creek
Decem: 20°. 1712.

Rev^d^. Sir,

I shall endeavour to be in town upon the day you appoint, I see nothing that can prevent my going, and I hope God will preserve me in health that I may not fail to meet and embrace you and my Brethren. My wife is so reasonable as to consent that you shoud do what you know is most convenient, she humbly salutes you.

I forgott to mention to you, that I had heard before of the Affection, with which you vindicated our Rights upon the occasion given to you in open vestry. We are much bound to you for your Zeal. If possible let all these hardships you are sensible of be remedyed. I'll advise with you how I ought to manage the matter, I am never the better, but rather the worse for my complaisance. I bear with patience what concerns me in particular, but I perceive my successors will suffer for some injustice done to me. What you tell me of those People's usage to Mr. Richbourg is afflicting. A friend did declare to me last week of their divisions and quarrell's and swords drawn at the Church door after divine Service. I thought our Brother had no share in all those affairs. I know you advised him to take no Party. I told him also the best that I coud, and that if I were in his place, I would content my self with the doing of my duty in the Pulpit and when sent for, but that I found it needless to give private advice to men who do not sin Ignorantly, and whom I find no ways dispos'd to follow it. for my part I have a very good Opinion of our Brother, and hope you will use your Authority that he may have comfort in his station. My humble Service to your family, I am with due respect

Rev^d^. Sir

your &c
Francis LeJaue.

To remedy all of these evils it is proposed:

1. That the episcopal authority and jurisdiction be established in its full extent, and that the writ de Excommunicato capiendo for the suppressing of profaneness and immorality be granted those here as well as at home.

2. That the right of presentation, institution and induction be in the Bishop, or at least that the Lords Proprietors have the right of presentation, and that the people be debarred from the electing or turning out of the Clergy under the pretense of an illegal election, and that the Clergy be hereafter instituted and inducted as they are in England.

3. That the granting of licences and administrations be in the hands of the Bishop or his Officer.

4. That the church and churchyard be declared the minister's freehold, and that he have the power of electing, and dismissing, his Clerk and Sexton.

5. That the Minister be president of the Vestry, or if the parish be vacant, that the minister of a neighbouring parish preside.

6. That the distribution of the £25 bounty to each Clergyman on arrival, be entirely in the Governor's power.

7. That the Country be obliged to keep the minister's houses, fences, and glebes in good repair, until the Clergy, by a better provision to be made for them are able to take the burden on themselves.
8. That some of the Clergy be always in the upper house or council, and that no law relating to church affairs be made without their consent.

9. That your Lordship with the Society would be pleased to find out some Expedient for the support and relief of the Province, while they remain in it; And that care be taken to provide for them after they have served abroad for seven years, or if want of health does not permit them to stay so long, that they be provided for as soon as they return, in case it appears that it is really that, and nothing else that forces them home.

10. That every parish writing for a Minister to his Lordship or the Society shall be obliged to receive the Person so sent as their true and lawful Minister without delay and that the Minister be entitled to receive his Salary from the date of his Institution or Licence. Lastly That the conversion of slaves among the People of that Province and of the neighbouring Indian Nations may be promoted by such Methods as his Lordship and the Society shall think most proper and convenient.

The Present State of the Clergy of South Carolina, with respect to that part of the Church Discipline, which more immediately concerns themselves.

When first I arrived in that Province, I assembled the Clergy at Charlestown, where we unanimously agreed among our selves to meet twice a year at least, (and oftener as occasion required) partly to preserve and cultivate a good correspondence among our selves and partly to give and receive mutual Advice, and to lay open our grievances to one another. Accordingly, we have ever since continued these meetings, but when want of health prevented us; And when anything occurred, that called upon us for our thanks, or oblidged us to complain, either to the Lord Bishop of London or the most Illustrious Society, we alwaies took those opportunities of joining with one another in publick Letters both to the one and the other.

I took it for granted that all of them religiously observ'd the canons and Rubrick, unless it were in some cases of impossibility, as the baptizing in private houses for want of Churches, or else because they were at too great a distance from them; the taking up with Godfathers and Godmothers, that never received the Communion, &cc. But concluded that in all other matters, which was within the compass of their own power, they were nicely and conscientiously scrupulous. In this belief & persuasion I continued for more than a year, during which time, my very great want of health did not permit me to inquire into as many things as I should otherwise have done. But as my strength encreas'd, so my acquaintance and knowledge of men and things enlarg'd in proportion; and I found Mr. Thomas, who died before I arriv'd there, made as bold with the canons and Rubrick, as People wou'd have him, for he baptized with or without the sign of the Cross, Godfathers and Godmothers and woud administer the Communion kneeling, sitting or standing as People would have him. By this means, tho' he never made one true convert to the Church, that I could hear of, yet it is certain he wonderfully ingratiated himself with our half faced Churchmen and dissenters, who cried him up, according to their usual Cant, for a peaceable and moderate Person. But whatever injury he did the Church of England, by thus playing fast and loose with the Canons and Rubrick, yet the great mischief of all was, that some of the Clergy observing the reputation he had acquired among the populace, by these base and unlawful condescensions, were too easily prevail'd upon to follow his Example.

Tis vile practice, I must own, seem'd to me so odious and abominable (in regard it was the betraying and giving up the best of Churches to Calvin and Knoxes schemes, contrary to their most solemn vows & subscription) that I could not forbear Expressing my self with some warmth and resentment against it. And as we alwaies have a sermon at every meeting, so I did not fail to animadvert upon this base and treacherous practice out of the Pulpit. "It is well known how fond and tenacious the Calvinists and dissenters are of their several waies and forms; And for us to be less zealously affected in a much better cause, is shameful and scandalous to the last degree. I am sensible there are some cases, in which it is not possible for us to observe the Canons and Rubrick; but when no such impossibilities lie in the way; I know of no dispensing power in the Church of England; Nor can all the Bishops of England put together, far less any single Bishop, or private Clergyman justly or legally pretend to any latitude or indifference, in things which are legally established, & are an Essential part of our present constitution. Certainly a Minister may be a peaceable, moderate, and good natur'd man, without being either asham'd or afraid of doing his duty; And from my own experience I have observ'd, that the more remiss and easy one is in these matters, ye higher will weak and unreasonable People rise in their demands upon him. But when the Minister has declared his fixed Resolution of conforming to the Churches Discipline in all things; and that he is once known to be inflexible this way; then he makes himself easy forever afterwards, by letting the People know what they are to expect from him. Shoud a Church of England man go to any of the reformed churches abroad, he woud find, that they woud not out of condescension to his scruples abate one jot of their forms and discipline; And the like may be said of all our dissenters at home; for which of them woud not rather suffer anything almost, than administer the Sacrament of the Lords Supper to those that kneel or baptize with the sign of the Cross out of complasance, or moderation, or call it what you will. This is what they have never yet been known to have done; And why any of us shoud be lukewarm in our way they are in theirs, especially considering the Justice of our cause, is what can never be well accounted for. Such are my sentiments of these things my Dear Brethren and according to this rule I mean to walk. And I am the more fully confirmed in this Resolution, because I am intirely persuaded, that abundance of charity, and good humour, and a bright and exemplary conversation is a much likelier way of gaining the Dissenters of every kind, than the giving up any part of our constitution to them or any other body of foreign Protestants amongst us. And I am the more confirm'd in this opinion, because, tho' they carp at our ceremonies, yet one of their grand objections and principal causes of separation from us is that prophaness & Immorality which is but too too visible among us".

All of these transactions I gave ye late Lord Bishop of London a full Account; and sent him all the original letters I had at any time received upon this subject, And that what I had said might make the more deep & lasting impression on them, I pray'd his Lordship to write a general Letter to all the Clergy, which he did; And this, with what has passed before, had so good an Effect upon them that at our next general Meeting, it was resolv'd unanimously, "that whereas, the People of that Province thro' their ignorance were formerly complied with by their Ministers in some particulars, not so conformable to the Canons and Rubrick, it is hereby unanimously declared & resolv'd, that the People being now sufficiently instructed in their duty, no Clergyman shall presume to dispense with these things for the future." This is the substance at least, if not the express words of the resolution then entered into, which after it was set down, in our journal, everyone signed; And of this I took care, to send an exact copy, by the very first opportunity, to his Lordship.

Those that were the Transgressors pleaded inadvertence and ignorance in those matters and urg'd that they were led into those mistakes, by the influence of Mr. Thomas's Example, who was a native of England, and might be well supposed to know the practice of the English Clergy in things of this nature much better than foreigners. The Persons chiefly guilty of these unfair and uncannonical proceedings were Messrs. Gignilat a Switzer, LaPierre, & Philip de Richbourg Frenchmen; but as Gignilat has quitted his parish, I have no more to say to him; As for Mr. LaPierre he has been just to his Engagements ever since; but I am sorry Mr. Richbourg is not a Man of that truth & sincerity, I took him for, as will easily appear in the following Account.

There are a great many French in the Rev^d^. Mr. Maule's Parish, who upon the Death of their Minister, had frequently declared and were fully resolved to join intirely in Communion with the Church of England for the future; & their Minister Mr. Truillart being dead, they did so accordingly for near two Months, till after the said Monsieur Philip de Richbourg's Arrival. This Gentleman being known to some of Mr. Maule's French Parishioners, was entreated to preach and administer the Sacrament of the Lords Supper to them in their own Language, as being most easy and familiar to them, as often as he coud be well absent from his Parish; Nor did that worthy good Man Mr. Maule make any difficulty to give his consent, provided everything was done as it shoud be according to the Cannons & Rubrick. This the other promised; but instead of being as good as his word, he basely and treacherously broke it, almost in every particular, and wholly made use of ye Geneva way; by which means he greatly indispos'd the French for uniting with us; & confirm'd them in their separation from Mr. Maule, for whom, till this unhappy occasion, they had alwaies a very great share of Esteem & Affection.

Mr. Maule being inform'd some time after this both by Eye & Ear witnesses of Mr. Richbourg's conduct, was extremely concern'd, not so much for himself, as for ye great disservice hereby done to ye Church of England. But being a very meek Man, he forbore to take any notice of what was done, till he had my opinion in the matter. I advised him to make his complaint publickly to me, at our next general meeting which was near at hand: which accordingly he did; Mr. Richbourg after some dodging & shuffling did confess enough of the charge to make him very criminal, & solemnly promised he woud do so no more. But I who well knew what complaints his Parishioners made of him to me, for leaving his own Parish & going to Mr. Maule's, absolutely charg'd him at his peril, never to officiate in any other Parish, directly or indirectly without mine, as well as ye Ministers express leave

& consent had thereto. And the like I said to them all, and an universal obedience was promised to this injunction. And indeed it must be own'd, that there is not a set of Clergy in the whole world that are so just & punctual to one another, in all other respects as they are. But since my coming away this unhappy Person has once more broke thro' all those Engagements, & has made himself an Exception to this general Rule; by which means the French are supported by one of our own false Brethren in their aversion to our church and they are so angry with me about this & Mr. LaPierre's affair, that I have intirely lost their friendship without the least hope of ever recovering it again. But all these things will best appear from the following passages extracted out of some of Dr. LeJaus, & my wifes letters.

In a letter from Dr. LeJau, dated the 30° of May last, there is the following Passage.

"Relating to our particular concerns I only say the promise made to do all things regularly has not been well kept by some; We will refer to setting of those affairs till you return, & content ourselves when we meet to express our dislike of what has been done: however I must observe, that the Persons, who exact a disobedience from any of us are sadly divided; so that we may hope things will return of themselves into the right course; this bids us wait patiently for Gods time."

There it is manifest, the Doctor points at Mr. Richebourg's ill conduct, & breach of promise in officiating for the French in Mr. Maules Parish, and this will be farther explained and confirm'd from the subsequent passage in my Wifes Letter of the 30th of August following, 1713.

"Mr. Richbourg behaves himself very ill in worthy Mr. Maules Parish, notwithstanding his Promises to you and to the whole Clergy, to ye contrary; he takes his opportunity when the good Gentleman is here serving for you. Mr. Maules patient temper was not for acquainting you with it, till you came; but I begg'd leave to let you know all that comes to my Ears while you are where perhaps you may take better measures for the redress of Errors, than you could here; No doubt that Mungrell sort of Clergy does a great deal to hurt, & greatly foment ye differences, & widen ye Breaches, between our Church & the French. I fancy it woud be much for your case as well as the Good of ye Church of this Province, if they coud be provided elsewhere, & sound Men put in their stead."

Thus your Lordship sees, how basely and unworthyly, this man behaves himself, without any regard to his vows & promises, & canonical subscriptions; and what trouble he gives us, & mischief he does the church of England by such false & perfidious practices; And it being in your Lordships power to withdraw his License, I am verily persuaded, it will be very much for the good of the Church, and the Clergy's satisfaction that you do so; & that he be transplanted to some other Province in America, where he may be wanted, & where this gentle chastisement, (which is too slight a Punishment indeed for so notorious an Offender) may perhaps teach him to be a little more sincere for the future. I will only take notice of one more particular in the foregoing Passage in the Doct^{rs}. Letter, and then I shall have done with Mr. Richbourg. "The Doctor there saies, that those, (meaning the French) who exact a Disobedience from any of us are sadly divided;" and it is certain they were so when I came away, especially in Mr. LaPierre's Cure. But I believe Mr. Richbourg makes his people pretty easy this way, as his Predecessors did; for certainly he that is a Calvinist in another Mans Parish, will not stick much at being one in his own; And it is certain, there in his Cure are absolutely the most factious & restless of all the French Refugees in that Province.

Mr. LaPierre indeed has not gone as far as Mr. de Richbourg did; but nevertheless he is not well satisfied with me for debarring him from gratifying his people as he formerly did, in every thing, they would have him. Of this my Wife has given me a short hint in her Letter of Aug ye 2^{d} 1713 in the following words which relate to the supply of my Cure in my Absence.

"Mr. Richbourg came to town in this town, but might as well have stay'd away; for as none can understand him, they grumbled as much as they do now, that there is none here at all. It is Mr. LaPierre's turn, I know not whether he has not baulk't it on purpose, in a kind of revenge."

Nothing indeed could persuade him that he was really guilty of an ill thing, in acting after so palpable a manner, contrary to the Rubrick, nor coud any Argument I made use of reclaim him, till I threatened him with the total loss & forfeiture of both the Cure & his salary. For I made him sensible that by the Laws of that Province, no Minister could be entitled to, or receive any salary from the Publick, but he that did in all things conform to the Liturgy; & ye moment he knowingly and willfully ceas'd to do so, he consequently ceas'd to be a Minister of the Church of England, And had no right to his Parish or salary, for the future. This indeed touched him to the Quick; & being assured by me, that I would have him infallibly turn'd out, if he did not do his duty as he ought, he solemnly promis'd me a full conformity in all things that were in his Power, tho' I coud plainly discern, he was not a little vext and dissatisfied with me on this occasion. But whatever ill he may bear me, for pressing him to do his duty contrary to his inclination; yet I must do him this Justice, that he has stood his ground, and been as good as his word ever since, by all that I can hear; tho' to speak my Mind freely, I wish your Lordship woud withdraw his License too; for let him or his Countryman Richbourg pretend what they will, their hearts are not with us, but at Geneva or Elsewhere, Nor woud they stick openly to profess & declare this to the world, did not the necessity of their Affairs, & the Love of our Loaves oblige them to dissemble.

But to make this difference between Mr. La Pierre & his People still plainer; It must be observ'd, that they pretend, when they desir'd Sr. Nath. Johnson to write to y[e] late Bishop for an Episcopal Minister for them, they at y[e] same time praied him, to acquaint his Lordship, that except they were permitted to receive Communion in y[e] Genevan Posture, it would be no Purpose for him to send one, in regard they would never admit him but under this condition; And this they say S[r]. Nathaniel Johnson faithfully promised them he woud do, & that it was in his power, as Governour & supreme ordinary to gratify them in that matter. The ill luck on't is, that S[r]. Nath[l]. Johnson died before this story was trumpt up, & all that had y[e] honour of knowing that worthy Gentleman do intirely acquit him from this Promise, & look upon it, to be a mere fiction, only to serve a present turn. But the truth on't is, tho' this Contest between Mr. LaPierre, his parishioners, & me was on foot a considerable time before S[r]. Nath[ls]. death, & that he coud, & woud be most certainly appeal'd to, as a material witness in this matter by Mr. LaPierre as well as his People, were there the least ground or occasion for it; yet neither the one nor the other ever spoke a word of S[r]. Nath[l]., till he was dead; And tho' Mr. La Pierre lived not far from S[r]. Nath[l]. & did often visit him, & converse with him, & had many opportunity's of knowing the truth of what was alledged he said to the French of Orange Quarter, yet to this very day Mr. LaPierre has never pretended to fasten anything of this kind upon that worthy Gentleman, who was a true member of the Church of England, & was to his dying day, the great Patron & Benefactor to all the poor Clergy of that Province. However let this thing be as it will, it is certain Mr. LaPierre does not in the least offer to say, that the late Bishop upon y[e] sending him to the French of St. Dennis's, did make the least mention of this matter, far less indulge him in administering the Sacrament of the Lords Supper, after ours or the Geneva way as the People woud have it. And because that good & worthy Bishop was well aware of the levity & fickleness of the French Nation in General; He of his own accord & out of the abundance of his prudence & foresight, gave Mr. LaPierre a copy of that Letter which the People writt to him; that in case of any controversy between him & them about his admission, subscriptions, & the like, this copy might be a lasting evidence against them. I, who read this Copy over & over, coud never discover the least syllable in it, that looked towards a Latitude in those things that are now contested; Nor indeed is there anything in it directly or indirectly, but what concerns the sending them a good Minister, & the Encouragement they promise to give him, by subscriptions, & otherwise, upon his coming among them.

But there is an other Argument, they insist on in favour of this practice, which indeed if true, is of some force against me & seems to excuse the liberty, which both the French Ministers & their People have taken as to the Rites & ceremonies of our Church; & tis this. They say, the late Bishop allow'd the French Episcopal Ministers in all the parts of his Diocess in England, to use the English or Genevan Liturgy indifferently, according as their People woud have it, & that nothing is more common in London, than for a French Episcopal Minister to pray & preach & administer the Sacrament of the Lords Supper in the Meeting houses of the Reformed, after the Genevan way; & that the Calvinist Ministers on the other hand preach with the same freedom at the Savoy & other Places belonging to those of the Church of England.

Whether such a promiscuous liberty was given to the French Clergy of both sides in London, or not, I can't tell; and far from countenancing any such practices in Carolina, I owne, I discourag'd and forbad it; for I lookt upon it to be very inconsistent & illegal; Nor coud I be ever persuaded to believe, that the good Bishop had at any time given way to such Latitude, till I saw it under his own hand, which I never did to this day. 'Tis possible the French Clergy of our Church are not so much in love with our constitution, as not to have a much greater fondness for their own old way; And perhaps an affected Moderation, & the desire of consolidating & uniting those of their nation among us in matters of religion might tempt them to take liberties, which was never given them; And therefore the utmost that I will venture to say in this matter is, that I believe what they did this way, was unknown to the Bishop, or at most but conniv'd at by him; But be this as it will, I am sure it neither is, or can be given to our own Clergy with respect to our English Dissenters; And why they should be indulged such Latitude expressly contrary to the Canons & Rubrick, & we excluded, when the Reasons for taking it are equal on both sides, is what I own I cannot comprehend. For if our own Dissentors are schismaticks, as we all say they are with one voice, then certainly the French Conventiclers who might, but will not join with the Established Church under Ministers of their own Nation, must of course & very justly fall under the same Character; in regard [to] their objections against our Communion, are the very same the Dissenters make. To be plain all of them, even those of the Episcopal way (a very few excepted) are little better than false Brethren & Enemies to our Constitution both in Church & State; And it is well known, how closely they are linkt in confederacy with those that woud feign disturb the publick tranquillity & peace, with groundless fears & false alarms; & are brethren in iniquity with the most factious & Seditious of our own sectaries, tho' at the same time, they are most ungrateful & worst of men for so doing.

But whether my opinion or the measures I have taken be right or wrong concerning these matters, yet it is certain Mr. LaPierre has been the original cause of all this trouble. For his warm & indiscreet temper has greatly inflam'd & exasperated the minds of his People; & tho' they were never so well agreed in the points now in debate, yet I believe they will hardly be ever thoroughly reconciled to one an other. The truth on't is, they look upon him to be a Man of No Principle, who woud do anything either this or that way indifferently, as it suited best with his ease or Advantage. And they did not spare to reproach him before my face for his double dealing & prevaricating in matters of Religion: "for when he began his Ministry among them, it was after the Geneva manner for the most part, tho' without the least force or constraint on their side for that purpose; And if he thought it lawful to do so then, why is it, said they, unlawful for him now to continue in that practice. But if it was not lawful, then he was a fool for knowing his duty no better; or else an ill Man for deceiving them & doing that for his own private ease and advantage, which in his conscience he knew he ought not to have done as a Minister of the Church of England." After this manner did Mr. LaPierres People lay the blame of all their contests & troubles about Genuflexion &c: at his door; Nor had he anything to plead against this, but a strangers Ignorance & inadvertence, & the examples of Mr. Thomas & others who trod in the same steps before him.

But to put an end to Mr. LaPierres affair once for all, Your Lordship will see by ye following Copy of a Letter sent me by Mr. Lescot, Minister of the French Congregation in Charlestown, to what a height the difference between Mr. LaPierre and his Parishioners is risen.

Epistola Gallorum Ecclesiae Auriacae in Carolina, ad Dominum Lapierre Pastorem suum, e Gallico Translata, qua declarant se ejus Ministerium abrenuntiare.

Domine

Per Epistolam nostram secunda superioris Novembris scriptam, et postridie tibi a nobis traditam, te rogaveramus ante, ne quenquam e nobis sollicitares de mutando Corporis statu in Receptione Sacrae Coenae, si optares officiis tui Ministerii inter nos depungi (defungi; Cui rogationi nostrae, quum obsequi nolueris, sed e contra nos ulterius ad eam mutationem, tum verbis, tum exemplis sollicitare, et Urgere perrexeris; Per hanc praesentem Epistolam superiori conjunctam et conformem tibi declaramus, quod nunc te non agnoscimus amplius, nec in futurum agnituri sumus tanquam Pastorem nostrum: Et si contingat te ulterius, in exercendis tui ministerii officiis pergere, iisque aliqui e Nostris vel per Obsequium, vel alia aliqua Ratione interfuerint; hoc superiori nostrae Declarationi praejudicare nullatenus posterit. Proinde tibi liberum est a nobis prout tibi libuerit, ad alium Gregem te transferas. De hoc te admonitum voluerunt, Domine, ex Nostris illi qui tui in hac Ecclesia Officiales nominati sunt, sicut et alii complures e familiarum nostrarum Patribus, qui se MM illis adjunxerunt. Interea Domine, sumus &ca.

Ego Infrascriptus fateor non fuisse notatam mihi a D^no. Lapierre Diem, qua scripta fuit haec Epistola, aut sibi data a Grege suo; sed apparere tantum scriptam, et ipsi datam fuisse, Mense vel Aprili vel Majo 1713. sed Testor me accepisse a D^no. Lapierre Apographum illius Epistolae ab ipso scriptum, et ad me missum Maii Mensis die 23^a. 1713

Paulus L'escot.

Dabam Carolopoli in Carolina
die 27^a. Augusti Mensis Anno 1713.

I will only subjoin the following Passage out of my wifes Letter of the 30th of August 1713 by which your Lordship will see in what ferment things were at that time, & how zealous Mr. Lescot has been in vindicating & defending the Church of England against his unreasonable Country men.

"You see here above how Mr. Lapierre is plagu'd by those headstrong fools, who after this sent their best orators with a Letter from the whole Body to Mr. Lescot, requiring to be admitted to communicate with him, which he woud by no means admit of; but remonstrated to them that not Conscience but Malice, or least groundless Prejudice, made them quarrel at so good a Church; & that his Conscience much better inform'd than theirs, did not permit him to admit to the Sacrament Persons out of charity as they are, not only with their Minister but even with their Church, nor to separate any lawful Assembly of Christians, particularly of a Church, which tolerates him, & his flock with so much Charity. In short, all you can expect of a Man of his sence & Principles he said. So that they are as angry with him as with Mr. LaPierre, and threaten him much, but reason & conscience startle not. He acquainted the chief of the English Clergy of these matters, who when next they mett, have endeavour'd to settle things: but being inform'd that it was writt of to ye Higher Powers, by these unruly People, they have as near as I can find, resolv'd to take no notice of it at all, but wait a decision from above."

This sufficiently speaks of ye worth & merit of this good Man, & I can't forbear adding, that he has often before me, blam'd both the French Ministers and their People for their scandalous & unjustifiable proceedings. He said every Church & Party of Christians had their own waies, which they strictly & religiously adhered to; And why they who were Members of the best of Churches, shoud not do so too, he coud not tell, nor could he call their lukewarmness or tergiversation in this matter by too hard a name. He has often solemnly declared that he woud not live a day without Episcopal Ordination, coud he bring his People to it, & heartyly wish'd, that all his countrymen were so wise, as to lay aside their groundless prejudices, & once forever to join in full & perfect communion with the Church of England. They are such men as Dr. LeJau, & he, that oblige me to entertain a charitable opinion of our French Refugees; & it is pity, both of them are not placed in a more advantageous Light; for certainly they are very deserving Men.

Thus I have given your Lordship a true Account of the steps I made in accomodating this difference, & in making both parties, especially the two Ministers sensible of the mistakes they had committed, & the duty tht was incumbent upon them. In the progress of this whole affair, I took special care to command my own temper; & instead of giving any of them just cause of offence or complaint against me, I made it my business to serve & oblidge them in all other matters according to the best of my skill & power, & that sometimes not without success. & I hope they will never be unthankful. Nevertheless it is certain that my standing in ye Gap after this manner has extremely prejudiced ye generality of that nation against me; & thinking that I had carried things too far, & that they had me at an Advantage, they did no doubt write to the late Lord Bishop of London; but his death prevented the determination of this controversy for that time. It is not improbable, but that they either have or will make Application to your Lordship, for your Opinion in this matter; & tho' they should not, yet I thought it my Duty, in regars I was entrusted with the care of the Church in that Province, to lay all these things before you, that you may give such Directions about them for the future as you shall think fit. I own I am very little concern'd at what the French say or think of me, being conscious to myself, that I have done nothing but what was my duty as a faithful Minister of the Church of England and as Commissary of that Province; And this is no small comfort to me, that I have your Lordship for my Judge, & some of the greatest Men in England justifying what I did. I will only add another passage out of my wifes Letter of ye 2^d^ of August 1713 concerning the Offence I have given the French; But tho' mention is made of but one particular in that Place, yet without doubt, they did not forget those other more weighty matters of Genuflexion & ca. at which are so mightily disgusted, The Letter runs thus,

"I had lately a great complaint made of you, of your severity in requiring the French Clergy to observe the strict discipline of the Church of England, & not permitting Mr. Richbourg to Preach at the French Church in Charleston, because it is not Episcopal, whereas (say they) the Biship of London lets them serve both sorts in London, & receive salarys from both. (the complaint came not from Mr. Richbourg to whom I must do that Justice, that he serv'd his week with all possible marks of respect to you & pleasure in doing you service) I neither know how far the good Bishops charity may connive at what they do among the French in those matters in London, nor am I a Judge how far it is fit but as I truly in my own heart approve your conduct in it, so I strongly Justify'd it, to which I was answer'd you might do what you Pleas'd, but that by it you had intirely lost y[e] Love & esteem of a People, who before woud have gone thro' fire & water to serve you, but were sorry you were not y[e] man they took you for. I write you this that you may make use of it, as you see fit at home, if you ever design to return hither."

As for the rest of the Clergy, I must needs say, that they are all of them very deserving Men. It is true Mr. Taylor did not hit it so well with his Parishioners, but how it is now with him I cannot tell. The misfortune is he has a Pack of bad People to deal with; & if things be not better with him since I came away, I shoud e'en advise him to leave them & goe elsewhere.

He was formerly a Presbyterian Teacher at Charleston, but being a man very well inclin'd before hand to our Church, he was the more easily prevail'd upon by me to forsake the Dissenters; & upon my recommending him to the Late Lord Bishop of London, he was ordain'd, & sent over as a Missionarie from the Society. Some of his People most maliciously & uncharitably say that it was the love of money made him a Convert, & for this reason they are prejudiced against him. But in all humane probability they do him a great deal of wrong in this particular, he being so far from want, that, before he came over to us, he was worth more than all the Clergy of the Province."

They are now building a large brick Church at Charleston 100 feet long in the clear, and 45 broad. It is proposed to have a ring of bells and an organ in it, all which will cost above £8000. There was but £600 raised when I left that country, and since I came to town, the Lords Proprietors, upon my application, have subscribed £500 more towards it, and I am in hopes I shall get 2 or £300 more among the merchants trading to that place. But I hope your Lordship will give me all the assistance you can for promoting so good and pious a work.

As to the difference of Numbers between the Churchmen & Dissenters, I believe the Advantage is our side & we are daily getting ground of them. But then I must say, that many of those I call Churchmen, can scarce tell what they are themselves, if they were put to the Test, being but a Mungrel Race, & Churchmen because the Church is uppermost, & very often continuing without receiving either of the Sacraments to their dying day; & of such sort of Churchmen Mr. Taylor's & indeed all our enemies more or less consist.

Next to the Presbyterians, the Anabaptists are most numerous, & after them the Independents, & last of all the Quakers.

There are three or four french setlements in that country, & they may be altogether computed at a sixth part of the Inhabitants. I will only add the Names & Characters of the several dissenting Teachers of every kind, & then I have done.

1. The worthy Mr. Paul Lescot, Minister of ye French congregation at Charlestown.
2. Mr. William Livingston, the Presbyterian teacher of the same town, a very good man, whom I almost made a proselyte before I came away and do no doubt with God's assistance of making him entirely one after my return.
3. Mr. Archibald Stobo, Presbyetrian teacher to the Southward, a rank Cameronian and a most fierce and violent man.
4. Mr. MacMurty, Presbyterian teacher on Cooper River, lately gone over, seems to be a person of a quiet and peaceable disposition.
5. Mr. Lord an Independent Teacher at Dorchester, a very good Man in his way. It appears by a Letter of his which was brought to me & which I transmitted to the late Bishop, that in his opinion it woud be of less ill consequence to the cause of God & Religion, for our Church to persecute the Dissenters, than to grant an universal indulgence to all sects.
6. Mr. Scriven, a Ship Carpenter, ye Anabaptist Teacher at Charleston; between whom & Mr. Livingston, there has been a sharp contention, concerning some of the town Presbyterians seduced by him.
7. Mr. Sandford, a Tallow Chandler, another Baptist teacher towards the Southward, both of them extremely ignorant, but this more seemingly modest than the other.

Mr. James Douglas is master of the Public school at Charleston at £100 per annum salary, of that country money, besides the advantages of his scholars and Mr. Joseph Barry is his usher at £30 per annum.

Letter to the Bishop of London. Original in Fulham Palace, London. South Carolina Letters.

South Carolina Parish of St. James
near Goose Creek. Feb. 7th 171 4/5

My Lord:

The clergy of this Province have received with all the respect they are capable of the letter with which Your Lordship has favored them with.

Some of us that live near each other have had the honour to read it at our particular meeting, and have imparted the comtents to our Brethren that live in the remotest parts of this Province. Our general Meeting is to be within a few weeks at which time the Clergy in a Body design to Renew the Assurance of their Duty and obedience which they have presumed to say to Your Lordship by a General letter, dated November last which we hope is come by this time to your Lordship's hand, and to return their most humble thanks to Your Lordship for your preventing goodness towards us. I am desired by my Brethren, Mr Maule and Mr Bull to join their humble duty with mine to Your Lordship. We beg leave to protest in the name of our absent Brethren and in our own, that we are resolv'd with the Grace of God, so to regulate our conduct as never to prove unworthy of the good opinion your Lordship has conceiv'd of us. And that we will take pains to deserve the honour of your Protection by our diligence in the Performance of our Dutyes, our submission to your Paternal Admonition our obedience to your Commands and by continuing in that Perfect Harmony and Brotherly Affection which through Divine Mercy do Reign amongst us. I had taken the liberty in my private Capacity to assure Your Lordship of my Respectful obedience by a letter of July 6 last past, for which I am in some apprehension, having no account of some others I wrote at the same time to the Secretary of the Venerable Society, and to Mr. Comm[ry] Johnston. Permit me My Lord to submit to Your Pious Consideration the suffering condition of My Brethren, those at least, that have the charge of a family, and to beg for me the Particular favour of your protection.

I crave in all humility Your Lordship's Blessing and ever praying for your health and prosperity, subscribe myself with profound veneration

My Lord
Your Lordship's
Most dutiful son and most humble and most obedient servant,
Francis LeJau.

Letter to the Bishop of London. Original in Fulham Palace, London. South Carolina Letters.

My Lord,

After having renewed the humble expressing of my perfect Duty and obedience to your Lordship, I think myself obliged to inform you of the loss we have lately sustained by the death of Mr. John Whitehead who departed this life in November last past, and of Mr. Robert Maule whom it pleased God to remove out of this world on the 23 of December last. This is the fourth Member of our Body we have lost since the beginning of the Indian Wars. Mr. Bull has been very ill but is well recovered God be praised and as for me I have laboured under a tedious and dangerous fit of sickness which I thought would have carried me out of the world, it has lasted near five months. But now through Divine Mercy I begin to recover, tho I am very weak as hardly to be able to write. By the death of Mr. Maule St. Johns Parish of the Province is vacant the inhabitants of it will very soon beg of Your Lordship a Minister able to comfort them in their affliction for the death of the very pious and honest man of whom they are deprived. I can assure your Lordship that that Parish which contains about 120 families has many worthy Persons among them with whom a minister will live very happily. They will write also to the Society praying that their Minister may be entertained as a Missionary, the miserable state of this Province laden with debts not permitting them to maintain their Minister according to their good inclination.

I was very sorry to hear often during my sickness that the inhabitants of the Parish of Charlestown had neglected to make their humble Application to Your Lordship for a Minister to succeed our late Comm^{ry} Mr. Johnston of whose unfortunate death I have taken the liberty to inform Your Lordship by two letters I writ some months since. But I am concerned above expression to hear and find that the cause of that neglect proceed from some disagreement among the inhabitants. It is too true the clergy here has many enemies, and it seems there is a set of people not conspicuous for any sense of religion who use all their endeavours to discourage the clergy, to multiply conventicles, and delude many poor people in order to gain an Assembly of their own by which means the interest of this Province both in Church and State is in a visible danger, should those men get once authoruty enough. But I hope God by his Grace will prevent those Evils, and your Lordship will help us. William Guy does attend the cure of Charlestown for the present time, but he has writ to me that as soon as the stormy season is over he will go to his Mission in New England so that we shall only remain five Missionaries and none of us able to do duty in Charlestown. I had an opportunity to discourse with a worthy Gentleman of Charlestown and exhorted him to endeavour to persuade his neighbours to write speedily to Your Lordship and the hon^{ble} Society for a Minister. That place wants a man of parts and temper.

I added that in these dear and scarce times our salaries being little or nothing worth they ought to contribute among themselves towards the support of their Minister and give an amount of what they engage to do for him to Your Lordship and the Society.

I said further that except they allow him and pay a Curate to assist him the Minister that comes will find great difficulties, the duty belonging to that Parish being very great chiefly in a time of sickness very frequent here. He promised to me he would do what he could.

When I have the honour of receiving Your Lordship's commands, I will assisted by Divine Grace obey them with all possible exactness.

I humbly crave Your Lordship's Blessing with the continuation of Your favour and Protection, and praying to Almighty God for your Prosperity and long and healthy life for the comfort of all true sons of the Church, I subscribe myself with profound respect,

My Lord
Your Lordship's
Most dutiful son, and most
humble and most
obedient servant
Francis LeJau.

South Carol. Parish of St. James, near Goose Creek,
Jan. 7th 171 6/7

British Transcripts, Library of Congress.
Fulham Palace MSS, Box 315, No. 116. Oct. 29, 1717.
(Fulham MSS, S. Carolina No. 116).

October ye 29th 1717

May it Please your Lordship

Wee the Vestrymen and Church Wardens of the Parish of St. James on Gooscreek in the Province of South Carolina; Do with grief & Affiection, but as our Duty obliges Us; hereby Inform your Lordship of the Death of our late Minister Dr. Francis Le Jau, who departed this Life on the 10th. day of September last past; After a very Long & tedious fitt of Sickness.

We do therefore humbly Pray your Lordship to Supply Us with an English Divine to Succeed him So Soon and So Qualified as in your great Wisdom you shall think fitt

Rt Revd. Sr our former Minister; being a Missioner from the Most Noble & Rt Honble. Society; for Propogateing ye Gospell in foreign Parts; the Bounty he Received from them; was the greatest Part of his Support Amongst Us; for tho' the Sallery here is £100 Pr. Annum; of this Country Mony; it is Not to be Value'd at Above £25 Sterling; Which is one of the ill Consequences; that has befell this Colony; by our Indian Warr; besides Which; the Vast Expences We have been at; and ye Present Charges we are forst to be at; daily to Defend ourSelves; from these our Barbarous Enemies; Renders Us So low; that we are truly Objects; worthy that Noble Societys Charity; and therefore are humble Petitioners to your Lordship; as A Member; of that Most Honble Christian Society: (to whom we have Address'd ourSelves by this Same Opportunity) to Advocate in our behalf, and we as in Duty bound, Shall Continue to Pray for your Lordships happiness, and Prosperity & Remain with all Dutyful Respect your Lordships Most Obedient humble Servants.

Edd. Smith
Jno. Gibbes
Churchwardens
Robt Howes
Arthur Middleton

Rog[r]. Moore
Benj[a] Schenckingh
Tho[s]. Smith
[Original Signatures]
Vestrymen

Addressed To
The R[t] Reverend
Father in God D[r]. Jn[o]. Robinson
Lord Bishop of London
In
London

fragment
of red
waxen
seal

Endorsed S. Carolina 1717 Ch. Wardens & Vestry of Goosecreek

Thomas Mellichamp's directions for making indigo, taken from John Tobler's *Almanac,* 1776.

Thomas Mellichamp's directions for making indigo equal to the best French for making which the public assembly of South Carolina allowed Mr. Mellichamp a reward of £1000 and is esteemed the best yet offered:

"Cut the herb in the morning and put it into the vat as soon as possible to prevent its wilting or heating, which are both prejudicial. Pump at least 3 or 4 inches of water above the herb, because the wash of this water cleanses and brings off with it the fine particles of indigo which might otherwise remain among the herb. Bore a small gimlet hole on the east side of the steeper about 2 inches from the bottom which stop with a small plug yet not so tight that you may have a continual dropping from it down the side of the steeper. This dropping is the impregnable rule to know when your liquor is impregnated and fit for the battery.

After your vat has been steeping 2 hours attention must be given to observe the changes of the water from this dropping. Lay a clean chip upon the ground, under the dropping which will be stained deeper as the liquor grows richer, of a fine green; and as soon as you discover the edges of this little stream down your vat to be coppery you must immediately draw off or your quality is soon destroyed: This will happen sooner or later according to the degrees of heat of the weather or water but generally happens with me from 3½ to 4, 5, and 6 hours; As the weather grows colder no doubt the appearances will be later. The liquor runs off of a bright green intermixed with a yellow, of a golden color and very bright. The water on the stop of the steeper must be the same as when it was put on the herb and not the least tinged with any green for that cannot be without a fermentation which when it happens kills the quality in the steeper and is absolutely impossible by any art to bring it to life in the battery The stems of the weed will be tinged green and not red, as about the steeper, only that it must be kept sweet and clean rinsed every time of steeping and when the *weeks' work is done throw out* the herb immediately and not let it lay in the vat until Monday as is usually the case to prevent its (the vats) leaking, but pump some water in, or depend on it your first vat is lost, though it will produce a very fine mud, and answer all the foregoing symptoms which when dry will be little better than mud.

The battery though less dangerous is more curious. As it is impossible as I said before to bring the quality to life there when it has been chilled in the steeper so it is almost impossible to kill it here when put in alive. I have tried every experiment I could think of and still the fine color remains, sometimes a fine copper at others a fine purple, and when properly managed, a fine Flora.

The fine copper is the product of beating, without lime water till the fine green is changed to purple or violet which generally happens in 2 hours and then a little lime water to settle it though it will do as well without.

The fine purple is made by beating from 5 to 10 minutes and then putting in lime water sparingly till the green as above changes to the purple or violet colour but *the fine Flora* which is the highest of our ambition is made in a different manner Every planter knows according to the charge of his steeper how deep it will fill his battery so that he may proportion his quantity of lime water 1/6 of lime water is to be let into his battery to be ready against the infallible symptoms appear from the drip of his little plug in the steeper. Draw off, to the lime water, which increases the beauty of the green from the steeper and when you begin to work with the buckets the drip from them looks as fine as the body of one of the green blowing flies. As soon as you begin to beat Start your lime plug again a litt,le and let it constantly run during the time of beating in the manner the steeper does at its last running. We will suppose to have a stream as large as a spike gimlet Continue beating until it is a fine violet Color on the top without having any regard to grains for while they are visible you are not perfect. The grains will appear after you draw off, before you begin to beat, being collected by the lime water which is a good rule to govern the maker in what proportion to put in. The salts thus collected are proof against all the assaults of air, and the liquor by heating will come to its proper colour which to an incurious maker will seem to be in half an hour. When fully beaten—on the top of the water is a fine violet cast and no appearance of grains till it has been put by in some small vessel or plate in a still place, for 4 or 5 minutes, the then flakes of water that fall from the bucket Seem purple and is occasioned by the reflection of a fine blue appearing through the yellowish water this is to come off when drawn, but the main body will still be green. Draw off in the morning or sooner if you have occasion, the waters on the top of the battery will then be green but the bottom of a straw colour. I now always beat 2 hours, but have beat 3 quarters for trial; the product was a coarse grain, but fine blue full of green specks, which disappear in drying and is maleable—in short you can't hurt it in the battery (beating vat) so as to spoil it otherwise than by letting in unssettled lime water and then the specks will be seen. The mud when beaten sufficiently is of a prodigious fine purple and when not—of a blue. The sieve and all your utensils with the true Flora will look pale which in our ordinary way of making indigo is an infallible sign of destruction, but in this is only disguise and a cover to defend it from the assaults of the sun in drying. for when you break it the hidden treasure appears. The thin case or crust I take to be the salts of the lime which it resists and throws off as it will suffer nothing impure to incorporate with it. It will be objected by some that by putting in lime water too soon they have spoiled their indigo I answer no. Their indigo was spoiled in the Steeper and the lime water proved it to be So [spoiled] for it could not stand the test for which reason most makers will not put it to the trial but steep soundly and beat roundly and when they have jumbled a parcel of corrupt filth together put it in lime water to subside it and when dry *they* are obliged to take the advantage of every every light to convince that it is Copper indigo

The best way of drawing the mud:

Make a frame with 4 boards, 3 inches deep at the bottom nail a woolen cloth. Dig up a piece of sandy ground and level it. Settle this box thereon, with the cloth next the ground, then bank it up half way at the sides and end very close Lay some Osnaburgs on the top of the woolen exactly the size of the bottom of the box Then take the liquor or mud out of the battery and strain into this box where it will perfectly drain and leave your mud cracked, when it is fit for the press."

Bodleian Library, Oxford. MSS Rawlinson C. 933 f136n.

I do hereby appoint the Bearer Mr. Albert Pouderous to be Minister of the French Congregation at St. James Sante in Carolina he having qualified himself for the Office & accord. I desire the Governour & all other Persons concern'd to receive and consider him as such.

Witnefs my hand this [ ] day of Nov. 1720.

British Transcripts, Library of Congress, Box 316, No. 277-278

A short memorial of ye Present State of the Church & Clergy in his Majesty's Province of S^{o}. Carolina in America.

The Province of S^{o}. Carolina is divided into thirteen Parishes.

In Berkley County there are Eight, viz—

1. S^{t}. Philip's Charles-City, the only Town of Note & Port of Trade in the Said Province, which Parish extends thro'out the S^{d}. City & a neck or Point of land between the two Navigable Rivers of Ashley & Cooper about six miles in length & two in Breadth & may contain between three & four hundred Christian Families. In the S^{d}. City there is a new erected Church, not yet entirely finished,

a large, regular & Beautiful Building, exceeding any that are in his Majesty's Dominions in America. The present Minister of the Sd. Church is the Revd. Mr. Alexander Garden (who hath enjoy'd that Living somewhat more than three years,) a learned & pious Divine, but of a Sickly & weak Constitution. The stated Salary of ye sd Church is one hundred & fifty Pounds per Annum Proclamation Money, ie, abt. One hundred & twenty pounds Sterling, paid out of the publick Treasury of the Province, besides the perquisites wch. in that Parish are considerable. There is likewise in the Sd. City a Grammar School now Setting up by the Revd. Mr. Thomas Morrit very lately arrived a Missionary from the honble. society for the Propagation of the Gospel in foreign Parts wth the Annual Allowance from yesd. Society of Thirty pounds Sterling. The Salary allow'd out of the publick Treasury to the sd. Schoolmaster is One hundred pounds pr. Annu· Proclamation Money, ie Eighty pounds Sterling, besides the Benefit of Scholars, which is settled by law at three pounds pr. Annum a Scholar in the sd. proclamation Money, or the value thereof in the Currency of Carolina. There are also in this City a Small Congregation of French Refugeès, who retain the Liturgy & Discipline of the reformed Churches of France. One of Presbyterians, Another of Anabaptists & a few Quakers, who have each a meeting House, but at present Neither of them have a Settled Minister or Teacher.

2 St. James at Goose Creek a rich & populous Parish. the Church which is abt. Sixteen miles from Charles City, is a neat & regular, but not a large Brick building. To this Church is lately gone over a Missionary from the Honble. Society for the Propagation of ye Gospel in foreign Parts, the Revd. Mr Ludlam, who was not arrived there the latter end of May last. The stated Salary allow'd out of the publick Treasury of the Province to this & to each of ye other Country Parishes is One hundred pounds pr. Annum of ye Said Proclamation money, or the value thereof in the Currency of Carolina. There is also a very handsome Parsonage House of Brick & a Glebe of about one hundred Acres of Land.

3d. St. Andrew's, The Church Twelve miles from Charles City—The Minister the Revd. Mr. Guy a worthy divine & well esteem'd of in the Parish, one of yeHonble. the Society's Missionary's & hath been so eleven years. There is a Decent Parsonage House & a Glebe of Twenty five Acres of Land. The Inhabitants are now enlarging & beautifying the Parish Church, wch. is built wth. Brick, having for that end obtained out of the publick Treasury four hundred pounds; & by Subscriptions among themselves five hundred pounds of the Currency of Carolina.

4. St. George's The Church 28 miles from Charles City a large & populous parish, wherein is an Handsome Brick Church, a Parsonage House built wth. timber & a Glebe of 250 Acres of Land. To this Church is now going over the Revd. Mr. Varnod Missionary from the honble. the Society &c.

5. S^{t}. John's a large populous & rich parish, in wch is a decent brick Church 25 miles from Charles City, lately adorned and beautifyed at ye Charge of the Parishioners, a very convenient brick Parsonage house pleasantly Scituated upon a Glebe of 300 Acres of land. The Rev^{d}. M^{r}. Brian Hunt Minister & Missionary from the hon^{ble}. the Society arrived there about March or April last & was kindly received by the People.

6. S^{t}. Thomas's a large & populous parish in which are two Churches & two Glebes, but no parsonage House as yet built. The Rev^{d}. M^{r}. Hasell who hath been Minister of the Parish & Missionary from ye hon^{ble}. Society fourteen years, & well esteem'd by his People residing upon an Estate & in an House of his own, whilst ye money appropriated from the Publick for ye building of an house is daily encreasing, being put out upon good Security at ye Legal Interest of ye Country.

7. S^{t}. Denis's, a Congregation of French Refugeès conforming to ye Church of England & within the bounds of S^{t}. Thomas's parish & made a distinct parish for a time 'till ye present inhabitants or their children attain the English tongue. The Minister, ye Rev^{d}. M^{r}. John La Pierre who hath enjoyed the Living about twelve years receiving an equal Salary from the Treasury with the other Country parishes: but is no Missionary.

8 Christ church a large parish but poor, There is a Timber Church thirteen miles from Charles City, a Parsonage house & Glebe of one hundred Acres of Land. the present Minister the Rev. M. Pownal one of ye Societyes Missionaryes came over to that parish in the Month of October last.

In Craven County are two Parishes.

9. S^{t}. James Santeè a Parish consisting chiefly of French Refugeès conforming to the Church of England, in which is a Church about Sixty miles from Charles City, a Parsonage house & a glebe of near 1000 Acres of land. The present Minister the Rev^{d}. M^{r}. Albert Powderous, a learned Divine & Convert from the Church of Rome hath been resident there above two years.

10. King-George's Parish, which being a new Settlement about ninety miles from Charles City was made a Parish by his Excellency General Nicholson his Majesty's present Governour ab^{t}. 18 Months agoe; The general Assembly having allowed One thousand pounds of the Currency of Carolina & his Excellency given One hundred pounds towards ye building of a Church there, wch is not yet begun.

In Colleton County are two Parishes viz—

11. St. Paul's now vacant & the parishioners humble Suppliants for Another Minister. They are a sober well-inclined people, kind & obliging to their late Minister, diligent in attending the Word of God & desirous of all good Instruction. The Church, wch is built of Brick & Stands 20 Miles from Charles City, being too small for the present Congregation is at this time enlarging and beautifying;

The Inhabitants having raised by Subscriptions among themselves upwards of One thousand pounds & obtain'd from the general Assembly 500^{ll} of the Currency of Carolina, besides a Legacy of 100^{ll} bequeathed to y^{t} use by M^{r}. John Whitmarsh of the S^{d}. parish lately deceased, & some few other presents. Near the Church is a glebe of Seventy Acres of Land, whereon was a very Convenient brick House & some other out buildings, wch were burnt down by ye Indians in the year 1715 & not yet rebuilt. The sum of 456^{ll} Carolina Money was allow'd out of ye Treasury there for to repair the same, wch having been let out to interest is now about 600^{ll}.

12 S^{t}. Bartholomew's. This parish hath been vacant since the year 1715 by the Death of the late incumbent M^{r}. Osborne one of ye hon^{ble}. the Society's Missionaryes. It was then entirely depopulated by the indian War, & very few of ye Inhabitants Since returned who live remote from one Another & have neither Church nor Parsonage House. There's a Glebe of 300 Acres of Land & some preparations were formerly making towards a Church & House. But ye War breaking out, ye Inhabitants dispersed & the Minister dead, nothing of late hath been done in it.

In Granville County there's but one Parish

13. S^{t}. Hellen's, in wch is neither Church nor parsonage House. The general Assembly hath lately allow'd 1000^{ll}: of ye Currency of Carolina & the Governour 100^{ll} towards ye Building of ye Church. This parish was also depopulated in ye Indian War, but many of ye Inhabitants since return'd. the Rev^{d}. M^{r}. Brayfield, Chaplain to his Majesty's Forces in Carolina officiates sometimes there. There's also a Prebyterian Teacher W^{o}: lives meanly & chiefly upon his own private Interest.

N.B. That near Charles City is a large handsome brick House and a Glebe of 17 Acres of land for the Parsonage, wch at present, wth. the Consent of ye Minister, is made use of for the School that is setting up there by M^{r}. Morritt; and an House within the City hired by the publick for ye use of the Minister.

N.B. That towards ye repairs of Parsonage houses, the Ministers, Church-Wardens & vestry of Each parish are empower'd to draw upon the publick Treasurer any sum not exceeding 25^{ll}. of ye abovesaid proclamation Money per Annu^{-}. And a certain sum for ye repairs of the Churches & to pay the Clerk, Sextons & Registers their Salaryes.

N.B. There are within ye several Parishes dissenters of several denominations, but there are no publick Teachers at present except among the Presbyterians or Independents, w^{o} have four or five, thô not above two or three of y^{m}, y^{t} are setled Teachers.

London Augt. 10th. 1723.

Wm Tredwell Bull, late Minister of S^{t}. Paul's Colleton County & Commissary to R^{t}. Rev^{d}. the Lord Bishop of London in S^{o}. Carolina.

ENDORSED Mr Bull's' Acct.
of S. Carolina
1723
Enter'd

British Transcripts, Library of Congress, Fulham Palace MSS, Box 315, No. 110. Apr. 15, 1724.

Queries to be answer'd by the persons who † were Commissaries to my Predecessor.

† In ye absence of Mr- Bull, I desire Mr- Garden to answer ye Queries.

in Bp. Gibson's hand.

WHAT publick Acts of Assembly have been made and confirm'd, relating to the Church or Clergy within that Government?

Answr. All such Acts, confirmd or not confirmd, your Lordship will find in Dr. Trott's printed Collection of the Ecclesiastical Laws of America (the late Act for advancing the Salarys of the Clergy, only excepted) several Copies of what were purchasd by the Honble Society—

HOW of hath it been usual to hold a Visitation of the Clergy? How oft have you call'd a Convention of them? And what has been the Business ordinarily done, and the method of proceeding in Such meetings?

Answr: (1) Once a year. (2) As oft as extraordinary Occasions have requird. (3) The Business ordinarily done, at the Annual Visitaon, has been, the Commissary's examining Letters of Ordinaon & Licenses; hearing Complaints, regulating Disorders, putting in mind of & enforcing the Bishop's Instructions with proper Motives & Arguments as Occasion may require; and in fine preparing the proper & necessary Accounts of the Church & Clergy to be transmitted to his Lordship & the Honble. Society: In occasional Meetings, the Business only of the Occasion: Method Visit: ut supra; in occasional Meetings not always Uniform.

DOES any Clergyman officiate, who has not the Bishops Licence for that Government? Answ: The revd. Messrs. Hunt & Morritt officiate without such License for this Government; the former as Minister of St John's Parish, the latter (licens'd only for Master of the free School) in supplying of any vacant Cure he thinks fit, at the rate of the Salary here allowd any regular Incumbent. The revd. Albert Poudrons of Santee has only the Bps private Letter signifying his Leave to officiate in the province.

WHAT Parishes are there, which have yet no Churches, nor Ministers. Answ: There are here Three Parishes which have yet no Churches nor Ministers (viz) the Parish of St. Helen Port royal, the Parish of St. Bartholomew, and a lately erected Parish calld King George's Winneaw. There is a Church a building in St. H. Portroyal, & Im informd almost finishd.

HOW is the revenue of the Church apply'd which arises during the Vacencies? Answ: The Church's Revenue being collected and paid by the publick Treasurer, during the vacancies 'tis apply'd for Contingencies of the Government.

WHAT are the ordinary prices of the Necessaries of Life there? Tis impossible to give your Lordship any direct Answer to this Q. Bread & flower of Wheat we have from New York & Pensyl: & according to the Quantity happens to be imported tis dearer or cheaper. The cheapest ten shill: P hundred. The Case is the same with regard to all Sorts of Liquors. Beef, Pork, Mutton, very much both in goodness & price according to the Season of the year. Beef in Winter sometimes 5ᵈ or 6ᵈ P pound, in Summer one penny or 3 half pence; Mutton often not to be had. Pork generally reasonable throughout the year. All sorts of Cloathes Cent P Cent at least dearer than in Europe. N.B. the above prices are meant in Sterling money.

CAN you Suggest anything that may be Serviceable to Religion, and conduce to the ease of the Clergy and their more comfortable Subsistence, which you believe to be fairly practicable, and which will no way interfere with the Authority of the Governour, nor be judg'd an infringement of the Rights of the People?

Answʳ. I beg leave of some longer time to Answer this Query—
I am
Your Lordships most dutiful & Obedᵗ
humble Servᵗ.
A Garden

Sᵒ. Carolina
Charlestown
Ap. 15/1724

Letter to the Bishop of London. Original in Fulham Palace, London. South Carolina Letters.

Milord

I have received the honour of your Lordship's command and sent the paper of quiries with the answers according to your Lordship's order, I give thanks to God Almighty that it pleased him to give us so mercifully a prelate full of Zeal and pastoral care for the Church of Christ; I hope Milord that your Lordship will not refuse me the same protection that your Lordship's predecessor granted me, and whatever Milord Archbishop of Canterbury honoured me continually. I am Milord a French Minister that abandoned everything for the cause of the Gospel and I have worked with great zeal for the oppressed Church in France, afterwards I suffered very much, I have embraced with all my heart the Church of England since many years finding her Conform with the work of God and with the primative Church I preached three years at London. I am sent by the late Milord Bishop of London and the Society by the recommending of Milord Archbishop to this parish, nevertheless I serve one of the biggest parishes of Carolina. It pleased not the Society to give me the same annual gratification as other ministers, for all that I am in more necessity, my parish is very poor, I am obliged without charity to assist the sick poor people and to keep physic to cure her. Some time there be at my charge two months before she recovered her health. I protest Milord I have no other benefit [than] my salary the parishioners be not able to help me in any thing, because the water-flood that ruined the plantations some time, the water came six foot high into the houses. The Society give me above Seventeen month thirty livres sterling to the gratificat for the damage that the water flood caused me, but it is not sufficient to the loss I had and more the first year I came in this country the salary of the ministers are no more than 25 livres sterling and I had a passage of seven months. I suffered very much by a shipwreck, all these unhappy circumstances is the cause that I am not yet recovered of my losses and my house is situated upon the common passage, every day I am obliged to lodge and to nourish passengers, being no taverns or inns in this parish and every thing is very dear because the parish is 60 miles distant from the town. I beg of your Lordship to consider my condition and to recommend me to the Society that I may obtain an annual gratificat to my subsistance. I will not prevail with importunacy. I declare Milord that the necessity constrained me and no covetousness. I am not so wretched man to undertake to the Saviour after I have abandoned father and Mother and a very good estate for the Cause of Christ, I desire no more as my necessary maintainance. I hope Milord being to your Lordship's care and a legal minister of your Lordship's Diocese you will not refuse me your Lordship's fatherly protection, as for my part, your Lordship may depend upon me as a faithful subject full of zeal and application for the present Government, and the Church of England, and principally upon mine constant application for the parishes that are committed to my care, my behaviour shall be found always even, upright and sincere. I pray ardently God Almighty to bless your Lordship's solitude, our merciful God will preserve your Lordship in all plentitude of grace for the best of the Church and State, I am with the profound respects,

Milord

Your Lordship's most humble obedient
and faithful servant
Albert Pouderous, min^{er} of
St. James.-Santee

In South Carolina
at Santee the
25 April 1724.

Letter to the Bishop of London. Original in Fulham Palace, London. South Carolina Letters.

My Lord,

I have received your Lordship's admonition good advice and favourable wishes with all humility, respect and thankfulness—

rather chusing to receive your checks than to be overlook'd among my brethren; but how much the happier would I count myself, My Lord, if I could obtain the same share in your favour and protection as I had once in that of your illustrious predecessor, by whome I was ordained and sent to the place wherein I am now officiating on the nineteenth year from my mission to a French colony, during which time I had the honour to wait upon several vaccant parishes of the English, besides my own parish of St. Dennis, without any molestation from the clergy or laity; but rather with all sorts of good encouragements, whereby upon recommendations, the honourable society was pleased to exstend their bounty upon me, having heard, withal of my helpless and chargeable family then consisting of five young children and my wife who lost her sight before our departure from England. The Reverend Mr. Garden was my first open adversary I had in this province, upon information that I had baptised a child of one of his parishioners, the case was this My Lord; the father of the child one Mr. Joseph Moor being at variance with his minister unknown to me, seeing me in his town on a certain day envited me to his house, and told me he had a young child to baptise if I would do it for him, whereupon I answered him that I thought it not convenient being in another minister's parish, he told me that Mr. Garden was very willing I should perform that office, but this did not prevail upon me till he added further that it was his wife's earnest desire being a French woman and formerly one of my hearers, the assistants likewise being of the French nation, but the father I suffered to be over persuaded, for want of a timely consideration, My Lord, and not out of any evil intent or contempt: for after I saw my name brought into question by my brother Garden, I would have made him all reasonable satisfaction in a meeting of the clery as our former custom was, without any need of troubling your Lordship: cases of obstinacy and stubbornness excepted. This so sudden and preposterous proceeding of Mr. Garden did lay upon me a necessity of vindicating and clearing myself before the people of this province by my appealing to a general arbitration and exposing to the light this slanderous lettre, which I make bold, My Lord, to propose here to your perusal in the following expressions:

Sir,

I have often heard of your insolent and disorderly practices in other parishes, but little suspected that I should have experienced them in my own. The following fact is so notorious that I am confident you will not dare to deny it: viz: that when you was last in my parish a few days ago, you did then and there: not only administer the Holy Sacrament of Baptism to a child of one of my parishioners without either my consent or privity, and whilst I was upon the spot and the child in good health, contrary to the express canons and rubricks of the Church; but also you did administer it in a public form and in a private house noless contrary to the said canons and rubricks and the known practice in my parish. This matter of fact Sir I charge you with which I am confident you will not dare to deny, so equally confident I am, that you can offer nothing tolerable either to justify or excuse, thus to break upon my charge is it to enter in by the door, or not rather to climb up some other way? is it the action of the shepherd or not rather of a thief and a robber thus to trample on the canons and rubricks of the church, is it the action of a faithful and obedient son and not rather of an apostate and faithless Traytor? I was in hopes that the late prevailing principles in your parish, of Dutarts I mean had been quite extinguish'd with those unhappy people, but alas, the reverend Mr. Lappierre daring thus to act in so open contempt and defiance of the ecclesiastical laws and constitutions savours so strongly of them that those hopes are almost choak'd and fears sprung up in their room. Pray Sir, could you flatter yourself either, that I shoud hear nothing of this clandestine piece of intrusion or that hearing of it I should yet pass it over in silence? Sure you are not so silly as to have flattered yourself of either of these. I heard of it the next day, I have already acquainted the Governor of it, and you may assure yourself that nothing but death shall prevent my transmitting it by him well attested in every circumstance to the Bishop of London and the honourable Society together of my complaint of it in the strongest terms. How little so ever you deserve it, yet I scorn to act any other than a fair and honourable part in this affair, and therefore give you this notice that I shall and to whom I shall complain that you may make such defence as you shall think proper against my complaint, I am your much provoak'd friend and servant

Charlestown
April 7th 8th 1725. A. Garden.

Your eyes may see My Lord how vile I am here made by a brother and I hope of your charity that if anything further should be alleged against me by the Reverend Mr. Garden, your Lordship will vouchsafe to hear me before I am condemned considering that I am as well as my adversary a labourer in the Lord's Vineyard under your inspection and patronage, and your Lordship, the most dutiful most humble and obedient servant,

John Lapierre.

St. Carolina in the parish
of St. Dennis.
January 7 . . 1 . . 1725/6

British Transcripts, Library of Congress
Fulham Palace MSS, Box 315, doc. No. 92, London, Mar. 27, 1731.
(Fulham MSS S. Carolina No. 92).

My Lord

Whe the Church wardens and Vestry of St. James Santy Mayde bold to humble adres. Our Selves to Your Grace Some time agoe and Direct Your Grace Our humble petition but as ye Dangers of y[e] Seas arre Great and it Might Be Miscar[ed] Whe In all humble Manor Do herre Lay a Coppy of y[e]. Same before Your Grace

Most Reverent S[r].

Being under y[e] Imidiat Eclesiatical of JuredDiction Your Grace wee the vestry of S[t]. James Santee In the Province of South Carolina doth Most humbly Pray that it May Plasse Your Grace to Suply this Our Parich with a Rector Y[e] Reve[t]. Do[r]: Poudrons whom Your Grace Send us being Desest Since y[e] 20 of Fab[ry]: 173°/1

Whe your Grace is most humble Peti[os]: being for y[e] most Part french refuges have alwais had a Ministor that Preached in their Own Langage and that by and under y[e]. Protection of Several Acts of y[e]. Commons of this Province in their favour but As by Succession of time Several English Gentlemen have seteled amonghts us and arre Deprived of y[e] hearing y[e] Explenation of y[e] holly Word of God When y[e] rector Can Preach Nothing but French as whe Our Selves Should be if on y[e] contrary he Could Preach Nothing but English to Eedefey y[e] holle Parrich whe most Earnestly Pray your Grace to Consider both our Casses and In your Great Zeal Goodnes and Charety Send us Such Minister as is quallified to preach in both Langages that wee May all be Edefied and rendered Capable of Glorefeying Allmity God in Our onne Langage Such as whe understand whe umblely pray your Grace if Possible not to Send us aney that hasse been of Roman Catholeck Church they being verry ap to have Some Eraneous Doctrine wch they Do Not Conseal in these remot Part with all y[e] Carre they do In England and may be of Dangerous Consequance the Extreme application Your Grace has Allwais Shown for y[e] Presarving and Incresing y[e] Church of England of whom Your Grace is so Illuster a doth unbolden us in our Littel Cappasety to Implorre Your Assistance having Nothing to return for Soe Great a Good but most humble thainks and Ever Lasting Prayers for y[e] Preservation of Your Grace is most Prescious Pearson being

Honored S[r] Your Grace is most
hum[e]: and most ob[t]: Servants y[e]
vestrey of S[t]. James Santy

Isaac Le Grand
Peter Robert
Peter Guerry
Isaac Dubose
John Barnet
(Orig[l]. Signatures)

Jaques Boisseau }
Paul Bruneau } Church Warden

A Coppy of y[e] Letter Datted 27 March
1731 and writ June y[e] 2/1731
Addressed To

His Grace Edmond by
Devine Providence Lord Bishop
of London
These

red
wax
seal
broken

Letter of the vestry and wardens of the Parish of St. James Santee, to the Bishop of London. Original in Fulham Palace, London, Letters North Carolina, South Carolina, and Georgia.

Most Reverend
S^{r}.

Your Lordship's Goodness towards us for sending the Rev^{d}. Mr. Coulet to be Rector of this your Lordship's Parish of St. James Santee is so infinite that we want for terms for to shew your Lordship our Gratitude and the Extreme Joy we have to be under the Pastoral Care of so tender a Bishop who extends his great Zeal and Charity even to these remote parts in providing us so good a Minister who is the greatest happiness that could happen us and our poor dispersed families for want of a good Pastor, leave us no room but to humbly pray Almighty God to continue your Lordship for ages in that Eminent Post full of health and all Prosperity which is the ardent wishes of your

Lordship's
Most humble and
most obedient
servants,

Isaac LeGrand
Peter Guerry
Jaques Guerry [Vestrymen]
Isaac Dulgec
Peter Roberts

Jacques Boisseau
Paul Bruneau
Wardens

Santee—
Dec 27. 1731.

Letter to the Bishop of London. Original in Fulham Palace, London. Letters North Carolina, South Carolina, and Georgia.

My Lord,

As I had the honour to have been ordained by your lordships predecessor in the year seventeen hundred and seven, who recommended me to the Governor of South Carolina, Sir Nathaniel Johnston to entitle me to a parish called the Parish of St. Dennis in a French colony which I was to serve till the death of the old Settlers who did not understand the English tongue. So in the time of the new generation who understood the said tongue in which they were born, I became an assistant to the Reverend Mr. Hazel in the parish of St.Thomas next to my parish, hoping of the two nations to make but one and the same people; though they were a distinct parish they indifferently followed the English Church and the French as well acquainted with both languages; and then seeing that my ministerial functions were not essentially required from a French minister, and hearing besides that in a province of North Carolina called Cape Fear, alias New Hanover they wanted a minister, the——— inhabitants of the place sent for me and the Reverend Mr. Garden your Lordship's Commissary in Concurrence with the rest of the clergy did actually consent that I should go and settle the Divine Service where it had never been, I readily complied to go thither, with the promise that they would inform your Lordship concerning my removal, but things succeeded otherwise than I expected: the first year I was regarded and respected of the inhabitants as St.Paul was at the first by the Galatians: Every one readily subscribed towards my salary; and though it fell short of near one hundred pounds yet was I ——— satisfied, out of consideration to a new country, which owed its good beginning less to the provision made by human laws than to the good discretion of some conscientious inhabitants. The second year, the Gentlemen of the vestry thought fit to lay an assessment upon the parish, the private subscribers should not be overburdened but this proved of none effect upon a mistake because what was called a parish was in reality no parish by law or act of public assembly, therefore I was entirely left to the good discretion of the several inhabitants against whom the vestry had no power of compulsion, therefore I fell short of my salary a second time, the third year the vestry—I confess did me that justice to engage that satisfaction to me that might be denied by the public—accordingly they promoted me a certain sum to lessen my loss but this fell a great deal short of my necessary living; after the third year I served the people of Cape Fear six months longer, but received nothing for it, only this answer: "who put you to work?" then I thought it was time to ask for my discharge, which after three times asking they granted me at last, and took in my stead one Mr. Richard Marsden now actually performing the Divine Service among them, a man whose whole study always was to undermine me. Now my Lord I am left to my own shifting and I am forced to work in the field for my living and for fear this people of my former charge should in any wise endeavour to impose upon your Lordship's probity as I hear that they petition for a new Minister. So I think myself in conscience bound to declare my mind, that any Clergyman that has a mind to come hither at their request will find a lawless place, a scattered people, no Glebe, no parsonage to receive him, without which Governor Barringtown told them that no minister should ever be sent to them from the society nor from your Lordship; however my Lord there is a certain Colony in this province that requires my help upon promise of subscribing towards my maintainance, with whom I will with your Lordship's good leave comply upon any reasonable terms sooner than to see the country destitute of The Light of the Gospel; the bearer my Lord can testify the truth of what I do here let forth before your Lordship whose most obedient servant and dutiful son I ever profess to be in the Gospel of Christ.

John Lapierre

New Brunswick in Cape Fear alias Cape Fear.
October 9th 1733.

Letter to the Bishop of London. Original in Fulham Palace, London. South Carolina Letters.

Milord, Mon très Reverend Père en Dieu.

J'ai pris la liberté d'ecrire le 20 du mois dernier a Votre Grandeur, que comme la Colonie de Purrysbourg n'etoit que d'environ soixante hommes je n'ai point pû obtenir de pension. La Province n'en accorde que pour les lieux que sont érigés en Paroisse composée de cent hommes; Et on ne peut pas espérer que celle-ci soit remplic, jusques après le retour de Monsieur Purry qui doit bientôt partu pour la Suisse. Et comme il suis chargé d'une nombreuse famille, d'une femme et de quatre petits enfrants et qu' il n'ai point de bien je ne scaurois subsister sans pension a l'avenir. C'est pourquai, ayant apris que l'Eglise de Santy stoit sans Ministre depuis près d'une année; Je leur ai affert mes services; Ils ont envoyé une lettre de vocation en ma faveur le 11 du mois passé a Monsieur le Commissaire Garden et qu'il a envoyée a Votre Grandeur avec ma premiere lettre. Je prends encore la liberté par cette seconde, de prier tres humblement Votre Grandeur, qu'au ca qu'elle n'eut point encore envoyé de Ministre pour Santy, de me faire la grace de m'accorder cette Cure, dont la pension est établie de cinq cent pieces de ce pays, avec quoi je serai en étet d'entretenir ma famille. J'ajoute a ma premiere lettre que j'espere d'y pouvoir faire plus de fruits et mieusc avonier le Regne de Jesus Christ, qu'ou il-y-a beaucoup d'Allemands qui n'entendent point la langue française et par consequent ne sauroyent etre edifies, mais a Santy ils sont passé les trois quarts de francois. D'ailleurs j'espere que dans quelque mois je serai capable de faire le Service en Anglais, j'etudie la langue pour cela. Monsieur Purry pourra amener un Ministre de son pays pour Purrysbourg, ou je demenurerai en attendant la response et les ordes de Votre Grandeur a cet égard. Je fais des voeux tris ardents pour la conservation de Votre Sacree Personne, et suis avec une parfaite soumission et un tris profond respect.

Milord, Mon tres Reverend Pere en Dieu
Votre tres humble et tres obes et tres
soumis serviteur,
Joseph Bugnion, V.D.M.

A Purrysbourg
15 Juille 1733.

LOSSES SUSTAINED BY FRENCH PROTESTANTS IN THE FIRE OF 1740, TOGETHER WITH THE BOUNTIES RECEIVED BY THEM.

MS. Col. Doc. S. C., volume XX. 559.

	Est. loss in currency	Est. loss in sterling	King's bounty rec'd.	American bounty rec'd.
Moses Audebert ...	359-00-0	57-05-8	16-19-1	5-06-2
Anthony Bonneau ..	1500-00-0	214-05-18	70-17-0	22-05-9
Peter Delmestre	691-05-0	98-15-0		32-13-0
Andrew Deveaux ...	700-00-0	100-00-0	33-01-3	10-07-1
Paul Douxsaint ...	1466-15-0	209-10-8	69-05-18	21-13-10
Benj. Godin	5584-12-3	797-16-0	263-15-11	82-12-1
Guignard & Gabriel*	650-00-0	92-17-1	30-14-0	9-12-3
Alex. Garden for David Guerard ...	8000-00-0	1142-17-1	377-17-9	118-06-8
*Hill & Guerard ...	228-10-0	32-12-10	10-15-10	3-07-7
Dan'l Huger	5000-00-0	714-05-8	236-03-7	73-19-2
Estate of Peter Horry	1234-12-1	176-07-5	58-06-4	18-05-2
Estate of Martha Horry ...	428-00-0	61-02-10	20-04-4	6-06-7
Esther Laurens	281-17-6	40-05-4	13-06-3	4-03-5
Peter Leger	573-15-0	81-19-3	27-02-0	8-09-8
Eliz. Laserre	1151-07-6	164-09-7	54-07-8	17-00-7
Ann LeBrasseur ..	3200-00-0	457-02-1	151-03-1	47-06-8
Mary Legare			29-01-4	1-06-2
Thomas Legare	276-10-0	39-10-0	13-01-2	4-01-9
Jacob Motte	12790-15-0	1827-05-0	604-03-9	189-03-11
Isaac Mazyck & his father's estate	934-00-0	133-08-6	44-02-4	13-16-3
John Neufville	840-00-0	120-00-0	39-13-6	12-08-6
Joel Poinsett	3075-00-0	439-05-8	145-05-0	45-09-8
P. Villepontoux ...	1147-00-0	163-17-1	54-03-7	16-09-3

An Account of a new Die from the Berries of a Weed in South Carolina; in a letter from Mr. Moses Lindo, dated at Charles Town, September 2, 1763 to Mr. Emanuel Mendez da Costa, Librarian of the Royal Society, London. copied from a MS (Natural History: LIII, 238-9) in the Library of the Royal Society, London:

"In August, 1757, I observed the mocking bird fond of a berry, which grows on a weed called Pouck, represented to me as of a poisonous quality; the juice of this berry being a blooming crimson. I was several times inclined to try, if I could extract a die from it; yet the very thoughts of its quality prevented me from proceeding, till observing these birds to void their excrement of the same color as the berry, on the Chinese rails in my garden, convinced me it

* Gabriel, not French.

* Hill, not French.

was not of the quality represented. I therefore made a tryal in the following manner.

1st. I ordered one of my negroes to gather me a pint of those berries, from which I extracted almost three quarters of a pint of juice, and boiled it with a pint of Bristol water, one quarter of an hour.

2dly. I then took two pieces of flannel and numbered them 1 and 2, boiled them in a separate tin pot with alum a quarter of an hour, and rinced them in cold water.

3dly. I then dipped the piece of flannel No. 1 into the pot, where the juice was, and left it to simmer five minutes, then took it out, and rinced it in cold water; when, to my surprise, I found a superior crimson dye fixed on the flannel than the juice of the berry.

4thly. I then dipped the piece of flannel No. 2 in the same juice, and being desirous to clean my hands from the stain, which No. 1 had caused, I ordered some lime water to be brought me, such as we use to settle our indico, and found the colour of the stain changed to a bright yellow. This unexpected change urged me to throw a wine-glass-full of lime water into the pot, where the piece of flannel No. 2 was simmering; on which, all the juice, as well as the flannel, became of a bright yellow, by which I find alum fixed the crimson, and lime the yellow.

5thly. Having then put a quart of fresh juice into two pint decanters, in one of which I put a small quantity of powdered alum, I laid them up: about six weeks after, I then examined them and found the juice in the decanter, which had no alum, was turned black, and the other retained its colour."

INDEX

www.ingramcontent.com/pod-product-compliance
Lightning Source LLC
Chambersburg PA
CBHW030234030426
42336CB00009B/94

* 9 7 8 1 6 3 9 1 4 0 6 1 9 *